THE MANAGER'S BOOKSHELF

A MOSAIC OF CONTEMPORARY VIEWS

Fourth Edition

JON L. PIERCE
University of Minnesota, Duluth

JOHN W. NEWSTROM
University of Minnesota, Duluth

 HarperCollins*CollegePublishers*

To the authors of management "best-sellers"
whose products have provided
a generation of readers
with food for thought
and a call to action.

Acquisitions Editor: Mike Roche
Project Coordination, and Text Design: York Production Services
Cover Design: Sarah Johnson
Manufacturing Manager: Hilda Koparanian
Electronic Page Makeup: R. R. Donnelley & Sons Company, Inc.
Printer and Binder: R. R. Donnelley & Sons Company, Inc.
Cover Printer: Color-Imetry Corp.

The Manager's Bookshelf: A Mosaic of Contemporary Views, Fourth Edition

Library of Congress Cataloging-in-Publication Data

The Manager's bookshelf: a mosaic of contemporary views/ [collected
  by] Jon L. Pierce, John W. Newstrom. — 4th ed.
       p. cm.
    Includes bibliographical references and index.
    ISBN 0-673-99452-X
    1. Management literature—United States. I. Pierce, Jon L. (Jon
Lepley) II. Newstrom, John W.
    HD70.U5M32 1995
    658—dc20   95-11313
                                                                CIP

7 8 9 10 11 12 13 14 15-DOC-02 01 00 99

CONTENTS

PART FIVE: ORGANIZATIONAL STRATEGY

PART SIX: MOTIVATION

PART SEVEN: EMPOWERMENT AND PARTICIPATION

PART ELEVEN: ORGANIZATIONAL CHANGE AND RENEWAL   **269**

PART TWELVE: MANAGING QUALITY IN CUSTOMER-DRIVEN ORGANIZATIONS   **297**

PART THIRTEEN: ETHICS AND MANAGEMENT   **321**

PREFACE

The last decade was marked by an intense fascination with, and a continued proliferation of, books on management, managers, and organizations. Bookstores around the country featured a larger number than ever before of management books, and many of these books found themselves on, or close to, the "best-sellers" list. Clearly, both managers and the general public are intrigued by, and searching for answers in, the popular business literature.

The Manager's Bookshelf: A Mosaic of Contemporary Views was prepared both for managers and management students. A significant number of individuals in both of these groups do not have sufficient time to read widely, yet many people find themselves involved in conversations where someone else refers to ideas like vision, self-directed workteams, or superleadership. We believe that a laudable goal for managers as well as all students of management is to remain current in their understanding of the views being expressed about organizational and management practices. To help you become a better informed organizational citizen, we prepared *The Manager's Bookshelf*, which introduces you to more than forty recently popular management books.

The Manager's Bookshelf, as a book of concise readings, does not express the views of one individual on the management of organizations, nor does it attempt to integrate the views of several dozen authors. Instead, *this book is a collage*—a composite portrait constructed from a variety of sources. It provides you with insights into many aspects of organizational management from the perspectives of a diverse group of management writers, including some highly regarded authors like Peter Drucker, Douglas McGregor, Warren Bennis, Stephen Covey, Bill Byham, Edward Lawler, Thomas Peters, and Rosabeth Kanter. Through this collection we will introduce you to the thoughts, philosophy, views, and experiences of a number of authors whose works have captivated the attention of today's management community.

This book contains a rich array of pieces. From a topical perspective there are inclusions that focus on ethics, global perspectives, participative practices, environmental trends, organizational culture, managing diversity, strategy, and managerial/leadership styles. This collection includes the views from a variety of individuals—some practitioners, some philosophers, some management consultants, and some management educators. The selections reflect a wide variety in terms of their tone and tenor, as well as the bases for their conclusions. Indeed, critics have characterized some of the authors' works as passionate, invaluable, and insightful, whereas others have been attacked as overly academic, superficial, or unrealistic.

The nature and source of the ideas expressed in this collection are diverse. Some inclusions are prescriptive in nature, whereas others are descriptive; some are philosophical, whereas others report on personal or organizational experiences; some of these works represent armchair speculation, whereas others are based on empirical study. Finally, the selections take a variety of forms. Some of the readings are excerpts extracted from the original book, some of the readings are articles written by the book's author in which part of their philosophy on management is revealed, and some of the inclusions are descriptive summaries of popular books that have been specially prepared for inclusion in *The Manager's Bookshelf*.

This collage can provide you with some useful insights, stimulate your thinking, and spark some stimulating dialogue with your colleagues about the management of today's organizations. We hope these readings will prompt you to raise questions of yourself and your peers about the viability of many of the ideas expressed by these authors regarding the practice of organizational management. If these goals are met, our purpose for assembling this collection will be realized.

ACKNOWLEDGMENTS

We would like to express our sincere and warm appreciation to several colleagues who read and prepared summaries of the contemporary books contained in this edition of *The Manager's Bookshelf*. Their commitment and dedication to students of organizations and management, coupled with their efforts, made this edition possible.

We would also like to express our appreciation to friend and colleague Larry L. Cummings (Carlson School of Management at the University of Minnesota, and The Institute) for his "reflections on the best-sellers" that is contained in the introduction to our book. We thank Larry for taking the time to reflect on this part of the organization and management literature and to offer an update to the insightful observations that he prepared for the earler editions.

The following individuals prepared book summaries for this edition of *The Manager's Bookshelf:*

INTRODUCTION

Diane Dodd-McCue, University of Richmond—Kilmann's *Managing Beyond the Quick Fix*

MANAGEMENT PARADIGMS

Brian Kalhbaugh, Hertz—Barker's *Paradigms: The Business of Discovering the Future*

Robert Marx, University of Massachusetts, Amherst—Quinn's *Beyond Rational Management* and Bolman and Deal's *Reframing Organizations*

Jean A. Grube, University of Wisconsin-Madison—Argyris' *Overcoming Organizational Defenses*

BEST-SELLER "CLASSICS"

Michael Bisesi, University of Houston—Ouchi's *Theory Z: How American Business Can Meet the Japanese Challenge*

Gayle Porter, Rutgers University—McGregor's *The Human Side of Enterprise*

Charles C. Manz, Arizona State University—Blanchard and Johnson's *The One Minute Manager*

HIGH-PERFORMING ORGANIZATIONS

Dorothy Marcic, Metropolitan State University, Minneapolis—Senge's *The Fifth Discipline*

Steve Gildersleeve, Carlson Florist and Greenhouses—Hammer and Champy's *Reengineering the Corporation*

Gary P. Olson, Center for Alcohol and Drug Treatment—Galbraith and Lawler's *Organizing for the Future*

ORGANIZATIONAL STRATEGY

Linda E. Parry, University of Minnesota-Duluth—Mintzberg's *The Rise and Fall of Strategic Planning*

Robert R. Wharton, University of Minnesota-Duluth—Tichy and Sherman's *Control Your Destiny or Someone Else Will*

MOTIVATION

Gail Porter, Rutgers University—Daniels' *Bringing Out the Best in People*

EMPOWERMENT AND PARTICIPATION

Constance Campbell, Georgia Southern University—Byham's *Zapp! The Lightning of Empowerment*

Charles C. Manz, Arizona State University and **Henry P. Sims Jr.**, University of Maryland—Manz and Sims', *SuperLeadership*

TEAMS AND TEAMWORK

R. Warren Candy, Minnesota Power—Katzenbach and Smith's *The Wisdom of Teams*

Cathy Hanson, University of Southern California—Wellins, Byham, and Wilson's *Empowered Teams*

LEADERSHIP

James R. Meindl, State University of New York, Buffalo—Gardner's *On Leadership*

Jim Laumeyer, Minnesota Department of Transportation—Conger's *The Charismatic Leader*

Gayle Baugh, The University of West Florida—Nanus' *Visionary Leadership*

Robert C. Ford, The University of Central Florida—Block's *Stewardship*

DIVERSITY

Linda E. Parry, University of Minnesota-Duluth, Loden and Rosener's *Workforce America!*

Scott L. Newstrom, Harvard University—Barrentine's *When the Canary Stops Singing*

ORGANIZATIONAL CHANGE AND RENEWAL

Kim A. Stewart, University of Denver—Belasco's *Teaching the Elephant to Dance*

Robert C. Ford, The University of Central Florida—Kanter's *When Giants Learn to Dance*

Jane Giacobbe-Miller, University of Massachusetts, Amherst—Peters' *The Tom Peters Seminar*

R. Warren Candy, Minnesota Power—Beer, et al.'s *The Critical Path to Corporate Renewal*

MANAGING QUALITY IN CUSTOMER-DRIVEN ORGANIZATIONS

William B. Gartner, Georgetown University and **M. James Naughton**, Expert-Knowledge Systems, Inc.—Deming's *Out of the Crisis*

Susan Zacur, University of Baltimore—Band's *Creating Value for Customers*

David A Wyrick, University of Minnesota-Duluth—Watson's *Strategic Benchmarking*

ETHICS AND MANAGEMENT

Stephen Rubenfeld, University of Minnesota-Duluth—Covey's *Principle-Centered Leadership*

Gregory Fox, University of Minnesota-Duluth—Kouzes and Posner's *Credibility*

GLOBAL DIMENSIONS

Robert R. Wharton, University of Minnesota-Duluth—Ohmae's *The Borderless World*

Kelly Nelson, U.S. Steel—Naisbitt's *Global Paradox*

PREPARING FOR THE TWENTY-FIRST CENTURY

Robert E. Heller, Wild Birds Unlimited—Reich's *The Work of Nations*

Richard S. Blackburn, University of North Carolina-Chapel Hill—Vaill's *Managing as a Performing Art*

We would like to express our appreciation to a number of individuals who provided us with a great deal of assistance and support for the preparation of this book. Many of our management colleagues took the time and effort to contribute to this book by carefully reading and preparing a summary of one of the selected books. Many of these individuals wanted to offer their personal opinions, offer their endorsements or criticisms, and surface elements of their own management philosophies, but they stuck to their task. To them we express our thanks for their time, energy, and commitment to furthering management education. To those who reviewed our proposal for this Fourth Edition and a draft of the final manuscript, we appreciate your recommendations. To Connie Johnson, who patiently helped us prepare the manuscript, we want to say *thank you once again* for helping us complete this project in a timely fashion. We appreciate the supportive environment provided by our colleagues in the Department of Management Studies here at the University of Minnesota-Duluth. We especially appreciate the continued project commitment and editorial assistance that we have received from Michael Roche and Melissa Rosati before her departure from HarperCollins. We wish Melissa fun and success as she samples "fine foods" and "robust wines" as part of her new editorial challenges!

Jon L. Pierce
John W. Newstrom

ABOUT THE EDITORS

John L. Pierce is Professor of Management and Organization in the School of Business and Economics at the University of Minnesota, Duluth. He received his Ph.D. in management and organizational studies at the University of Wisconsin-Madison. He is the author of more than sixty papers that have been published or presented at various professional conferences. His publications have appeared in the *Academy of Management Journal, Academy of Management Review, Journal of Management, Journal of Occupational Behavior, Journal of Applied Behavioral Science, Organizational Dynamics, Organizational Behavior and Human Decision Processes,* and *Personnel Psychology.* His research interests include sources of psychological ownership, employee ownership systems, and organization-based self-esteem. He has served on the editorial review board for the *Academy of Management Journal, Personnel Psychology,* and *Journal of Management.* He is the coauthor of five other books— *Management, Managing,* and along with John W. Newstrom, *Alternative Work Schedules, Windows into Management,* and *Leaders and the Leadership Process.*

John W. Newstrom is Professor of Human Resource Management in the School of Business and Economics at the University of Minnesota, Duluth. He completed his doctoral degree in management and industrial relations at the University of Minnesota and then taught at Arizona State University for several years. His work has appeared in publications such as *Personnel Psychology, California Management Review, Journal of Management, Academy of Management Journal,* and *The Journal of Occupational Behavior.* He has served on the editorial review boards for the *Academy of Management Review, Academy of Management Journal, The Personnel Administrator, Human Resource Development Quarterly,* and *The Journal of Management Development.* He is the coauthor of fourteen books, including *Organizational Behavior: Human Behavior at Work* (Ninth Edition, with Keith Davis), *Supervision: Managing for Results* (Seventh Edition, with Lester Bittel), *Transfer of Training* (with Mary Broad), and *The Complete Games Trainers Play* (with Ed Scannell).

1

INTRODUCTION

Part One contains four pieces. The first, "Understanding and Using the Best-Sellers," prepared by the editors of *The Manager's Bookshelf*, provides insight into why such a large number of management-oriented books have found themselves in the downtown bookstores, on our coffee tables, and on the bookshelves of those who manage today's organizations. Pierce and Newstrom discuss the rationale for this mosaic of contemporary views on organizations and management, and they provide you with insight into the nature and character of *The Manager's Bookshelf: A Mosaic of Contemporary Views*. They challenge you to read and reflect upon this collection of thoughts and experiences. They invite you to debate the ideas and philosophies that are presented here. They encourage you to let these contemporary management books stimulate your thinking, motivate you to look more systematically into the science of organizations and management, and provide you with the fun of learning something new.

As a result of their concern that these contemporary books will be seen as "quick and dirty" cures for organizational woes, Pierce and Newstrom encourage you to read Ralph H. Kilmann's *Managing Beyond the Quick Fix*.

Several years ago Ralph Kilmann, in his earlier book *Beyond the Quick Fix: Managing Five Tracks to Organizational Success*, attempted to provide us with a valuable message, one that should serve as the backdrop to your consumption and assessment of the myriad of purported "one minute" cures for organizational problems and for the management of today's complex organizations. Kilmann encourages you to stop perpetuating the myth of organizational and management simplicity, and to develop a more complete and integrated approach to the management of today's complex organizations. In *Managing Beyond the Quick Fix*, Kilmann showcases his framework for understanding and managing organizational success by using his integrated five-track approach: culture, management skills, team building, strategy-structure, and reward systems. After describing the five tracks, he offers an account of Eastman Kodak's successful implementation of the five-track program. Ralph H. Kilmann is a Professor of Business Administration and Director of the Program in Corporate Culture at the University of Pittsburgh.

Currently two types of voices create "messages" relevant to management education. One is the organizational scholar (e.g., Edward Lawler, Lyman Porter, and Charles Perrow), who offers us rich theories of management and organization and rigorous empirical observations of organizations in action. The other source includes management consultants and management practitioners (e.g., William Byham, Tom Peters, Stephen Covey, and Bill Gates) who offer us perspectives from their lives on the "organizational firing line."

Traditional academics—students of tight theory and rigorous empirical study of organizational behavior—often find a large disparity between these two perspectives on management and organization. Confronted with the increasing popularity of the "best sellers," the editors of *The Manager's Bookshelf* began to ask a number of questions about this nontraditional management literature. For example:

◆ Is this material "intellectual pornography" as some have claimed?

◆ Do we want our students to read this material?

◆ Should managers of today's organizations be encouraged to read this material and to take it seriously?

◆ What contributions to management education and development come from this collection of management books?

◆ How should this management literature be approached?

For answers to these questions we turned to colleague and friend Professor Larry L. Cummings.

We asked Professor Cummings to reflect upon the current and continuous popularity of this literature. Professor Cummings is a distinguished management scholar, organization and management consultant, and educator of MBA and Ph.D. students. The questions we asked Professor Cummings are intended to help us frame, and therefore critically and cautiously consume, this literature. Professor Cummings' reflections on the role of the popular books in management education is presented as a part of this introductory chapter.

Business Week (September 28, 1987) referred to Peter F. Drucker as the "Dr. Spock of Business." For generations of managers, Peter F. Drucker probably is "the most read, most listened-to, and most enduring guru of professional management" (pp. 61–65). Since 1971 he has been a professor of social sciences at Claremont Graduate School in California.

Peter Drucker, in *The New Realities*, addresses a comprehensive array of topics in the social superstructure: economics, politics, society, education, and social organizations. Although the book addresses Drucker's concerns for the knowledgeable worker, an information-based organization, and the need for dramatic educational changes, he is perhaps most quoted when commenting on the state of management today and its needs in the future. Specifically, Drucker lays out seven essential principles defining management. He concludes that it is truly a liberal art, because it is the practice and application of fundamental knowledge and wisdom.

READING 1

Understanding and Using the Best Sellers

Jon L. Pierce and John W. Newstrom

A large number of books treating various aspects of management have been in high demand at local bookstores. Several individuals have authored books that have sold millions of copies, among them are Tom Peters (e.g, *In Search of Excellence*), Bill Byham (e.g., *Zapp! The Lightning of Empowerment*), Stephen Covey (e.g, *Seven Habits of Highly Effective People*), Lee Iacocca (e.g., *Iacocca: An Autobiography*), and Kenneth Blanchard and Spencer Johnson (e.g., *The One Minute Manager*). Some of their books have stayed on "best-seller" lists for many weeks. What are the reasons for their popularity? Why have business books continued to catch the public's attention as we move through the decade of the 1990s? Frank Freeman, of the Center for Creative Leadership, suggests simply that we are living in the "business decade."[1] Corporate America, he says, is back in good standing with the public, and there has been a resurgence of pride and hope in the business community.

We have heard stories about, and many have felt the shockwaves of, downsizing, restructuring, and reengineering of the organization. We've all heard stories about the success of foreign organizations. We have continued to watch bigger and bigger portions of our markets being dominated by foreign-owned and -controlled organizations. And we have witnessed foreign interests purchase certain segments of America. Perhaps in response to these trends, a tremendous thirst for *American* success stories has arisen. In essence, the public is receptive and the timing is right for the sale of popular management books at bookstores everywhere.

A second reason for the upsurge in management books stems from another form of competition. Many management consultants, fighting for visibility, have written books they hope will become best-sellers.[2] Through the printed word they hope to provide a unique take-home product for their clients, communicate their management philosophies, gain wide exposure for themselves or their firms, and occasionally profit handsomely.

Third, the best-sellers also provide an optimistic message to a receptive market. In difficult economic times, managers may be as eager to swallow easy formulas as sick patients are to drink their prescribed medicine. Sensing this, the authors of the best-sellers (and of many other books with lesser records) often claim, at least implicitly, to present managers with an easy cure for their organizational woes, or with an easy path to personal success.

Fourth, we are witnessing an increased belief in and commitment to proactive organizational change. An increasing number of managers are rejecting the notion that "if it ain't broke, don't fix it," and instead are adopting a *bias toward action*. These managers are seriously looking for and experimenting with different approaches toward organizational management. Many of the popular books provide managers with insights into new and different ways of managing.

In their search for the "quick fix," generations of American managers have adopted a series of organizational management concepts, such as management by objectives (MBO), job enlargement, job enrichment, flextime, and a variety of labor-management participative schemes (such as quality circles and quality of work-life programs).[3] Each has been widely heralded, frequently implemented, and sometimes later abandoned and replaced by another emerging management technique. As a consequence of this managerial tendency to embrace ideas and then soon discard them, many viable managerial techniques have received a tarnished image. For example, many of the Japanese participative management systems that are being copied by American managers today found their way into the garbage cans of an earlier generation of American managers. With the demand for quick fixes there is a ready market for new, re-born, and revitalized management ideas. We encourage you to read and seriously reflect on Ralph Kilmann's views on the quick fix that follows in this opening part. The search for solutions to major organizational problems in terms of "one-minute" answers reflects a band-aid approach to management and one that is condemned by Kilmann and destined to ultimate failure.

We alert you to this managerial tendency to look for "new" solutions to current organizational problems. The rush to resolve problems and take advantage of opportunities frequently leads to the search for simple remedies for complex organizational problems. Yet very few of today's organizational problems can be solved with any single approach. Concepts such as high-involvement management, learning organizations, and corporate culture advocated in today's generation of popular management books may also join the list of tried-and-abandoned solutions to organizational woes. We especially hope that the quick fix approach to organizational problem solving that characterizes the management style of many will *not* be promoted as a result of this mosaic (i.e., *The Manager's Bookshelf*) of today's popular business books.

❖ RATIONALE FOR THIS BOOK

The business world has been buzzing with reference to terms like *vision, paradigms, stewardship,* the *learning organization,* the *spirit of work* and the *soul of business, transformational and charismatic leaders, high-involvement manage-*

ment and organizations, and *corporate cultures.* On the negative side, these new terms feed the management world's preoccupation with quick fixes and the perpetuation of management fads. On the positive side, many of these concepts serve as catalysts to the further development of sound management philosophies and practices.

In earlier decades a few books occasionally entered the limelight (e.g., *Parkinson's Law, The Peter Principle, My Years with General Motors, The Money Game*), but for the most part they did not generate the widespread and prolonged popularity of the current generation of business books. Then, too, many weren't written in the readable style that makes most contemporary books so easy to consume.

Managers seem to find the current wave of books not only interesting, but enjoyable to read. For example, a small survey by the Center for Creative Leadership found that a significant number of managers who participated in a study of their all-around reading selections chose one or more *management* books as their favorite! Of the 179 business or management books identified in total, *In Search of Excellence* accounted for more than half of the books that were read by managers.[1] The point is, many of the popular management books *are* being read by managers—probably because the books are often supportive of their present management philosophies! Many managers report that these books are insightful, interestingly presented, and seemingly practical. Whether or not the prescriptions in these books have had (or ever will have) a real and lasting impact on the effective management of organizations remains to be determined.

Despite best-sellers' overall popularity, some managers don't read *any* current management books, and many other managers have read only a limited number or small parts of a few.* Similarly, many university students studying management have heard about some of these books but have not read them. *The Manager's Bookshelf: A Mosaic of Contemporary Views* presents perspectives from (but not a criticism of) a number of those popular management books. *The Manager's Bookshelf* was prepared for two audiences: managers who are interested in the ideas presented in many of the popular management books but don't have time to read them in their entirety, and students of management who want to be well informed as they prepare for entry into the work world. Reading about the views expressed in many of the best-sellers will expand the knowledge of both groups and enable them to engage in meaningful conversations with their managerial colleagues.

Although reading the forty-five summaries provided here can serve as a useful introduction to this literature, they should not be viewed as a substitute for immersion in the original material, nor do they remove the need for further reading of the more substantive management books and professional

---

*For those of you who incorporate these types of management books into your management training programs you might find the following article useful: "The potential role of popular business books in management development programs," by J. W. Newstrom and J. L. Pierce in *Journal of Management Development,* 1989, *8,* 2, 13–24.

journals. The *good news* is that the popularity of these books suggests that millions of managers are reading them and they are exhibiting an interest in learning about what has worked for other managers and firms. This an important step toward the development of an open system paradigm for themselves and for their organizations.

We strongly advocate that both managers and students be informed organizational citizens. Therefore, we believe it is important for you to know and understand what is being *written* about organizations and management. We also believe that it is important for you to know what is being *read* by the managers who surround you, some of which is contained in best-sellers, much of which is contained in more traditional management books, as well as in professional and scientific journals.[5]

❖ CONTENTS OF THE BEST-SELLERS

What *topics* do these best-selling books cover, what is their *form,* and what is their *merit?* Although many authors cover a wide range of topics and others don't have a clear focus, most fall into one of several categories. Some attempt to describe the more successful and unsuccessful companies and identify what made them successes or failures. Others focus on "micro" issues in leadership, motivation, or ethics. And yet others turn their attention toward broad questions of corporate strategy and competitive tactics for implementing strategy. Some focus on pressing issues facing the contemporary organization such as social responsibility, globalism, workforce diversity, and the "virtual workplace."

In terms of form, many contain apparently simple answers and trite prescriptions. Others are built around literally hundreds of spellbinding anecdotes and stories. Some have used interviews of executives as their source of information, and others have adopted the parable format for getting their point across. As a group their presentation style is rich in diversity.

Judging the merits of best-sellers is a difficult task (and one that we will leave for readers and management critics to engage in). Some critics have taken the extreme position of calling these books "intellectual wallpaper" and "business pornography." Certainly labels like this, justified or not, should caution readers. A better perspective is provided by an assessment of the *sources,* often anecdotal, of many of the books. In other words, much of the information in best-sellers stems from the experiences and observations of a single individual and is often infused with the subjective opinions of that writer. Unlike the more traditional academic literature, these books do not all share a sound scientific foundation. Requirements pertaining to objectivity, reproducibility of observations, and tests for reliability and validity have not guided the creation of much of the material. As a consequence, the authors are at liberty to say whatever they want (and often with as much passion as they desire!).

Unlike authors who publish research-based knowledge, authors of best-sellers do not need to submit their work to a panel of reviewers who then critically evaluate the ideas, logic, and data. The authors of these popular management books are able to proclaim as sound management principles virtually anything that is intuitively acceptable to their publisher and readers. Therefore, *readers need to be cautious consumers.* The ideas presented in these books need to be critically compared with the well-established thoughts from more traditional sources of managerial wisdom.

❖ CRITIQUING THESE POPULAR BOOKS

While the notion of one-minute management is seductive, Jim Renier, former CEO of Honeywell notes that, "There are no fast-acting cures for what ails business." Recognizing that simple solutions are not likely to be found and that the best-sellers frequently present (or appear to present) quick fixes and simple solutions, we strongly encourage readers to read these popular books, looking less for simple solutions and more toward using them to stimulate their thinking and challenge the way they go about doing their business. We encourage you to not only achieve comprehension and understanding, but to ultimately arrive at the level of critique and synthesis.

In order to help you approach these works more critically, we encourage you to use the following questions to guide your evaluation.[6]

■ Author credentials:	How do the authors' backgrounds and characteristics uniquely qualify them to write this book? What relevant experience do they have? What unique access or perspective do they have? What prior writing experience do they have, and how was it accepted by others? What is their research background (capacity to design, conduct, and interpret the results of their observations)?
■ Rationale:	Why did the authors write the book? Is their reason legitimate?
■ Face validity:	On initial examination of the book's major characteristics and themes, do you react positively or negatively? Are you inclined to accept or reject the author's conclusions? Does it fit with your prior experience and expectations, or does it rock them to the core?
■ Target audience:	For whom is this book uniquely written? What level of managers in the organizational hierarchy would most benefit from reading the book and why?

■ Integration of existing knowledge: A field of inquiry can move forward only if it draws on and extends existing knowledge. Was this book written in isolation of existing knowledge? Do the authors demonstrate an awareness of and build upon existing knowledge?

■ Readability/Interest: Do the authors engage your mind? Are there relevant, practical illustrations that indicate how the ideas have been or could be applied?

■ Internal validity: To what degree do the authors provide substantive evidence that the phenomenon, practice, or ideas presented actually produce a valued result? Is there an internally consistent presentation of ideas that demonstrates the processes through which *causes* for their observations are understood?

■ Reliability: To what degree do the author's conclusions converge with other sources of information or methods of data collection.

■ Distinctiveness: Is the material presented new, creative, and distinctive, or is it merely a presentation of "old wine in new bottles?"

■ Objectivity: To what extent do the authors have a self-serving or political agenda, or have the authors presented information that was systematically gathered and evaluated? Have the authors offered both the pros and cons of their views?

■ External validity: Will the authors' ideas work for me in my unique situation, or are they bound to the context within which the author operates?

■ Practicality: Are the ideas adaptable? Does the author provide suggestions for application? Are the ideas readily transferable to the workplace in such a way that the typical reader could be expected to know what to do with them a few days later at work?

These are only some of the questions that should be asked as you read and evaluate any popular management book.

❖ NATURE OF THIS BOOK

This is the Fourth Edition of *The Manager's Bookshelf.* The First Edition was published in 1988. Recent editions have appeared in Italian and Chinese, pointing to the international popularity of these books as well. The Fourth Edition includes many books that were not previously summarized, representing approximately a 50-percent revision. *The Manager's Bookshelf* provides a comprehensive introduction to many of the major best-sellers in the management field during recent years.

The selections are of two types: excerpts of original material and summaries by a panel of reviewers. In some cases, we provide the reader with not only the main ideas presented by the author of a best-seller, but also the *flavor* (style or nature) of the author's approach. For some selections, we obtained permission to excerpt directly a chapter from the original book, especially when the chapter was the keystone presentation of the author's major theme. In other cases, the author's original thoughts and words were captured by selecting an article (representing part of the book) that the author had written for publication in a professional journal. Here again, the reader will see the author's ideas directly, though only sampled or much condensed from the original source.

The other major format chosen for inclusion is a comprehensive *summary* of the best-seller prepared by persons selected for their relevant expertise, interest, and familiarity. These summaries are primarily descriptive, designed to provide readers with an overall understanding of the book. These summaries are not judgmental in nature, nor are they necessarily a complete or precise reflection of the authors' management philosophy.

Determining what constituted a "best-seller" worthy of inclusion was easy in some cases and more difficult in others. From the hundreds of books available for selection, the ones included here rated highly on one or more of these criteria:

1. *Market acceptance:* Several books have achieved national notoriety by selling hundreds of thousands, and occasionally millions, of copies.
2. *Provocativeness:* Some books present thought-provoking viewpoints that run counter to "traditional" management thought.
3. *Distinctiveness:* A wide variety of topical themes of interest to organizational managers are presented.
4. *Representativeness:* In an attempt to avoid duplication from books with similar content within a topical area, many popular books were excluded.
5. *Author reputation:* Some authors (e.g., Peter Drucker, Edward Lawler III) have a strong reputation for the quality of their thinking and the insights they have historically generated, and, therefore, some of their newer products were included.

❖ AUTHORS OF THE BEST-SELLERS

It is appropriate for a reader to inquire of a best-seller, "Who is the author of this book?" Certainly the authors come from varied backgrounds. Some have previously developed a respected academic and professional record and have subsequently integrated their thoughts into book form. Others have spent their entire careers working in a single organization and now share their reflections from that experience base.

Some of the authors have been described as self-serving egotists who have little to say constructively about management, but do say it with a flair and passion such that reading their books may be very exciting! Some books are seemingly the product of armchair humorists who set out to entertain their readers with tongue in cheek. Other books on the best-seller lists have been written with the aid of a ghost writer (that is, by someone who takes information that has been provided by another and then converts it into the lead author's story). In summary, it may be fascinating to read the "inside story" as told by the CEO of a major airline or oil conglomerate, but the reader still has the opportunity and obligation to challenge the author's credentials for making broad generalizations from that experience base.

❖ CONCLUSIONS

We encourage you to read and reflect on this collection of thoughts from the authors of today's generation of management books. We invite you to expand and enrich your insights into management as a result of learning from this set of popular books. We challenge you to question and debate the pros and cons of the ideas and philosophies that are presented by these authors. We hope you will ask when, where, how, and why these ideas are applicable. Examine the set of readings provided here, let them stimulate your thinking, and, in the process, learn something new. You'll find that learning can be fun and addictive!

❖ NOTES

1. Frank Freeman, "Books That Mean Business: The Management Best Sellers," Academy of Management Review, 1985, 345–350.
2. Dan Carroll, "Management Principles and Management Art." Paper presented to the Academy of Management annual meeting, Chicago, Illinois, August, 1986.
3. "Business Fads: What's In—And Out." *Business Week* (1986, January 20). Armstrong, W. W. "The Boss Has Read Another New Book!" *Management Review*, (1994, June), 61–64.

4. Freeman, "Books That Mean Business."
5. See, for example, a report on executive reading preferences by Marilyn Wellemeyer in "Books Bosses Read," *Fortune,* April 27, 1987.
6. See, John W. Newstrom and Jon L. Pierce, "An Analytic Framework for Assessing Popular Business Books," *Journal of Management Development,* 1993, *12,* 4, 20–28.

READING 2

Managing Beyond the Quick Fix

Ralph H. Kilmann
Summary prepared by Diane Dodd-McCue

Diane Dodd-McCue is an Assistant Professor of Management at the University of Richmond, Virginia. Her writings have appeared in *Journal of Management, Business Horizons, Journal of Management Education, Personnel, Academy of Management Review,* and other academic publications. Dr. Dodd-McCue's current research interests include the impact of gender, family, and job structure on professionals' perceived stress, retention of women in accounting, and corporate responses to child and elder care needs. She received her D.B.A. in organizational theory from the University of Kentucky.

Understanding "the essence" of organizational activity—success—demands a fully integrated, holistic program and patience. Organizations can be revitalized, but only by rejecting the myth of simplification. Quick fixes—simple solutions to complex problems—will not produce lasting change.

Managers must don a new world view. Viewing the world as a complex hologram best captures the dynamic complexity of contemporary life because it emphasizes the interconnectedness of the open system. Through the holographic lens organizational problems, now seen as complex and interrelated, demand multiple problem-solving approaches. For multiple approaches to success, breadth of knowledge and information are needed. Participative management, coupled with the contributions of internal and external consultants, is the only way to combine expertise with commitment. However, even with these implementations long-term success is doomed without *top management's commitment to an integrated program of planned change.*

The holographic approach goes far beyond the "quick fix" programs often adopted by firms today. It accents a five-track formula for managing an organization successfully. Each of the five tracks—culture, management skills,

Ralph H. Kilmann, *Managing Beyond the Quick Fix*. San Francisco: Jossey-Bass, 1989.

team building, strategy-structure, and reward systems—will be briefly described. Then, to illustrate this approach in action, an account of Eastman Kodak's successful implementation of the five-track program is included. In this discussion theoretical concepts and recommendations come to life in an extensive "real world" laboratory.

❖ THE FIVE TRACKS

The five tracks to organizational success comprise an all-encompassing program. Implementing each of the tracks requires a participative effort among managers, consultants, and organizational members. In planning the integrated program, scheduling within and across tracks demands coordination, sharing, and flexibility.

◆ THE CULTURE TRACK

The *Culture Track* emphasizes establishing trust, information sharing, and adaptiveness. To achieve these culture-change objectives, the organization needs to survey actual norms, establish desired norms, identify and close the culture gap, and sustain culture change.

There are four types of cultural norms—task support, task innovation, social relationships, and personal freedom. *Task support norms* focus on information sharing, helping other groups, and efficiency concerns; extreme examples include "supporting others" as opposed to "them versus us." *Task innovation norms* emphasize creativity and innovation and reflect the organization's stance on status quo versus change. *Social relationships norms* suggest the extent to which socializing and mixing work with pleasure are condoned or even encouraged. *Personal freedom norms* reflect the organization's norms for self-expression, the exercise of personal discretion, and self-satisfaction. Each of these four types of cultural norms can be characterized across two dimensions: technical or human, short term or long term.

An adaptive culture is imperative for all other improvement efforts beyond the quick fix for two reasons. First, an adaptive culture allows managers to accept their shortcomings and learn how to address tough, complex problems. Second, the openness of an adaptive culture allows organizational members to participate in the team-building efforts which are critical to improvement. Only in an adaptive culture can efforts in the remaining tracks proceed successfully.

◆ THE MANAGEMENT SKILLS TRACK

The *Management Skills Track* builds on the assumption that a variety of skills—conceptual, analytic, administrative, social, and interpersonal—are vital in successfully managing complex problems. Problem management involves sensing problems, defining problems, deriving solutions, implementing solutions, and evaluating outcomes. Further complicating the problem management process is the psychological baggage managers bring with them to the process.

Among the management skills needed is *assumption analysis,* a systematic method of addressing the most difficult aspects of problem management, problem definition, and solution implementation. Assumption analysis involves categorizing the assumptions that underlie conclusions in light of certainty and importance. Through a series of integrated group and individual exercises managers can evaluate whether their assumptions represent fantasy and habit, or reality and choice. Nested in an organizational culture of openness and trust, managers can be comfortable altering faulty assumptions to lay the groundwork for dealing with the complexity of their new holographic world.

◆ THE TEAM–BUILDING TRACK

The *Team-Building Track* emphasizes infusing new cultures and skills throughout the organization. At this third stage in the organization-improvement program, the culture and management skills tracks have been addressed. The Team-Building Track provides an arena for the organization to capitalize on its new and emerging adaptive culture and its members' new and improved talents.

The Team-Building Track focuses on three areas: managing troublemakers, team building, and interteam building. Successful implementation within the Team-Building Track creates a (positive) domino effect. If troublemakers curtail their disruptive behavior, others will feel more comfortable and free to express themselves. If work groups evolve into effective teams, they will manage their work-related setbacks more effectively. If interconnected work groups become cooperative teams, difficult organizational problems that span traditional group boundaries will be managed successfully.

At this stage managers should take notice: successes within the first three tracks have yet to be translated into formally documented systems. Only at this point is the organization ready to face the gritty issues of the strategy-structure and reward system tracks.

◆ THE STRATEGY-STRUCTURE TRACK

The *Strategy-Structure Track* addresses how the organization can align objectives, tasks, and people, and develop written statements specifying where an organization is going and how it will get there. For the Strategy-Structure Track process a *Problem Management Organization (PMO)* is created, which is a diverse collection of organizational members from varying levels and areas in the organization who spend part of their time away from their formal responsibilities addressing complex organizational issues.

The Strategy-Structure Track proceeds from classifying and synthesizing strategic assumptions, to strategy formation, to operationalizing strategies through structure. Particular attention is given to making the structure succeed: (1) those assigned to work units are given the resources needed to translate plans into action; and (2) sequential and reciprocal interdependencies ("more costly task flows") are grouped *within* subunits.

◆ THE REWARD SYSTEM TRACK

The *Reward System Track* aims high: to motivate high performance and sustain all previous improvements. Addressing the organization's reward system assumes that the organization is moving the "right" direction, with the "right" strategies and the "right" resources. A good reward system also provides employees with an opportunity to experience intrinsic rewards. If the other tracks have been implemented successfully, employees would be working within an open, trusting environment where their contributions are valued; they would have refined skills that lead to their job successes and are recognized by others; they are contributing members in effective teams; and their jobs and groupings are designed to allow them some autonomy and to see the results of their efforts. Thus, the formal reward system can then focus on ways to extrinsically reward these desirable behaviors and outcomes.

How implementation of the Reward System Track unfolds is again a function of a Program Management Organization (PMO), although the desired membership may include different individuals than PMO members from the Strategy-Structure Track PMO. A broad representation of different perspectives from different areas within the organization is desired because what is being rewarded—desired performance—may vary across subunits. With this attempt to create a synthesized reward system, the "final" reward system usually is marked by five characteristics:

1. The entire organization is guided by a unified policy of performance-based evaluations and rewards.
2. Within this holistic framework, autonomous subunits have the freedom to tailor a subunit-specific reward system to fit their needs.
3. Even with subunit-specific reward systems, similarities surface: measures for short and long term evaluations, schedules for adjustments, recognition of individual and group contributions, formulas for superior rewards.
4. Relevant business information (i.e., financial, marketing, human resource, manufacturing) is needed and must be accessible to organizational members; this information is vital if they are to make well-informed decisions about how they can achieve high levels of performance, and hence high levels of reward.
5. Each subunit offers a wide range of intrinsic and extrinsic rewards to satisfy their employees' needs and personalities.

In summary, the Reward System Track ties together the Kilmann program and marks the point at which the program has gone the full circle. The improvement program has progressed from the early tracks, which have required external consultants to provide needed resources, to this final stage, during which the program has been internalized and formalized by the organization.

❖ THE EASTMAN KODAK EXPERIENCE

◆ THE FIVE TRACKS COME ALIVE

The previous discussion presented the complete organizational success program, one track at a time. However, given a holographic view of organizations, it is unrealistic to evaluate the program without attempting to fit these interrelated pieces into an integrated whole. Fortunately Eastman Kodak provided this opportunity, using its 125-member Market Intelligence (MI) group as the target.

Kodak's program was conceived in 1984, the brainchild of Vince Barabba, who headed this division. Barabba, brought into Kodak with a mandate to develop the corporate function of market intelligence, was familiar with the five-track program and sympathetic to the idea of managing beyond the quick fix.

Although the five-track program demands patience and commitment, the Kodak experience initially raced along. The key ideas were presented to top managers; then fifty members of the MI organization and twenty-five key external stakeholders were interviewed. From these interviews emerged an initial diagnosis of organizational problems, with emphasis on their links to the five tracks and a schedule of implementing the five tracks, plus a *shadow track*. The *shadow track* was a special steering committee that included Barabba, the three directors of MI divisions, and an additional director who was responsible for coordinating program logistics. The shadow track's role was to monitor the entire program and do whatever was necessary to ensure its success.

All 125 members of MI participated in the first three tracks, although employees were separated by job level for the culture and skills tracks. The culture track and skills track both involved a series of monthly workshops scheduled on alternate weeks over a three-month period. The team-building track, which marked the first time natural work groups would be united during the improvement program, involved inter- and intra-group workshops begun a few months later. The strategy-structure track, undertaken by a PMO of fifteen members representing all levels and areas of Kodak's MI worked to develop a recommended plan. The reward system track, steered by a different PMO, was slated to initiate its work thereafter and complete it six months later.

The culture and skills building tracks got off to a timely start but soon participants began complaining that they could no longer attend the workshops because of time demands. At this point some members of the shadow track suggested canning the improvement program altogether. In a compromise move the workshops were rescheduled to include a working lunch, and one skills-building workshop was refocused on time management. This near-derailment proved a blessing in disguise.

Targeting time management as a skills workshop topic brought several issues out on the table. Participants confronted "time-wasters" and "time-gaps" much like they had confronted culture. Their new-found openness and ability to communicate were evidenced both within and between work groups.

The Team-Building Track began as scheduled. A participant from each group served as a process observer for each group and provided feedback at the end of each session. During the workshops participants analyzed *team-gaps,* the difference between actual and desired dimensions of work-group functioning, and sought solutions for narrowing these gaps.

A demanding workload for MI members led to a two-month delay for the Strategy-Structure Track. Even with a continuing heavy workload, the PMO developed and presented its recommendations for strategy-structure changes to the shadow track on schedule. Among the major recommendations of the PMO were: (1) defining the function of the MI group as *business intelligence,* and renaming it accordingly; (2) defining the role of the MI group to include providing Kodak decision makers not only information but also the *implications* of the information; (3) enhancing the organization's "people" orientation through enhanced employee orientation, mentoring, and increased opportunities for employee participation. Within one year the majority of these recommendations were implemented, often without any modifications.

Implementation of the final track—reward system—was delayed because of the increased work load and resistance by several members of the shadow track to relinquish their prerogative to manage the reward system. Further complications also surfaced. Leadership of the MI unit changed; Barabba, the continuing program sponsor, left Kodak and was replaced by an insider who also affirmed his support of the program. Kodak issued corporate mandates that all divisions were required to design a Special Recognition Plan and that all divisions were to postpone recommendations for improving the formal rewards system until after a corporate-wide revamping was completed. Thus, the focus of the Reward System Track was limited to only one aspect of the reward system: special recognitions.

Even with these changes and limitations the Reward System Track presented its recommendations for the Special Recognition Plan to the shadow track on schedule. The plan was approved and implemented without modifications. Key characteristics of the plan included a committee to oversee implementation, no limits on employee eligibility for rewards, and endorsement of any combination of tangible, informal, or cash rewards deemed appropriate.

◆ THE STORY REVISITED

Follow-up observations tend to validate the success of the fully-integrated five-track program.

First, the organizational culture had extinguished employee class differ-ence. Prior to the program, employees had been identified by salary and man-agerial/non-managerial labels; now the fundamental and equal contributions of different types of employees were valued.

Second, there was corporate-wide respect for Business Research, and not just by top executives. Prior to the program market intelligence personnel had been criticized for their lack of "street smarts;" now they were respected be-cause they effectively provided information and analysis on its implications with greater knowledge of the consumer.

Third, the program had become so well ingrained into Business Research that employees hired *after* the program could recognize its outcomes even though they were unfamiliar with the separate tracks leading to those out-comes. For example, new employees commented on the warm nurturing cul-ture, the participative, team-oriented work environment, and their qualified, articulate coworkers. Although they voiced dissatisfaction with Kodak's over-all reward system, they pointed to the Special Recognition Award system as a timely celebration of excellent performance.

Kodak's experience at a completely integrated program—managing be-yond the quick fix—had proved a worthwhile experience for members and consultants. Top management's commitment to the five-track program had not wavered, even in the midst of increased workloads, personnel changes, and pressures for bottom-line results. The five-track implementations had continued to focus on the evolving needs of the organization even though the original implementation schedule had undergone extensive revision. But, most significantly, the organization's ongoing adaptability had shown the pro-gram's effectiveness at creating an organization devoted to vibrant change and relevance for its key stakeholders, the basics needed to create and maintain success.

READING 3

Reflections on the Best-Sellers—A Cautionary Note

Jon L. Pierce and John W. Newstrom, with Larry L. Cummings

This reading provides our reflections upon management (both the body of knowledge and its practice), as well as upon the wave of management books that have become part of the popular press. We hope it will provide some helpful perspectives and point you in some new directions.

Management can be defined as the skillful application of a body of knowledge to a particular organizational situation. This definition suggests to us that management is an art form as well as a science. That is, there is a body of knowledge that has to be applied with the fine touch and instinctive sense of the master artist. Execution of the management role and performance of the managerial functions are more complex than the simple application of a few management concepts. The development of effective management, therefore, requires the development of an in-depth understanding of organizational and management concepts, as well as the capacity to grasp when and how to apply this knowledge.

The organizational arena presents today's manager with a number of challenges. The past few decades have been marked by a rapid growth of knowledge about organizations and management systems. As a consequence of this growth in management information, we strongly believe that it is important for today's manager to engage in *lifelong learning,* by continually remaining a student of management. It is also clear to us that our understanding of organizations and management systems is still in the early stages of development. That is, there remain many unanswered questions that pertain to the effective management of organizations.

Many observers of the perils facing today's organizations have charged that the crises facing American organizations are largely a function of "bad management." Similarly, Tom Peters and Bob Waterman have observed that the growth of our society during the earlier part of this century was so rapid that almost any management approach appeared to work and work well. The real test of effective management systems did not appear until the recent decades, when competitive, economic, political, and social pressures created a form of environmental turbulence that pushed existing managerial tactics beyond their limits. Not only are students of management challenged to learn about effective management principles, but they are also confronted with the need to develop the skills and intuitive sense to apply that management knowledge.

Fortunately, there are many organizations in our society that they can learn from, and there is a wealth of knowledge that has been created that focuses on effective organizational management. There are, at least, two literatures that provide rich opportunities for regular reading. First, there is the traditional management literature that is found in management and organization textbooks and academic journals (e.g., *Academy of Management Journal, Administrative Science Quarterly,* and *California Management Review*). Second, this past decade has seen the emergence of a nontraditional management literature written by management practitioners and management consultants who are describing their organizational experiences and providing a number of other management themes. Knowledge about effective and ineffective management systems can be gleaned by listening to the management scholar, philosopher, and practitioner.

Since not all that is published in the academic journals or in the popular press meets combined tests of scientific rigor and practicality, it is important that motivated readers immerse themselves in *both* of these literatures. Yet, neither source should be approached and subsequently consumed without engaging in critical thinking.

❖ CRITICAL THINKING AND CAUTIOUS CONSUMPTION

We believe that the ideas promoted in these best-sellers should not be blindly integrated into any organization. Each should be subjected to careful scrutiny in order to identify its inherent strengths and weaknesses; each should be examined within the context of the unique organizational setting in which it may be implemented; and modifications and fine-tuning of the technique may be required in order to tailor it to a specific organizational setting and management philosophy. Finally, the process that is used to implement the management technique may be as important to its success as the technique itself.

This is an era of an information-knowledge explosion. Perhaps consumers of that information need to be reminded of the relevance of the "caveat emptor" from the product domain, because there are both good and questionable informational products on the market. Fortunately, advisory services like *Consumer Reports* exist to advise us on the consumption of consumer goods. There is, however, no similar guide for our consumption of information in the pop-management press. Just because something has been a best-seller or widely promoted does not mean that the information contained therein is worthy of direct consumption. It may be a best-seller because it presents an optimistic message, it is enjoyable reading, or because it has been successfully marketed to the public!

The information in all management literature should be approached with caution; it should be examined and questioned. The pop-management literature should not be substituted for more scientific-based knowledge about effective management. In addition, this knowledge should be compared and contrasted with what we know about organizations and management systems from other sources—the opinions of other experts, the academic management literature, and our own prior organizational experiences.

We invite you to question this literature. In the process there are a myriad of questions that should be asked. For example: What are the author's credentials, and are they relevant to the book? Has the author remained an objective observer of the reported events? Why did the author write this book? What kind of information is being presented (e.g., opinion, values, facts)? How reliable and valid is the information that is being presented? Does this information make sense when it is placed into previously developed theories (e.g., from a historical context)? Could I take this information and apply it to another situation at a different point in time and in a different place, or was it unique to the author's experience? These and similar questions should be part of the information screening process.

❖ INTERVIEW WITH PROFESSOR L. L. CUMMINGS

As we became increasingly familiar with the "best-sellers" through our roles as editors, we found ourselves asking a number of questions about this type of literature. For example,

1. Is this material "intellectual pornography," as some have claimed?
2. Do we want our students to read this material?
3. Should managers of today's organizations be encouraged to read this material and take it seriously?
4. What contributions to management education and development come from this collection of management books?
5. How should this management literature be approached?

As a part of our reflection upon the currently popular literature, we talked with a distinguished management scholar, organization and management consultant, and educator of MBA and Ph.D. students: Professor L. L. Cummings. Following are excerpts from that interview:

QUESTION Larry, during the past decade we have witnessed an explosion in the number and type of books that have been written on management and organizations for the trade market. Many of these books have found themselves on the "best-sellers" list. What, in your opinion, has been the impact of these publications? What is the nature of their contribution?

ANSWER   Quite frankly, I think these books have made a number of subtle contributions, most of which have not been labeled or identified by either the business press or the academic press. In addition, many of their contributions have been misappropriately or inaccurately labeled.

Permit me to elaborate. I think it is generally true that a number of these very popular "best-seller list" books, as you put it, have been thought to be reasonably accurate translations or interpretations of successful organizational practice. While this is not the way that these books have been reviewed in the academic press, my interactions with managers, business practitioners, and MBA students reveal that many of these books are viewed as describing organizational structure, practices, and cultures that are thought to contribute to excellence.

On the other hand, when I evaluate the books myself and when I pay careful attention to the reviews by respected, well-trained, balanced academicians, it is my opinion that these books offer very little, if anything, in the way of *generalizable* knowledge about successful organizational practice. As organizational case studies, they are the most dangerous of the lot, in that the data (information) presented has not been systematically, carefully, and cautiously collected and interpreted. Of course, that criticism is common for case studies. Cases were never meant to be contributions to scientific knowledge. Even the best ones are primarily pedagogical aids.

The reason I describe the cases presented in books like *When Giants Learn to Dance* and *In Search of Excellence* as frequently among the most dangerous is because they are so well done (i.e., well done in a marketing and journalistic sense), and therefore, they are easily read, and so believable. They are likely to influence the naive, those who consume them without critically evaluating their content. They epitomize the glamour and the action orientation, and even the machoism of American management practice; that is, they represent the epitome of competition, control, and order as dominant interpersonal and organizational values.

Rather, I think the contributions of these books, in general, have been to provide an apology, a rationale, or a positioning, if you like, of American management as something that is not *just* on the defensive with regard to other world competitors. Instead, they have highlighted American management as having many good things to offer: a sense of spirit, a sense of identification, a sense of clear caricature. This has served to fill a very important need. In American management thought there has emerged a lack of self-confidence and a lack of belief that what we are doing is proactive, effective, and correct. From this perspective these books have served a useful role in trying to present an upbeat, optimistic characterization.

QUESTION   In addition to a large volume of sales, surveys reveal that many of these books have been purchased and presumably read by those who are managing today's organizations. Does this trouble you? More specifically, are there any concerns that you have, given the extreme popularity of these types of books?

ANSWER   I am of two minds with regard to this question. First, I think that the sales of these books are not an accurate reflection of either the degree, the extent, nor the carefulness with which they have been read. Nor do I believe that the sales volumes tell us anything about the pervasiveness of their impact. Like many popular items (fads), many of these books have been purchased for desktop dressing. In many cases, the preface, the introduction, and the conclusion (maybe the summary on the dust jacket) have been read such that the essence of the book is picked up so that it can become a part of managerial and social conversation.

Obviously, this characterization does not accurately describe everyone in significant positions of management who have purchased these books. There are obviously many managers who make sincere attempts to follow the management literature thoroughly and to evaluate it critically. I think that most of the people that I come in contact with in management circles, both in training for management and in actual management positions, who have carefully read the books are not deceived by them. They are able to put them in the perspective of representations or characterizations of a fairly dramatic sort. As a consequence, I am not too concerned about the books being overly persuasive in some dangerous, Machiavellian, or subterranean sense.

On the other hand, I do have a concern of a different nature concerning these books. That concern focuses upon the possibility that the experiences they describe will be taken as legitimate bases or legitimate directions for the study of management processes. These books represent discourse by the method of emphasizing the extremes, in particular the extremes of success. I think a much more fruitful approach to studying and developing prescriptions for management thought and management action is to use the *method of differences* rather than the *method of extremes.*

The method of differences would require us to study the conditions which gave rise to success at Chrysler, or which gave rise to success at McDonald's, or which currently gives rise to success at Merck, or any of the other best-managed companies. However, through this method we would also contrast these companies with firms in the same industries which are not as successful. The method of contrast (differences) is likely to lead to empirical results which are much less dramatic, much less exciting, much less subject to journalistic account (i.e., they're likely to be more boring to read), but it is much more likely to lead to observations that are more generalizable across managerial situations, as well as being generative in terms of ideas for further management research.

Thus, the issue is based on the fundamental method that underlies these characterizations. My concern is not only from a methodological perspective. It also centers on our ethical and professional obligations to make sure that the knowledge we transmit does not lead people to overgeneralize. Rather, it should provide them with information which is diagnostic rather than purely prescriptive.

The method of extremes does not lead to a diagnostic frame of mind. It does not lead to a frame of mind which questions why did that happen, under what conditions will it happen, or under what conditions will it not happen. The method of differences is much more likely to lead to the discovery of the conditional nature of knowledge and the conditional nature of prescriptions.

QUESTION   A CEO or middle manager is about to take a sabbatical and has on his/her agenda the reading of a number of these "best-sellers." What advice would you like to offer?

ANSWER   Let me make the assumption that the CEO's sabbatical is for three months. My first advice would be to make an absolute public commitment to spend not more than one month of the sabbatical (i.e., not more than one third of it) reading these best-sellers. That would be the absolute maximum! Because of the lack of generalizability and validity of much of this information, any more time than this would be poorly spent. A crash course of one month, supplemented by perhaps video and audio tapes, would be sufficient to get the manager up to the place where he or she knows basically what is in these books. At this point the manager would have a working knowledge of the material as well as be capable of carrying on a reasonable conversation about the contents of the books.

Far more important, and worthy of at least two thirds of the time, would be reading of a different sort. Reading and study of the classics, both the intellectual and the philosophical classics, as well as the spiritual classics and historical classics would be of significant value.

I think one of the most important disciplines for the study of management, particularly for an experienced manager on sabbatical, is the study of history—the study of the development and decline of nation states and religious empires. They should look at history from a strategic perspective (i.e., what things did important nations and leaders take into consideration and what did they fail to take into consideration; what were their points of vulnerability and how could that have been prevented). It seems to me that this kind of knowledge is far more likely to lead to the discovery of useful diagnostics than the knowledge that is likely to be gained from reading the "best-seller" list.

❖ CONCLUSION

We hope that you have enjoyed reading the views of management scholar Professor Cummings regarding recent popular management books. In addition, we hope that these readings will serve to stimulate your thinking about effective and ineffective practices of management. We reiterate that there is no single universally applicable practice of management, for management is the skillful application of a body of knowledge to a particular situation. We invite you to continue expanding your understanding of new and developing management concepts. In a friendly sort of way, we challenge you to develop the skills to know when and how to apply this knowledge in the practice of management.

READING 4

The New Realities

Peter F. Drucker

When Karl Marx was beginning work on *Das Kapital* in the 1850s, the phenomenon of management was unknown. So were the enterprises that managers run. The largest manufacturing company around was a Manchester cotton mill employing fewer than three hundred people and owned by Marx's friend and collaborator Friedrich Engels. And in Engels's mill—one of the most profitable businesses of its day—there were no "managers," only "charge hands" who, themselves workers, enforced discipline over a handful of fellow "proletarians."

Rarely in human history has any institution emerged as quickly as management or had as great an impact so fast. In less than one hundred fifty years, management has transformed the social and economic fabric of the world's developed countries. It has created a global economy and set new rules for countries that would participate in that economy as equals. And it has itself been transformed. Few executives are aware of the tremendous impact management has had. Indeed, a good many are like M. Jourdain, the character in Moliäre's *Bourgeois Gentilhomme*, who did not know that he spoke prose. They barely realize that they practice—or mispractice—management. As a result, they are ill-prepared for the tremendous challenges that now confront them. The truly important problems managers face do not come from technology or politics; they do not originate outside of management and enterprise. They are problems caused by the very success of management itself.

To be sure, the fundamental task of management remains the same: to make people capable of joint performance through common goals, common values, the right structure, and the training and development they need to perform and to respond to change. But the very meaning of this task has changed, if only because the performance of management has converted the workforce from one composed largely of unskilled laborers to one of highly educated knowledge workers.

❖ THE ORIGINS AND DEVELOPMENT OF MANAGEMENT

Eighty years ago, on the threshold of World War I, a few thinkers were just becoming aware of management's existence. But few people even in the most advanced countries had anything to do with it. Now the largest single group in the labor force, more than one third of the total, are people whom the U.S. Bureau of the Census calls "managerial and professional." Management has been the main agent of this transformation. Management explains why, for the first time in human history, we can employ large numbers of knowledgeable, skilled people in productive work. No earlier society could do this. Indeed, no earlier society could support more than a handful of such people. Until quite recently, no one knew how to put people with different skills and knowledge together to achieve common goals. Eighteenth-century China was the envy of contemporary Western intellectuals because it supplied more jobs for educated people than all of Europe did—some twenty thousand per year. Today, the United States, with about the same population China then had, graduates nearly a million college students a year, few of whom have the slightest difficulty finding well-paid employment. Management enables us to employ them.

Knowledge, especially advanced knowledge, is always specialized. By itself it produces nothing. Yet a modern business, and not only the largest ones, may employ up to ten thousand highly knowledgeable people who represent up to sixty different knowledge areas. Engineers of all sorts, designers, marketing experts, economists, statisticians, psychologists, planners, accountants, human-resources people—all working together in a joint venture. None would be effective without the managed enterprise.

There is no point in asking which came first, the educational explosion of the last one hundred years or the management that put this knowledge to productive use. Modern management and modern enterprise could not exist without the knowledge base that developed societies have built. But equally, it is management, and management alone, that makes effective all this knowledge and these knowledgeable people. The emergence of management has converted knowledge from social ornament and luxury into the true capital of any economy.

Not many business leaders could have predicted this development back in 1870, when large enterprises were first beginning to take shape. The reason was not so much lack of foresight as lack of precedent. At that time, the only large permanent organization around was the army. Not surprisingly, therefore, its command-and-control structure became the model for the men who were putting together transcontinental railroads, steel mills, modern banks, and department stores. The command model, with a very few at the top giving orders and a great many at the bottom obeying them, remained the norm for nearly one hundred years. But it was never as static as its longevity might suggest. On the contrary, it began to change almost at once, as specialized knowledge of all sorts poured into enterprise. The first university-trained engineer in manufacturing industry was hired by Siemens in Germany in 1867—his name was Friedrick von Hefner-Alteneck. Within five years he had built a research department. Other specialized departments followed suit. By World War I the standard functions of a manufacturer had been developed: research and engineering, manufacturing, sales, finance and accounting, and a little later, human resources (or personnel).

Even more important for its impact on enterprise—and on the world economy in general—was another management-directed development that took place at this time. That was the application of management to manual work in the form of training. The child of wartime necessity, training has propelled the transformation of the world economy in the last forty years because it allows low-wage countries to do something that traditional economic theory had said could never be done: to become efficient—and yet still low-wage—competitors almost overnight.

Adam Smith reported that it took several hundred years for a country or region to develop a tradition of labor and the expertise in manual and managerial skills needed to produce and market a given product, whether cotton textiles or violins. During World War I, however, large numbers of unskilled, pre-industrial people had to be made productive workers in practically no time. To meet this need, businesses in the United States and the United Kingdom began to apply the theory of scientific management developed by Frederick W. Taylor between 1885 and 1910 to the systematic training of blue-collar workers on a large scale. They analyzed tasks and broke them down into individual, unskilled operations that could then be learned quite quickly. Further developed in World War II, training was then picked up by the Japanese and, twenty years later, by the South Koreans, who made it the basis for their countries' phenomenal development.

During the 1920s and 1930s, management was applied to many more areas and aspects of the manufacturing business. Decentralization, for instance, arose to combine the advantages of bigness and the advantages of smallness within one enterprise. Accounting went from "bookkeeping" to analysis and control. Planning grew out of the "Gantt charts" designed in 1917 and 1918 to plan war production; and so did the use of analytical logic and statistics, which employ quantification to convert experience and intuition into definitions, information, and diagnosis. Marketing evolved as a result of applying management concepts to distribution and selling. Moreover, as early as the mid-1920s and early 1930s, some American management pioneers such as Thomas Watson, Sr., at the fledgling IBM, Robert E. Wood at Sears, Roebuck, and George Elton Mayo at the Harvard Business School, began to question the way manufacturing was organized. They concluded that the assembly line was a short-term compromise. Despite its tremendous productivity, it was poor economics because of its inflexibility, poor use of human resources, even poor engineering. They began the thinking and experimenting that eventually led to "automation" as the way to organize the manufacturing process, and to teamwork, quality circles, and the information-based organization as the way to manage human resources. Every one of these managerial innovations represented the application of knowledge to work, the substitution of system and information for guesswork, brawn, and toil. Every one, to use Frederick Taylor's term, replaced "working harder" with "working smarter."

The powerful effect of these changes became apparent during World War II. To the very end, the Germans were by far the better strategists. Having much shorter interior lines, they needed fewer support troops and could match their opponents in combat strength. Yet the Allies won—their victory achieved by management. The United States, with one fifth the population of all the other belligerents together, had almost as many men in uniform. Yet it produced more war matériel than all the others taken together. It managed to transport the stuff to fighting fronts as far apart as China, Russia, India, Africa, and Western Europe. No wonder, then, that by the war's end almost all the world had become management-conscious. Or that management emerged as a recognizably distinct kind of work, one that could be studied and developed into a discipline—as happened in each country that has enjoyed economic leadership during the postwar period.

After World War II we began to see that management is not *business* management. It pertains to every human effort that brings together in one organization people of diverse knowledge and skills. It needs to be applied to all third-sector institutions, such as hospitals, universities, churches, arts organizations, and social service agencies, which since World War II have grown faster in the United States than either business or government. For even though the need to manage volunteers or raise funds may differentiate nonprofit managers from their for-profit peers, many more of their responsibilities are the same—among them defining the right strategy and goals, developing people, measuring performance, and marketing the organization's services. *Management worldwide has become the new social function.*

❖ MANAGEMENT AND ENTREPRENEURSHIP

One important advance in the discipline and practice of management is that both now embrace entrepreneurship and innovation. A sham fight these days pits "management" against "entrepreneurship" as adversaries, if not as mutually exclusive. That's like saying that the fingering hand and the bow hand of the violinst are "adversaries" or "mutually exclusive." Both are always needed and at the same time. And both have to be coordinated and work together. Any *existing* organization, whether a business, a church, a labor union, or a hospital, goes down fast if it does not innovate. Conversely, any *new* organization, whether a business, a church, a labor union, or a hospital, collapses if it does not manage. Not to innovate is the single largest reason for the decline of existing organizations. Not to know how to manage is the single largest reason for the failure of new ventures.

Yet few management books paid attention to entrepreneurship and innovation. One reason was that during the period after World War II when most of these books were written, managing the existing rather than innovating the new and different was the dominant task. During this period most institutions developed along lines laid down clearly thirty or fifty years earlier. This has not changed dramatically. We have again entered an era of innovation, and it is by no means confined to "high tech" or to technology generally. In fact, social innovation—as this book tries to make clear—may be of greater importance and have much greater impact than any scientific or technical invention. Furthermore, we now have a "discipline" of entrepreneurship and innovation (see my *Innovation and Entrepreneurship*, 1986). It is clearly a part of management and rests, indeed, on well-known and tested management principles. It applies to both existing organizations and new ventures, and to both business and non-business institutions, including government.

❖ THE LEGITIMACY OF MANAGEMENT

Management books tend to focus on the function of management inside its organizations. Few yet accept its social function. But it is precisely because management has become so pervasive as a social function that it faces its most serious challenge. To whom is management accountable? And for what? On what does management base its power? What gives it legitimacy?

These are not business questions or economic questions. They are *political* questions. Yet they underlie the most serious assault on management in its history—a far more serious assault than any mounted by Marxists or labor unions: the hostile takeover. An American phenomenon at first, it has spread throughout the non-Communist developed world. What made it possible was the emergence of the employee pension funds as the controlling shareholders of publicly owned companies. The pension funds, while legally "owners," are economically "investors"—and, indeed, often "speculators." They have no interest in the enterprise and its welfare. In fact, in the United States at least they are "trustees," and are not supposed to consider anything but immediate pecuniary gain. What underlies the takeover bid is the postulate that the enterprise's sole function is to provide the largest possible *immediate* gain to the shareholder. In the absence of any other justification for management and enterprise, the "raider" with his hostile takeover bid prevails—and only too often immediately dismantles or loots the going concern, sacrificing long-range, wealth-producing capacity to short-term gains.

Management—and not only in the business enterprise—has to be accountable for performance. But how is performance to be defined? How is it to be measured? How is it to be enforced? And to *whom* should management be accountable? That these questions can be asked is in itself a measure of the success and importance of management. That they need to be asked is, however, also an indictment of managers. They have not yet faced up to the fact that they represent power—and power has to be accountable, has to be legitimate. They have not yet faced up to the fact that they matter.

❖ WHAT IS MANAGEMENT?

But what is management? Is it a bag of techniques and tricks? A bundle of analytical tools like those taught in business schools? These are important, to be sure, just as thermometer and anatomy are important to the physician. But the evolution and history of management—its successes as well as its problems—teach that management is, above all else, a very few, essential principles. To be specific:

1. Management is about human beings. Its task is to make people capable of joint performance, to make their strengths effective and their weaknesses irrelevant. This is what organization is all about, and it is the reason that management is the critical, determining factor. These days, practically all of us are employed by managed institutions, large and small, business and non-business. We depend on management for our livelihoods. And our ability to contribute to society also depends as much on the management of the organizations in which we work as it does on our own skills, dedication, and effort.

2. Because management deals with the integration of people in a common venture, it is deeply embedded in culture. What managers do in West Germany, in the United Kingdom, in the United States, in Japan, or in Brazil is exactly the same. How they do it may be quite different. Thus one of the basic challenges managers in a developing country face is to find and identify those parts of their own tradition, history, and culture that can be used as management building blocks. The difference between Japan's economic success and India's relative backwardness is largely explained by the fact that Japanese managers were able to plant imported management concepts in their own cultural soil and make them grow.

3. Every enterprise requires commitment to common goals and shared values. Without such commitment there is no enterprise; there is only a mob. The enterprise must have simple, clear, and unifying objectives. The mission of the organization has to be clear enough and big enough to provide common vision. The goals that embody it have to be clear, public, and constantly reaffirmed. Management's first job is to think through, set, and exemplify those objectives, values, and goals.

4. Management must also enable the enterprise and each of its members to grow and develop as needs and opportunities change. Every enterprise is a learning and teaching institution. Training and development must be built into it on all levels—training and development that never stop.

5. Every enterprise is composed of people with different skills and knowledge doing many different kinds of work. It must be built on communication and on individual responsibility. All members need to think through what they aim to accomplish—and make sure that their associates know and understand that aim. All have to think through what they owe to others—and

make sure that others understand. All have to think through what they in turn need from others—and make sure that others know what is expected of them.

6. Neither the quantity of output nor the "bottom line" is by itself an adequate measure of the performance of management and enterprise. Market standing, innovation, productivity, development of people, quality, financial results—all are crucial to an organization's performance and to its survival. Non-profit institutions, too, need measurements in a number of areas specific to their mission. Just as a human being needs a diversity of measures to assess his or her health and performance, an organization needs a diversity of measures to assess its health and performance. Performance has to be built into the enterprise and its management; it has to be measured—or at least judged—and it has to be continuously improved.

7. Finally, the single most important thing to remember about any enterprise is that results exist only on the outside. The result of a business is a satisfied customer. The result of a hospital is a healed patient. The result of a school is a student who has learned something and puts it to work ten years later. Inside an enterprise, there are only costs.

Managers who understand these principles and function in their light will be achieving, accomplished managers.

❖ MANAGEMENT AS A LIBERAL ART

Thirty years ago, the English scientist and novelist C. P. Snow talked of the "two cultures" of contemporary society. Management, however, fits neither Snow's "humanist" nor his "scientist." It deals with action and application; and its tests are results. This makes it a technology. But management also deals with people, their values, their growth and development—and this makes it a humanity. So does it concern with, and impact on, social structure and the community. Indeed, as everyone has learned who, like this author, has been working with managers of all kinds of institutions for long years, management is deeply involved in spiritual concerns—the nature of man, good and evil.

Management is thus what tradition used to call a liberal art—"liberal" because it deals with the fundamentals of knowledge, self-knowledge, wisdom, and leadership; "art" because it is practice and application. Managers draw on all the knowledges and insights of the humanities and the social sciences—on psychology and philosophy, on economics and history, on the physical sciences and ethics. But they have to focus this knowledge on effectiveness and results—on healing a sick patient, teaching a student, building a bridge, designing and selling a "user-friendly" software program.

For these reasons, management will increasingly be the discipline and the practice through which the "humanities" will again acquire recognition, impact, and relevance.

2

MANAGEMENT PARADIGMS

Management consultants comment that the management philosophy reflected by the notion "If it ain't broke, don't fix it," needs to be discarded if organizations are going to survive the decade of the 1990s and enter the twenty-first century as viable and competitive social systems. In its place, Peters argues, is the need for the philosophy which espouses "If it ain't broke, fix it anyway"—reasoning which, if working today, in highly turbulent environments, will most likely be short-lived. In order to make this change, managers need to make a major paradigm shift. The three books summarized in this section of *The Manager's Bookshelf* focus on management paradigms and the need for managers to identify theirs, change them as needed, and work with multiple (and sometimes competing) paradigms.

Joel Barker continues his interest in paradigms and the business context with the publication of a new book *Paradigms: The Business of Discovering the Future.* A paradigm is a set of rules and regulations that establishes boundaries and tells people how to behave within the boundaries in order to be successful. Barker discusses innovation and anticipation as the keys to organizational survival as we move into the twenty-first century. An organization's position relative to the dominant paradigms and paradigm shifts within its industry will also play a critical role. He discusses paradigm leaders—those who change the rules by shifting the paradigms—and the forces that are associated with paradigm shifts.

Joel Barker has been a teacher, advertising executive, and served as the director of the Future Studies Department of the Science Museum of Minnesota. In addition to his writing, he is a corporate consultant.

Robert E. Quinn, in *Beyond Rational Management: Mastering the Paradoxes and Competing Demands of High Performance*, contends that the successful manager of the future cannot find answers to critical organizational questions in one-dimensional frameworks offered by such theories as Theory Y and Theory Z. The successful manager, who may have thrived as a professional engineer employing rational approaches and technical skills, will have to find a way to deal with the irrational world of organizational politics and employee morale.

Quinn, who is Professor of Organization Studies and Public Administration at the State University of New York, Albany, introduces the idea of a *master manager,* outlines how one can be developed, and lays out the master manager's journey to excellent performance. In particular, the master manager must acquire the ability to apply flexibly (and live with) competing values systems.

Lee G. Bolman and Terrence E. Deal's book, *Reframing Organizations: Artistry, Choice, and Leadership,* focuses on ways of becoming a more versatile manager and artistic leader. They approach these issues by focusing their attention on structure, human resources, political, and symbolic frames for bringing about major leadership and organizational change.

Lee Bolman is a Lecturer on Education at the Harvard Graduate School of Education, and Terrence Deal is Professor of Education at the Peabody College at Vanderbilt University. They also serve as codirectors of the National Center for Educational Leadership.

Chris Argyris' book *Overcoming Organizational Defenses* portrays ways of overcoming the defenses that tend to slow down change and inhibit the organization's ability to significantly improve performance. Shifting from established tradition, which focuses on morale, loyalty, and satisfaction as the foundation for the achievement of organizational excellence, Argyris argues that a more realistic base for excellence may come from an emphasis placed upon learning, competence, and justice. He alerts managers to the dangers of defensive reasoning, and argues that they must learn to engage in double-loop learning. Chris Argyris is the James Bryant Conant Professor on the Business and Education faculties at Harvard University.

READING 1

Paradigms: The Business of Discovering the Future

Joel A. Barker
Summary prepared by Brian E. Kahlbaugh

Brian Kahlbaugh is a manager of administration, operations, human resources, and customer relations for a Hertz car rental franchise in Duluth, Minnesota. He graduated with honors from the University of Minnesota, Duluth, with a degree in Business Administration.

> What is impossible to do in your business (field, discipline, department, division, technology, etc.) but, if it could be done, would fundamentally change it (p. 141)?

Joel Barker's quote encourages consideration of three complementary routes to success: creative thought (innovation), concern for the development of quality in ongoing business operations (excellence), and thought with regard to future opportunities and their consequences (anticipation). These three elements—innovation, excellence, and anticipation—are seen as necessary ingredients for organizational systems to move successfully into and through the twenty-first century. *Paradigms: The Business of Discovering the Future* focuses on innovation and anticipation within the key context of paradigms.

Creative thinking involves *innovation,* which is the key to gaining and maintaining a competitive advantage. Innovation is crucial for a system to survive in a constantly changing environment. Managerial attitudes and actions (their paradigms) within a system can either enhance or inhibit the ability of the system to innovate. Paradigms become a major factor affecting innovation and survival, especially when the system is confronted with rapid change.

Anticipation is founded in exploration of changing trends while keeping an eye open for possibilities arising as an outcome of change. Anticipation forces proactive thought, which seeks to prevent problems by staying ahead of

Joel A. Barker, Paradigms: *The Business of Discovering the Future.* New York: Harper-Collins, 1993.

them as opposed to responsive thought, which seeks to solve problems after they have arisen. An ability to accurately anticipate the future is as much, or more, artistic in nature as it is scientific. The ability to anticipate a successful direction for the future of a system based on uncertainty and lack of proof is art. The art of good anticipation is based on strategic exploration, which consists of the following elements:

◆ *Understanding influence* To understand what influences perception.

◆ *Divergent thinking* To seek more than one answer.

◆ *Convergent thinking* To assess all the perceived options and information and then focus and prioritize among choices.

◆ *Mapping* To highlight the routes that will get the system from here to the future.

◆ *Imaging* To picture in words, drawings, or models the results of your exploration of the future.

Good anticipation provides a system with tools to move into the future and gives the system a greater likelihood of succeeding through accelerating change.

What are paradigms? A *paradigm* can be defined as, *"A set of rules and regulations (written or unwritten) that does two things: (1) establishes or defines boundaries, and (2) tells you how to behave inside the boundaries in order to be successful* (p. 32)."

For example, consider the fast-food industry. Employees in a fast-food restaurant must comply with both formal and informal rules. Formal rules may include policies and standards of operation defined by management and laws regarding cleanliness. Informal rules may include unwritten expectations regarding how customers are treated, readiness, food preparation, and how employees should interact with each other. Together, the written and unwritten rules and regulations establish the boundaries for the fast-food restaurant. Fast food will be served by the rules and methods defined. New York Strip steak and lobster served in a quiet, private atmosphere is out of bounds for a fast-food restaurant. If the food preparers, order takers at the front counter and at the drive-up window, and other employees at the restaurant comply with the established rules within the established boundaries, a lot of tasty fast food will be sold, employees will keep their jobs, and the fast-food restaurant will be successful.

A *paradigm shift* is a change to a new paradigm having new rules, boundaries, and behaviors. Consider the paradigm of the cigarette industry. How might trends in the environment, such as recent legal and public health issues and changes in the public's attitudes, affect the prosperous cigarette manufacturing industry in the future? Could a profound paradigm shift be forthcoming?

Paradigms are not exclusive to business organizations. Paradigms exist in all areas of human interaction where the interactions have established boundaries (limits placed on participants within the paradigm) and where the interactions require success-oriented behaviors of the participants within these boundaries. Any particular sport, education, marriage, business organization, or even a whole society may be considered a paradigm. The list of all possible paradigms would be endless.

"Successful" is a key word in the definition of paradigm. A paradigm's degree of success is measured by its ability to solve increasingly difficult problems. If a paradigm is not able to solve increasingly difficult problems, it will have short-lived success. This suggests that paradigms have an identifiable life-span. Paradigms are born all the time, but the length of their life depends on their ongoing problem-solving ability. Paradigm shifts involve the birth of new paradigms and the death (or at least obsolescence) of old paradigms. As established paradigms lose their ability to solve new problems, new paradigms with the ability to solve new sets of problems need to emerge.

The long-term survival of a business is dependent on the business' ability to innovate and its ability to anticipate the future. If these activities are done well the probability increases that the business will be able to avoid or solve future problems.

❖ WHEN DO PARADIGM SHIFTS OCCUR?

During the life span of a system, problems are encountered and solved. As more and more increasingly difficult problems are solved, the system goes through a period of success. The success convinces participants that the rules for *"doing things"* are correct, and a mindset may develop whereby participants no longer are able or allowed to solve new problems in any way other than in the ways that have, historically, proven themselves to be the *"right"* ways! Sooner or later, however, the system encounters problems that it does not solve, perhaps as a result of the established mindset. When this happens participants within the system, and others external to the system who are in some way aware of the problems, observe the unsolved problems. Both frustration and opportunity reveal themselves. The time is now ripe for change. When unsolved problems are not dealt with and start accumulating within a system, a paradigm shift is likely to occur. Someone sees the unsolved problems and goes about forming a new paradigm to take on the unsolved problem set. *The status quo becomes challenged.*

If a system is aware of where it is in this process, it can better anticipate what is ahead, and perhaps even stimulate a search for new paradigms.

❖ WHO ARE THE PARADIGM SHIFTERS?

There are basically four types of paradigm shifters. Three of the four exist outside of, or are new to, an established system. *All* types of paradigm shifters face conflict and resistance to their ideas for change. This occurs as a result of the prevailing mindset in most systems. Because the existing paradigms have performed well and because the rules/boundaries have become so potent inside the system, suggestions for change seem unnecessary and almost insulting. Those who are resistant to suggestions for change proclaim that, *"I have done well for a long time, and I don't need you telling me anything different!"* The problem with this attitude is that it bases itself in past successes as though the ways in which the system has solved problems before are the same ways in which future problems will be solved. These individuals neglect to anticipate changing trends or new paradigms, and they will not allow themselves to acknowledge the new types of problems that will be encountered.

The first type of paradigm shifter is the "green horn." This person knows of a system only through study, not through personal experience. This person has not learned the rules/boundaries of the system through hard knocks as have those who have been working within the system for some time. The mind of the green horn has not been constricted by the established rules of the system and, therefore, is capable of perceiving problems and solutions in a fresh light.

The second type of paradigm shifter is the veteran of one system changing over to a new system. These people have become proficient in one system, and, as a result, they bring with them actual problem-solving experience that may be adapted to solve different sets of problems in the new paradigm. They also bring with them a mind not constricted by the established rules/boundaries and, therefore, can offer ideas and perspectives unique to the new system.

An important element shared by the first two types of paradigm shifters is a combination of naiveté and creativity due to a lack of familiarity with the new system. This can be a powerful resource for a system willing to tap into it.

The third type of paradigm shifter is the "maverick." These people are insiders of a system who see the unsolved problems stacking up, who know the existing rules/boundaries of the system will not provide the necessary solutions, and who challenge the existing system in an attempt to force a paradigm shift from within the system. The unique aspect of mavericks is that they are practitioners of a system, but are not shackled by the system's rules/boundaries.

The fourth type involves people in scientific and technical systems. These people have a natural curiosity that motivates them to play around with unsolved problems in an attempt to come up with new solutions.

The four types of paradigm shifters are important resources for systems concerned with longevity. Their value can support both the process of innovation and the process of anticipation.

❖ WHO FOLLOWS THE PARADIGM SHIFTERS?

The group of people who follow someone who has initiated change share important traits. Their primary traits are courage and intuition. To choose to follow someone into uncharted territories takes courage. To choose to follow a new path treaded by someone who has met resistance along the way involves intuition and trust. A new path presents unknown risk. To follow someone into a new system requires a gut-feeling that the risk is worth the attempt. These people face high risk, but they also face the potential of high gain if the new paradigm (system) is successful. The followers provide energy and momentum for the new paradigm.

❖ WHAT IS THE PARADIGM EFFECT?

> "When someone offers us a paradigm-enhancing innovation—one that improves upon what we are already practicing—we see that easily. But when someone offers us a paradigm-shifting innovation, we find ourselves resistant to it, because it just doesn't fit the rules we are so good at." (p. 92)

Opportunity is in the future. Changing trends provide hints about the future, but they do not provide certainty. The future and dynamic change are inevitable. Without a doubt, there will be new paradigms that seek to capitalize on the problems of the future. The rules will change. *The tendency, however, is for practitioners of an established paradigm to resist participating in new paradigms and the opportunities they present.*

Perception is shaped by the established paradigm, which limits the ability to recognize and internalize new rules that are developing with the process of changing trends. An established paradigm has been functioning for a period of time. This leads to a logical belief that things are being done right (and for the time being they are), that the rules, as they are, are sufficient for continued success. We see what has worked and stand by it. It is very difficult to argue with what has worked out well. Because of these shaped perceptions it is also very difficult to acknowledge changing rules and changing trends in the environment. It is easier to acknowledge the success of rules that have previously worked within the established paradigm and, further, to assume that those same rules will continue to be successful. For progress and long-term survival, it becomes necessary to challenge existing perceptions and realize that the future is coming, times will change and the rules will change. To take part in the future requires acceptance of new paradigms. No one stays on top forever. The *paradigm effect* is a process whereby we are forced to review our own perceptions, shaped by our own paradigm, and begin considering the merits of other perceptions being shaped by newly developing paradigms.

Understanding when paradigms shift, who initiates paradigm shifts, who follows into the new paradigm, and how paradigms and paradigm shifts affect the perceptions of people are key elements in anticipating future trends. These are the elements that help in a proactive approach to change.

The paradigm principles are seven fundamental generalizations about the characteristics and operation of paradigms and are presented as a part of the focus on anticipating your future and increasing your innovative capacity. The *paradigm principles* include:

1. *Paradigms are common*—They exist in all areas of society—some on a small scale and some on a large scale. All paradigms, however, provide the participants with specific understanding and specific problem-solving abilities.

2. *Paradigms are functional*—They provide rules and directions for weaving a route through complex environments. Good paradigms focus our perceptions and our resources on what is important and keep us from straying into areas that are not immediately important. They also combine talents of diverse participants into problem-solving endeavors.

3. *The paradigm effect reverses the commonsense relationship between seeing and believing*—We normally believe something when we see it. The paradigm effect forces us to see something when we believe it. Before we can change our perceptions to acknowledge the value and the inevitability of new paradigms that differ from our own, we must first come to believe in their value and their inevitability. Only then will we come to acknowledge their merit and their potential for opportunity.

4. *There is almost always more than one right answer*—By acknowledging paradigm shifts our perceptions are broadened so that we see our world from a new standpoint. This does not mean either our old perceptions or our new perceptions are the right or wrong perceptions, only that we can now see there are more ways to solve problems.

5. *Paradigms too strongly held can lead to paradigm paralysis, a terminal disease of certainty*—A paradigm achieves power through its ability to solve problems. A very powerful paradigm is one that has been successful. This leads to *paradigm paralysis*—a belief that the existing paradigm is *the* paradigm and any other alternatives are wrong. ("*This* is the way we do things around here!") The result may be that new ideas are quashed or do not even get a chance to be known. This is a dangerous place to be in, especially in times of rapid change, and may lead to obsolescence of the strongly held paradigm.

6. *Paradigm pliancy is the best strategy in turbulent times*—Greater opportunity can be recognized when practitioners of an established paradigm actively promote *paradigm pliancy*—a tolerance of suggested alternative paradigms for solving new problem sets created by a rapidly changing environment. Practitioners of paradigm pliancy encourage and genuinely consider suggested alternative paradigms.

7. *Human beings can choose to change their paradigms*—People have a demonstrated ability to adapt to change and to survive through seemingly overwhelming obstacles. It often times is an arduous process and would not be possible without our determination to prevail. This determination forces us, as a whole, to *choose* to find new ways of solving problems. Not everyone makes this choice, and not everyone will prevail through rapid change by holding on to existing paradigms. We do, however, have the options of

leading, or following, into new paradigms, taking with us our skills and abilities developed in our existing paradigms.

The future is coming. What are we going to do with it, what kind of problems will it present, and what can we do now to ready ourselves? The answers lie in our understanding and use of paradigms.

READING 2

Beyond Rational Management: Mastering the Paradoxes and Competing Demands of High Performance

Robert E. Quinn
Summary prepared by Robert Marx

Robert Marx is Associate Professor of Management at the University of Massachusetts in Amherst. He received his doctorate in clinical psychology from the University of Illinois. His research efforts have focused on the problem of skill retention following management development programs. He has published on the topic of relapse prevention.

❖ THE JOURNEY FROM NOVICE TO MASTER MANAGER

There is hardly a consultant, social scientist, or practicing manager who does not have an opinion about what makes a master manager. The search for answers to this critical question wanders through a veritable dictionary of management panaceas exploring everything from the danger of Type A behavior[1] to the promise of theories Y[2] and Z.[3] These prescriptive models offer novice managers widely varying responses to a myriad of managerial problems.

The master manager, however, has learned that these prescriptive approaches are "one-dimensional bromides"[4] that explain only a small part of the managerial arena. Master managers recognize that organizations are "gyrating in constant chameleonic flux."[5] Behavioral consistency and logic, when overused, fail to cope effectively with such pervasive change. Master man-

Robert E. Quinn. *Beyond Rational Management*. San Francisco: Jossey-Bass, 1988.

agers must develop the capacity to use *contradiction and paradox*. The real world of organizations is not characterized by stable, predictable patterns that easily lend themselves to structured, analytical solutions. The higher levels of managing occur in complex dynamic systems that include change, ambiguity, and contradiction.

An engineer who has thrived professionally by solving complex technical problems may begin the journey to management mastery with a simplistic technical approach to management success. However, the rational technical skills that worked so well solving engineering problems are based on a set of assumptions that are unlikely to work well in the irrational world of organizational politics and employee morale.

The master manager must learn to use contradictory paradoxical frames that respond to existing circumstances. Unfortunately, such abilities do not come easily or naturally to most individuals. Because people develop a set of values and a world view from which they take action, contradictory perspectives may appear initially to be wrong or evil. The entrepreneur excels at innovation and seizing the moment. Development of the formal systems necessary to *maintain* the innovation are seen as unimportant by the novice manager. Conversely, the keeper of the systems sees the entrepreneur as a "loose cannon" who must be brought under control before an entire operation is blown to bits. Master managers transcend several competing values and assumptions. They see no contradiction in loose cannons and secure systems operating in tandem. The path from novice to master manager crosses many streams of thought and acknowledges how each one contributes to the flow of organizational life.

Research has shown that master managers have greater cognitive complexity than novices, thus allowing for more discrimination of cues and greater differences in responses to situations.[6] Master managers also evolve to higher levels of ego development.[7]

Whereas novice managers are likely to function at the technician stage of ego development characterized by a high degree of logic, bureaucracy, and detail orientation, master managers reach the strategist stage generating new orders, delighting in paradoxes, and understanding "the uniqueness of each individual and situation."[8]

The path to mastery evolves from the *novice stage* where facts and rules dominate[9] to the *advanced beginner stage* where experience becomes critical. Just as a novice chess player begins by learning the rules and experiencing exceptions in play, so does the evolving manager. With the *competence stage* comes the ability to appreciate the complexity of the task and to take risks that go beyond rational analysis. The *proficiency stage* brings with it "flow," pattern recognition, and intuitive moves that indicate a holistic view of the game or the workplace. The chess masters and master managers evolve to the *expert stage* where they have transcended the rules and personal styles and can deal with existing contradictions. The master manager can simultaneously function at the level of detail and vision, task and person, coach and politician, and with this flexibility achieves a high level of productivity.

❖ ACHIEVING EXCELLENCE THROUGH PARADOX

The master manager's journey to excellent performance must proceed through a dynamic cycle of events called the *transformational cycle.* The cycle begins with the *initiation phase,* where the person has a desire to improve and is willing to take risks to explore the unknown. Fear of failure can end the cycle, but high performers see failure as a stepping-stone. "Contrary to rational-technical thinking, the initiation of action under conditions of risk is an important step to begin performance."[10] The *uncertainty phase* is entered once the new action is taken. This uncertainty is epitomized by a youngster learning to ride a two-wheel bike. As she tries to keep the bike upright, a natural response is to stop pedaling and manage the impending fall. If she can overcome the fear and keep pedaling, the bike will stay upright and "excellence" will be experienced. As she begins to gain control over the bike, the youngster experiences the *transformation phase.* Here the risk of falling has been challenged and supplanted with a new set of accomplishments. The child and parents feel the excitement and exhilaration of the moment. Then the *routinization phase* sets in. She "knows" how to ride. There is little risk, but logical, systematic practice prevail. Sustaining excellence is difficult over the long term. Risk and intuition that led to transformation and exhilaration must yield to control and rationality to consolidate gains. The master manager does not forget to repeat the risk-taking behavior that brought her to new levels of exhilaration and transformation.

❖ THE COMPETING VALUES MODEL: REDEFINING ORGANIZATIONAL EFFECTIVENESS AND CHANGE

It is inherently difficult for people to think in contradictory ways. Bateson[11] describes the natural tendency of Western thought to be "schismogenic," where one value is chosen *over* another, eliminating contradiction and paradox. Schismogenic thinking thus eliminates competing positive values from consideration because they are not logically consistent with the "best" choice.

Rather than be trapped in any single set of values and assumptions about organizational life, master managers can tolerate several competing sets of assumptions simultaneously. They may be purposive in temporarily choosing to solve a specific management problem. Yet they are not schismogenic or *stuck* in any single frame.

The ways that managers process information culminate in strong predispositions and values that determine what they believe good managers should do. Often managers are unaware of these underlying values, but they become "emotionally held moral positions" about what "good" managers do. Unfortunately, these deeply held positions are only effective part of the time. Instead of remaining consistent and logical and clinging to a single set of values, it is frequently advantageous to see problems from a contradictory set of values.

Indeed, master managers must free themselves from "their preferred way of seeing and behaving"[12] and learn to balance a set of competing values. The competing values model makes explicit the contradictions that managers must constantly live with. Organizations must be adaptable and at the same time be stable. They must emphasize the value of people, while maintaining productivity.

The competing values framework, displayed in Figure 1, is scaled along two bipolar axes, which yield four quadrants. The vertical axis measures the degree of control exerted by the organization. High control is exemplified by values that support centralization, hierarchy, and integration, which allow the organization to maintain stable procedures and develop plans. High flexibility at the other pole of the axis is exemplified by decentralization, self-management, and differentiated action, which allows the organization to respond quickly to changing circumstances and avoid the dysfunctional elements of bureaucracy.

The horizontal axis measures the degree of internal versus external emphasis of the organization. The external emphasis is exemplified by an orientation toward competition, growth, and response to the world outside the organization. The internal emphasis is exemplified by values oriented toward maintaining the sociotechnical systems within the organization. It focuses on internal structure, information systems, clear job descriptions, morale, and decision-making.

Each of the four competing values is based on a mode of information processing. As presented here, each perspective comprises a combination of two factors: (a) flexible or tight controls and (b) external or internal forces. Thus the commonality and contrast of each of the competing values' orientations can be seen within an integrated framework. Effective managers recognize the delicate blend of contradictory perspectives necessary for effective organizational problem solving. The four cells include the *human relations, internal process, open systems,* and *rational goal* perspectives.

◆ HUMAN RELATIONS PERSPECTIVE

This cell combines the values of internal emphasis and flexibility. The approach prefers long time lines and low certainty. The primary information of importance is that of process, where the nature of human interaction is observed. Organizations emphasizing process are often managed as a team. The prevailing concern in this culture is for members of the organization. Commitment and morale are maintained by openness, participation, and discussion. Human resources are valued, and training, autonomy, and delegation are common-place. Career management, fair salaries, incentives, and matching jobs to the skill of the individual are concrete expressions of this value system. This culture emphasizes the importance of understanding the needs of employees. However, when used to the extreme this perspective can be perceived as the irresponsible country club where human relations criteria are emphasized to the point of encouraging laxity and negligence.

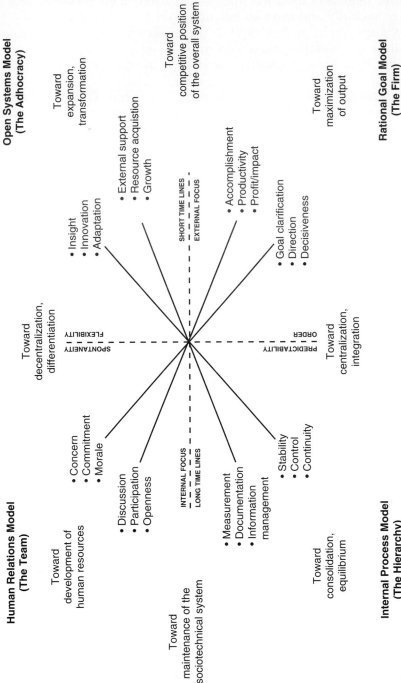

Human Relations Model (The Team)

Toward development of human resources

Toward maintenance of the sociotechnical system

- Concern
- Commitment
- Morale

- Discussion
- Participation
- Openness

- Measurement
- Documentation
- Information management

Toward consolidation, equilibrium

Open Systems Model (The Adhocracy)

Toward expansion, transformation

Toward competitive position of the overall system

Toward maximization of output

- Insight
- Innovation
- Adaptation

- External support
- Resource acquistion
- Growth

- Accomplishment
- Productivity
- Profit/impact

- Goal clarification
- Direction
- Decisiveness

Rational Goal Model (The Firm)

Toward decentralization, differentiation

Toward centralization, integration

- Stability
- Control
- Continuity

Internal Process Model (The Hierarchy)

FLEXIBILITY
SPONTANEITY

ORDER
PREDICTABILITY

SHORT TIME LINES
EXTERNAL FOCUS

INTERNAL FOCUS
LONG TIME LINES

FIGURE 1
Competing Values Framework: Culture

Source Figure 6. p. 51. Robert Quinn, Beyond Rational Management Mastering the Paradoxes and Competing Demands of High Performance, San Francisco Josey-Bass, 1988. Used with permission.

◆ THE INTERNAL PROCESS PERSPECTIVE

This model represents the values of internal focus and high control. The internal process approach processes information with long time lines and high certainty. It emphasizes rational problem-solving and perpetuation of the status quo. Organizations based on this information processing style are often managed as bureaucracy.[13] This model works "best when the task to be done is well understood and when time is not an important factor."[14]

The prevailing concerns of this value system are maintaining the hierarchy, which provides the organization with the stability and continuity to make effective long-range decisions. In this framework, information management and documentation allow for efficient integration. An organization that emphasizes these values has an accessible and comprehensive data base. There are clear job descriptions, role expectations, and procedures for resolving conflicts over unclear procedures. This culture emphasizes an internally organized company. However, when used to the extreme this perspective can be perceived as the "frozen bureaucracy," where the organization becomes atrophied as a result of excessive measurement and documentation and everything is done "by the book" regardless of its effectiveness.

◆ OPEN SYSTEMS PERSPECTIVE

The values of flexibility and an external focus define the third quadrant. This perspective organizes information along short time lines and low certainty. The open systems approach seeks risk, variation, intuitive thought, and a future orientation. The system is always open to new feedback. Organizations based on this information processing style are organized as "adhocracies," preferring organic matrix forms that are easily modified. The adhocracy functions well when the task is not well understood, and when quick completion is essential.

The prevailing concerns of this value system are expansion and adaptation to the changing business environment. Readiness to make decisions is viewed as the key to growth and resource acquisition. The open systems perspective is designed to produce in a competitive market through constant innovation and change. This culture emphasizes adaptability to the marketplace. However, when used to the extreme this perspective can be perceived as the "tumultuous anarchy," where the emphasis on insight and innovation results in disastrous experimentation, political expediency, and an obsession with competitive advantage at the expense of continuity and control over work.

◆ RATIONAL GOAL PERSPECTIVE

This model combines the values of external focus and high control. The prevailing concerns of this value system are productivity and efficiency. The rational goal approach organizes information along short time lines and high certainty, and requires short-term goals and rapid decision-making. Organizations based on this information processing style are often managed as "firms" with the emphasis on the bottom line. These are achieved through planning, goal setting, goal clarification, and direction. The rational goal perspective values the control inherent in planning and goal setting and builds in feedback systems to modify procedures when goals are not accomplished. This culture emphasizes the maximization of output in a competitive environment. However, when used to the extreme, this perspective can be perceived as the "oppressive sweatshop," where the emphasis on productivity and effectiveness yields perpetual exertion, and eventual burnout, and limited opportunity for individual differences and employee input.

Each of these four perspectives represents an important set of values that yield an entirely different set of managerial activities. The team-oriented manager would emphasize the needs of the individual, while the firm-oriented manager would emphasize goal accomplishment. Master managers see these contrasting value orientations as complementary rather than competing. They learn to play each of these roles as necessary in the changing environment, avoiding schismogenic thought and appreciating the strengths and weaknesses of each perspective.

❖ THE FRAMEWORK AS A DIAGNOSTIC TOOL

This framework can be used to diagnose organizational problems and suggest appropriate interventions. For example, a fast-growing high tech firm used the competing values framework to diagnose that it had become very good at functioning in the open systems model by adapting rapidly to a changing marketplace. However, the internal process model, which should provide a system for decision-making, was sorely neglected. The firm had bought flexibility at the cost of internal integrity.[15] The human relations model, which champions cohesiveness and morale, also suffered because of the extreme external emphasis of this firm. Strategies were developed to emphasize competing values to bring the firm into balance and renew its creative thrust.

Because values change in organizations over time, new emphases must be adopted. The competing values framework explains how different values may be emphasized during various stages of organizational growth. Organizations move through four distinct transitional stages, each of which requires a different values emphasis. The *entrepreneurial stage* of an organization is typified by innovation and creativity and fits the open systems model. The *collectivity stage* follows with a strong emphasis on informal communication, commitment, and a sense of family. Focusing human motivation and energy is a strength of the human relations model. As the organization matures during the *formalization stage,* organizational stability and efficiency of productivity become paramount. The internal process model provides necessary rules and procedures, while the rational goal model highlights goal accomplishment and productivity. In the fourth stage, *elaboration of structure,* the organization turns its emphasis toward the external environment to renew itself or expand. Otherwise it risks stagnation beneath a structure that is static in nature and unresponsive to the changing environment.

Failure to recognize the changes in culture as a firm develops can spell disaster. Don Burr of People Express used his creativity to build a dynamic organization that was creative and humanistic. However, when confronted with the formalization stage requiring policies, procedures, and coordination, he could not adapt. Burr's inability to emphasize internal stabilization represented a failure to utilize competing values and transcend his personal style.[16]

By contrast, Bill Gates of Microsoft (now the world's largest software firm) survived a similar formalization crisis by bringing in professional managers who understood how to create internal stability. Gates was able to maintain his own entrepreneurial and technological focus, while simultaneously maintaining a secure infrastructure. By not perceiving the need to formalize a competing, either-or value, Gates was able to move from one set of values to another. Effective managers of today must understand how to manage change. The competing values model offers a powerful tool.

❖ APPLICATIONS OF THE COMPETING VALUES MODEL: THE ROLES OF LEADERSHIP

While many models of leadership recommend espousing one leadership style over another, the competing values model recognizes the importance of avoiding either-or considerations. It simply asks what leadership skills are needed to manage specific organizational concerns. This model identifies eight leadership roles and integrates them with the four competing values perspectives:

The open systems model supports leadership activities that are creative and risk-taking, externally oriented, and flexible. Leaders operating from this perspective function in the *innovator role,* envisioning the future and risking needed change. The *broker role* requires political astuteness in order for an individual to serve as an effective external liaison to acquire needed resources.

The rational goal model encourages leadership activities that are competitive and structured, with goal orientation and productivity of greatest importance. The *producer role* requires task orientation and understanding of how to motivate employees to accomplish stated goals. The *director role* emphasizes defining and designing goals, roles, and tasks for high-output performance.

The internal process model focuses on leadership activities that develop necessary internal stability. This conservative, structured approach includes the *monitor role,* which controls and analyzes information to facilitate logical problem solving, and the *coordinator role,* which maintains continuity through careful planning and organizing, linking the performance of producers with the evaluation of the monitors.

The human relations model highlights leadership activities that emphasize interpersonal collaboration. The leadership style is supportive and based on people's need for affiliation. The *facilitator role* develops group cohesion and participative decision making, and mediates conflict. The *mentor role* develops people through skill building, availability, and trust.

Each of the four perspectives has perceptual biases about the assumptions and roles of leadership. The cautious, stable approach of the internal process perspective contrasts starkly with the risk-taking predilection of the open systems approach. However, the competing values models asks managers to move from the either-or schismogenic position of the novice to the both/and frame of mind of the master manager.

A preliminary study of effective and ineffective managers[17] suggests that *balance* is the key. Ineffective managers scored below average on all eight leadership roles or emphasized only one or two at the expense of others. Effective managers were above average on five or more roles, thus allowing flexibility in leadership behavior despite a few weak areas.

❖ TRANSFORMING MANAGEMENT STYLES

The journey from novice to master manager requires diagnosing and confronting one's weak quadrants. Such transformations require taking risks and dealing with fear of the unknown or of the underdeveloped side of oneself. Such transformations can take place *spontaneously* when a manager in crisis discovers that old strategies won't solve new problems. In one example, a manager indoctrinated in the hierarchical approach to leadership found that when a crisis required him to set up task forces to solve problems, motivation, trust, and performances unexpectedly improved dramatically. Leadership activities previously associated with "bad management" suddenly proved their worth. Out of the chaos came a valuable lesson about balancing polarities.

Transformation can also occur through *self-examination*. Managers can learn about themselves through self-assessment, feedback from peers and subordinates, and maintaining a journal. Using the competing values framework and its related assessment instruments, managers can become more aware of their prevailing value systems and develop change strategies for improving weak areas.

The journey from novice to master manager requires a balance between logical, purposive behavior, and holistic, intuitive flow. Managers get stuck by being too predisposed to values in a given quadrant. What has started out as a positive value becomes negative when it is overused. When managers get in trouble they often continue to do whatever they have been doing, only harder. The competing values framework allows managers to dismantle polarities. It makes available to master managers both ends of the continuum and the middle as well. It provides a meaningful framework to help managers respond to change in their organizations and to risk change within themselves.

❖ NOTES

1. Friedman, M., and R. H. Rosenman, *Type A Behavior and Your Heart.* New York: Alfred Knopf, 1974.
2. McGregor, D., *The Human Side of Enterprise.* New York: McGraw-Hill, 1960.
3. Ouchi, W. G., *Theory Z: How American Business Can Meet the Japanese Challenge.* Reading, MA: Addison-Wesley, 1981.
4. Quinn, R. E., *Beyond Rational Management: Mastering The Paradoxes and Competing Demands of High Performance.* San Francisco: Jossey-Bass, 1988, p. 3.
5. Ibid., p. xiv.
6. Streufert, S. and R. W. Swezey, *Complexity, Managers and Organizations.* Orlando, FL: Academic Press, 1986.
7. Torbert, W. R., *Managing the Corporate Dream: Restructuring for Long-Term Success.* Homewood, IL: Dow Jones-Irwin, 1987.
8. Quinn, p. 7.
9. Dreyfus, H. L., S. E. Dreyfus, and T. Albanasion, *Mind Over Machine: The Power of Human Intuition and Expertise in the Era of the Computer.* New York: Free Press, 1986.
10. Quinn, p. 18.
11. Bateson, G., *Mind and Nature.* New York: Bantam Books, 1979.
12. Quinn, p. 90.
13. Weber, M., *Theory of Social and Economic Organization.* Translated by A. M. Henderson and T. Parsons. London: Oxford University Press, 1921.
14. Quinn, p. 39.
15. Quinn, p. 53.
16. Hackman, J. R., "The Transition That Hasn't Happened." In J. R. Kimberly and R. E. Quinn (eds.), *Managing Organizational Transitions.* Homewood, IL: Dow Jones-Irwin, 1984.
17. Quinn, R. E., S. R. Faerman, and N. Dixit, "Perceived Performance: Some Archetypes of Managerial Effectiveness and Ineffectiveness." Working paper, Institute for Government and Policy Studies, Department of Public Administration, State University of New York at Albany, 1987.

READING 3

Reframing Organizations: Artistry, Choice, and Leadership

Lee G. Bolman and Terrence E. Deal
Summary prepared by Robert Marx

Robert Marx is an Associate Professor of Management at the University of Massachusetts at Amherst. He is the coauthor of *Management Live! The Video Book.* Marx was the 1991 recipient of the Bradford Outstanding Educator Award from the Organizational Behavior Teaching Society in recognition of his excellence in teaching.

❖ THE POWER OF REFRAMING

In this century, our society has evolved from a simple, local lifestyle where people could manage their own affairs to a global, technologically sophisticated world dominated by large, complex organizations. These new organizations have proliferated because they have been enormously successful at producing a wide range of goods and services, including better health care, education, and communication linkages. Yet, for all their successes, there are flaws in these large companies and government organizations.

Indifferent salespersons, meaningless work, contradictory and unethical policies, and shoddy products represent the price paid for creating these unwieldy groups of people that comprise organizations. Despite the best efforts to improve these organizations through new management techniques, the use of consultants, and government interventions, organizations still do more of the same, handling problems the "only way"[1] they could be handled. *Managers and leaders must be able to expand their repertoire of ideas to handle the complex problems of organizations.* They must be able to "reframe" their thinking.

Lee G. Bolman and Terrence E. Deal, *Reframing Organizations: Artistry, Choice, and Leadership.* San Francisco: Jossey-Bass, 1991.

❖ THE FOUR FRAMES

"The truly effective leader will need multiple tools, the skill to use each of them, and the wisdom to match frames to situations."[2]

Based on insights from research and experience working with many organizations and managers, four perspectives or frames have emerged. Each frame views the world from a particular set of values and basic assumptions. They are:

◆ THE STRUCTURAL FRAME

Based on rational systems theory, the structural frame emphasizes the rational aspect of organizational life. The organization is viewed as a machine whose parts must be run and maintained efficiently. Organizations create structures to fit their environment and technology. Formal roles, clear rules, and responsibilities are necessary for efficient functioning. When problems arise, reorganizing is the primary method for restoring equilibrium.

◆ THE HUMAN RESOURCES FRAME

Based on theories of human behavior from the psychological sciences, the human resources frame views the organization as a family. People are the heart of the organization and they have needs and feelings which must be understood and addressed. There must be a good fit between the organization's structure and the needs of its people. That is, people must be able to get the job done and feel good about what they're doing. When problems arise, communication and support are required.

◆ THE POLITICAL FRAME

Based on theories of power, the political frame sees the organization as a jungle where different interest groups compete for scarce resources. Conflict is a part of everyday life in organizations because each interest group has its own agenda. Effective managers must understand how to build power bases and coalitions and manage conflict as productively as possible. When problems arise, power may be concentrated in the wrong places and negotiating may be required.

◆ THE SYMBOLIC FRAME

Based on anthropological theory, the symbolic frame emphasizes the meaning of organizational activity. It views the organization as a theater, in which stories, rituals, and myths make up a culture which helps to give employees a sense of shared values and mission. The symbolic frame considers the importance of history and tradition in building a strong culture that employees can believe in. Problems may develop when symbols lose their meaning. The culture may be improved by developing meaningful rituals, traditions, and visions.

Taken one by one, each frame offers its own perspective on a problem and each frame provides a set of ideas and techniques that managers can employ in order to enhance organizational efficiency and effectiveness. For example, an executive trying to reduce turnover among middle managers might receive the following suggestions from consultants representing each of the four frames.

"As your firm has grown, managers' responsibilities have probably become blurred and overlapping. When reporting relationships are confused, you get stress and conflict. You need to restructure." (Structural)

"You are probably neglecting your managers' needs for autonomy and for opportunities to participate in important decisions. You need an attitude survey to pinpoint the problems." (Human Resource)

"Your real problem is that you have been ignoring the realities of organizational politics. The union has too much power and top management has too little. No one knows how to deal with conflict. There's turf protection everywhere. You have to bring politics out of the closet and get people to negotiate." (Political)

"Your company has never developed a strong value system, and growth has made the situation worse. Your managers don't find any meaning in their work. You need to revitalize your company's culture." (Symbolic)[3]

Each of these suggestions is based on a different frame and would result in very different courses of action. However, managers who adhere too tightly to one frame that is most consistent with their professional training or personal values are *unnecessarily limiting themselves to a single tool for solving organizational problems* that are complex, changing, and ambiguous.

Some problems in organizations have little to do with rational and quantitative analysis, but are caused by poor interpersonal communication. Other problems are essentially based on a cloudy picture of the organization's mission and values and have little to do with power and influence. All managers must develop self-awareness of their prevailing frames and their blind spots, and they must develop the ability to view complex organizational activities through *each of the four frames* from a multiple perspectives point of view. Managers must be able to think and act in more than one way and to ask new questions that will reveal creative possibilities for effective action.

❖ GETTING ORGANIZED: THE STRUCTURAL FRAME

The structural frame inquires about the best way to structure the organization given the goals that it is pursuing. This frame is based upon the work of Frederick Taylor and a German sociologist, Max Weber. Taylor introduced time and motion studies as a way to determine scientifically the most efficient way for a laborer to complete a task. Weber introduced the concept of bureaucracy as a rational approach to structuring organizations.

McDonald's and Harvard University are both highly successful organizations, yet each has a radically different structure that is designed to fit its circumstances. All organizations, for example, have goals, boundaries, levels of authority, and procedures, yet they differ widely on how these structural characteristics appear.

McDonald's is highly centralized. Most decisions are made at the top and efforts are made to ensure conformity, so that a "Big Mac" tastes the same at McDonald's franchises all over the world.

Harvard is highly decentralized, with each school of the University controlling its own destiny. Unlike the McDonald's employees, who have little discretion about how they carry out their tasks, Harvard faculty have enormous autonomy over what they research and how they run their classes. People therefore expect a predictable product from McDonald's but a unique learning experience from a Harvard professor.

Organizations such as McDonald's, which have highly specific and easily measurable goals such as profitability, growth, and market share, are able to structure themselves tightly through written procedures and detailed checklists. Harvard's teaching and research goals are much less routine and predictable. Producing knowledgeable students and "important research" are rather diffuse goals that require a more decentralized and loosely connected structure.

Organizations change their structure to fit a changing environment. A simple structure that worked with a boss and a small number of employees will likely give way to a machine bureaucracy for routine tasks or a professional bureaucracy for more creative activities. Divisional forms serve specific areas or products within the larger organization while adhocracy and matrix structures are helpful for adapting to a rapidly changing, turbulent environment.

Groups and teams must grapple with the same kinds of design questions that face the large organization. Likewise, it has been shown that the structure of the group may need to change significantly over the group's life as the group develops and different tasks are required.

When the structural frame is overutilized by the manager, adherence to the rulebook and established procedures may interfere with creative input. Management may be cold and impersonal. Good ideas may not be implemented because of insufficient power and influence. Work may be done without a clear set of values or mission.

When the structural frame is underutilized, the organization may not be designed in a manner that optimizes output. Role confusion and unclear job descriptions may result in repeated conflict. An appropriate emphasis on structure will help the organization cope with these problems.

❖ PEOPLE AND ORGANIZATION: THE HUMAN RESOURCE FRAME

The human resource frame is grounded in psychological theories of human behavior, including the work of Maslow, McGregor, and Argyris. This frame "starts from the premise that people's skills, insights, ideas, energy and commitment are an organization's most critical resource. Organizations, however, can be so alienating, dehumanizing, and frustrating that human talents are wasted and human lines are distorted."[4] This frame assumes that organizations exist to serve human needs, and a good fit between the individual and the organization benefits both. People find meaningful work, and organizations receive people's talents and commitment.

Numerous strategies have been developed to improve human resource management. These activities generally involve listening more closely to the ideas of employees and allowing them a voice in how their work is carried out. These interventions include management training, job enrichment, participative management, survey feedback, organization development consultation, and self-managed work teams.

When managers overuse the human resource frame, they may focus too heavily on resolving problems by open communication and support while overlooking structural flaws that may precipitate such conflict. Overuse of this frame may also fail to give proper acknowledgment of the role of power and authority in dealing with competitive issues. Overuse of the human resources frame may result in an overly optimistic view that all organizational issues can be resolved through consensus and collaborative activities.

Underuse of the human resource frame may be seen in organizations which have not bothered to ask what the needs and aspirations of their workers are. Such organizations may not experience the increased creativity, commitment, and communication from employees who feel that they are heard and supported.

❖ POWER, CONFLICT, AND COALITIONS: THE POLITICAL FRAME

The tragic explosion of the space shuttle Challenger with seven astronauts aboard was in part caused by political forces which created a context for conflict and power plays among individuals and groups.

The procedure had always been clear. Before any space vehicle could be launched, NASA and their contractors had to prove that it was safe to fly. But on the night of January 27, 1986, Morton Thiokol senior managers overruled the no-launch decision by their engineers; the next day seven astronauts were killed and the nation's space program was in a shambles. Technically, the record cold temperature on the launch pad had caused the "O-rings" to fail, thus allowing hot gases to escape. Further investigation revealed that the decision-making process had changed significantly since NASA's early days when decisions were made on the lowest possible level. Clearly the evolution of NASA since the heady days of the Apollo moon landing had changed the structure of the organization so that the people making the important decisions were getting farther and farther away from the people getting their hands dirty.

In addition to these structural problems, the human resource view of NASA showed an organization whose morale had diminished since the days of generous funding and national commitment to push back the frontiers of space. The fit between the organization's needs and the needs of its employees had eroded. The space pioneers of the early years had given way to the shuttle program's "box car in space."[5] But correcting the structural and human resource problems in the space program may not have prevented the tragedy of the space shuttle Challenger.

The political forces in Washington, in NASA, and in Morton Thiokol (the contractor responsible for the O-rings) collectively overruled the advice of technical experts and put the space shuttle in harm's way.

The political frame views organizations as living political arenas that house a complex variety of individual and group interests. Because of competition for scarce resources (time, money, positions), conflict is inevitable in organizations and members of different coalitions must know how to bargain and negotiate for their positions.

In the Challenger case there were many political forces that affected the decision-making process.

NASA ran the space program because a complex coalition of Congress, the White House, the media, and the public supported them. Crista McAuliffe, the teacher-in-space, was aboard the Challenger because having an ordinary citizen as a member of the crew built public support for the program.

The president intended to mention the launch of the Challenger in his State of the Union speech to Congress and to a national TV audience, but Morton Thiokol engineers recommended against the launch for valid scientific reasons. However, corporate executives feared that more delays would put their lucrative government contract in jeopardy. Similarly, NASA managers were aware that NASA's credibility was slipping, deemed the engineering data inconclusive, and recommended the launch.

On the night before the fateful launch, a coalition of managers from NASA and Morton Thiokol brought together by the dwindling space budget combined forces to overrule the scientists, who in the end had made the right recommendation.

The political frame focuses on situations of scarce resources and incompatible preferences and thus the collision of different needs. If a group of graduate students, for example, wants the university to become more democratic and responsive to their needs, while the faculty wishes to tighten controls and standards, the political theorist might emphasize how each group articulates its preferences and mobilizes the power to get what it wants. The structural view assumes that some solutions are better than others and urges rational problem-solving methods to reach a discussion. The human resource approach seeks a win-win outcome of this conflict where the needs of both groups are shared and an integrative solution is reached. For the political manager, scarcity and conflict are enduring facts of organizational life, and they are less optimistic than the structural- and human-resource-oriented managers of achieving the "best" or "win-win" resolutions.

The political frame is focused on the use of power and the tactics of conflict. Power can come from authority, expertise, control of rewards and punishments, alliances and networks, control of agendas, control of meetings and symbols, and personal power. Most managerial jobs are characterized by an imbalance where responsibility seems to be larger than the authority to get things done. As a consequence, other forms of power (e.g., reward) must be enlisted to manage effectively.

Within the political frame, conflict is not necessarily seen as something bad and to be avoided. Therefore, its focus is not always on the resolution of conflict, as is often the case for the human resource and structural frames. The political frame asserts that conflict has benefits, such as encouraging innovative approaches to problem solving, challenging the status quo, and reducing complacency. Because conflict is not going to disappear, the political frame asks how groups and individuals can make the best use of it. To use the political frame effectively, managers must understand the strategy and tactics of conflict. According to the political frame, not only do the authorities have power, but there are many in the organization who have different forms of power. Those who get and use power best see their ideas implemented. The use of power does not need to be destructive. Constructive use of power is necessary to create effective organizations.

Managers who underutilize the political frame may be ignoring an enduring reality of organizational life. The political perspective can be a powerful antidote to the rationality of the structural frame.

Overuse of the political frame can be equally restrictive. The political frame can be cynical and pessimistic, overestimating the inevitability of conflict and understating the potential for rational analysis and interpersonal collaboration.

❖ ORGANIZATIONAL CULTURE AND SYMBOLS: THE SYMBOLIC FRAME

When Martin Luther King spoke to the huge throng that participated in the march on Washington in August 1963, he said to them, "I have a dream." In that memorable speech, Dr. King spoke with conviction and passion about American values. He included many of the most cherished symbols of our country. His speech included "My country 'tis of thee, sweet land of liberty," and other songs and phrases uttered daily in every school in our land. He reminded his listeners of the basic values and principles that our country was founded upon when its first settlers sought refuge from political persecution nearly two centuries earlier.

The symbolic frame emphasizes the symbolic aspect of the human experience. It departs from the rational, linear view of organizations and recognizes the importance of culture, rituals, stories, and metaphors. Just as the earliest tribal rituals may have required a youngster at puberty to kill a lion and be circumcised, large corporations have their modern-day versions of initiation rituals.

In a strong culture, the message to newcomers will be "you are different and not yet one of us." The newcomer (in this example, a woman) may say "I know this place is hostile to women and I expect that to change." In this symbolic interchange, newcomers have a part to play by bringing new ideas and perspectives into the organization. At the same time, old-timers act as a force for cohesion, stability and the wisdom of the past.[6]

The basic assumption of the symbolic frame is that what is important about any event is not what happened, but *what it means to people.* Because organizations are so complex, it is often hard to know what is happening and why it is happening. With such uncertainty and ambiguity, it is difficult to analyze rationally the causes of problems and their solutions. People create symbols to reduce confusion and provide direction in their lives. The core values of McDonald's, the golden arches, and the stories of its founder, Ray Kroc, give direction to franchise holders. The history and rituals of Harvard University offer professors and students a common set of values from which to work.

In Martin Luther King's memorable "I have a dream" speech, he was able to articulate how a set of values based on our country's history could serve as a vision for our future. A more structural Dr. King might have spoken about "I have a plan" while a human resource or political leader would have emphasized feelings and coalition-building. But in that moment, he chose to reach people with his vision. Managers who understand the importance of the symbolic frame appreciate the power of rituals, ceremonies, and stories, and they use them to articulate a set of shared values called *culture.*

The symbolic frame views the organization as theater. For example, the structure of an organization may be seen as more than the structural view, which emphasizes the network of interdependent roles and linkages that are determined by goals, technology and environment. To the symbolic manager, the structure may be more like a stage design and props that make the organization look credible to its audience. For example, because of their elusive goals and underdeveloped technologies, schools have symbols of effectiveness and modern appearance. Certified teachers, American flags, and computers are part of the props. The schools achieve legitimacy by maintaining an appearance "that conforms to the way society thinks they should look."[7]

There are two faces of the symbolic perspective. Symbols can be used to camouflage or distort. The certified teacher may be incompetent. The corporation that states "People come first" may have an abysmal record in dealing with people. Managers who emphasize vision and charisma may be inept at enacting their vision. The symbolic frame is on dangerous ground when symbols are not congruent with reality. On the other hand, *symbols offer order and predictability in an ambiguous and uncertain world.* When the space shuttle Challenger exploded, killing its precious crew, people engaged in rituals to help them deal with their collective loss. In this way the symbolic frame can give meaning and hope to organizational activities that defy explanation in more rational terms.

❖ INTEGRATING FRAMES FOR EFFECTIVE PRACTICE

While each of the frames emphasizes a different slice of organizational life, each one alone serves only as an incomplete map of a complex terrain. Each frame has a unique comparative advantage. For example, the structural frame will be most salient under conditions of stable authority, clear goals, and well-developed technologies. Human resource issues are likely to become prominent in an organization where employee motivation is important but problematic, and when resources are abundant. When goals and values are in conflict, resources are scarce, and the distribution of power is unstable, the political frame is likely to stand out. The symbolic frame is likely to be important under conditions of high ambiguity and inadequate information.

Taken together, the frames remind us that people and organizations try to behave in rational ways, but they are also affected by their needs and biases. They are adaptable but not infinitely so. They often will be dealing with scarce resources, and the importance of power and politics cannot be underestimated. Finally, the symbolic frame reminds us that we attribute meaning to organizational events. It is only in this multiple-perspective mode that we can begin fully to understand organizational activity at the level of complexity that is experienced by managers.

Multiple-perspective managers are able to interpret the same event in many different ways. A simple meeting can, for example, be a formal occasion for making decisions. Besides this structural interpretation, it can serve human resource needs by being an occasion for sharing feelings and building commitment to an idea. Meetings can serve as occasions to gain power and win points, and they can symbolically reaffirm values or transform the culture. Managers who can apply all of these frames and diagnose which perspectives are being used by the meeting's participants are likely to be more effective than those limited to a single perspective.

❖ REFRAMING CHANGE

Modern organizations are being buffeted by powerful external forces that threaten the status quo.

Globalization requires organizations to enter new markets, adapt to new cultures, and reorganize their management structure. New technologies introduce new production and communication strategies. Deregulation in the airline and communications fields has forced these industries to shift from a service emphasis to a marketing emphasis. Demographic shifts have meant a changing workplace which is more diverse and multicultural, resulting in a sense of loss for some members.

The four frames can help managers anticipate the impact of change and act in ways to reduce resistance to change. The four approaches to change may look like this:

1. *Structural*—Change alters existing structural arrangements, causing confusion and ambiguity. Formal patterns and policies need to be realigned.
2. *Human Resource*—Change causes people to feel incompetent and powerless to handle new situations and behaviors. Training and psychological support are necessary when employees feel insecure.
3. *Political*—Change causes conflict and creates winners and losers. Managers must create arenas where issues can be negotiated.
4. *Symbolic*—Change creates loss of meaning and purpose. When attachments to symbols are severed, transition rituals are required and new symbols created.

"A fully effective change requires attention to all four issues: structure, needs, conflict, and loss. Changes in one frame inevitably reverberate through the others and the frame that is ignored is very likely to be the one that distorts or undermines the effort."[8]

❖ REFRAMING LEADERSHIP: LEADERS AS ARCHITECTS, CATALYSTS, ADVOCATES, AND PROPHETS

Many current views of leadership have been based on oversimplified models. Each of the frames offers a different perspective on how leaders might behave when they are effective and ineffective.

Effective leaders are more likely to have the skills to lead from a multiple perspectives framework, and they are more likely to know which frame might be the most appropriate fit for the situation at hand. Effective leaders can develop rational systems but avoid leading too heavily by the rules. They can support and empower people but avoid abdicating their leadership role. Effective leaders are able to build coalitions and advocate for their constituents, but use power fairly and judiciously. They can inspire others by giving meaning to their experience and by communicating a vision, but they can avoid the use of hollow symbols and balance their vision with concrete action.

❖ ARTISTRY, CHOICE, AND LEADERSHIP

The best managers and leaders understand their prevailing frames and know how those frames both benefit and limit their effectiveness. Wise leaders know how to build teams that can provide leadership across all four frames as the situation requires. They will be able to create a balance between core values and elastic strategies. They can be dramatically explicit about their core values and beliefs but apply frames flexibly in pursuit of their mission.

In a world of constant change, leaders of complex organizations will need the ability to see new possibilities and to discover choices, even when options seem severely constrained. The ability to reframe their thinking can give them new power and new skills.

❖ NOTES

1. Bolman, Lee G., and Terrence E. Deal, *Reframing Organizations: Artistry, Choice, and Leadership.* San Francisco CA: Jossey-Bass, 1991. p. 4.
2. Bolman and Deal, p. 12.
3. Bolman and Deal, p. 10.
4. Bolman and Deal, p. 120.
5. Bolman and Deal, p. 184.
6. Bolman and Deal, p. 249.
7. Bolman and Deal, p. 275.
8. Bolman and Deal, p. 402.

Reading 4

Overcoming Organizational Defenses

Chris Argyris
Summary prepared by Jean A. Grube

Jean A. Grube is a Lecturer in Management at the University of Wisconsin, Madison, where she received her Ph.D. Her current research interests include organizational commitment, stress and coping behaviors, and organizational change.

Managers have long focused on morale, satisfaction, and loyalty as foundations for the achievement of organizational excellence. A more realistic base for excellence may come from organizational members' *learning* (how to detect and correct organizational errors), *competence* (solving problems such that they remain solved and increase the members' ability to solve future problems), and *justice* (promoting values about organizational health that are applicable to all organizational members). These are the underpinnings for *Overcoming Organizational Defenses.*

Although the concept of organizational defenses is not a new one, approaches to understanding how and why such defenses develop have historically focused primarily on *first-order errors*—those caused by "not knowing." This book is directed at understanding how organizational defenses develop from *second-order errors*—those errors that humans actively design and produce.

We need to examine managerial activities that belie sound management practice (puzzles) and how they result from defensive reasoning. It is important to understand how and why defensive reasoning develops in organizational members, and which activities are used to routinize defensiveness and ensure its survival in organizations. Interestingly, the usual help procedures (e.g., consulting practices and organizational surveys) actually compound the problem. Specific advice for dealing with organizational defensiveness (Model II) is needed. New mindsets about management are needed if Model II theories-in-use are to survive in organizations. Organizational defenses and their

Chris Argyris, *Overcoming Organizational Defenses.* Needham, Mass.: Allyn & Bacon, 1990.

potential contribution to the "ethical pollution" in organizations must be examined continually.

❖ PUZZLES

The actions of modern management are characterized by *puzzles* that depict weaknesses of modern management behavior. Individuals engage in activities that produce and proliferate errors, even when the results run counter to what they say they want and to what they believe reflects sound management. If organizational players are free to choose activities and elect to choose those that are contrary to good management, then defensive reasoning must be taking place.

According to Argyris, *defensive reasoning* occurs when individuals: (1) hold premises the validity of which is questionable yet they think it is not; (2) make inferences that do not necessarily follow from the premises yet they think they do; and (3) reach conclusions that they believe they have tested carefully yet they have not because the way they have been framed makes them untestable. Defensive reasoning is caused by programs in individuals' heads that are skillfully deployed to deal with errors that are embarrassing or threatening. Utilization of these mental managerial programs results in the creation of organizational defense routines, and activities used to protect the defensive routines emerge as a self-sealing device.

To understand how and why organizational members develop these programs, one must consider the issue of skilled incompetence.

❖ HUMAN THEORIES OF CONTROL: SKILLED INCOMPETENCE

Skilled incompetence has its origins in the fact that human beings seek to be in control of their actions because they feel good when they are able to produce intended results. When faced with situations that could lead to lack of control (i.e., embarrassing or threatening conditions), people look for guidelines to direct their actions. Two programs that exist in the minds of individuals serve as guidelines. The first program, *espoused theories of action*, is comprised of the beliefs and values people hold about how to manage their lives. The second program, *theories-in-use*, contains rules people use to manage their beliefs.

Most people follow a *Model I* theory-in-use which directs them to achieve unilateral control, to win, and to suppress negative feelings. Such theories-in-use are learned at an early age and are supported by such social virtues as caring, helping, and respecting others. Model I action strategies include selling, persuading, and face-saving. Some of these strategies are counterproductive. For example, people tell "little white lies" to salvage another person's pride (face-saving). This requires people to (1) bypass the errors others make, and act as if they are not making errors because one can only save another's face by not revealing what is happening; (2) make the bypass undiscussable, because errors cannot be bypassed successfully if others discuss it, and (3) make the undiscussability of the undiscussable also undiscussable. Consequently, important thoughts and feelings are not communicated honestly and fully by organizational members. This pattern leads to misunderstandings and distortions, making it unlikely that managers or others will be able to detect and correct errors. Ironically, Model I strategies require great skill at doing counterproductive things (e.g., it is difficult to change the mind of an individual without upsetting him or her) and hence are illustrated by the term *skilled incompetence.*

Although such strategies are counterproductive, they are repeated because they have become automatic, spontaneous, and taken for granted by organizational members. Furthermore, such actions are supported by a society that sees giving approval, offering praise, and deferring to others as virtues. Skilled incompetence becomes even more counterproductive when routinized in organizations.

❖ ORGANIZATIONAL DEFENSIVE ROUTINES

Because most individuals' actions are guided by Model I theories-in-use, these activities become organizational norms. Subsequently, *organizational defensive routines* (actions or policies that are established to protect individuals or segments of the organization from experiencing embarrassment or threat) develop. Managers and other organizational members construct the framework for these defensive routines in accordance with Model I: (1) messages are crafted that contain inconsistencies, and yet, individuals act as if the messages are not inconsistent; (2) the inconsistencies of the message are made undiscussable; (3) the undiscussability of the undiscussable is also made undiscussable.

Defenses present a "double bind" for many organizational members. They recognize that organizational performance will suffer if they are not able to discuss errors. However, they find it difficult to change defensive routines because "opening this can of worms" invokes more defensive routines, thus worsening the situation. So they continue to massage the truth, which serves to reinforce and proliferate defenses. The actions becoming self-fulfilling and self-sealing.

How do individuals live with this "double bind"? Many do not, which may be the most fundamental cause of burnout and turnover in upper level management. Others rely on fancy footwork in order to live with their inconsistencies.

❖ FANCY FOOTWORK AND MALAISE

To deal with the "double bind," some organizational members use *fancy footwork* (actions that permit them to ignore inconsistencies in their actions, deny that inconsistencies exist, or place the blame on other people). Eventually, a sense of malaise develops in which members recognize that fancy footwork permeates the organization but feel helpless to change it. There are three symptoms associated with *organizational malaise*. First, members seek and find fault with the organization but do not accept responsibility for correcting its failures. Second, individuals begin to accentuate and magnify negative aspects of the organization. In fact, they find pleasure in doing so because it helps them to justify their own distancing and helplessness behaviors. Finally, people espouse values that everyone knows cannot be implemented. Because they are never implemented they eventually lose credibility.

The result of skilled incompetence, organizational defensive routines, fancy footwork, and malaise is an *organizational defensive pattern (ODP)*. ODP is generic to all human organizations and, unfortunately, traditional techniques are ineffective in reducing its effects.

❖ SOUND ADVICE: IT COMPOUNDS THE PROBLEM

If executives who want to deal with ODP followed the advice of the "best and the brightest," they would find themselves in trouble for a variety of reasons. Management consultants, for instance, rarely deal with ODP. When they do, the advice is too abstract to be of help. The vast majority of leadership books focus on "espoused theories" and, therefore, offer little in the way of correcting the actual behaviors that are guided by theory-in-use. Similarly, problems occur when solutions are sought through organizational surveys, because respondents reply based on their espoused theories of action.

Another problem with advice is that it can reinforce errors and organizational defensive routines. For example, management literature advises that feedback be obtained in a manner that allows subordinates not to worry about negative consequences of being honest. However, the very act of using a third "trusted" party reinforces that subordinates cannot be honest with their supervisors in situations that may be threatening or cause embarrassment. Actions like these further justify defensive routines.

For advice to be implementable or enactable, it must possess certain characteristics. First, it must show *causality* (engaging in this behavior will produce these results). Second, advice must be *concrete* (this is exactly what must be done). Finally, the advice must *make explicit the values* that govern the suggested actions (this action is suggested so that I can monitor the outcome of my decision). Conventional advice does not meet these criteria.

❖ REDUCING THE ORGANIZATIONAL DEFENSE PATTERN

If traditional techniques are ineffective, what should managers do to reduce ODP? The answer lies in double-loop learning.

Model I theory-in-use is characterized as a *single-loop model* because it focuses on the presenting problem (symptom) and does not direct attention to the cause. Consequently, it is only a matter of time before the problem resurfaces. To correct ODP, the initial values that governed the actions that led to errors must be changed. This is termed *double-loop learning*. To sustain double-loop learning, an organization's managers must develop a culture that rewards individuals who learn how to divorce themselves from Model I actions that contribute to ODP. In essence, a new theory-in-use model (*Model II*) must be taught.

To learn new actions for handling situations that are embarrassing or threatening, organizational members must first see how they presently deal with problems under such conditions. Next, the individuals must be shown how these actions are counterproductive. Third, individuals are taught how to use Model II as a theory-in-use and are encouraged to practice this step. Finally, these three steps are repeated for each new problem that arises.

The values governing Model II theory-in-use are valid information, informed choice, and responsibility for evaluating the quality of choice implementation. The actions that flow from Model II are those that invite inquiry into one's stated position and minimize face-saving behaviors. Model II assumes that productive reasoning is occurring; individuals make clear to others what premises and inferences they are using, they develop conclusions that others can test, and they actively look for inconsistencies in their own logic and invite others to do the same. This necessarily means that members must openly deal with organizational defensive routines, fancy footwork, and malaise. Otherwise, Model II theory-in-use cannot survive.

❖ MAKING THE NEW THEORY OF MANAGING HUMAN PERFORMANCE COME TRUE

There are other compelling reasons why Model II theory-in-use must become a reality in organizations. Over the last twenty years, a new theory of managing human performance has evolved. It focuses on employee energy and initiative that can be tapped through the experience of psychological success. It emphasizes the need for commitment and involvement over more traditional values of unilateral control, dependency, and submissiveness. However, some suggest that this new management approach will bring with it new contradictions and dilemmas. Furthermore, some learning through trial and error will naturally occur as managers shift away from a more traditional view of managing employees. This implies that embarrassing and threatening situations will occur which invites ODP to develop. Unless a Model II theory-in-use is utilized, it is difficult to envision how nontraditional management practices can survive.

❖ GETTING FROM HERE TO THERE

How can managers move organizational members from Model I to Model II? Several modes can facilitate the transition. Although there are variations, all modes have features in common. An organizational member writes a case that depicts a particular problem and how he or she responded. Guided by professionals, other participants review the case and offer insights into how the actions contributed to ODP and what corrective actions are available. A six-step procedure can help individuals overcome organizational defenses.

1. Diagnose the problem.
2. Connect the diagnosis to the actual behavior of participants.
3. Show participants how their behavior creates organizational defenses.
4. Help them change their behavior.
5. Change the defensive routine that reinforced the old behavior.
6. Develop new organizational norms and culture that reinforce the new behavior.

❖ UPPING THE ANTE

Some managers are able to ignore or deny the existence of ODP because the building of, and negative consequences associated with, these defenses is an insidious process. Additionally, managers introduce activities that attempt to minimize the likelihood of embarrassment or threat. One such activity is to objectify methods for monitoring actions of the organization in order to minimize the effects of the human element. However, since humans have to implement the systems, such "correcting" methods ultimately fail. Another strategy is to create greater tolerance for embarrassment and threat in organizational members through the development of involvement and internal commitment (the nontraditional management practice). The assumption is that individuals who are more involved and committed will show more initiative for detecting and correcting errors. The problem with such an approach is that it is difficult to use as a foundation for a major organizational strategy, and it does not take into account the ingenious ways that members seek to protect themselves when they encounter situations of threat or embarrassment.

For new management practices to be successful, a new mindset is necessary. There are four activities that will promote the mindset needed to foster new management approaches. First, members must stop taking for granted what is taken for granted (i.e., they must learn to examine more carefully what they assume is obvious). Second, members must make learning as sacred as they make other activities or policies (e.g., such as the policy of face-saving). Third, members must evaluate how they contribute to ODP and accept individual responsibility for reducing defenses in the organization. Finally, members must come to understand that productive reasoning is as critical for human problems as it is for those technical in nature.

❖ ETHICS AND THE ORGANIZATIONAL DEFENSES PATTERN

Many have cited openness and trust as critical to ethical behavior in organizations. By engaging in cover-up behaviors, organizational members may unknowingly be contributing to the "ethical pollution" in organizations. The solution lies within each manager as each must learn to manage and accept responsibility for his or her own actions and help the organization develop rewards for this self-responsible behavior.

3

Best-Seller "Classics"

Many of those books that have found their way into earlier editions of *The Manager's Bookshelf* as a part of our *mosaic of contemporary views* continue to have a message that many managers reference and still want to hear. As a result, for the Fourth Edition of *The Manager's Bookshelf* we have created this new part, which contains summaries of selected books published in earlier years that continue to be popular among managers today.

While working as partners for McKinsey & Company (a management consulting firm), Thomas J. Peters and Robert H. Waterman Jr. conducted research that led to their book *In Search of Excellence.* The results of their study of management practices in several dozen companies in six industries led to the identification of eight attributes that were practiced consistently and appeared to be related to organizational success. Peters and Waterman's work also sparked an interest in looking at management through a different set of lenses and defined management's role as coach, cheerleader, and facilitator. Subsequently, Peters co-authored *A Passion for Excellence, Thriving on Chaos, Liberation Management,* and *The Tom Peters Seminar.* Waterman wrote *The Renewal Factor* and *What America Does Right.*

William Ouchi, a Professor at the University of California, Los Angeles, shocked the managerial community in the early 1980s with his contention that American businesses have a lot to learn from Japanese corporations. His *Theory Z* book suggests that U.S. firms should create and follow a corporate philosophy that builds upon trust, understanding of personalities, and intimacy at work. Theory Z firms (such as Hewlett-Packard, Dayton-Hudson, Rockwell, Intel, and Eli Lilly) demonstrate their commitment to these values and their employees through vehicles such as quality control (Q-C) circles.

Kenneth Blanchard and Spencer Johnson, in the widely read book *The One Minute Manager,* build their prescriptions for effective human resource management on two basic principles. First, they suggest that *quality time* with the subordinate is of utmost importance. Second, they adopt Douglas McGregor's notion that employees are basically capable of *self-management.* These two principles provide the basis for their prescriptions on goal setting, praising, and reprimanding as the cornerstones of effective management.

Kenneth Blanchard was a professor of management at the University of Massachusetts, and has been active as a management consultant. With Norman Vincent Peale, Blanchard has also published *The Power of Ethical Man-*

agement. Spencer Johnson, the holder of a medical doctorate, is interested in stress and has written extensively about medicine and psychology.

A true classic in the management literature is Douglas McGregor's *The Human Side of Enterprise,* first published in 1960. Because of the book's popularity, its timeless theme, and genuine relevance for organizations as they prepare to enter the twenty-first century, there was a twenty-fifth anniversary printing of McGregor's seminal work.

McGregor identifies two sets of assumptions that managers might hold and that drive two very different approaches to the management of organizations and their employees. Through the presentation of two sets of assumptions—labeled *Theory X* and *Theory Y*—McGregor urges managers to see employees as capable of innovation, creativity, commitment, high levels of sustained effort, and the exercise of self-direction and self-control.

Douglas McGregor received his Ph.D. at Harvard University. Before his death in 1964, he served on the faculties of Harvard University and the Massachusetts Institute of Technology and was president of Antioch College. McGregor is also the author of *The Professional Manager.*

READING 1

In Search of Excellence

Thomas J. Peters and Robert H. Waterman, Jr.

What makes for excellence in the management of a company? Is it the use of sophisticated management techniques such as zero-based budgeting, management by objectives, matrix organization, and sector, group, or portfolio management? Is it greater use of computers to control companies that continue to grow even larger in size and more diverse in activities? Is it a battalion of specialized MBAs, well-versed in the techniques of strategic planning?

Probably not. Although most well-run companies use a fair sampling of all these tools, they do not use them as substitutes for the basics of good management. Indeed, McKinsey & Co., a management consultant concern, has studied management practices at thirty-seven companies that are often used as examples of well-run organizations and has found that they have eight common attributes. None of those attributes depends on "modern" management tools or gimmicks. In fact, none of them requires high technology, and none of them costs a cent to implement. All that is needed is time, energy, and a willingness on the part of management to think rather than to make use of management formulas.

The outstanding performers work hard to keep things simple. They rely on simple organizational structures, simple strategies, simple goals, and simple communications. The eight attributes that characterize their managements are:

- A bias toward action.
- Simple form and lean staff.
- Continued contact with customers.
- Productivity improvement via people.
- Operational autonomy to encourage entrepreneurship.
- Stress on one key business value.

◆ Emphasis on doing what they know best.

◆ Simultaneous loose-tight controls.

Although none of these sounds startling or new, most are conspicuously absent in many companies today. Far too many managers have lost sight of the basics—service to customers, low-cost manufacturing, productivity improvement, innovation, and risk-taking. In many cases, they have been seduced by the availability of MBAs, armed with the "latest" in strategic planning techniques. MBAs who specialize in strategy are bright, but they often cannot implement their ideas, and their companies wind up losing the capacity to act. At Standard Brands Inc., for example, Chairman F. Ross Johnson discovered this the hard way when he brought a handful of planning specialists into his consumer products company. "The guys who were bright [the strategic planners] were not the kinds of people who could implement programs," he lamented to *Business Week*. Two years later, he removed the planners.

Another consumer products company followed a similar route, hiring a large band of young MBAs for the staffs of senior vice-presidents. The new people were assigned to build computer models for designing new products. Yet none of the products could be manufactured or brought to market. Complained one line executive: "The models incorporated eighty-three variables in product planning, but we were being killed by just one—cost."

Companies are being stymied not only by their own staffs but often by their structure. McKinsey studied one company where the new product process required 223 separate committees to approve an idea before it could be put into production. Another company was restructured recently into 200 strategic business units—only to discover that it was impossible to implement 200 strategies. And even at General Electric Co., which is usually cited for its ability to structure itself according to its management needs, an executive recently complained: "Things become bureaucratic with astonishing speed. Inevitably when we wire things up, we lose vitality." Emerson Electric Co., with a much simpler structure than GE, consistently beats its huge competitor on costs—manufacturing its products in plants with fewer than 600 employees.

McKinsey's study focused on ten well-managed companies: International Business Machines, Texas Instruments, Hewlett-Packard, 3M, Digital Equipment, Procter & Gamble, Johnson & Johnson, McDonald's, Dana, and Emerson Electric. On the surface, they have nothing in common. There is no universality of product line: Five are in high technology, one is in packaged goods, one makes medical products, one operates fast-food restaurants, and two are relatively mundane manufacturers of mechanical and electrical products. But each is a hands-on operator, not a holding company or a conglomerate. And while not every plan succeeds, in the day-to-day pursuit of their businesses these companies succeed far more often than they fail. And they succeed because of their management's almost instinctive adherence to the eight attributes.

❖ BIAS TOWARD ACTION

In each of these companies, the key instructions are *do it, fix it, try it.* They avoid analyzing and questioning products to death, and they avoid complicated procedures for developing new ideas. Controlled experiments abound in these companies. The attitude of management is to "get some data, do it, then adjust it," rather than to wait for a perfect overall plan. The companies tend to be tinkerers rather than inventors, making small steps of progress rather than conceiving sweeping new concepts. At McDonald's Corp., for example, the objective is to do the little things regularly and well.

Ideas are solicited regularly and tested quickly. Those that work are pushed fast; those that don't are discarded just as quickly. At 3M Co., the management never kills an idea without trying it out; it just goes on the back burner.

These managements avoid long, complicated business plans for new projects. At 3M, for example, new product ideas must be proposed in less than five pages. At Procter & Gamble Co., one-page memos are the rule, but every figure in a P&G memo can be relied on unfailingly.

To ensure that they achieve results, these companies set a few well-defined goals for their managers. At Texas Instruments Inc., for one, a typical goal would be a set date for having a new plant operating or for having a designated percent of a sales force call on customers in a new market. A TI executive explained: "We've experimented a lot, but the bottom line for any senior manager is the maxim that more than two objectives is no objective."

These companies have learned to focus quickly on problems. One method is to appoint a "czar" who has responsibility for one problem across the company. At Digital Equipment Corp. and Hewlett-Packard Co., for example, there are software czars, because customer demand for programming has become the key issue for the future growth of those companies. Du Pont Co., when it discovered it was spending $800 million a year on transportation set up a logistics czar. Other companies have productivity czars or energy czars with the power to override a manufacturing division's autonomy.

Another tool is the task force. But these companies tend to use the task force in an unusual way. Task forces are authorized to fix things, not to generate reports and paper. At Digital Equipment, TI, HP, and 3M, task forces have a short duration, seldom more than ninety days. Says a Digital Equipment executive: "When we've got a big problem here, we grab ten senior guys and stick them in a room for a week. They come up with an answer and implement it." All members are volunteers, and they tend to be senior managers rather than junior people ordered to serve. Management espouses the busy-member theory: "We don't want people on task forces who want to become permanent task force members. We only put people on them who are so busy that their major objective is to get the problem solved and to get back to their main jobs." Every task force at TI is disbanded after its work is done, but within three months the senior operations committee formally reviews and assesses the results. TI demands that the managers who requested and ran the task force justify the time spent on it. If the task force turns out to have been useless, the manager is chided publicly, a painful penalty in TI's peer-conscious culture.

How 10 Well-Run Companies Performed in 1979

	Millions of dollars		Percent	
	Sales	Profits	Return on sales	Return on equity
IBM	$22,862.8	$3,011.3	14.8%	21.6%
Procter & Gamble	10,080.6	615.7	5.6	19.3
3M	5,440.3	655.2	12.2	24.4
Johnson & Johnson	4,211.6	352.1	6.5	19.6
Texas Instruments	3,224.1	172.9	5.1	19.2
Dana	2,789.0	165.8	6.1	19.3
Emerson Electric	2,749.9	208.8	7.5	21.5
Hewlett-Packard	2,361.0	203.0	8.2	18.1
Digital Equipment	2,031.6	207.5	9.7	19.7
McDonald's	1,937.9	188.6	8.7	22.5
BW composite of 1,200 companies			5.1	16.6

❖ SIMPLE FORM AND LEAN STAFF

Although all ten of these companies are big—the smallest, McDonald's, has sales in excess of $1.9 billion—they are structured along "small is beautiful" lines. Emerson Electric, 3M, J&J, and HP are divided into small entrepreneurial units that—although smaller than economies of scale might suggest—manage to get things done. No HP division, for example, ever employs more than 1,200 people. TI, with ninety product customer centers, keeps each notably autonomous.

Within the units themselves, activities are kept to small, manageable groups. At Dana Corp., small teams work on productivity improvement. At the high-technology companies, small autonomous teams, headed by a product "champion," shepherd ideas through the corporate bureaucracy to ensure that they quickly receive attention from the top.

Staffs are also kept small to avoid bureaucracies. Fewer than 100 people help run Dana, a $3 billion corporation. Digital Equipment and Emerson are also noted for small staffs.

❖ CLOSENESS TO THE CUSTOMER

The well-managed companies are customer driven—not technology driven, not product driven, not strategy driven. Constant contact with the customer provides insights that direct the company. Says one executive: "Where do you start? Not by poring over abstract market research. You start by getting out there with the customer." In a study of two fast-paced industries (scientific instruments and component manufacturing), Eric Von Hippel, associate professor at Massachusetts Institute of Technology, found that 100 percent of the major new product ideas—and eighty percent of the minor new product variations—came directly from customers.

At both IBM and Digital Equipment, top management spends at least 30 days a year conferring with top customers. No manager at IBM holds a staff job for more than three years, except in the legal, finance, and personnel departments. The reason: IBM believes that staff people are out of the mainstream because they do not meet with customers regularly.

Both companies use customer-satisfaction surveys to help determine management's compensation. Another company spends twelve percent of its research and development budget on sending engineers and scientists out to visit customers. One R&D chief spends two months each year with customers. At Lanier Business Products Inc., another fast growing company, the twenty most senior executives make sales calls every month.

Staying close to the customer means sales and service overkill. "Assistants to" at IBM are assigned to senior executives with the sole function of processing customer complaints within 24 hours. At Digital Equipment, J&J, IBM, and 3M, immense effort is expended to field an extraordinarily well-trained sales force. Caterpillar Tractor Co., another company considered to have excellent management, spends much of its managerial talent on efforts to make a reality of its motto, "24-hour parts delivery anywhere in the world."

These companies view the customer as an integral element of their businesses. A bank officer who started his career as a J&J accountant recalls that he was required to make customer calls even though he was in a financial department. The reason: to ensure that he understood the customer's perspective and could handle a proposal with empathy.

❖ PRODUCTIVITY IMPROVEMENT VIA CONSENSUS

One way to get productivity increases is to install new capital equipment. But another method is often overlooked. Productivity can be improved by motivating and stimulating employees. One way to do that is to give them autonomy. At TI, shop floor teams set their own targets for production. In the years since the company has used this approach, executives say, workers have set goals that require them to stretch but that are reasonable and attainable.

The key is to motivate all of the people involved in each process. At 3M, for example, a team that includes technologists, marketers, production people, and financial types is formed early in a new product venture. It is self-sufficient and stays together from the inception to the national introduction. Although 3M is aware that this approach can lead to redundancy, it feels that the team spirit and motivation make it worthwhile.

Almost all of these companies use "corny" but effective methods to reward their workers. Badges, pins, and medals are all part of such recognition programs. Outstanding production teams at TI are invited to describe their successes to the board, as a form of recognition. Significantly, the emphasis is never only on monetary awards.

❖ AUTONOMY TO ENCOURAGE ENTREPRENEURSHIP

A company cannot encourage entrepreneurship if it holds its managers on so tight a leash that they cannot make decisions. Well-managed companies authorize their managers to act like entrepreneurs. Dana, for one, calls this method the "store manager" concept. Plant managers are free to make purchasing decisions and to start productivity programs on their own. As a result, these managers develop unusual programs with results that far exceed those of a division or corporate staff. And the company has a grievance rate that is a fraction of the average reported by the United Auto Workers for all the plants it represents.

The successful companies rarely will force their managers to go against their own judgment. At 3M, TI, IBM, and J&J, decisions on product promotion are not based solely on market potential. An important factor in the decision is the zeal and drive of the volunteer who champions a product. Explains one executive at TI: "In every instance of a new product failure, we had forced someone into championing it involuntarily."

The divisional management is generally responsible for replenishing its new product array. In these well-managed companies, headquarters staff may not cut off funds for divisional products arbitrarily. What is more, the divisions are allowed to reinvest most of their earnings in their own operations. Although this flies in the face of the product-portfolio concept, which dictates that a corporate chief milk mature divisions to feed those with apparently greater growth potential, these companies recognize that entrepreneurs will not be developed in corporations that give the fruits of managers' labor to someone else.

Almost all these companies strive to place new products into separate startup divisions. A manager is more likely to be recognized—and promoted—for pushing a hot new product out of his division to enable it to stand on its own than he is for simply letting his own division get overgrown.

Possibly most important at these companies, entrepreneurs are both encouraged and honored at all staff levels. TI, for one, has created a special group of "listeners"—138 senior technical people called "individual contributors"—to assess new ideas. Junior staff members are particularly encouraged to bring their ideas to one of these individuals for a one-on-one evaluation. Each "contributor" has the authority to approve substantial startup funds ($20,000 to $30,000) for product experimentation. TI's successful Speak'n'Spell device was developed this way.

IBM's Fellows Program serves a similar purpose, although it is intended to permit proven senior performers to explore their ideas rather than to open communications lines for bright comers. Such scientists have at their beck and call thousands of IBM's technical people. The Fellows tend to be highly skilled gadflies, people who can shake things up—almost invariably for the good of the company.

The operating principle at well-managed companies is to do one thing well. At IBM, the all-pervasive value is customer service. At Dana it is productivity improvement. At 3M and HP, it is new product development. At P&G it is product quality. At McDonald's it is customer service—quality, cleanliness, and value.

❖ STRESS ON A KEY BUSINESS VALUE

At all these companies, the values are pursued with an almost religious zeal by the chief executive officers. Rene McPherson, new dean of Stanford University's Graduate School of Business but until recently Dana's CEO, incessantly preached cost reduction and productivity improvement—and the company doubled its productivity in seven years. Almost to the day when Thomas Watson Jr. retired from IBM he wrote memos to the staff on the subject of calling on customers—even stressing the proper dress for the call. TI's ex-chairman Patrick Haggerty made it a point to drop in at a development laboratory on his way home each night when he was in Dallas. And in another company, where competitive position was the prime focus, one division manager wrote 700 memos to his subordinates one year, analyzing competitors.

Such single-minded focus on a value becomes a culture for the company. Nearly every IBM employee has stories about how he or she took great pains to solve a customer's problem. New product themes even dominate 3M and

HP lunchroom conversations. Every operational review at HP focuses on new products, with a minimum amount of time devoted to financial results or projections—because President John Young has made it clear that he believes that proper implementation of new-product plans automatically creates the right numbers. In fact, Young makes it a point to start new employees in the new-product process and keep them there for a few years as part of a "socialization" pattern. "I don't care if they do come from the Stanford Business School," he says. "For a few years they get their hands dirty, or we are not interested." At McDonald's the company's values are drummed into employees at Hamburger U., a training program every employee goes through.

As the employees who are steeped in the corporate culture move up the ladder, they become role models for newcomers, and the process continues. It is possibly best exemplified by contrast. American Telephone & Telegraph Co., which recently began to develop a marketing orientation, has been hamstrung in its efforts because of a lack of career telephone executives with marketing successes. When Archie J. McGill was hired from IBM to head AT&T's marketing, some long-term employees balked at his leadership because he "wasn't one of them," and so was not regarded as a model.

Another common pitfall for companies is the sending of mixed signals to line managers. One company has had real problems introducing new products despite top management's constant public stress on innovation—simply because line managers perceived the real emphasis to be on cost-cutting. They viewed top management as accountants who refused to invest or to take risks, and they consistently proposed imitative products. At another company, where the CEO insisted that his major thrust was new products, an analysis of how he spent his time over a three-month period showed that no more than 5 percent of his efforts were directed to new products. His stated emphasis therefore was not credible. Not surprisingly, his employees never picked up the espoused standard.

Too many messages, even when sincerely meant, can cause the same problem. One CEO complained that no matter how hard he tried to raise what he regarded as an unsatisfactory quality level he was unsuccessful. But when McKinsey questioned his subordinates, they said, "Of course he's for quality, but he's for everything else, too. We have a theme a month here." The outstanding companies, in contrast, have one theme and stick to it.

❖ STICKING TO WHAT THEY KNOW BEST

Robert W. Johnson, the former chairman of J&J, put it this way: "Never acquire any business you don't know how to run." Edward G. Harness, CEO at P&G, says, "This company has never left its base." All of the successful companies have been able to define their strengths—marketing, customer contact, new product innovation, low-cost manufacturing—and then build on them. They have resisted the temptation to move into new businesses that look attractive but require corporate skills they do not have.

❖ SIMULTANEOUS LOOSE-TIGHT CONTROLS

While this may sound like a contradiction, it is not. The successful companies control a few variables tightly, but allow flexibility and looseness in others. 3M uses return on sales and number of employees as yardsticks for control. Yet it gives management lots of leeway in day-to-day operations. When McPherson became president of Dana, he threw out all of the company's policy manuals and substituted a one-page philosophy statement and a control system that required divisions to report costs and revenues on a daily basis.

IBM probably has the classic story about flexible controls. After the company suffered well-publicized and costly problems with its System 360 computer several years ago—problems that cost hundreds of millions of dollars to fix—Watson ordered Frank T. Cary, then a vice-president, to incorporate a system of checks and balances in new-product testing. The system made IBM people so cautious that they stopped taking risks. When Cary became president of IBM, one of the first things he did to reverse that attitude was to loosen some of the controls. He recognized that the new system would indeed prevent such an expensive problem from ever happening again, but its rigidity would also keep IBM from ever developing another major system.

By sticking to these eight basics, the successful companies have achieved better-than-average growth. Their managements are able not only to change but also to change quickly. They keep their sights aimed externally at their customers and competitors, and not on their own financial reports.

Excellence in management takes brute perseverance—time, repetition, and simplicity. The tools include plant visits, internal memos, and focused systems. Ignoring these rules may mean that the company slowly loses its vitality, its growth flattens, and its competitiveness is lost.

READING 2

Theory Z: How American Business Can Meet the Japanese Challenge

William G. Ouchi
Summary prepared by Michael Bisesi

Michael Bisesi is Associate Dean of the College of Business Administration at the University of Houston. He teaches the "Business and Society" course and has research interests involving the business-government-education relationship. His articles have appeared in such journals as *Sloan Management Review, Journal of Policy Analysis and Management*, and the *British Journal of Educational Studies.*

What business phenomenon will be recalled as the hallmark of the 1980s? Some will argue that the "Reagan Revolution," with its emphasis on getting government "off the backs" of business, will be most significant. Others will suggest that past government intervention, such as the Chrysler bailout, will be most memorable. What about mergers and acquisitions, "greenmail," "golden parachutes," and other aspects of what Robert Reich calls "paper entrepreneurialism"? What about trade imbalances, Third World debt, or the deregulation of London's financial markets?

While all of these are important, the most enduring revelation of all is that *Japan is much more interested in effective management than America.* While Americans may have written the dominant management textbooks, the Japanese have actually read them. And while we may have started the trend toward the establishment of global markets, the Japanese have actually mastered them.

The unfair advantages that foreign countries enjoy were the topic of many business conversations in the 1980s. Japan, some said, has a central planning authority in MITI (the Ministry of International Trade and Industry) and thus benefits from government assistance. (These same individuals usually oppose

William Ouchi, *Theory Z: How American Business Can Meet the Japanese Challenge.* Reading, MA: Addison-Wesley, 1981.

government involvement in the American economy, of course.) Japan, said others, is a homogeneous culture, and what they have will not work here. (These same individuals usually ignore the adaptation of our American practices in Japan and the success of Japanese-managed American plants.)

In *Theory Z*, William Ouchi tells us not about the obvious economic challenge from Japan, but about a more difficult challenge: *refocusing the corporate culture from technology to people.* Ouchi argues that productivity gains are the direct result of an involved work force; that coordinating and organizing people is the most important task of management; and that productivity is a matter of sound social organization.

Just as a nation and a people have a culture, so does an organization. Ouchi's theme is that American organizations can draw on the success of the Japanese without imitating them. Further, there are specific principles of organization that have nothing to do with national cultures and have everything to do with organizational cultures.

More precisely, American managers will have to act in ways that many find publicly uncomfortable. *Trust* is necessary, for both employees and managers. *Subtlety of personalities,* or understanding who works well with whom, must be acknowledged, regardless of bureaucratic rules. *Intimacy* (in the sense of personal concern), an essential ingredient in any healthy society, must become more commonplace at work.

Old plants and equipment are not the cause of the American Problem, Ouchi claims. The cause seems to be how American organizations treat their people. Americans who work for Japanese companies continually marvel at their emphasis on competence, quality, and personal interest. In fact, the contrasts in operating philosophies between Japanese and American organizations are quite revealing.

❖ CHARACTERISTICS OF JAPANESE ORGANIZATIONS

If one characteristic stands out above all others, it is that many Japanese companies are distinguished by their policies of lifetime employment. Companies tend to hire only once a year, usually promote from within, and generally retain employees until the mandatory retirement age of fifty-five years.

Evaluation and promotion of employees is another distinctive feature of Japanese businesses. Two new employees simultaneously entering a typical Japanese firm would receive the same pay raises and promotions for the first *ten years* of their employment. Differentiation would only begin after that point, regardless of prior performance levels. The advantages of such an approach seem to be a reduction of game-playing for short-term gain and a general reduction of colleague competition and backstabbing.

Career development is another interest of Japanese firms. Typical career paths promote the learning of many functions rather than one function. The personnel officer is more important than the financial officer. This emphasis on "people management" builds organizational loyalty instead of a narrowly functional perspective.

Shared experiences and common frames of reference enhance the ability of Japanese employees to communicate effectively. Since overall company philosophies and objectives are already accepted, decision making becomes a participative and collective activity. Discussion is focused on how to reach the goal, and the view is long-term. Responsibility is taken by a team or a group rather than by a single individual.

Finally, there is a holistic concern for people that molds business and social life together. In general, while there may be some variance, all organizations in Japan exhibit the above characteristics to some degree.

❖ THE AMERICAN CONTRAST

American organizations are characterized by comparatively short-term employment. Rapid turnover requires quick evaluation and promotion, with considerable employee unrest if a promotion takes more than three years. Because of the competition for promotions and raises, people tend to work alone rather than collaboratively. Career paths tend to be highly specialized. Standardization is the main method of control, and integration and coordination are almost impossible because of the emphasis on specialization. Decision making and responsibility are individual matters. The organizational concerns tend to be segmented and impersonal rather than holistic.

❖ THE "THEORY Z" ORGANIZATION

Can Japanese management practices work in American business? Ouchi argues that "Theory Z" may be the answer.

A Theory Z organization is one that has a policy of long-term employment, accompanied by an investment in training and a policy of slow evaluation and promotion. It plans career development *across* functional areas. Quantitative analysis *informs* decisions rather than *controlling* them. "Theory Z" organizations are *not* culturally restricted to Japan, as evidenced by successful adaptations in such American corporations as Hewlett-Packard, Dayton-Hudson, Rockwell International, Intel, and Eli Lilly.

A company has to decide to adopt such a style. Value is more than an advertising slogan, because profits will only come to those maintaining high value in products and services and high value in how employees are treated. In fact, the presence of lifetime employment and general trust facilitates the Theory Z organizations. And what is "lost" in terms of professional specialization is gained in terms of group membership.

❖ MAKING "THEORY Z" WORK

Ouchi contends that organizations, like marriages, must be built and maintained. For those who want to implement a Theory Z organization, Ouchi provides a step-by-step guide (*not* a cookbook). The process itself will take patience and time (at least two years). Theory Z must be compared to the current organizational philosophy. The desired philosophy must be defined with the active involvement and support of the top executive. Both organizational structures and motivational incentives will be involved. Interpersonal skills will require more complete development, emphasizing listening and participative decision making, and paying equal attention to the process as well as the content of communication. Questionnaires or other testing devices must be used. Workers (union or otherwise) must be involved, since people support that which they help to create. A system for slow evaluation and promotion must be decided upon, which will really be best for the long-run perspective of the organization. The development of career paths must be broadened, which should enhance employee enthusiasm, effectiveness, and satisfaction. The process must start from the top, and must be organizationally holistic. Such change is gradual, and instant results cannot be expected.

❖ WHY COMPANY PHILOSOPHY IS CRITICAL

None of the above can happen without an awareness and acceptance of organizational values, goals, and philosophy. Moreover, if the stated philosophy is not implemented, the whole exercise becomes meaningless. An organization can use many methods to ensure implementation, ranging from survey-feedback measures to operating procedures. Moreover, there must be a willingness to accept non-quantitative objectives.

A "Theory Z" corporate culture is one based on a tradition and climate in which the commitment to people is the most important organizational philosophy. This commitment is based on trust and teamwork. Ouchi concludes that American organizations will survive, learn from, and prosper from the Japanese challenge if they balance corporate goals with the needs of individual employees.

❖ CASE HISTORIES OF SUCCESSFUL Z COMPANIES

Two appendices add a valuable dimension to this book. Appendix One lists the Company Z philosophies of the five Fortune 500 organizations mentioned above. In each of these firms, the emphasis was on deliberate and gradual change to a new culture.

Hewlett-Packard selects and develops people in a conscious fashion. It recognizes that intelligent ideas can be found at all levels of the organization, and that people need to have latitude in reaching objectives. While profit is the first objective, a customer-oriented approach that has teams of people working on organization-wide problems is one of its distinguishing characteristics. Most important are its people-related objectives: performance-based job security, fostering of initiative and creativity, and recognition of its corporate citizenship responsibilities.

Dayton-Hudson, the diversified retailing firm, has high values for its people and for its products. It is concerned with honesty, integrity, and responsiveness in its retail operations. It is concerned with enhancing the personal and professional development of its employees. While striving to provide shareholders with "an attractive financial return," it also wants "to serve the communities in which we operate."

Rockwell International established a "culture profile" of itself, examining where it was in the mid-1970s, what it has accomplished, where it is now, and what its future direction might be. It assessed itself on a variety of important dimensions, including such Z issues as short- versus long-term environment, organization communication, information sharing, individual orientation, and job security. In all cases, the company decided it should move toward Z attributes.

Intel ties individual and corporate success together. While people are individuals, they are also part of a team. Managers "must be capable of recognizing and accepting their mistakes and to learn from them." Management also is committed to open communication, ethical decisions, employee development, long-term commitments, and teamwork.

Eli Lilly Co. is concerned with fairness, responsibility to the employee, and responsibility to the community.

❖ THE Q-C CIRCLE

An important tool in many Theory Z firms is the Q-C (quality-control) circle. The Q-C circle is a management-employee group effort for finding and solving production and coordination problems. This form of high worker involvement results in some fifty to sixty implemented suggestions per worker per year in Japan!

A typical Q-C circle has from two to ten employees. All workers are encouraged to become involved in these groups, with the goal of studying any problem that involves the group's work. Whether the issue is product quality, production time, or other related issues, the people closest to the problem—the workers—systematically study it and make recommendations. American firms should accept the fact that "a firm can realize the full potential of its employees only if it both invests in their training and then shares with them the power to influence decisions."

❖ CONCLUSION

Ouchi effectively refutes those arguments that suggest that a Theory Z approach is culture-bound to Japan tradition. *Theory Z* provides a rich resource of information and illustrations for those who want to do further study on the subject of Japanese management and its adaptation to American firms. For many American managers, the Japanese challenge is one that will require substantial reexamination and reorientation of some comfortable ways of thinking.

READING 3

The One Minute Manager

Kenneth Blanchard and Spencer Johnson
Summary prepared by Charles C. Manz

Charles C. Manz is an Associate Professor of Strategic Management and Organization in the College of Business at Arizona State University. He holds a Ph.D. in Organizational Behavior from Pennsylvania State University. His professional publications and presentations concern topics such as self-leadership, vicarious learning, self-managed work groups, leadership, power and control, and group processes. He has co-authored a book focusing on self-leadership and leading others to be self-leaders. He is the author of the book *The Art of Self-Leadership*.

The most distinguishing characteristic of *The One Minute Manager* by Kenneth Blanchard and Spencer Johnson is its major philosophical theme: Good management does not take a lot of time. This dominant theme seems to be based on two underlying premises: (1) *Quality* of time spent with subordinates (as with one's children) is more important than quantity; and, (2) in the end, people (subordinates) should really be managing themselves.

The book is built around a story that provides an occasion for learning about effective management. The story centers on the quest of "a young man" to find an effective manager. In his search he finds all kinds of managers, but very few that he considers effective. According to the story, the young man finds primarily two kinds of managers. One type is a hard-nosed manager who is concerned with the bottom line (profit) and tends to be directive in style. With this type of manager, the young man believes, the organization tends to win at the expense of the subordinates. The other type of manager is one who is concerned more about the employees than about performance. This "nice" kind of manager seems to allow the employees to win at the expense of the organization. In contrast to these two types of managers, the book suggests, an effective manager (as seen through the eyes of the young

Kenneth Blanchard and Spencer Johnson, *The One Minute Manager*. La Jolla, CA: Blanchard Johnson Publishers, 1981.

man) is one who manages so that both the organization and the people involved benefit (win).

The dilemma that the young man faces is that the few managers who do seem to be effective will not share their secrets. That is only true until he meets the "One Minute Manager." It turns out that this almost legendary manager is not only willing to share the secrets of his effectiveness, but is so available that he is able to meet almost any time the young man wants to meet, except at the time of his weekly two-hour meeting with his subordinates. After an initial meeting with the One Minute Manager, the young man is sent off to talk to his subordinates to learn, directly from those affected, the secrets of One Minute Management. Thus the story begins, and in the remaining pages, the wisdom, experience, and management strategies of the One Minute Manager are revealed as the authors communicate, through him and his subordinates, their view on effective management practice.

In addition to general philosophical management advice (e.g., managers can reap good results from their subordinates without expending much time), the book suggests that effective management means that both the organization and its employees win, and that people will do better work when they feel good about themselves; it also offers some specific prescriptions. These prescriptions center around three primary management techniques that have been addressed in the management literature for years: goal setting, positive reinforcement in the form of praise, and verbal reprimand. The authors suggest that applications of each of the techniques can be accomplished in very little time, in fact in as little as one minute (hence the strategies are labeled "one minute goals," "one minute praisings," and "one minute reprimands"). The suggestions made in the book for effective use of each of these strategies will be summarized below.

❖ ONE MINUTE GOALS

"One minute goals" are said to clarify responsibilities and the nature of performance standards. Without them, the authors suggest, employees will not know what is expected of them, being left instead to grope in the dark for what they ought to be doing. A great deal of research and writing has been done on the importance of goals in reaching a level of performance (c.f., Locke, Shaw, Saari, and Latham, 1981). The advice offered in *The One Minute Manager* regarding effective use of performance goals is quite consistent with the findings of this previous work. Specifically, the authors point out through one of the One Minute Manager's subordinates that effective use of One Minute Goals includes:

◆ agreement between the manager and subordinate regarding what needs to be done;

◆ recording of each goal on a single page in no more than 250 words that can be read by almost anyone in less than a minute;

♦ communication of clear performance standards regarding what is expected of subordinates regarding each goal;

♦ continuous review of each goal, current performance, and the difference between the two.

These components are presented with a heavy emphasis on having employees use them to manage themselves. This point is driven home as the employee who shares this part of One Minute Management recalls how the One Minute Manager taught him about One Minute Goals. In the recounted story, the One Minute Manager refuses to take credit for having solved a problem of the subordinate, and is in fact irritated by the very idea of getting credit for it. He insists that the subordinate solved his own problem and orders him to go out and start solving his own future problems without taking up the One Minute Manager's time.

❖ ONE MINUTE PRAISING

The next employee encountered by the young man shares with him the secrets of "one minute praising." Again, the ideas presented regarding this technique pretty well parallel research findings on the use of positive reinforcement (c.f., Luthans and Kreitner, 1986). One basic suggestion for this technique is that managers should spend their time trying to catch subordinates doing something *right* rather than doing something wrong. In order to facilitate this, the One Minute Manager monitors new employees closely at first and has them keep detailed records of their progress (which he reviews). When the manager is able to discover something that the employee is doing right, the occasion is set for One Minute Praising (positive reinforcement). The specific components suggested for applying this technique include:

♦ letting others know that you are going to let them know how they are doing;

♦ praising positive performance as soon as possible after it has occurred, letting employees know specifically what they did right and how good you feel about it;

♦ allowing the message that you really feel good about their performance to sink in for a moment, and encouraging them to do the same;

♦ using a handshake or other form of touch when it is appropriate (more on this later).

Again, these steps are described with a significant self-management flavor. The employee points out that after working for a manager like this for a while you start catching yourself doing things right and using self-praise.

❖ ONE MINUTE REPRIMANDS

The final employee that the young man visits tells him about "One Minute Reprimands." This potentially more somber subject is presented in a quite positive tone. In fact, the employee begins by pointing out that she often praises herself and sometimes asks the One Minute Manager for a praising when she has done something well. But she goes on to explain that when she has done something wrong, the One Minute Manager is quick to respond, letting her know exactly what she has done wrong and how he feels about it. After the reprimand is over, he proceeds to tell her how competent he thinks she really is, essentially praising her as a *person* despite rejecting the undesired *behavior*. Specifically, the book points out that One Minute Reprimands should include:

◆ letting people know that you will, in a frank manner, communicate to them how they are doing;

◆ reprimand poor performance as soon as possible, telling people exactly what they did wrong and how you feel about it (followed by a pause allowing the message to sink in);

◆ reaffirm how valuable you feel the employees are, using touch if appropriate, while making it clear that it is their *performance* that is unacceptable in this situation;

◆ make sure that when the reprimand episode is over it is over.

❖ OTHER ISSUES AND RELATED MANAGEMENT TECHNIQUES

These three One Minute Management techniques form the primary applied content of the book. Good management does not take a lot of time; it just takes wise application of proven management strategies—One Minute Goals, Praisings, and Reprimands. Beyond this, the book deals with some other issues relevant to these strategies, such as "under what conditions is physical touch appropriate?" The book suggests that the use of appropriate touch can be helpful when you know the person well and wish to help that person succeed. It should be done so that you are giving something to the person such as encouragement or support, not taking something away.

The authors also address the issue of manipulation, suggesting that employees should be informed about, and agree to, the manager's use of One Minute Management. They indicate that the key is to be honest and open in the use of this approach. They also deal briefly with several other issues. For example, the book suggests that it is important to move a subordinate gradually to perform a new desired behavior by reinforcing approximations to the behavior until it is finally successfully performed. The technical term for this is "shaping." A person's behavior is shaped by continuously praising improvements rather than waiting until a person completely performs correctly. If a manager waits until a new employee completely performs correctly, the authors suggest, the employee may well give up long before successful performance is achieved because of the absence of reinforcement along the way.

The authors also suggest substituting the strategies for one another when appropriate. With new employees, for instance, they suggest that dealing with low performance should focus on goal setting and then trying to catch them doing something right rather than using reprimand. Since a new employee's lack of experience likely produces an insufficient confidence level, this makes reprimand inappropriate, while goal setting and praise can be quite effective (so the logic goes). The authors also suggest that if a manager is going to be tough on a person, the manager is better off being tough first and then being supportive, rather than the other way around. Issues such as these are briefly addressed through the primary story and the examples described by its primary characters, as supplemental material to the management philosophy and specific management techniques that have been summarized here.

Eventually, at the end of the story, the young man is hired by the One Minute Manager and over time becomes a seasoned One Minute Manager himself. As he looks back over his experiences, the authors are provided with the occasion to summarize some of the benefits of the management approach they advocate—more results in less time, time to think and plan, less stress and better health, similar benefits experienced by subordinates, and reduced absenteeism and turnover.

❖ THE ONE MINUTE MANAGER IN SUMMARY

Perhaps one bottom-line message of the book is that effective management requires that you care sincerely about people but have definite expectations that are expressed openly about their behavior. Also, one thing that is even more valuable than learning to be a One Minute Manager is having one for a boss, which in the end means you really work for yourself. And finally, as the authors illustrate through the giving attitude of the young man who has now become a One Minute Manager, these management techniques are not a competitive advantage to be hoarded but a gift to be shared with others. This is true because, in the end, the one who shares the gift will be at least as richly rewarded as the one who receives it.

❖ References

Locke, E., K. Shaw, L. Saari, and G. Latham. "Goal Setting and Task Performance 1969–1980." *Psychological Bulletin* 90(1981), 125–152.

Luthans, F. and T. Davis. "Behavioral Self-management (BSM): The Missing Link in Managerial Effectiveness." *Organizational Dynamics* 8(1979), 42–60.

Luthans, F. and R. Kreitner. *Organizational Behavior Modification and Beyond.* Glenview, IL.: Scott, Foresman and Co., 1986.

Manz, C.C. *The Art of Self-leadership: Strategies for Personal Effectiveness in Your Life and Work.* Englewood Cliffs, NJ: Prentice-Hall, 1983.

Manz, C.C. "Self-leadership: Toward an Expanded Theory of Self-influence Processes in Organizations." *Academy of Management Review* 11(1986), 585–600.

Manz, C.C. and H.P. Sims, Jr. "Self-management as a Substitute for Leadership: A Social Learning Theory Perspective." *Academy of Management Review* 5(1980), 361–367.

READING 4

The Human Side of Enterprise

Douglas McGregor
Summary prepared by Gayle Porter

Gayle Porter obtained her Ph.D. from The Ohio State University in Organizational Behavior and Human Resource Management and is now at Rutgers University–Camden. Articles and ongoing research interests include the effects of dispositional differences in the workplace, group perceptions of efficacy and esteem, and the comparison of influence on employees through reward systems, leadership, and employee development efforts. Her prior experience includes positions as Director of Curriculum Development for a human resource management degree program; consultant on training programs, financial operations, and computer applications; financial manager for an oil and gas production company; and financial specialist for NCR Corporation.

The Human Side of Enterprise was written during an ongoing comparative study of management development programs in several large companies. In McGregor's view, the making of managers has less to do with formal efforts in development than with how the task of management is understood within that organization. This fundamental understanding determines the policies and procedures within which the managers operate, and guides the selection of people identified as having the potential for management positions. During the late 1950s McGregor believed that major industrial advances of the next half century would occur on the human side of enterprise and he was intrigued by the inconsistent assumptions about what makes managers behave as they do. His criticism of the conventional assumptions, which he labels Theory X, is that they limit options. Theory Y provides an alternative set of assumptions that are much needed due to the extent of unrealized human potential in most organizations.

Douglas McGregor, *The Human Side of Enterprise*. New York: McGraw-Hill, 1960.

❖ THE THEORETICAL ASSUMPTIONS OF MANAGEMENT

Regardless of the economic success of a firm, few managers are satisfied with their ability to predict and control the behavior of members of the organization. Effective prediction and control are central to the task of management, and there can be no prediction without some underlying theory. Therefore, all managerial decisions and actions rest on a personally held theory, a set of assumptions about behavior. The assumptions management holds about controlling its human resources determine the whole character of the enterprise.

In application, problems occur related to these assumptions. First, managers may not realize that they hold and apply conflicting ideas and that one may cancel out the other. For example, a manager may delegate based on the assumption that employees should have responsibility, but then nullify that action by close monitoring, which indicates the belief that employees can't handle the responsibility. Another problem is failure to view control as selective adaptation, when dealing with human behavior. People adjust to certain natural laws in other fields; e.g., engineers don't dig channels and expect water to run uphill! With humans, however, there is a tendency to try to control in direct violation of human nature. Then, when they fail to achieve the desired results, they look for every other possible cause rather than examine the inappropriate choice of a method to control behavior.

Any influence is based on dependence, so the nature and degree of dependence are critical factors in determining what methods of control will be effective. Conventional organization theory is based on authority as a key premise. It is the central and indispensable means of managerial control and recognizes only upward dependence. In recent decades, workers have become less dependent on a single employer, and society has provided certain safeguards related to unemployment. This limits the upward dependence and, correspondingly, the ability to control by authority alone. In addition, employees have the ability to engage in countermeasures such as slowdowns, lowered standards of performance, or even sabotage to defeat authority they resent.

Organizations are more accurately represented as systems of *inter*dependence. Subordinates depend on managers to help them meet their needs, but the managers also depend on subordinates to achieve their own and the organization's goals. While there is nothing inherently bad or wrong in the use of authority to control, in certain circumstances it fails to bring the desired results. Circumstances change even from hour to hour, and the role of the manager is to select the appropriate means of influence based on the situation at a given point in time. If employees exhibit lazy, indifferent behavior, the causes lie in management methods of organization and control.

Theory X is a term used to represent a set of assumptions. Principles found in traditional management literature could only have derived from assumptions such as the following, which have had a major impact on managerial strategy in organizations:

1. *The average human being has an inherent dislike of work and will avoid it if possible.*
2. *Because of this human characteristic of dislike of work, most people must be coerced, controlled, directed, and threatened with punishment to get them to put forth adequate effort toward the achievement of organizational objectives.*
3. *The average human being prefers to be directed, wishes to avoid responsibility, has relatively little ambition, and wants security above all.*

These assumptions are not without basis, or they would never have persisted as they have. They do explain some observed human behavior, but other observations are not consistent with this view. Theory X assumptions also encourage us to categorize certain behaviors as human nature, when they may actually be symptoms of a condition in which workers have been deprived of an opportunity to satisfy higher-order needs (social and egoistic needs).

A strong tradition exists of viewing employment as an employee's agreement to accept control by others in exchange for rewards that are only of value outside the workplace. For example, wages (except for their symbolism as status differences), vacation, medical benefits, stock purchase plans, and profit sharing are of little value during the actual time on the job. Work is the necessary evil to endure for rewards away from the job. In this conception of human resources we can never discover, let alone utilize, the potentialities of the average human being.

Many efforts to provide more equitable and generous treatment to employees and to provide a safe and pleasant work environment have been designed without any real change in strategy. Very often what is proposed as a new management strategy is nothing more than a different tactic within the old Theory X assumptions. Organizations have progressively made available the means to satisfy lower-order needs for subsistence and safety. As the nature of the dependency relationship changes, management has gradually deprived itself of the opportunity to use control based solely on assumptions of Theory X. A new strategy is needed.

Theory Y assumptions are dynamic, indicate the possibility of human growth and development, and stress the necessity for selective adaptation:

1. *The expenditure of physical and mental effort in work is as natural as play or rest.*
2. *External control and the threat of punishment are not the only means for bringing about effort toward organizational objectives. People will exercise self-direction and self-control in the service of objectives to which they are committed.*
3. *Commitment to objectives is a function of the rewards associated with their achievement (satisfaction of ego and self-actualization needs can be products of effort directed toward organizational objectives).*
4. *The average human being learns, under proper conditions, not only to accept but to seek responsibility.*

5. *The capacity to exercise a relatively high degree of imagination, ingenuity, and creativity in the solution of organizational problems is widely, not narrowly, distributed in the population.*

6. *Under the conditions of modern industrial life, the intellectual potentialities of the average human being are only partially utilized.*

The Theory Y assumptions challenge a number of deeply ingrained managerial habits of thought and action; they lead to a management philosophy of integration and self-control. Theory X assumes that the organization's requirements take precedence over the needs of the individual members, and that the worker must always adjust to needs of the organization as management perceives them. In contrast, the principle of *integration* proposes that conditions can be created such that individuals can best achieve their own goals by directing their efforts toward the success of the enterprise. Based on the premise that the assumptions of Theory Y are valid, the next logical question is whether, and to what extent, such conditions can be created. How will employees be convinced that applying their skills, knowledge, and ingenuity in support of the organization is a more attractive alternative than other ways to utilize their capacities?

❖ THEORY Y IN PRACTICE

The essence of applying Theory Y assumptions is guiding the subordinates to develop themselves rather than developing the subordinate by telling them what they need to do. An important consideration is that the subordinates' acceptance of responsibility for self-developing (i.e., self-direction and self-control) has been shown to relate to their commitment to objectives. But the overall aim is to further the growth of the individual, and it must be approached as a managerial strategy rather than simply as a personnel technique. Forms and procedures are of little value. Once the concept is provided, managers who welcome the assumptions of Theory Y will create their own processes for implementation; managers with underlying Theory X assumptions cannot create the conditions for integration and self-control no matter what tools are provided.

The development process becomes one of role clarification and mutual agreement regarding the subordinate's job responsibilities. This requires the manager's willingness to accept some risk and allow mistakes as part of the growth process. It also is time-consuming in terms of discussions and allowing opportunity for self-discovery. However, it is not a new set of duties on top of the manager's existing load. It is a different way of fulfilling the existing responsibilities.

One procedure that violates Theory Y assumptions is the typical utilization of performance appraisals. Theory X leads quite naturally into this means of directing individual efforts toward organizational objectives.

Through the performance appraisal process, management tells people what to do, monitors their activities, judges how well they have done, and rewards or punishes them accordingly. Since the appraisals are used for administrative purposes (e.g., pay, promotion, retention decisions), this is a demonstration of management's overall control strategy. Any consideration of personal goals is covered by the expectation that rewards of salary and position are enough. If the advancement available through this system is not a desired reward, the individuals are placed in a position of acting against their own objectives and advancing for the benefit of the organization only. The alternative (for example, turning down a promotion) may bring negative outcomes such as lack of future options or being identified as employees with no potential.

The principle of integration requires active and responsible participation of employees in decisions affecting them. One plan that demonstrates Theory Y assumptions is *The Scanlon Plan.* A central feature in this plan is the cost-reduction sharing that provides a meaningful cause-and-effect connection between employee behavior and the reward received. The reward is directly related to the success of the organization and it is distributed frequently. This provides a more effective learning reinforcement than the traditional performance appraisal methods. The second central feature of the Scanlon Plan is effective participation, a formal method through which members contribute brains and ingenuity as well as their physical efforts on the job. This provides a means for social and ego satisfaction, so employees have a stake in the success of the firm beyond the economic rewards. Implementation of the Scanlon Plan is not a program or set of procedures; it must be accepted as a way of life and can vary depending on the circumstances of the particular company. It is entirely consistent with Theory Y assumptions.

Theory X leads to emphasis on tactics of control, whereas Theory Y is more concerned with the nature of the relationship. Eliciting the desired response in a Theory Y context is a matter of creating an environment or set of conditions to enable self-direction. The day-to-day behavior of an immediate supervisor or manager is perhaps the most critical factor in such an environment. Through sometimes subtle behaviors, superiors demonstrate their attitudes and create what is referred to as the psychological "climate" of the relationship.

Management style does not seem to be important. Within many different styles, subordinates may or may not develop confidence in the manager's deeper integrity, based on other behavioral cues. Lack of confidence in the relationship causes anxiety and undesirable reactions from the employees. No ready formula is available to relay integrity. Insincere attempts to apply a technique or style—such as using participation only to manipulate subordinates into believing they have some input to decisions—are usually recognized as a gimmick and soon destroy confidence.

In addition to manager-subordinate relationships, problems connected to Theory X assumptions can be observed in other organizational associations such as staff-line relationships. Upper management may create working roles for staff groups to "police" line managers' activities, giving them an influence that equates psychologically to direct line authority. Top management with Theory X assumptions can delegate and still retain control. The staff function provides an opportunity to monitor indirectly, to set policy for limiting decisions and actions, and to obtain information on everything happening before a problem can occur.

Staff personnel often come from a very specialized education with little preparation for what their role should be in an organization. With full confidence in their objective methods and training to find "the best answer," they often are unprepared for the resistance of line managers who don't share this confidence and don't trust the derived solutions. The staff may conclude that line managers are stupid, unconcerned with the general welfare of the organization, and care only about their own authority and independence. They essentially adopt the Theory X assumptions and readily accept the opportunity to create a system of measurements for control of the line operations.

To utilize staff groups within the context of Theory Y, managers must emphasize the principle of self-control. As a resource to all parts and levels of the organization, staff reports and data should be supplied to all members who can use such information to control their own job—not subordinates' jobs. If summary data indicate something wrong within the manager's unit of responsibility, the manager would turn to subordinates, not to the staff, for more information. If the subordinates are practicing similar self-control using staff-provided information, they have most likely discovered the same problem and taken action before this inquiry occurs. There is no solution to the problem of staff-line relationships in authoritative terms that can address organizational objectives adequately. However, a manager operating by Theory Y assumptions will apply them similarly to all relationships—upward, downward, and peer level—including the staff-line associations.

❖ THE DEVELOPMENT OF MANAGERIAL TALENT

Leadership is a relationship with four major variables: the characteristics of the leader; the attitudes, needs and other personal characteristics of the followers; the characteristics of the organization, such as its purpose, structure, and the nature of its task; and the social, economic and political environment in which the organization operates. Specifying which leader characteristics will result in effective performance depends on the other factors, so it is a complex relationship. Even if researchers were able to determine the universal characteristics of a good relationship between the leader and the other situational factors, there are still many ways to achieve the same thing. For example, mutual confidence seems important in the relationship, but there are a number of ways that confidence can be developed and maintained. Different personal characteristics could achieve the same desired relationship.

Also, because it is so difficult to predict the situational conditions an organization will face, future management needs are unpredictable. The major task, then, is to provide a heterogeneous supply of human resources from which individuals can be selected as appropriate at a future time. This requires attracting recruits from a variety of sources and with a variety of backgrounds, which complicates setting criteria for selection. Also, the management development programs in an organization should involve many people rather than a few with similar qualities and abilities. Finally, management's goal must be to develop the unique capacities of each individual, rather than common objectives for all participants. We must place high value on people in general—seek to enable them to develop to their fullest potential in whatever role they best can fill. Not everyone must pursue the top jobs; outstanding leadership is needed at every level.

Individuals must develop themselves and will do so optimally only in terms of what each of them sees as meaningful and valuable. What might be called a "manufacturing approach" to management development involves designing programs to build managers; this end product becomes a supply of managerial talent to be used as needed. A preferred alternative approach is to "grow talent" under the assumption that people will grow into what they are capable of becoming, if they are provided the right conditions for that growth. There is little relationship (possibly even a negative one) between the formal structure for management development and actual achievement of the organization, because programs and procedures do not *cause* management development.

Learning is fairly straightforward when the individual desires new knowledge or skill. Unfortunately, many development offerings soon become a scheduled assignment for entire categories of people. Learning is limited in these conditions, because the motivation is low. Further, negative attitudes develop toward training in general, which interferes with creating an overall climate conducive to growth. In many cases, managers may have a purpose in sending subordinates to training that is not shared with or understood by that individual. This creates anxiety or confusion, which also interferes with learning. It is best if attendance in training and development programs are the result of joint target-setting, wherein the individual expresses a need and it can be determined that a particular program will benefit both the individual and the organization.

Classroom learning can be valuable to satisfying needs of both parties. However, it can only be effective when there is an organizational climate conducive to growth. Learning is always an active process, whether related to motor skills or acquisition of knowledge; it cannot be injected into the learner, so motivation is critical. Practice and feedback are essential when behavior changes are involved. Classroom methods such as case analysis and role playing provide an opportunity to experiment with decisions and behaviors in a safe environment, to receive immediate feedback, and to go back and try other alternatives. Some applications of classroom learning may be observed directly on the job. In other cases, the application may be more subtle, in the form of increased understanding or challenging one's own preconceptions. Care must be taken so that pressures to evaluate the benefits of classroom learning don't result in application of inappropriate criteria for success while the true value of the experience is overlooked.

Separate attention is given to management groups or teams at various levels. Within Theory X assumptions, direction and control are jeopardized by effective group functioning. On the other hand, a manager who recognizes interdependencies in the organization—one who is less interested in personal power than in creating conditions so human resources will voluntarily achieve organization objectives—will seek to build strong management groups. Creating a managerial team requires unity of purpose among those individuals. If the group is nothing more than several individuals competing for power and recognition, it is not a team. Again, the climate of the relationships and the fundamental understanding of the role of managers in the organization will be critical. One day the hierarchical structure of reporting relationships will disappear from organizational charts and give way to a series of linked groups. This shift in patterns of relationships will be a slow transition, but will signify recognition of employee capacity to collaborate in joint efforts. Then we may begin to discover how seriously management has underestimated the true potential of the organization's human resources.

❖ SUMMARY COMMENTS

Theory X is not an evil set of assumptions, but rather a limiting one. Use of authority to influence has it place, even within the Theory Y assumptions, but it does not work in all circumstances. A number of societal changes suggest why Theory X increasingly may cause problems for organizations needing more innovation and flexibility in their operating philosophy. It is critically important for managers honestly to examine the assumptions that underlie their own behavior toward subordinates. To do so requires first accepting the two possibilities, Theory X and Theory Y, and then examining one's own actions in the context of that comparison. Fully understanding the implications on each side will help identify whether the observed choices of how to influence people are likely to bring about the desired results.

4

HIGH–PERFORMING ORGANIZATIONS

Most organizations don't want merely to survive; they want to be effective, or even excellent, at what they do. To do so requires a prior definition of success, and this often encourages the managers of an organization to examine the actions of their best competitors for comparative models (benchmarks). The assumption is that if they can identify the organizational characteristics that allow others to succeed, perhaps these attributes can be transplanted (or adapted) to facilitate their own success. There is, therefore, considerable interest across a wide variety of organizations and management groups in what "high-performing organizations" actually do and what the guiding principles are.

The three books in this section concern themselves with issues pertaining to organizational effectiveness. High-performing organizations, according to Peter Senge, place an emphasis on learning, competence, and justice. They are learning organizations. Michael Hammer and James Champy suggest that the high-performing organizations have reengineered themselves by organizing around processes. According to Jay Galbraith and Edward E. Lawler III, competitive pressures have revealed the shortcomings of the functional design, thus creating a need for new organizational designs. James C. Collins and Jerry Porras have learned that the truly exceptional and long-lasting companies have not found their essence in visionary leaders and corporate vision. These organizations are more concerned about visionary product concepts, visionary products, and/or visionary market insights.

Peter M. Senge is the Director of the Systems Thinking and Organizational Learning Program at MIT's Sloan School of Management. His book *The Fifth Discipline: The Art and Practice of the Learning Organization* emphasizes the importance of organizations developing the capacity to engage in effective learning. Senge identifies and discusses a set of disabilities that are fatal to organizations, especially those operating in rapidly changing environments. The fifth discipline—*systems thinking*—is presented as the cornerstone for the learning organization. Personal mastery, mental models, shared vision, and team learning are presented as the core disciplines and the focus for building the learning organization.

Michael Hammer and James Champy, authors of *Reengineering the Corporation,* claim that most American companies need to make radical changes if they are to survive long-term. Success, they claim, will require that organizations organize themselves around *processes,* and not around individual tasks or functions. Environmental changes are quickly rendering many organization structures and management principles incapable of the flexibility and responsiveness needed for survival in the turbulent and highly competitive markets of today.

Michael Hammer (Ph.D.) is the president of Hammer and Company, a management education and consulting firm. James Champy is the chairman of CSC Index, a management consulting firm. Both authors have worked with firms as they have undertaken reengineering efforts. Champy is also the author of *Reengineering Management,* and Hammer has written *The Reengineering Revolution.*

Authors of *Organizing for the Future,* Jay R. Galbraith and Edward E. Lawler III are professors of management and members of the Center for Effective Organizations at the University of Southern California. Observing the shortcomings of the functional unit design revealed by competitive pressures, they offer several suggestions about organizing for the future. Their high-involvement model of organization is seen as an alternative to the slow and inflexible hierarchical organization. In order for the high-involvement model to emerge, management must adopt a new paradigm based on the assumption that *the key to maximizing organizational effectiveness is to maximize the employee's ability to respond directly to changing conditions.* This calls for a new approach to information access, decision-making influence, reward systems, and knowledge (i.e., skills and abilities within the organization).

James C. Collins and Jerry I. Porras, authors of *Built to Last: Successful Habits of Visionary Companies,* are on the faculty at the Stanford University Graduate School of Business. Based upon a six-year research project conducted at Stanford's Business School, *Built to Last* provides insight into the question, "What makes the truly exceptional companies different from other companies?" Eighteen truly exceptional and long-lasting companies (e.g., Boeing, Disney, General Electric, 3M, Merck, Motorola, Procter & Gamble, and Philip Morris) who have outperformed the general stock market since the late 1920s were the focus of their research.

Collins and Porras argue that the popular model that attributes organizational high-performance to visionary leadership fails to account for the success of many organizations. For example, the charismatic visionary leader model fails to account for the success of 3M: " . . .neither its current nor past CEOs fit this model. 3M's chief executive officers over the years have been highly competent and effective managers, but from all reports were not the 'larger than life' type of leader commonly associated with . . . charismatic visionaries" (p. 7). Those organizations "built to last" possess characteristics that differentiate them from other organizations. Their findings organize themselves around (a) characteristics of the leadership during the formative years, and (b) characteristics (e.g., a well understood and enduring core ideology) of the organization.

READING 1

The Fifth Discipline

Peter Senge
Summary prepared by Dorothy Marcic

Dorothy Marcic is Professor of Management in the graduate program at Metropolitan State University in Minneapolis, where she teaches organizational behavior and strategy. In addition, she has conducted over 350 training programs for managers. Her doctorate is from the University of Massachusetts in Amherst and she is the author of 12 books, including *Organizational Behavior: Experiences and Cases* and *Management International.*

Learning disabilities can be fatal to organizations, causing them to have an average life span of only 40 years—half a human being's life. *Organizations need to be learners, and often they aren't.* Somehow some survive, but never live up to their potential. What happens if what we term "excellence" is really no more than mediocrity? Only those firms which become learners will succeed in the increasingly turbulent, competitive global market.

❖ LEARNING DISABILITIES

There are seven learning disabilities common to organizations.

IDENTIFICATION WITH ONE'S POSITION   American workers are trained to see themselves as what they do, not who they are. Therefore, if laid off, they find it difficult, if not impossible, to find work doing something else. Worse for the organization, though, is the limited thinking this attitude creates. By claiming an identity related to the job, workers are cut off from seeing how their responsibility connects to other jobs. For example, one American car had three assembly bolts on one component. The similar Japanese make had only one bolt. Why? Because the Detroit manufacturer had three engineers for that component, while a similar Japanese manufacturer had only one.

EXTERNAL ENEMIES   This belief is a result of the previously-stated disability. External enemies refers to people focusing blame on anything but them-

Peter Senge, *The Fifth Discipline*. New York: Doubleday, 1990.

selves or their unit. Fault is regularly blamed on factors like the economy, the weather, or the government. Marketing blames manufacturing, and manufacturing blames engineering. Such external fault-finding keeps the organization from seeing what the real problems are, and prevents them from tackling the real the issues head-on.

THE ILLUSION OF TAKING CHARGE Being proactive is seen as good management—doing something about "those problems." All too often, though, being proactive is a disguise for reactiveness against that awful enemy out there.

THE FIXATION ON EVENTS Much attention in organizations is paid to events—last month's sales, the new product, who just got hired, and so on. Our society, too, is geared toward short-term thinking, which in turn stifles the type of generative learning that permits a look at the real threats—the slowly declining processes of quality, service or design.

THE PARABLE OF THE BOILED FROG An experiment was once conducted by placing a frog in boiling water. Immediately the frog, sensing danger in the extreme heat, jumped out to safety. However, placing the frog in cool water and slowly turning up the heat resulted in the frog getting groggier and groggier and finally boiling to death. Why? Because the frog's survival mechanisms are programmed to look for sudden changes in the environment, and not to gradual changes. Similarly, during the 1960s, the U.S. auto industry saw no threat by Japan, which had only four percent of the market. Not until the 1980s when Japan had over twenty-one percent of the market did the Big Three begin to look at their core assumptions. Now with Japan holding about a thirty percent share of the market, it is not certain if this frog (U.S. automakers) is capable of jumping out of the boiling water. Looking at gradual processes requires slowing down our frenetic pace and watching for the subtle cues.

THE DELUSION OF LEARNING FROM EXPERIENCE Learning from experience is powerful. This is how we learn to walk and talk. However, we now live in a time when direct consequences of actions may take months or years to appear. Decisions in R & D may take up to a decade to bear fruit and their actual consequences may be influenced by manufacturing and marketing along the way. Organizations often choose to deal with these complexities by breaking themselves up into smaller and smaller components, further reducing their ability to see problems in their entirety.

THE MYTH OF THE MANAGEMENT TEAM Most large organizations have a group of bright, experienced leaders who are supposed to know all the answers. They were trained to believe there are answers to all problems and they should find them. People are rarely rewarded for bringing up difficult issues or for looking at parts of a problem which make it harder to grasp. Most teams end up operating below the lowest IQ of any member. What results are "skilled incompetents"—people who know all too well how to keep *from* learning.

❖ SYSTEMS THINKING

There are five disciplines required for a learning organization: personal mastery, mental models, shared vision, team learning, and systems thinking. The fifth one, systems thinking, is the most important. Without systems thinking, the other disciplines do not have the same effect.

◆ THE LAWS OF THE FIFTH DISCIPLINE

Today's Problems Result from Yesterday's Solutions.   A carpet merchant kept pushing down a bump in the rug, only to have it reappear elsewhere, until he lifted a corner and out slithered a snake. Sometimes fixing one part of the system only brings difficulties to other parts of the system. For example, solving an internal inventory problem may lead to angry customers who now get late shipments.

Push Hard and the System Pushes Back Even Harder.   Systems theory calls this compensating feedback, which is a common way of reducing the effects of an intervention. Some cities, for example, built low-cost housing and set up jobs programs, only to have more poor people than ever. Why? Because many moved to the cities from neighboring areas so that they, too, could take advantage of the low-cost housing and job opportunities.

Behavior Gets Better Before it Gets Worse.   Some decisions actually look good in the short term, but produce *compensating feedback* and crisis in the end. The really effective decisions often produce difficulties in the short run, but create more health in the long term. This is why behaviors such as building a power base or working hard just to please the boss come back to haunt you.

The Best Way Out is to Go Back In.   We often choose familiar solutions, ones that feel comfortable and not scary. But the effective ways often mean going straight into what we are afraid of facing. What does *not* work is pushing harder on the same old solutions (also called the "what we need here is a bigger hammer" syndrome).

The Cure Can be Worse Than the Disease.   The result of applying nonsystematic solutions to problems is the need for more and more of the same. It can become addictive. Someone begins mild drinking to alleviate work tension. The individual feels better and then takes on more work, creating more tension and a need for more alcohol, and the person finally becomes an alcoholic. Sometimes these types of solutions only result in shifting the burden. The government enters the scene by providing more welfare and leaves the host system weaker and less able to solve its own problems. This ultimately necessitates still more aid from the government. Companies can try to shift their burdens to consultants, but then become more and more dependent on them to solve their problems.

Faster Is Slower.   Every system, whether ecological or organizational, has an optimal rate of growth. Faster and faster is not always better. (After all, the tortoise finally did win the race.) Complex human systems require new ways of thinking. Quickly jumping in and fixing what *looks* bad usually provides solutions for a problem's symptoms and not for the problem itself.

Cause and Effect Are Not Always Related Closely in Time and Space.   *Effects* here mean the symptoms we see, such as drug abuse and unemployment, while *causes* mean the interactions of the underlying system which bring about these conditions. We often assume cause is near to effect. If there is a sales problem, then incentives for the sales force should fix it, or if there is inadequate housing, then build more houses. Unfortunately, this does not often work, for the real causes lie elsewhere.

Tiny Changes May Produce Big Results; Areas of Greatest Leverage Are Frequently the Least Obvious.   System science teaches that the most obvious solutions usually don't work. While simple solutions frequently make short-run improvements, they commonly contribute to long-term deteriorations. The *non*-obvious and *well-focused* solutions are more likely to provide leverage and bring positive change. For example, ships have a tiny trim tab on one edge of the rudder that has great influence on the movement of that ship, so small changes in the trim tab bring big shifts in the ship's course. However, there are no simple rules for applying leverage to organizations. It requires looking for the structure of what is going on rather than merely seeing the events.

You Can Have Your Cake and Eat it Too—But Not At the Same Time.   Sometimes the most difficult problems come from "snapshot" rather than "process" thinking. For example, it was previously believed by American manufacturers that quality and low cost could not be achieved simultaneously. One had to be chosen over the other. What was missed, however, was the notion that improving quality may also mean eliminating waste and unnecessary time (both adding costs), which in the end would mean lower costs. Real leverage comes when it can be seen that seemingly opposing needs can be met over time.

Cutting the Elephant in Half Does Not Create Two Elephants.   Some problems can be solved by looking at parts of the organization, while others require holistic thinking. What is needed is an understanding of the boundaries for each problem. Unfortunately, most organizations are designed to prevent people from seeing systemic problems, either by creating rigid structures, or by leaving problems behind for others to clean up.

There is No Blame. Systems thinking teaches that there are not outside causes to problems; instead, you and your "enemy" are part of the same system. Any cure requires understanding how that is seen.

❖ THE OTHER DISCIPLINES

◆ PERSONAL MASTERY

Organizations can learn only when the individuals involved learn. This requires personal mastery, which is the discipline of personal learning and growth, where people are continually expanding their ability to create the kind of life they want. From their quest comes the spirit of the learning organization.

Personal mastery involves seeing one's life as a creative work, being able to clarify what is really important, and learning to see current reality more clearly. The difference between what's important, what we want, and where we are now produces a "creative tension." Personal mastery means being able to generate and maintain creative tension.

Those who have high personal mastery have a vision which is more like a calling, and they are in a continual learning mode. They never really "arrive." Filled with more commitment, they take initiative and greater responsibility in their work.

Previously, organizations supported an employee's development only if it would help the organization, which fits in with the traditional "contract" between employee and organization ("an honest day's pay in exchange for an honest day's work"). The new, and coming, way is to see it rather as a "covenant," which comes from a shared vision of goals, ideas, and management processes.

Working towards personal mastery requires living with emotional tension, not letting our goals get eroded. As Somerset Maugham said, "Only mediocre people are always at their best." One of the worst blocks to achieving personal mastery is the common belief that we cannot have what we want. Being committed to the truth is a powerful weapon against this, for it does not allow us to deceive ourselves. Another means of seeking personal mastery is to integrate our reason and intuition. We live in a society which values reason and devalues intuition. However, using both together is very powerful and may be one of the fundamental contributions to systems thinking.

◆ MENTAL MODELS

Mental models are internal images of how the world works, and they can range from simple generalizations (people are lazy) to complex theories (assumptions about why my co-workers interact they way they do). For example, for decades the Detroit automakers believed people bought cars mainly for styling, not for quality or reliability. These beliefs, which were really unconscious assumptions, worked well for many years, but ran into trouble when competition from Japan began. It took a long time for Detroit even to begin to see the mistakes in their beliefs. One company which managed to change its mental model through incubating a business worldview was Shell.

Traditional hierarchical organizations have the dogma of organizing, managing and controlling. In the new learning organization, though, the revised "dogma" will be values, vision and mental models.

Hanover Insurance began changes in 1969 designed to overcome the "basic diseases of the hierarchy." Three values espoused were:

1. *openness*—seen as an antidote to the dysfunctional interactions in face-to-face meetings.
2. *merit*, or making decisions based on the good of the organization—seen as the antidote to decision-making by organizational politics.
3. *localness*—the antidote to doing the dirty stuff the boss doesn't want to do.

Chris Argyris and colleagues developed "action science" as a means for reflecting on the reasoning underlying our actions. This helps people change the defensive routines which lead them to skilled incompetence. Similarly, John Beckett created a course on the historical survey of main philosophies of thought, East and West, as a sort of "sandpaper on the brain." These ideas exposed managers to their own assumptions and mental models, and provided other ways to view the world.

◆ SHARED VISION

A shared vision is not an idea. Rather it is a force in people's hearts, a sense of purpose which provides energy and focus for learning. Visions are often exhilarating. Shared vision is important because it may be the beginning step to get people who mistrusted each other to start working together. Abraham Maslow studied high-performing teams and found that they had shared vision. Shared visions can mobilize courage so naturally that people don't even know the extent of their strength. When John Kennedy created the shared vision in 1961 of putting a man on the moon by the end of the decade, only fifteen percent of the technology had been created. Yet it led to numerous acts of daring and courage.

Learning organizations are not achievable without shared vision. Without that incredible pull toward the deeply felt goal, the forces of *status quo* will overwhelm the pursuit. As Robert Fritz once said, "In the presence of greatness, pettiness disappears." Conversely, in the absence of a great vision, pettiness is supreme.

Strategic planning often does not involve building a shared vision, but rather announcing the vision of top management, asking people to, at best, enroll, and, at worst, to comply. What Senge talks of is gaining commitment from people. This is done by taking a personal vision and building it into a shared vision. In the traditional hierarchical organization, compliance is one of the desired outcomes. For learning organizations, commitment must be the key goal. Shared vision, though, is not possible without personal mastery, which is needed to foster continued commitment to a lofty goal.

◆ TEAM LEARNING

Bill Russell of the Boston Celtics wrote about being on a team of specialists whose performance depended on one another's individual excellence and how well they worked together. Sometimes that created a feeling of magic. He is talking about *alignment,* where a group functions as a whole unit, rather than as individuals working at cross purposes. When a team is aligned, its energies are focused and harmonized. They do not need to sacrifice their own interests. Instead, alignment occurs when the shared vision becomes an extension of the personal vision. Alignment is a necessary condition to empower others and ultimately empower the team.

Never before today has there been greater need for mastering team learning, which requires mastering both dialogue and discussion. *Dialogue* involves a creative and free search of complex and even subtle issues, while *discussion* implies different views being presented and defended. Both skills are useful, but most teams cannot tell the difference between the two. The purpose of dialogue is to increase individual understanding. Here, assumptions are suspended and participants regard one another as on the same level. *Discussion,* on the other hand, comes from the same root word as *percussion* and *concussion* and involves a sort of verbal ping-pong game whose object is winning. Although this is a useful technique, it must be balanced with dialogue. A continued emphasis on winning is not compatible with the search for truth and coherence.

One of the major blocks to healthy dialogue and discussion is what Chris Argyris calls *defensive routines.* These are habitual styles of interacting that protect us from threat or embarrassment. These include the avoidance of conflict (smoothing over) and the feeling that one has to appear competent and to know the answers at all times.

Team learning, like any other skill, requires practice. Musicians and athletes understand this principle. Work teams need to learn that lesson as well.

❖ OTHER ISSUES

Organizational politics is a perversion of truth, yet most people are so accustomed to it, they don't even notice it anymore. A learning organization is not possible in such an environment. In order to move past the politics, one thing needed is openness—both speaking openly and honestly about the real and important issues, and being willing to challenge one's own way of thinking.

Localness, too, is essential to the learning organization, for decisions need to be pushed down the organizational hierarchy in order to unleash people's commitment. This gives them the freedom to act.

One thing lacking in many organizations is time to reflect and think. If someone is sitting quietly, we assume they are not busy and we feel free to interrupt. Many managers, however, are too busy to "just think." This should not be blamed on the tumultuous environment of many crises. Research suggests that, even when given ample time, managers still do not devote any of it to adequate reflection. Therefore, habits need to be changed, as well as how we structure our days.

READING 2

Reengineering the Corporation

Michael Hammer and James Champy
Summary prepared by Steve Gildersleeve

Steve Gildersleeve is the general manager of Carlson Florist and Greenhouses in Duluth, Minnesota. He has also worked in the Controller's Department for 3M in Austin, Texas, and in Corporate Accounting for The Carlson Companies in Minneapolis, MN.

He is actively studying and applying systems thinking principles and methods at Carlson's along with searching for methods to teach it to his co-workers and friends.

Another interest is developing a "no-excuses management" system that creates a supportive work environment in addition to focusing employees' efforts on the achievement of daily and long-term business goals.

"Why do we do what we do at all?" This is the key question for organizations to answer as they approach the twenty-first century. No longer will "How can we do what we do faster?" or "How can we do what we do better?" or even, "How can we do what we do at a lower cost?" succeed as questions on which to focus managerial attention. Most American companies have come to a point where radical changes are required in order to survive. The change process required is called business reengineering.

"If I were recreating this company today, given what I know and given current technology, what would it look like?" This question directly expresses the focal point of reengineering.

The basic premise of reengineering is simple, yet, like most simple prescriptions, it can be very difficult to swallow. Success in the marketplace requires that companies become the best in their business at the fundamentals: inventing products and services, manufacturing or providing them, marketing or selling them, and serving customers. To do this, companies must organize around processes, not individual tasks or functions. This dramatic approach may virtually require some to recreate their organizations.

Michael Hammer & James Champy, *Reengineering the Corporation*. New York: Harper Business, 1993.

❖ THE REASONS FOR REENGINEERING

The performance of American companies today is suffering for the very same reasons that their performance used to be so strong. *Most businesses are trying to compete in a world that has changed so drastically that their organizational structures and management principles no longer have any hope of adjusting or adapting.* It is important to note that these are the same structures and principles that propelled these same American businesses to the forefront in years past.

The historical patriarchs of today's companies are men like Henry Ford and Alfred Sloan and the railroad barons of the nineteenth century. They further developed Adam Smith's eighteenth-century principle of the division of labor by adding the pyramidal organization or bureaucracy, true assembly-line production, decentralized divisions, managing by the numbers, and elaborate centralized planning.

These once-crucial managerial techniques certainly had weaknesses, but those were far outweighed by the level of control they allowed and the results they achieved. However, these same techniques are now creating a managerial myopia that is leading businesses toward extinction.

Three forces have been the catalysts for this reversal. They are the three Cs: customers, competition, and change. First, *customers have taken charge.* In the past, customers bought what was offered, whether or not it was what they wanted or needed. They had no choice. Today, customers no longer are a "mass market." Customers demand and receive products and services with the features and prices they want—at least to a degree never known before. This force requires a responsiveness and flexibility previously unknown to the business world.

The second force driving the need for reengineering is *intensifying competition.* In the past, the best price would obtain the customer. Now, niche marketing has created an environment where similar products and services sell for entirely different reasons in different markets. One competitor in almost any part of the world can redefine the playing field for a whole industry virtually overnight through the introduction of new features or a different product that satisfies consumers' needs more effectively. Furthermore, technology has changed the very nature of competition itself, making available all sorts of market data previously unavailable and even eliminating whole segments of industries, such as wholesalers and distributors.

The third force is that *change has become constant.* The pace of change has accelerated, and it relentlessly and continuously alters almost every aspect of every segment of every industry. Life cycles have diminished exponentially. Most importantly, the significant changes will likely come from totally unexpected directions or sources.

These three basic forces have so radically changed the business environment that companies designed to function effectively in the business environment encountered even just a decade or less in the past, not to mention thirty to forty years ago, cannot hope to compete effectively today without totally reinventing their methods of doing business.

◆ REENGINEERING DEFINED

Reengineering is the fundamental rethinking and radical redesign of business processes to achieve dramatic improvements in critical, contemporary measures of performance, such as cost, quality, service, and speed. It's the search for new models of organizing work. It's starting over.

There are four key words in the definition. The first is *fundamental;* reengineering asks the most basic questions and ignores what is in favor of what should be. The second key word is *radical;* reengineering is about reinvention, not improvement. The third key word is *dramatic;* improvements in cost, quality, speed, or service are exponential, not incremental. The final key word is *processes;* reengineering focuses on a collection of activities that creates an output that is valuable to a customer rather than on the individual tasks, departments, or structures created by the Adam Smith mindset.

Reengineering is not automation, which just creates more efficient methods of doing the wrong things. It isn't restructuring or downsizing, which only involve doing less with less. Nor is reengineering similar to reorganizing or flattening out an organization. These processes only impose a new organizational structure over the same flawed operational system. Finally, although reengineering shares some of the same ideas as the various modern quality movements, it transcends them by not trying to work within the existing structure. Reengineering looks for continuous incremental improvement. It seeks breakthroughs, not enhancements.

◆ CHARACTERISTICS OF REENGINEERED BUSINESS PROCESSES

SEVERAL JOBS ARE COMBINED INTO ONE   Formerly distinct and separate tasks are reunited. Frequently the end result is a case worker or case team that accomplishes what used to be spread across many departments and people.

WORKERS MAKE DECISIONS   The creation of a case worker is a form of horizontal compression. This is vertical compression. Decision making becomes part of the work.

THE STEPS IN THE PROCESS ARE PERFORMED IN A NATURAL ORDER   They are no longer constrained by the artificiality created by the assembly line mentality.

PROCESSES HAVE MULTIPLE VERSIONS   Instead of one process that tries to deal with every possible variable, a "triage" step is used to determine which of several versions of the process is most appropriate.

Work Is Performed Where It Makes the Most Sense   Each department might purchase its own supplies, vendors might take over inventory management for their customers, or customers might even become trained repair people for their vendors (e.g., office copiers).

Checks and Controls Are Reduced   Frequently, the cost of "policing" a traditional process outweighs the benefits, or the inherent risk has been greatly exaggerated. Instead of the traditional methods, companies can often enforce the desired behavior by awarding preferred vendor status with the threat of ending the relationship if excesses occur, for example.

Reconciliation Is Minimized   The number of external contact points for a typical process is greatly reduced, along with the number of chances for errors requiring reconciliation.

A Case Manager Provides a Single Point of Contact   Instead of requiring a customer to contact the shipping department to check on a lost order, accounts receivable to adjust an invoice, and sales to place an order, a customer deals with the same person or team who can take care of everything the typical customer needs.

Hybrid Centralized/Decentralized Operations Are Prevalent   Information technology allows organizations to operate as though their units were completely autonomous, while still enjoying the advantages of the economies of scale that centralization creates. In addition, everyone in an organization can know the details of events happening anywhere in their organization without the meddling bureaucracy this would normally entail.

◆ **Other Changes That Occur in a Reengineered Organization**

Work Units Change   The work of a business will no longer be done by representatives of its various functional departments but by a process team that replaces departments.

Jobs Change   The performance of a highly specialized task or set of tasks will be transformed into the performance of a multidimensional role as a member of a team. The once-clear boundaries between engineering and sales, for example, will be blurred. Specialists will become generalists.

People's Roles Change   Traditional companies expect employees to follow the rules and procedures. Reengineered companies expect their employees to use their judgment to find the best solution in each situation.

JOB PREPARATION CHANGES   Training people to perform a specific set of tasks is replaced with educating people to figure out what their job really is and then letting them do it.

THE FOCUS OF PERFORMANCE MEASURES AND COMPENSATION SHIFTS When people are assigned specific tasks and are not responsible for the outcome of the process they're part of, there is no choice but to pay people solely for their time. In a reengineered organization, the results a person generates can be directly measured, and compensation can be tied directly to those results.

ADVANCEMENT CRITERIA CHANGE   A person must demonstrate the required abilities for a new position in order for a job change or a promotion to be warranted. Exceptional performance in a current job is no longer an acceptable justification.

VALUES CHANGE   The belief system a reengineered company reinforces and requires of its people shifts from ideas such as, "No matter what everybody says, the reality is I must keep those above me happy—they pay my salary," to "Customers pay my salary—I need to do whatever makes them happy."

MANAGERS' ROLES CHANGE   The traditional company requires managers to be supervisors who design and allocate work. The reengineered company requires managers who act as mentors and coaches.

EXECUTIVES CHANGE   Their perspective and focus has been primarily a financial one. It changes to ensuring that the organization's performance measurement and compensation systems motivate the team members to define and accomplish their jobs.

Reengineering changes all aspects of a company—because all aspects are interrelated. This fact is represented by the business system diamond. Its four points are business processes, values and beliefs, management and measurement systems, and jobs and structures. If you change one aspect, the others will necessarily adjust, and all four points on the diamond must work together to achieve success.

◆ **THE HUNT FOR REENGINEERING OPPORTUNITIES**

A good way to understand the processes at work in an organization is to give them names that reflect the work that actually gets done from start to finish. For example, product development is more accurately named the concept to prototype process; sales becomes the prospect to order process. Create a process map to illustrate how work flows through a company and to use as a starting point for discussions on reengineering.

Organizations will generally use three criteria to identify the processes to reengineer.

◆ *Dysfunction* Which processes are causing the most trouble?

◆ *Importance* Which processes have the greatest effect on customers?

◆ *Feasibility* Which processes are the best candidates for a successful redesign?

Once a *process* has been selected and a reengineering team formed, they must next reach an accurate understanding of the current process. The best method to accomplish this is to see it from the customer's perspective. Literally becoming a customer, in some cases, or at least working closely with them, is imperative for an accurate understanding.

Benchmarking—identifying excellent industry practices—can also be used, but a team should benchmark the best in the world, not just the best in the industry, to prevent their company from readopting a different version of the industry's current paradigm.

It is important to remember that a team should be studying the old process solely to learn what parts of it are critical for its performance, not because they are considering its redesign.

◆ THE EXPERIENCE OF PROCESS REDESIGN

Teams have used a number of techniques to generate creative redesign ideas. Teams can apply a reengineering principle to the process. An example of a principle: "As few people as possible should be involved in the performance of a process." Use this principle as a goal, and redesign the process in an attempt to achieve it. Another technique is to identify and annihilate assumptions. Find the deeply held beliefs about who can do what or about how things must be done and throw them out or reverse them to observe the effect that would have on the process. A third technique is to survey the current and cutting-edge abilities of information technology and find ways to apply them to the process, seeing what that would allow the company to do.

When asked what lessons they learned during the redesigning phase of the process, team members generally report very similar answers:

1. You don't need to be an expert to redesign a process.
2. Being an outsider helps.
3. You have to discard preconceived notions.
4. It's important to see things through the customer's eyes.
5. Redesign is best done in teams.
6. You don't need to know much about the current process.

7. It's not hard to have great ideas.

8. Redesign can be fun.

◆ EMBARKING ON REENGINEERING

Two key messages must be articulated and communicated clearly, consistently, and repeatedly for reengineering to be a success. First, *all people involved must understand where their company currently is and why it can't stay like that.* Second, *they must understand what their company needs to become.* The process of reengineering is a selling job that is never really over.

◆ REENGINEERING MISTAKES

Successfully reengineered companies know the rules, follow them, and don't make the common and avoidable mistakes. Some of the most common errors:

TRYING TO FIX A PROCESS INSTEAD OF CHANGING IT Don't make changes to the existing process and call it reengineering.

NOT FOCUSING ON BUSINESS PROCESSES By focusing on processes, most other concerns like empowerment and innovation are addressed. The opposite is not true.

IGNORING EVERYTHING EXCEPT PROCESS DESIGN The management systems, organizational structures, and job designs associated with the process also require changes.

NEGLECTING PEOPLE'S VALUES AND BELIEFS Managers must help their people rise to the challenges of reengineering by fostering and supporting effective beliefs and values.

SETTLING FOR MINOR RESULTS Marginal improvements make it more difficult to figure out how things really work. They discourage additional time and capital investments because the original return on investment didn't meet expectations. They also create a company that lacks courage.

QUITTING TOO EARLY Some companies lose their nerve, while others end the effort once they have their first success to display. Both lose the huge benefits that lie further down the road.

TRYING TO MAKE THINGS HAPPEN FROM THE BOTTOM UP Any person not at the top of an organization lacks the perspective and the authority to transform a process effectively.

Skimping on the Resources Devoted to Reengineering   Management must assign the best people and give them plenty of time and other resources to accomplish the reengineering efforts. Anything less signals a lack of true commitment that everyone else in the organization will read as an excuse to ignore and impede the efforts.

Dissipating Energy Across a Great Many Reengineering Projects   It requires focus and discipline, which can't be achieved if a large number of projects demand attention.

Concentrating Exclusively on Design   Quality ideas are required but are no less important than active and effective follow-through.

Pulling Back When People Resist Reengineering's Changes   Powerful resistance is to be expected and it must be acknowledged and dealt with without losing momentum.

❖ CONCLUSION

People are remarkably resourceful at finding new ways to drop the ball. However, *if reengineering efforts fail, the major cause will always be lack of understanding or commitment at the top of an organization.*

Despite the numerous opportunities for failure, there are many organizations with reengineering successes. Organizations that undertake reengineering with understanding, commitment, and strong executive leadership will succeed. The payoffs of successful efforts are spectacular for a company, its employees, and the economy. The time for hesitation is gone; the time for action is now.

READING 3

Organizing for the Future

Jay R. Galbraith and Edward E. Lawler III & Associates
Summary prepared by Gary P. Olson

Gary P. Olson is the Executive Director of the Center for Alcohol & Drug Treatment, Inc. He received his M.B.A. from the University of Minnesota, Duluth. He has consulted with businesses in the creation of virtual workplaces and employee involvement.

Businesses do not operate in a vacuum. The business environment has become, like society, increasingly complex and unpredictable. Competitive pressures have increased, and what were once considered to be profound competitive advantages have proved short-term or nonexistent. The pace of technological and other changes appears to be increasing. New forms of organization and approaches to management will be needed to enable the business organization to compete effectively in the future.

Traditional organizations were created to achieve stability and predictability. Large corporations offered economies of scale and well-defined career paths for their managers. Shareholders realized good returns on companies whose market value usually exceeded real asset value. Success in a stable environment, however, has not translated into effectiveness in a dynamic, rapidly changing milieu.

In response to competition, strategic initiatives to increase productivity, quality, and customer satisfaction have become commonplace. Instead of creating a sustainable advantage, these initiatives have served mainly to meet basic competitive requirements. Only companies that have been able to implement competitive strategies quicker or better than their competitors have obtained a competitive advantage, and that has often been only temporary.

In the future it is likely that only the *ability of a company to organize effectively and manage change will form the basis for achieving a longer term advantage*. Companies must acquire and adopt business strategies more quickly than the competition and do a better job implementing these strategies.

Jay R. Galbraith & Edward E. Lawler, *Organizing for the Future*. New York: Jossey-Bass, 1993.

❖ DESIGNING ORGANIZATIONS

Organizational design is not only the process of creating a structure, but it also includes alignment of management functions, information systems, human resources, and other elements within that structure. New models attempt to negotiate tradeoffs between the benefits of large scale and reduced cycle times and also to resolve conflicts that are inherent in these models.

The design of *new organizational forms is driven by competitive forces including service and product quality, cost, and the need to make rapid adjustments to external market conditions and internal demands.* Also, increased research and development expenditures due to complex product technology require expanded markets just to cover fixed costs. At the same time, technology has contributed to the emergence of new organizational forms. Organizational control methods are changing due to the power of buyers, who demand decision making at the point of buyer-seller contact. Also, buyers expect a functional relationship with the seller where speed of delivery, installation, and service are perceived as product features. The scarcity of highly skilled knowledge workers has required the relocation of work to sites where the workers are located or, alternately, the creation of *"virtual"* worksites using information technology. Several of these forces have resulted in a *power shift away from top-level management control structures and into the workplace.*

Organizational design is, at best, a temporary response to a continuously changing environment. In the future, an increased allocation of resources will be needed to insure the development of knowledgeable, skilled human resources. Speed and flexibility are key advantages of laterally integrated systems. Networking with other organizations enhances organizational learning. A variety of practices and designs can exist within the same organization in order to create a flexible response to change. Top management needs to formulate and articulate a clear vision and strategy.

❖ STRATEGY AND STRUCTURE

Business strategy has always influenced structure. Single-product businesses have used *functional* models, whereas diversified businesses have tended to use a *divisional* structure. In single-product businesses, management has assumed full operational control. In diversified companies, management control was more strategic, aligning the operation of divisions to reduce duplication and insure cooperation among divisions.

The emergence of conglomerates, and the creation of holding companies with their portfolios of unrelated businesses, resulted in a third strategy-structure model. In most cases, managers of a *holding* company exert mainly financial control over its diversified holdings. They specify return-on-investment (ROI) targets and acceptable inventory turnover ratios, provide access to capital markets, and so forth. Contrary to widespread belief, little evidence supports the claim that diversification leads to diminished performance. There is evidence that the optimal number of businesses to manage effectively is usually three or four.

New structural models are emerging, driven by competitive forces and the internal adjustments required to successfully respond to them. The *front-end/back-end model* is a hybrid form that separates a front-end unit (organized around customers), from a back-end system or product-oriented area. This hybrid model is often seen in the computer industry, where the customer deals with a single face for a problem-solving system (including software), while the back-end supplies some, but not all of the hardware to meet the requirements. This model requires some decentralization due to market and product diversity (the front-end may be geographically widespread), but strategic and operational control are exercised by the corporation. The front-end and back-end functions also need to be carefully integrated to avoid the conflicts inherent in this model. For example, sourcing arrangements by the front-end may conflict with the back-end's desire to be a sole supplier.

Divisionalized forms are moving toward what looks more like the holding company model. This occurs when the need for a coordinated response to market forces exceeds the need for divisional coordination. One of the shortcomings of the traditional divisional form is that divisions must suboptimize in order to adopt a common corporate policy or share a corporate resource. Achieving coordination is expensive and may handicap the division unnecessarily. Decentralization and a move toward divisional autonomy is an outgrowth of this strategic response.

When financial markets, through "sell" recommendations, force up price-earnings ratios of conglomerates (reducing stock prices), the breakup value of the company may exceed the market value. This results in pressure to divest some units or be taken over. Conglomerates will continue to exist, however, and clustering may be a way to deal with the mixed strategies required by both related and unrelated businesses in a portfolio. Where advantage can be achieved (given the cost of managing it), clustering brings together seemingly-diverse businesses in a portfolio that share a common market, a common product, or other major factors.

The strategic business unit (SBU) is the building block of structure. An *SBU* is a logical or economic entity with its own set of customers, products, and competitors. Although the divisional profit center is still seen, there is a new focus on the modification of the functional unit, as well as the creation of new models.

Competitive pressures have revealed the shortcomings of the functional unit design. The functional unit, with its own set of rewards and performance measures, tends to create barriers to interfunctional cooperation. Reductions in the number of specialties and hierarchical levels have moved functional performance, particularly of routine activities, closer to the front lines. Still, total quality service and other initiatives require extensive cooperation.

Lateral units are groups that are formally or informally organized across functional boundaries. They are developed around a logical business requirement. Sales functions grouped geographically and engineering organized around similar manufacturing processes would be examples of lateral units. An assembly function may be organized around each component of a complex system. Technology has enabled such units to organize without being tied to a physical location.

Increasingly, management functions need to be diffused into the lateral organization in order to achieve effective integration. Particularly in front-end/back-end structures, the quality of the lateral integrating process is a key to avoiding interfunctional conflicts. Integrated planning and budgeting activities create shared responsibilities for targets, outcomes, and rewards.

Business network units have emerged as an alternative to the autonomous division. One company can assume the role of integrator to a network of efficient single-product or single-service organizations. The integrator must negotiate the interests of the members based on trust and mutual advantage. Business network units are most successful when the integrator performs a dominant functional task such as large-scale buying or intensive R & D.

❖ FLATTER IS SMARTER

The movement toward less hierarchical structures in business is the direct result of competitive pressures that demand greater speed, quality, and productivity. Achieving continuously higher levels of performance demands dramatic changes in the management of internal operations that hierarchical forms cannot produce.

The way organizations acquire, adopt, and implement change will be a critical factor in their ability to adopt new organizational forms and strategy. Organizations "learn" when they alter processes ahead of, or in response to, changes in their environment.

Organizational learning includes innovation, process improvement, and organizational redesign; all of these involve organizational change. Several important conclusions about change stand out:

◆ Change does not happen without a compelling reason.
◆ Leadership is crucial to the change process.
◆ Change in one part of a system creates pressure for change in other parts.
◆ Change involves conflict.
◆ Change is not an orderly process.
◆ Change will be a continual fact of life in the coming decades.

Lateral integration is emerging as an important organizing principle. In hierarchical organizations, integration is achieved within the top-to-bottom structure. An organizational model that is designed to produce stability and predictability cannot adequately respond to multiple products, markets, and customers while simultaneously producing lower cost, achieving high-quality performance, and attracting highly skilled, motivated employees.

The compromises and adjustments of effective lateral design require a continuum of integrating mechanisms. Formalizing the integrating role in management or team structures ensures organizational support of the·process. Less formal approaches can co-locate with formal systems within the same organization.

❖ HIGH-INVOLVEMENT ORGANIZATIONS

Up to the present, employee involvement has been limited in its application or undertaken to achieve tactical advantages within the organization. Quality circles, for example, are top-down undertakings that neither transform job design nor permit worker discretion over quality. Companies have also used employee involvement as a tactic to avoid unionization. Even "Japanese-style management" that employs practices like consensus decision making mask the deeper reality of a traditional, control-type practice. The degree of employee autonomy is limited, even though employee suggestions for process improvement are sought and encouraged.

Employee involvement practices exist along a continuum ranging from suggestion systems to the truly high-involvement organization. Intermediate variations like job involvement, job enrichment, or semi-autonomous work teams give employees more control over decisions that directly affect their jobs. High-involvement organizations extend employee participation toward managing the business as a whole.

The four key variables in employee involvement are (1) access to information, (2) the opportunity to influence decision-making, (3) participation in rewards, and (4) knowledge. Without knowledge, information cannot be properly interpreted, and the resulting decisions will be flawed. Without accurate and timely information, good decision making is not possible. Without participation tied to rewards, the program has no incentive to succeed.

Working examples of high-involvement models are rare, not because they have proven ineffective, but because they are relatively new and run contrary to the dominant management ideology: control and internal stability. For high-involvement models to emerge, management must adopt a new paradigm based on the assumption that *the key to maximizing organizational effectiveness is to maximize the employee's ability to directly respond to changing conditions.* Currently, many managers verbally support involvement but often fail to see the implications for their own behavior. Managers must be educated and coached to translate theory into practice.

Implementing employee involvement as a means to achieving organizational performance goals is probably the best way to legitimize the effort and ensure full organizational support. Although it is not necessary to use the process of employee involvement to implement a program, unless management is committed to the effort and can experience it firsthand the program will not develop effectively.

Employee involvement, however, is not suited to all organizations. Examples of businesses where employee involvement is unlikely to lead to improved effectiveness are those that involve routine technology and little innovation, where employee attitudes are unrelated to business performance, or where the business operates in an unusually stable environment. *In organizations where it is appropriate, successful employee involvement programs can be expected to increase the speed of decision making, reduce overhead costs, and improve flexibility.* Because management style and organizational design can be sources of competitive advantage, employee participation will be adopted in a number of industries in the near future.

❖ TEAMWORK, PARTNERSHIP, AND LEADERSHIP

If business units are the building blocks of structure, teams and teamwork mechanisms have been the building blocks of performance in many organizations. *What is changing is the way teams are integrated into the organizational structure.* The same competitive forces that are driving organizational redesign are creating an increased interest in teamwork and giving teams more autonomy and power. The use of teams to achieve lateral integration, an important organizing principle discussed earlier, is becoming increasingly evident.

Collaborative networked teams, parallel teams, project teams, and work teams are some of the designs that are used. Teams operate along three dimensions. Teams may be permanent or temporary within a time dimension. They may do the basic work of the organization, as in autonomous work groups, or be dedicated to process improvement, as in the quality circle. A third dimension is the way the team functions within the organization's authority structure. Teams may transcend divisional boundaries or exist within a defined unit and report through existing hierarchical channels.

Human resource management departments were once devoted to the administrative and legal aspects of dealing with employees. Forces such as global competition, the need to manage change, increased knowledge about human resource management, information technology, and the emergence of the knowledge worker have moved human resource managers to the center of the new organizational models. At the same time, these departments must justify their existence by adding value and cutting costs.

Managing change will require new selection, training, appraisal, and reward systems to match new organizational designs, management styles, and work structures. *Human resource functions will contribute to both planning and implementing change.* These departments will not only be involved in the implementation of strategic initiatives, such as employee involvement and teams, but will be integral to planning these strategies and providing expertise about how to organize and conduct the strategizing process.

In addition to the flattening of hierarchical structures, lateral integration, and increased employee involvement, *the importance of leadership has emerged as a critical factor for achieving and maintaining competitive advantage.* Competitive crises may have created a "survival of the fittest" environment from which gifted leaders have emerged. Leadership practices that have been known for decades (setting clear goals, involving people in decision making, motivating through challenge) have reemerged in the search for excellence. It is not enough, however, to assume good leadership will emerge on its own. Leaders can, and must, learn skills and develop attitudes that will help them adapt to the changes that confront the organizations of the future. Their ability to convert missions into reality, align people with direction, develop trust based on integrity, be comfortable with uncertainty, develop self-awareness, and learn from experience will be the keys to future success.

READING 4

Visionary Companies: Why Do They Endure?

Jerry I. Porras and James C. Collins

What is a visionary organization, and what makes it successful over long periods of time? We explored this question in a research project begun in 1988, a point in time in which the concept of visionary organizations had yet to be fully developed. Previously, the focus of management thinking had been on charismatic visionary leadership, and any visionary behavior by an organization was attributed to the visionary leader. We began to wonder how an organization like 3M could be explained using the charismatic visionary leader model, since it seemed that, for 3M, neither its current nor past CEOs fit this model. 3M's chief executive officers over the years have been highly competent and effective managers, but from all reports were not the "larger than life" type of leader commonly associated with the concept of charismatic visionaries. This observation led us to two conclusions. First, our focus should be on the organization and its characteristics, rather than the leader. Second, the type of leadership to be found in 3M-like organizations must be different than the one prescribed by the charismatic visionary leadership model.

❖ METHOD

A survey of 700 CEOs drawn from the two Fortune 500 lists (50 percent sample stratified by industry and size) plus the two *Inc. Magazine* lists of public and private companies (100 CEOs randomly selected from each of these lists) provided the companies we studied. Each CEO was asked to nominate the five companies he/she thought most visionary (using whatever definition of visionary company they personally held). The CEO response rate was approxi-

Excerpted, with permission of the publisher, from *Built to Last: Successful Habits of Visionary Companies* (New York: HarperCollins, 1994).

mately 23 percent and was representative of the entire sample. Companies were rank ordered according to frequency of nomination with the top twenty selected for study. This list was reduced to eighteen when we concluded that longevity was a key explanatory factor, thereby eliminating both Compaq (eight years old at the time our research began) and Apple (twelve years old). The remaining companies were all forty-five years old or older (company founding dates ranged from 1945 back to 1812) fitting the criteria for longevity.

The age issue also drove our next methodological decision, which was to study the nominated organizations from their founding date forward rather than over a more recent period, say the last five or ten years. We wanted to know the principles that guided these organizations and their designs over decades and ultimately over their entire history. We believed that this method had the potential to yield principles that would be more fundamental.

Finally, we selected a comparison group of companies by matching each visionary company with a company founded in approximately the same time period, in the same industry, often a chief competitor of the visionary company, rarely mentioned in the CEO survey as highly visionary, and still alive in 1990.

Since we wished to study these companies over their entire history, our search for information had to be extremely comprehensive. Sources of data included company archival material (provided by the company), published books (over 100 of them, each focused primarily on one company), published and unpublished cases, and magazine and newspaper articles going back to the founding era of each company. A conservative estimate of the number of pages was accomplished using the variables proposed in Porras.[1]

❖ FINDINGS

After our initial analysis of the data, we derived the following general descriptions of a visionary company: Visionary companies are organizations widely admired by their peers, with a history of having made a significant impact on the environments in which they operate, and having been highly successful through multiple cycles of leadership, multiple product cycles, and multiple industry cycles.

Visionary companies are highly respected, well-known and, over the long term, economically very successful. We explored their economic success by creating three mythical stock portfolios and exploring the performance of each. These were: (a) the market as a whole, (b) the set of comparison companies, and (c) the set of visionary companies. We invested one dollar in each portfolio beginning in 1926 and by reinvesting dividends and properly accounting for stock splits, swaps, and so forth, we tracked the investments until 1990. A dollar in the market grows to $415, while a dollar in the comparison company portfolio grows to $955 (more than two times the market performance). A dollar in the visionary company portfolio grows to $6355 (over fifteen times better than the market and six and a half times better than the comparison companies).

Our primary findings can be clustered in two categories: (1) Characteristics of the founding leader or the leader during key formative years of the company, and (2) characteristics of the companies themselves. The findings reported in both of these categories obtained in a preponderance of the visionary companies and not in the comparison companies.

◆ LEADER CHARACTERISTICS

Leaders of visionary companies tended to focus on building the capabilities of their companies to behave in visionary ways rather than on playing a central role in the development of great ideas, strategies, marketing approaches, and so on. We call these leaders "organizational visionaries." In contrast, leaders of comparison companies focused mainly on developing the great product or service, devising innovative marketing and promotions approaches, creating comprehensive strategies, or, in general, being key initiators of activities that already determined the company's success. As a result, the performance of the comparison organizations was heavily predicated on their leaders being the center of decision activity for the organization. We call this type of leader a "product or service visionary."

We came to use a metaphor to describe these two types of visionary leaders: "Organizational visionaries are clock-builders" and product/services visionaries are "time-tellers." Clock builders built an "organizational clock," so that the time could be told without their having to be there. Time-tellers, on the other hand, were the only ones who knew how to tell the time, so that whenever people needed to "know the time," they were dependent on the time-teller to provide it.

We found that throughout the history of the visionary and comparison companies, the former tended to be led by clock-builders, while the latter by time-tellers. All the comparison companies were founded on a successful product idea, while with only three exceptions, the visionary companies were not founded on a successful product idea. For example, Hewlett-Packard's first products were an automatic urinal flusher, a bowling foul line indicator, a shock machine for weight reduction, and a clock-drive for a telescope. In contrast, Texas Instruments, H-P's comparison, had a very successful first product, a seismographic sensing device used in oil exploration. Hewlett and Packard built a great company that then created great products. Texas Instrument built their company around the great product they started with.

George Westinghouse was a great inventor holding patents for hundreds of products and founding his company on the principle of alternating current electricity. Charles Coffin, founder of General Electric, developed the first industrial research laboratory to invent the great products that made GE successful, even though his company originally had been based on the direct current principle, which initially was a failure. Coffin built a clock: Westinghouse told the time.

◆ CORE IDEOLOGY AND A DRIVE FOR PROGRESS

Our analysis of the entire history of the two sets of companies indicated that they possessed two key dimensions—a core ideology (core values plus enduring purpose) and a powerful, almost primal drive for progress (change, adaptation, innovation, experimentation). These two dimensions play themselves out in the organization in terms of two sets of processes; the first serves to preserve the core while the second results in stimulating progress. These processes are enacted through a variety of concrete organizational mechanisms. Although both sets of companies possessed many mechanisms in common, we identified six that provided discrimination between the two sets. Visionary companies preserved their core by (a) having a purpose beyond maximization of profits, (b) creating cult-like cultures, and (c) growing their management (especially the CEO and the top-most executives) from within the company. They stimulate progress doing one or more of the following: (a) creating and achieving audacious goals, (b) promoting purposeful evolution, and (c) engaging in continual self-improvement.

◆ PRESERVE THE CORE

The core values and enduring purpose were much more well understood (often codified, e.g., Hewlett-Packard Way, Johnson & Johnson Credo, Sony Pioneer Spirit, 3M Manifesto) in the visionary companies than in the comparisons. Core values are those very most fundamental values the organization will continue to hold and behave consistently with even if punished by the environment. Johnson & Johnson's first core value in their credo is, "Our first responsibility is to our customers." Their response to the Tylenol tampering incident demonstrates their commitment to the core value. It included removing the product from all the shelves in the United States, redesigning the bottle's sealing system, and informing the public through a massive information effort that involved approximately 2500 people. All these efforts were estimated to have cost the company $100 million—a pretty significant cost for living a core value. Contrast this to Bristol-Meyers, Squibb who had a somewhat similar event occur with Excedrin a few weeks later. Although the Bristol-Meyers pledge (created in 1987) appears to emphasize a similar core value of commitment to customers, the organization did not behave consistently with it when the "chips were down." This means that this value is not truly a core value of the organization.

Visionary companies preserve and protect their core ideology. As a result, it rarely changes. We found evidence of consistent core values for periods of over 100 years in some cases, and of consistent purpose for over sixty years. Visionary companies tend to think of their purpose as accomplishing an end beyond maximization of profit or shareholder wealth. In seventeen out of eighteen companies, the visionary companies were more ideological driven and less product-maximization driven that the comparison companies. They don't lose sight of their true purpose by letting profit maximization dominate their decision making. Rather, they see profit as a consequence instead of a cause. Disney's purpose is to bring happiness to millions; Merck's is to preserve and improve human life; Marriott's is to make people away from home feel they are among friends and really valued; Hewlett-Packard's is to make a technical contribution; Johnson and Johnson's is to alleviate pain and disease. These companies believe in the words of George Merck II, CEO of Merck, when he said in 1950, "We try never to forget that medicine is for the people. It's not for the profits. The profits follow, and if we remembered that, they have never failed to appear. The better we have remembered it, the larger they have been."

There should be no question that visionary companies are interested in profits, but they believe that if they serve their purpose well, profits will follow, not the other way around.

Core ideology is also preserved by creating strong, cult-like cultures, cultures so tight that if a person doesn't fit, over the longer run, they are "ejected like a virus." Cults are characterized by strong ideologies, extensive indoctrination processes, tightness of fit between the system and the individual, and a sense of elitism among members. Visionary companies hold similar characteristics and do so to a much greater extent than the comparison companies. Disneyland teaches new employees how to frame their job (a role in the show) what language to use (guests rather than tourists, costumes rather than uniforms, on-stage versus off-stage, casting rather than personnel), and generally define the specific behaviors desired from their cast members. Nordstrom has a one-page employee manual that gives substantial autonomy within the context of providing outstanding customer service. Smile contests, most Nordstrom-like contests, phantom shoppers, and sales per hour feedback all result in tight social control of employees and highly consistent behavior.

Core ideology is also preserved in visionary companies by practicing a policy of growing their management from within the corporation. Rarely have visionary companies gone outside the company for a CEO. As of our data collection cut-off date (1992), only two visionary companies had gone outside— Disney, when it hired Michael Eisner, and Phillip Morris, early in the 1900s when it went outside three times for CEOs. In contrast, thirteen comparison companies have brought in outside CEOs at least once in their history. Looked at another way, of the 113 visionary company CEOs for which we have data, only 3.5 percent came from outside. Of the 140 comparison company CEOs, 22.1 percent were outsiders.

In order to preserve the core ideology, a CEO must really have that ideology buried deep in their psyche, put there through countless experiences in which the ideology comes into play and guides behavior. Outsiders don't have that fundamental understanding and as a consequence, wind up changing it as they make difficult decisions.

◆ STIMULATE PROGRESS

Change and adaptation are fundamental for survival. The comparison companies were much more adept at stimulating progress than they were at knowing and protecting their core ideology. Perhaps this is why they have survived and performed quite well. The visionary companies, however, create tangible mechanisms that preserve the core *and* stimulate progress.

Visionary companies stimulate progress in three ways that are not commonly used by the comparisons. First, they set audacious, stretching major goals that coalesce and motivate the organization. Goals that challenge the organization, that aren't easily achievable, excite the imagination, provide substantial innovation and change. We have come to call these "Big Hairy Audacious Goals" (BHAGs) to capture their magnitude and impact. BHAGs can range from "bet the company" types of goals to ones that just are quite audacious (Boeing bet the company on the 707 and 747. Had they failed, the company probably wouldn't have survived. IBM bet the company on the 360 computer series: A $5 billion investment that, had it gone sour, may have sunk the company). (In 1991 Wal-Mart set the goal of being a $125 billion company by the year 2000. At the time they set this goal, they were a $30 billion company, and only GM had attained the $125 billion level.)

Purposeful evolution is a second prominent approach to stimulating change used by visionary companies. Just as biological species evolve through variation and selection processes, so do visionary companies "try a lot of stuff and keep what works." By creating policies and strategies that promote experimentation and innovation, then keeping the experiments that are both successful and consistent with the core ideology, a visionary company evolves and adapts. 3M requires technical employees to dedicate 15 percent of their work time to dreaming up new ideas. It requires divisions to generate 30 percent of annual sales from products or services introduced in the previous four years. It provides "Genesis Grants" which are internal venture capital funds of up to $50,000 for researchers to develop prototypes and do market tests.

Visionary companies also stimulate progress by continuous self-improvement. In contrast to the more recent management "fad" of self-improvement, visionary companies have been practicing this concept since their early founding periods, which for some means all the way back to the early 1900s. Johnson and Johnson created their product management structure as a way to keep themselves number one. They believed that if they competed against the best (i.e., themselves) they would always be number one. Motorola cuts off mature product lines while they are still profitable, forcing itself to fill the gap with new products, and have been doing so since they were in the radio business in the late 1920s. David Packard preached continuous improvement beginning in the 1950s.

Never being satisfied and constantly striving for improvement has also played itself out in the ways visionary companies invest for the long term. By analyzing financial statements for the two sets of companies, going all the way back to 1925, we found that for these companies for which data existed that: (a) Visionary companies consistently invested more heavily in new property, plant, and equipment as a percentage of annual sales, than did the comparisons (thirteen out of fifteen cases); (b) Visionary companies plow back a greater percentage of each year's earnings into the company, paying out less in cash dividends to share-holders (twelve of fifteen cases with one case being indistinguishable); (c) Visionary companies invest more heavily in R&D as a percentage of sales (eight of eight cases); (d) Broadly, visionary companies invest more aggressively in human capital via extensive recruiting, training, and professional development, as well as in technical know-how, new technologies, and innovative industry practices.

The mechanisms described above differentiate visionary companies from their comparisons. As such, they provide a picture of the key dimensions of highly successful companies.

One final result remains to be described. Visionary companies were more consistently aligned than the comparisons. The mechanisms described above, as well as many other dimensions of the organization's architecture, were highly aligned to deliver consistent messages about desired behavior. Clearly, they are not perfectly aligned systems, but more aligned than their comparisons and, therefore, generating more "organized" behavior from their employees.

In summary, visionary companies possess characteristics that differentiate them from their early competitors. The differences they exhibit appear to have led to significantly different levels of performance over very long time periods. Certainly, more lessons are left to be learned from these companies, but we believe that the results of our study have provided a useful platform for increasing our understanding of what it takes for a company to be truly visionary.

❖ NOTES

Porras, J.I. (1987). *Stream analysis: A powerful new way to diagnose and manage organizational change.* Reading, MA: Addison-Wesley.

5

ORGANIZATIONAL STRATEGY

Many of the authors in this book have suggested that organizations can benefit by defining their own standard of effectiveness, especially after examining other successful firms. An organization's external environment has a powerful influence on organizational success and needs to be monitored for significant trends and influential forces. In addition, effective executives need to recognize when internal changes are necessary to adapt to the external environment.

The two readings in this section are designed to stimulate thinking about strategic management through a focus on the management and leadership of the internal environment, and the management of the organization relative to its external context.

Taken collectively, these two readings suggest that organizations can (and should) proactively *take control of their destinies.* One way of doing this is by articulating and following a set of organizational strategies and plans that can systematically guide them into the future and help deal with current affairs. In effect, managers are urged to have a master plan that defines their mission, identifies their unique environmental niche, builds on their strengths, and adapts to changing needs.

The authors whose work is summarized here are Henry Mintzberg, Noel M. Tichy, and Stratford Sherman. Henry Mintzberg is a professor in the faculty of management at McGill University in Montreal, Canada. Noel Tichy is on the faculty at the University of Michigan's School of Business and director of the school's Global Leadership Program, and Stratford Sherman, a management specialist, has covered the world of business for *Fortune* magazine.

Henry Mintzberg recently noted that ever since the 1950s corporations have heavily invested time and resources in strategic planning. General Electric, for example, had approximately two hundred senior-level planners by 1980. In spite of this effort the results associated with strategic planning are mixed. General Electric's Jack Welch felt that planners had taken over the business and were paying attention to data rather than market instincts and information about customer preferences. Thus, he decimated the corporate planning group. In his book, *The Rise and Fall of Strategic Planning*, Mintzberg explores the differences between strategy and planning and then examines the role of the planning specialist. He presents reasons why planning fails and proposes conditions under which strategic planning could be successful.

In their book *Control Your Destiny or Someone Else Will,* Noel M. Tichy and Stratford Sherman document the transformation of GE under the leadership of Jack Welch, its CEO during the 1980s and 1990s. Welch's vision was to create an organization that depends more on shared values and open communications than one dependent on hierarchy and coercion in order to achieve efficiency and competitiveness. Tichy and Sherman discuss the *six rules* that served to guide Welch's revolution (e.g., control your destiny, or someone else will; don't manage, lead; change before you have to; and if you don't have a competitive advantage, don't compete), his *vision for GE* (e.g., every GE business must be No. 1 or No. 2 in its market; integrated diversity; boundarylessness; speed, simplicity, and self-confidence), and the process of *vision implementation* through the three strands (i.e., technical, political, and cultural) of organizational behavior.

READING 1

The Rise and Fall of Strategic Planning

Henry Mintzberg
Summary prepared by Linda E. Parry

Linda E. Parry is an Assistant Professor of Organizational Studies at the University of Minnesota–Duluth. She received her Ph.D. at the State University of New York at Albany. Her current research interests include the strategic impact of technological, societal, and legal factors on organizations. She has published articles in *Technology Innovation and Human Resources, Journal of Social Behavior and Personality, Journal of Staff, Program, & Organization Development* and numerous conference proceedings including the Decision Science Institute, Southern Academy of Management, and ORSA/TIMS. She teaches organizational theory and strategic management.

Ever since the 1950s, organizations have been consumed with strategic planning. Great amounts of time and resources have been spent to derive the "perfect strategy." For example, General Electric Corporation had approximately two hundred senior level planners by 1980. However, even after expending all this energy, the results were mixed. What are the possible causes for this lack of success? *The Rise and Fall of Strategic Planning* explores the differences between strategy and planning, examines the role of planners, presents reasons why planning failed, and proposes conditions under which strategic planning could be successful.

❖ STRATEGY AND PLANNING

Although the words *strategy* and *planning* are often used interchangeably, it is possible to draw a sharp distinction between the two activities. *Strategy*, also known as strategic formation, encompasses the four activities of planning, patterning, positioning, and perspective:

◆ First, strategy can be a *plan* in the sense that it guides the organization's actions into the future.

Henry Mintzberg, *The Rise and Fall of Strategic Planning*. New York: Free Press, 1994.

- ◆ Second, strategy can be a *pattern* of behavior that develops over a period of time. Strategy as a pattern is different from strategy as a plan. A plan implies deliberate actions on the part of management, whereas a pattern can emerge as organizations cope with events external to the organization.

- ◆ Strategy as *position* is evident when an organization attempts to bring specific products to specific markets and, therefore, occupies a certain position in the marketplace. For example, Coca Cola wanted to be the number one producer of soft drinks in the United States.

- ◆ Finally, strategy as *perspective* involves knowing what type of organization you are and building on that competency. For example, McDonald's introduced the Egg McMuffin successfully because they knew that their expertise was in the area of fast food.

Planning, a formalized system to meet organizational goals, takes into account only one aspect of strategy. The concept of formalization is critical to planning. Formalization implies rationality. Moreover, it involves decomposing strategies into a series of steps that can be carried out throughout the organization. Formalization also implies that the plans, which are the products of planning, are clearly articulated.

The difference between strategic formation and formal planning is the same as the difference between a manager who thinks strategically about how to gain competitive advantage and a manager who focuses on how to make strategy work and formally carries out those activities within an organization.

❖ WHY PLAN?

Although planning is only one aspect of strategy, it has its function within the organization. Planning allows organizations to coordinate their activities. It ensures that organizations think in terms of how their present actions will impact the future. It formalizes decision making and controls activities throughout the organization. Because of these benefits, managers moved forward to adopt a basic model for planning.

❖ THE BASIC PLANNING MODEL

The original basic planning model analyzes the strengths and weaknesses of the organization to uncover its distinctive competencies. At the same time, the threats and opportunities in the environment are examined to uncover key success factors. The planning model assumes that strategy is a controlled process of thought and the exclusive domain of the chief executive. Strategies should also be simple, explicit, and implemented throughout the organization with particular attention to objectives, budgets, and programs. Expanding on the model, H. Igor Ansoff introduced the concepts of gap analysis and synergy. *Gap analysis* is a four-step process. First, an organization sets objectives.

Second, the difference (gap) between the firm's position and its objectives is measured. Finally, courses of action for narrowing the gap are determined and then tested to judge their effectiveness. *Synergy* refers to combining all the components in the organization so that the sum is greater than the whole, and competitive advantage is achieved.

Other models added even greater detail, providing checklists and steps to ensure that everything in the process of planning was taken into account. There was a hierarchy of objectives, budgets, strategies, and programs. Objectives were decided on by the top manager and passed down through the organization for implementation. Budgets were like objectives and flowed down the organization. They were often applied to every subunit of the organization. This brought up the question of whether the strategy controlled the budget or did the budget dictate the strategy? Corporate strategies led to business strategies that led to functional strategies. The assumption was that all these strategies would be perfectly coordinated and done on a timely basis. This assumption is contradicted by all the evidence that *real strategic change is sporadic*. Programs were developed to bridge the gap between planning and budgeting, although there is little evidence that this was accomplished.

However, with all this attention to process, one important detail was missing. The whole process never addressed how strategies were created. The planning models showed managers how to collect information, how to evaluate strategies, and how to implement strategy, but they neglected to state how to derive a strategy.

❖ DOES PLANNING PAY?

Managers are ultimately interested in the question "Does planning pay?" The answer is not always encouraging. As noted earlier, GE had over two hundred planners when Reginald Jones was CEO. In the early 1980s, when Jack Welch took over as CEO, he decimated the corporate planning group and purged planners from GE's operating sectors, groups, and divisions. He, along with many of his division managers, felt that the planners had taken over the business, relying on data rather than market instincts, and ignoring those people who were closest to consumer preference. Other downsides to planning and planners surfaced. Oftentimes, the people who approved strategies were too distant from the process. It was not unusual for plans to be summarized to such an extent that they contained little relevant information on which to make a decision. In addition, decisions on strategies often depended on the credibility of the sponsor as opposed to the credibility of the plan. Lastly, managers tend to be risk averse. Decisions were made incrementally even when there was overwhelming evidence for dramatic action.

Nevertheless, even with all these limitations, the benefits of planning remain. Planning still allows a formal, systematic method for agreeing on goals, instituting action plans, and evaluating a strategy's success. Also, planning can expose gaps in the organization and introduce an information network that helps managers reduce their uncertainty about the future and engage in long-range thinking. Finally, managers can use planning as a tool to gain control of their organizations.

❖ THE PITFALLS OF PLANNING

Even though planning has its benefits, there are pitfalls in successful implementation. *One pitfall is top management's lack of commitment to the planning process.* This caveat appears counter-intuitive as so much of the literature talks about planning beginning with the CEO. In actuality, however, many organizations have installed planning systems that are so automatic that top management is only in the planning loop two or three times a year.

Another pitfall, limited participation, can be avoided if everyone in the organization is included in the process and not just the planners. Avoiding this pitfall can facilitate ideas and eliminate some of the competitive feelings that can emerge between planners and doers.

A third pitfall is the tendency of planners to centralize all control, which sends the clear message to employees that there is "one best way of doing things" and stifles creativity.

By its nature, planning can be very analytical in the formulation stage. Consequently, it tends to impede creativity and flexibility in the implementation stage. To compound the problem, it is often easier to dictate the terms of planning rather than explain its purposes. Therefore, workers become accustomed to just following orders. This may not be in the organization's long-term best interests. For instance, communist countries planned very effectively during the 1960s, but when their economies began to sour, employees did not step forward to offer solutions because they were not accustomed to participation.

Finally, in addition to the more obvious pitfalls of plans being too inflexible, incremental, and political, *plans can also give managers the illusion of control.* As an example, the King in Saint-Exupery's *The Little Prince* claimed that he had the power to order the sun to rise and set—but only at a certain time of the day. Does a planner's obsession with control merely reflect an illusion of control?

Certainly, the pitfalls of planning can account for some of the failures that organizations have encountered in planning. However, such pitfalls only address the more superficial problems with planning. The problems often go deeper. These difficulties can be labeled the fundamental fallacies of strategic planning.

❖ THE FUNDAMENTAL FALLACIES OF STRATEGIC PLANNING

There are numerous basic assumptions that are made about strategic planning. One is that the strategy-making process can be programmed with the use of systems. This is equivalent to believing that if you build a baseball field, a team will play there. Establishing a system for planning does not guarantee that a strategy will be created anymore than building a field ensures a baseball franchise. Another misconception is that plans are objective and quantifiable even though there is ample evidence to suggest just the opposite.

Planning helps organizations plan for the future. The unspoken assumption here is that planning will help predict the future. However, *planning does not help predict when discontinuities, such as new technological advances or earthquakes, will appear.* The difficulty is that a model cannot be built that takes into account one-time events. Managers who are successful in managing abrupt changes in the environment are those who have a strong understanding of their industry and its context. No sophisticated model, including those that use artificial intelligence or expert systems, has yet to match the exercise of human judgment. Nevertheless, people still see plans as a "cure-all."

The fact that planners use "hard data" has also led managers to put too much credence in the results. The difficulties come with the nature of hard data, which is often limited in scope and too aggregated for effective use in strategic thinking. For example, before 1980, the planners at GE sought to aggregate all the strategic business units' plans into a single plan for CEO Reginald Jones to review. Jones was elated with the result because he could quickly read through the report. When Jack Welch became CEO, he quickly abolished this system because he saw that it distanced him too far from the actual business of the organization. Finally, hard data often arrives too late, and when it does arrive it is often unreliable.

Another assumption about planning is that it will assist companies in taking a broader view of themselves and their mission. A common illustration is that railroads could have seen themselves as transportation companies. Although many companies rushed out to redefine themselves, the question remains whether they really have the technology, distribution channels, or production capabilities to branch out into these new expanded markets.

All of these assumptions lead to the planning school's grand fallacy—*strategic planning does not equate with strategy formation.* This is a critical concept. Establishing a plan (analysis) will not ensure the creation (formation) of a strategy.

❖ THE ROLE OF PLANNING, PLANS, AND PLANNERS

While there are many pitfalls and fallacies to strategic planning, planning still has a purpose. Managers need to recognize it for what it is, accept its benefits, and at the same time introduce other factors, such as intuition and "soft data," into their organizations to encourage strategic thinking. Formal planning should then be used to operationalize these strategies.

Although all organizations can engage in planning, there are conditions that appear favorable to its successful use. For example, environmental stability helps to forecast events. Industry maturity provides information on how consumers will react. Heavy capital investment also provides incentive to plan because the more resources that have to be applied to a project, the more these resources need to be controlled. Large size is also beneficial to planning since planning can be expensive, and larger companies tend to engage in programs that require heavy capital investment and market control. The ideal organization for planning also has a highly structured organization whose units are tightly coupled and yet engages in relatively simple operations. Using the same logic, certain "types" of organizations (e.g., adhocracy, professional) perform better with planning than others. For example, mechanistic organizations are more successful than entrepreneurial organizations because entrepreneurial organizations, by their nature, are always facing new environments and situations.

Just as planning serves a function, plans have numerous functions for organizations. First, they provide a communications media to ensure that everyone in the organization works in the same direction. Communication works externally as well as internally since it provides the public, as well as investors, with a sign that the company knows where it is going. Plans also act as control mechanisms that assist in scheduling and specifying goals and targets. They should not, however, become barriers to implementing emergent strategies.

Although many managers were quick to terminate planners when organizations began to have difficulties in the 1980s, planners still have a real function. Planners can encourage future thinking within the organization. They can be the finders of strategies. They can also follow patterns of action within organizations to look for emergent or deliberate strategies. They can also analyze internal and external data that can assist managers in developing strategies. Finally, they can act as a catalyst for change within the organization. *None of these planning roles precludes the planner from acting as the strategist.* Nevertheless, it is incumbent on senior management to comprehend that planners, important as they can be to the organization, will never be the panacea for the organization.

READING 2

Control Your Destiny or Someone Else Will

Noel M. Tichy and Stratford Sherman
Summary prepared by Robert R. Wharton

Robert R. Wharton is an Assistant Professor of Management at the University of Minnesota-Duluth. He received his Ph.D. from Rutgers University. His current research interests include cooperative business information systems, innovation management, and comparative management issues.

Managers are growing increasingly concerned about what businesses of the future will need to do in order to prosper in the face of intensified domestic and global competition. Based on the premise that the rules for succeeding in business have changed radically, *Control Your Destiny* details these changes as it profiles the organizational transformation of one of the country's industrial giants into a global business power.

As the story opens, recently hired junior managers at General Electric are sitting around a conference table at the company's management training center engaged in a heated discussion of Jack Welch, GE's Chief Executive Officer. Scrawled on a flip chart at the front of the room are the two competing propositions under debate:

"Jack Welch is the greatest CEO GE has ever had," and,
"Jack Welch is an a____hole."

A few years earlier, such irreverent behavior on company time would have cost these young managers their jobs. Jack Welch had already spent nearly five years pushing a radical agenda of change that had fundamentally altered GE and its way of doing business. Welch's vision was to create an organization that depends more on shared values and open communication than one dependent on hierarchy and coercion in order achieve efficiency and competitiveness.

Noel M. Tichy and Stratford Sherman, *Control Your Destiny or Someone Else Will*. New York: Harper Business, 1993.

When Welch became CEO of GE, it was already one of the strongest and most admired firms in the United States. Founded over a century earlier by Thomas Edison, GE scarcely seemed to be in trouble. But Welch saw an organization ill-equipped to deal with a changing world. Lagging productivity in the face of increasing global competition was the warning sign, and Welch recognized it as a threat to GE's long-term survival.

In the following years, Welch would preside over the elimination of dozens of the company's businesses and over 100,000 jobs. He would also challenge every remaining employee to rethink how they worked and managed in order to be competitive. Often reviled in the press and among hostile employees, the GE that has emerged is among the world's most potent competitors. *Control Your Destiny* documents the story of this transformation.

❖ SIX RULES

GE is a large and highly *diversified* business; nonetheless, the ideas behind Jack Welch's revolution are so basic that they may serve as a set of principles for managing almost any organization of the future. Welch distilled his standards down to six rules:

1. Control your destiny, or someone else will.

2. Face reality as it is, not as it was or as you wish it were.

3. Be candid with everyone.

4. Don't manage, lead.

5. Change before you have to.

6. If you don't have a competitive advantage, don't compete.

The rules may be simple, but acting on them and managing by them can be painful. For Welch, it meant confronting the painful reality that many of GE's products were costlier to produce, yet were worth less, than those of its competitors. Welch decided that every GE business had to be number one or number two in its market; any business that failed to rise to that standard would be fixed, sold, or closed. In the end he made good on his threats, selling $14 billion of profitable but under-performing businesses, and buying $21 billion of new businesses.

At the same time, Welch realized that drastic changes in the competitive environment were creating a need for a new form of management and organization. Mergers and acquisitions forced the *consolidation* of scores of industries so that competition was dominated by enormous firms with overwhelming financial power. In addition, *globalization* was forcing companies to expand beyond their nation's borders, even as foreign competitors were invading their home markets. The drive to improve productivity had forced corporations to adopt *just-in-time* (JIT) inventory controls and other techniques that resulted in an unprecedented dependence on suppliers. New technologies shortened product development cycles, increasing the expectations of customers and increasing the emphasis on speed.

The painful reality that Welch recognized was that *success in the future would require all the resources of a large corporation and all the agility of an entrepreneurial start-up.* Yet, while GE had enormous financial resources, it still organized work as it had at the turn of the century. These methods, exemplified in Henry Ford's assembly lines and based on the teachings of the *scientific management* school of thought, called for top managers to analyze the work that needed to be done, and then break down the process into simple tasks to be performed repeatedly and efficiently by an unskilled workforce.

As effective as these methods had been, they would not serve GE well in the emerging competitive environment. The new management techniques that Welch sought to implement would seek to liberate workers, rather than control them. It would involve a painful process of stripping away layers of management, with the goal of producing a fluid and agile organization equipped to face the new and dynamic competition.

❖ THE VISION

Rather than present a detailed strategic plan, Welch presented to GE workers and managers a vision or a handful of central ideas that would guide the company into the future. These ideas drove the revolution, and Welch's dedication to constantly and clearly communicating them increased the understanding and acceptance of the new vision throughout GE.

The first vision was that every GE business must be No. 1 or No. 2 in its market, an idea that was repeated so often that GEers began to slur it into a single word, *number-one-or-number-two.* However, there were other ideas that would drive the transformation at GE.

Integrated diversity was one of these visions, the idea that each of GE's highly diversified businesses could maintain their operating independence and yet still be able to work together as a team for the good of GE as a whole. Welch suggested the image of GE as a "business engine," with each unit working like the cylinders of an engine to drive cash, information, expertise, and the best practices into the corporation, for the benefit of all.

To drive the organizational transformation that was necessary, Welch offered the vision of *boundarylessness,* an idea that underlies GE's increasingly fluid organizational form. The boundaryless organization should break down all the internal *bureaucratic* barriers that separate people and inhibit communication based on hierarchy or geographic location or functional specialty. It also pushes the company into closer partnerships with its customers and suppliers.

Finally, Welch communicated the vision of *speed, simplicity, and self-confidence.* It takes self-confidence to take individual initiative and to simplify complex issues. Simple procedures and individual initiative, in turn, are prerequisites for the speed and responsiveness that will enable GE to win in the marketplace.

❖ THE IMPLEMENTATION

Ultimately, what is revolutionary is not the ideas themselves. Lots of companies have ideas. Rather, the revolution was in GE's insistence on weaving them into the fundamental fabric of its organization. This process of implementation can be summarized in terms of three main aspects of organizational behavior: the *technical, political, and cultural* (or *TPC*). Together they can be seen as a three-stranded rope that must be tightly interwoven for the organization to be strong. When the rope unravels, as it certainly will when an organization is transformed, each strand must be carefully braided with the others into a new rope.

The first strand is the *technical*, and is focused on technique rather than technology. In general, this refers to the ordinary, everyday, strategic and decision-making concerns that high-ranking executives have the authority to execute without input from others. Traditional scientific management methods encourage managers to focus on the technical strand. The rule of No. 1 or No. 2 in market share was central to his implementation of the technical strand, as was his insistence that GE fix, close, or sell any business that didn't measure up to that standard.

The second element of the TPC rope is the *political* strand. Here managers need to be concerned with the often fragile matter of power relationships among people. This strand involves hiring and firing, replacing opponents with allies, and encouraging people to work together as a team. Welch focused on the technical strand for nearly five years before taking political action.

Within GE, there were many people who resisted change in general, and Welch's new vision of GE in particular. Some were hourly workers, but others included some of GE's highest-ranking business leaders. Few, if any, dared to oppose Welch openly. But they would stand aside passively, rather than actively pushing for change. Welch learned that such passive resistance can slow progress down to a crawl.

In 1985, GE "delayered" its top management, eliminating some of the most powerful positions in the company. It then reshuffled its top management, removing high-level resisters and replacing them with hand-picked executives who were committed to change. A new entity, the Corporate Executive Council, or CEC, was formed to help Welch consolidate these political gains. The members of the CEC, top managers from GE's diverse businesses, are directly accountable to the CEO.

Serving as a central information exchange, the CEC promotes the *integration* aspect of Welch's main political idea: integrated diversity. To encourage the other aspect, *diversity,* Welch granted greater autonomy to the top managers of each business area, while cutting corporate headquarters staff in half and redefining their role. Instead of directing each of the businesses from headquarters, corporate staffers were instructed to assist them. One result is that GE replaced its single, corporate-wide compensation system with dozens of unique schemes, adapted to the unique needs of each individual business.

The third and final strand of the TPC rope is the *cultural*. This is the most difficult area of management to define with precision, and it also offers the greatest challenges. Changing the culture of a company involves changing the basic and often unspoken values and beliefs that drive an organization. Alone, the CEO can do little to change a corporate culture; the voluntary cooperation of an organization's employees and managers is essential. As a result, the task is so difficult that most leaders place cultural change last on their agendas. However, no organizational transformation is complete without it. Long after the most far-reaching technical and political changes have been effected, holdovers from the previous culture will continue to impact people's behaviors, often in undesirable ways.

Welch started the process of cultural change at GE by initiating and orchestrating a dialogue of ideas. To the extent that employees get involved in thinking about big ideas, they will become accustomed to thinking for themselves on the job—an important goal at GE. For example, the company urges its business units to develop compensation systems that directly reward employee behaviors that support GE's values. The CEO has promoted committed allies to head businesses where there had been resistance to change. Welch has also encouraged company-wide debates about what GE's values should be. Together, he hopes that these methods will transform new ideas into accepted habits; as that occurs, the culture will have changed.

❖ MECHANISMS OF CHANGE

In his drive to create a new organization at GE, Welch could not allow the old one to squirm out from under his thumb. He had to be able to reach out to GE's 400,000 employees without relying on the existing, and still resistant, chain of command. Welch, in a move to consolidate his power, seized the three main levers of control necessary to any revolutionary: the police, the media, and the schools.

Organizations have their equivalents of the police, media, and schools. GE's "police" were the ranks of corporate strategic planners and finance staffs, those employees who reviewed every operating decision and provided oversight to the allocation of capital. Once Welch gained control of these staffs, every one of these reviews became an opportunity to police the behavior of GE's managers.

The police caught GE's business managers in a tight grip. To gain approval of plans, budgets, and capital requests, executives now had to satisfy the CEO's demands: consistent increases in quarterly earnings and market leadership as defined by the No. 1 or No. 2 rule. These demands forced managers to slash their costs while rethinking their businesses from the ground up. The process forced thousands of layoffs in the short run, but eventually purged almost all of the underperforming operations from GE's business *portfolio*.

The "schools" at GE were the company's management training facilities at Crotonville. Welch made certain that his allies were in control of the programs at Crotonville, and then used the facility to teach the new brand of management that GE would need. In one project, cohorts of new managers, entering in the same teams in which they would later work on the job, received intensive training in teamwork and team development. Later, and still under the watchful eyes of the Crotonville trainers, the managers would tackle, as a team, a real problem faced by their business unit. After their experience at Crotonville, managers were expected to use and develop the team skills they had acquired.

GE's "media" included executive's speeches, along with a range of publications, from employee magazines to GE's corporate annual report. Welch was acutely aware of the importance of the media, and took pains to write his own speeches and prepare his own charts. The CEO has been alert to the need to repeatedly reiterate his vision for GE and the need for change. Whether in personal talks, Q&A sessions with GE personnel, or through corporate publications, Welch has been determined that his message be heard—and heard again.

❖ THE TWENTY-FIRST CENTURY ORGANIZATION

Welch's definition of an effective corporate executive is "someone who can change the tires while the car's still rolling." The CEO's own challenge has been to create a *boundaryless organization* in a technologically sophisticated and rapidly globalizing world, while fighting a life-or-death battle with first-rate competitors. How successful has Welch been?

Once begun, the revolutionary process never ends. New challenges constantly emerge to confront the manager. Welch can now boast a portfolio of efficient businesses and a willing workforce, but his vision of a truly *boundaryless organization* is still not completely realized. The process of cultural change continues and remains an urgent priority.

Welch still foresees a future of brutal competition. As companies across the globe bring the quality of their products up to world-class standards, businesses have little other basis on which to compete except through lower prices, innovation, and speedier delivery. To prevail against the competition, GE must continue to improve its productivity. But most of the fat Welch inherited in 1981 is long gone. The company has more than doubled its revenues while greatly reducing total employment. The only way such a lean, efficient organization can continue to improve its performance may be by inspiring the remaining workers to produce more.

Cultural change may be the critical future test of GE's leadership. In any event, change will remain a constant for GE, or for any viable organization, and self-renewal will remain the mark of success.

6

♦ ♦ ♦

MOTIVATION

A number of readings contained in the Fourth Edition of *The Manager's Bookshelf* attempt to focus the manager's attention on the social-psychological side of the organization. Authors, concepts, and suggestions for proactive management call our attention to the importance of recognizing that all organizations have a natural (human) resource that, when appropriately managed, can lead to dramatic performance effects.

Part Six has two readings. In the first, Alfie Kohn, drawing from his book *Punished by Rewards,* discusses the problems associated with the use of incentives. In the second, Aubrey C. Daniels applies concepts from learning theory and organizational behavior modification to present his approach to the management of employee motivation.

Alfie Kohn argues that it is common to believe that "people will do a better job if they have been promised some sort of incentive." As a result many organizations have a motivational program that attempts to tie compensation to some index of performance. Yet, according to Kohn, it is common to observe rewards *undermining* that which they were intended to enhance. In his article "Why Incentive Plans Cannot Work," Kohn discusses this motivational problem.

Alfie Kohn is the author of four books and is a corporate lecturer. Mr. Kohn has written on competition and incentive plans.

Aubrey C. Daniels, in his book *Bringing Out the Best in People,* discusses the use and effects associated with the application of positive reinforcement as a motivational technique. Daniels, a behavioral psychologist, boldly suggests that managers can forget such fads as reengineering, self-directed work teams, and organizational cultural changes. There is, he argues, a management system that can and has produced short- and long-term results.

According to Daniels, the solution to organizational productivity, for example, can be found in the laws of human behavior. *People engage in those behaviors that get reinforced.* Through the skillful management of organizational reinforcers, you can attain the kinds of individual performance that add up to organizational performance. Thus, Daniels calls for defining reinforcers that work; setting fair performance measurement standards; building effective reinforcers into every area of your organization; and eliminating those management practices that have been shown not to bring out the best in people.

Aubrey C. Daniels (Ph.D.) is the president of Aubrey Daniels & Associates and Precision Learning Systems—two firms that work with companies to find solutions to quality, productivity, education, and morale problems.

READING 1

Punished by Rewards

Alfie Kohn

It is difficult to overstate the extent to which most managers and the people who advise them believe in the redemptive power of rewards. Certainly, the vast majority of U.S. corporations use some sort of program intended to motivate employees by tying compensation to one index of performance or another. But more striking is the rarely examined belief that people will do a better job if they have been promised some sort of incentive. This assumption and the practices associated with it are pervasive, but a growing collection of evidence supports an opposing view. According to numerous studies in laboratories, workplaces, classrooms, and other settings, rewards typically undermine the very processes they are intended to enhance. The findings suggest that the failure of any given incentive program is due less to a glitch in that program than to the inadequacy of the psychological assumptions that ground all such plans.

❖ TEMPORARY COMPLIANCE

Behaviorist theory, derived from work with laboratory animals, is indirectly responsible for such programs as piece-work pay for factory workers, stock options for top executives, special privileges accorded to Employees of the Month, and commissions for salespeople. Indeed, the livelihood of innumerable consultants has long been based on devising fresh formulas for computing bonuses to wave in front of employees. Money, vacations, banquets, plaques—the list of variations on a single, simple behaviorist model of motivation is limitless. And today even many people who are regarded as forward thinking—those who promote teamwork, participative management, continuous improvement, and the like—urge the use of rewards to institute and maintain these very reforms. What we use bribes to accomplish may have changed, but the reliance on bribes, on behaviorist doctrine, has not.

Moreover, the few articles that appear to criticize incentive plans are invariably limited to details of implementation. Only fine-tune the calculations and delivery of the incentive—or perhaps hire the author as a consultant—and the problem will be solved, we are told. As Herbert H. Meyer, professor emeritus in the psychology department at the College of Social and Behavioral Sciences at the University of South Florida, has written, "Anyone reading the literature on this subject published twenty years ago would find that the articles look almost identical to those published today." That assessment, which could have been written this morning, was actually offered in 1975. In nearly forty years, the thinking hasn't changed.

Do rewards work? The answer depends on what we mean by "work." Research suggests that, by and large, rewards succeed at securing one thing only: temporary compliance. When it comes to producing lasting change in attitudes and behavior, however, rewards, like punishment, are strikingly ineffective. Once the rewards run out, people revert to their old behaviors. Studies show that offering incentives for losing weight, quitting smoking, using seat belts, or (in the case of children) acting generously is not only less effective than other strategies but often proves worse than doing nothing at all. Incentives, a version of what psychologists call extrinsic motivators, do not alter the attitudes that underlie our behaviors. They do not create an enduring *commitment* to any value or action. Rather, incentives merely—and temporarily—change what we do.

As for productivity, at least two dozen studies over the last three decades have conclusively shown that people who expect to receive a reward for completing a task or for doing that task successfully simply do not perform as well as those who expect no reward at all. These studies examined rewards for children and adults, males and females, and included tasks ranging from memorizing facts to creative problem-solving to designing collages. In general, the more cognitive sophistication and open-ended thinking that was required, the worse people performed when working for a reward. Interestingly enough, the researchers themselves were often taken by surprise. They assumed that rewards would produce better work but discovered otherwise.

The question for managers is whether incentive plans can work when extrinsic motivators more generally do not. Unfortunately, as author G. Douglas Jenkins, Jr., has noted, most organizational studies to date—like the articles published—have tended "to focus on the effects of *variations* in incentive conditions, and not on whether performance-based pay per se raises performance levels."

A number of studies, however, have examined whether or not pay, especially at the executive level, is related to corporate profitability and other measures of organizational performance. Often they have found slight or even *negative* correlations between pay and performance. Typically, the absence of such a relationship is interpreted as evidence of links between compensation and something other than how well people do their jobs. But most of these data could support a different conclusion, one that reverses the causal arrow. Perhaps what these studies reveal is that higher pay does not produce better performance. In other words, the very idea of trying to reward quality may be a fool's errand.

Consider the findings of Jude T. Rich and John A. Larson, formerly of McKinsey & Company. In 1982, using interviews and proxy statements, they examined compensation programs at ninety major U.S. companies to determine whether return to shareholders was better for corporations that had incentive plans for top executives than it was for those companies that had no such plans. They were unable to find any difference.

Four years later, Jenkins tracked down twenty-eight previously published studies that measured the impact of financial incentives on performance. (Some were conducted in the laboratory and some in the field.) His analysis, "Financial Incentives," published in 1986, revealed that sixteen, or 57 percent, of the studies found a positive effect on performance. However, all of the performance measures were quantitative in nature: a good job consisted of producing more of something or doing it faster. Only five of the studies looked at the quality of performance. And none of those five showed any benefits from incentives.

Another analysis took advantage of an unusual situation that affected a group of welders at a Midwestern manufacturing company. At the request of the union, an incentive system that had been in effect for some years was abruptly eliminated. Now, if a financial incentive supplies motivation, its absence should drive down production. And that is exactly what happened, at first. Fortunately, Harold F. Rothe, former personnel manager and corporate staff assistant at the Beloit Corporation, tracked production over a period of months, providing the sort of long-term data rarely collected in this field. After the initial slump, Rothe found that in the absence of incentives the welders' production quickly began to rise and eventually reached a level as high or higher than it had been before.

One of the largest reviews of how intervention programs affect worker productivity, a meta-analysis of some 330 comparisons from ninety-eight studies, was conducted in the mid-1980s by Richard A. Guzzo, associate professor of psychology at the University of Maryland, College park, and his colleagues at New York University. The raw numbers seemed to suggest a positive relationship between financial incentives and productivity, but because of the huge variations from one study to another, statistical tests indicated that there was no significant effect overall. What's more, financial incentives were virtually unrelated to the number of workers who were absent or who quit their jobs over a period of time. By contrast, training and goal-setting programs had a far greater impact on productivity than did pay-for-performance plans.

❖ WHY REWARDS FAIL

Why do most executives continue to rely on incentive programs? Perhaps it's because few people take the time to examine the connection between incentive programs and problems with workplace productivity and morale. Rewards buy temporary compliance, so it looks like the problems are solved. It's harder to spot the harm they cause over the long term. Moreover, it does not occur to most of us to suspect rewards, given that our own teachers, parents, and managers probably used them. "Do this and you'll get that" is part of the fabric of American life. Finally, by clinging to the belief that motivational problems are due to the particular incentive system in effect at the moment, rather than to the psychological theory behind all incentives, we can remain optimistic that a relatively minor adjustment will repair the damage.

Over the long haul, however, the potential cost to any organization of trying to fine-tune reward-driven compensation systems may be considerable. The fundamental flaws of behaviorism itself doom the prospects of affecting long-term behavior change or performance improvement through the use of rewards. Consider the following six-point framework that examines the true costs of an incentive program.

1. "PAY IS NOT A MOTIVATOR"   W. Edward Deming's declaration may seem surprising, even absurd. Of course, money buys the things people want and need. Moreover, the less people are paid, the more concerned they are likely to be about financial matters. Indeed, several studies over the last few decades have found that when people are asked to guess what matters to their coworkers—or, in the case of managers, to their subordinates—they assume money heads the list. But put the question directly—"What do you care about?"—and pay typically ranks only fifth or sixth.

Even if people were principally concerned with their salaries, this does not prove that money is motivating. There is no firm basis for the assumption that paying people more will encourage them to do better work or even, in the long run, more work. As Frederick Herzberg, Distinguished Professor of Management at the University of Utah's Graduate School of Management, has argued, just because too little money can irritate and demotivate does not mean that more and more money will bring about increased satisfaction, much less increased motivation. It is plausible to assume that if someone's take-home pay was cut in half, his or her morale would suffer enough to undermine performance. But it doesn't necessarily follow that doubling that person's pay would result in better work.

2. REWARDS PUNISH   Many managers understand that coercion and fear destroy motivation and create defiance, defensiveness, and rage. They realize that punitive management is a contradiction in terms. As Herzberg wrote in HBR some twenty-five years ago ("One More Time: How Do You Motivate Employees?" January–February 1968), a "KITA"—which, he coyly explains, stands for "kick in the pants"—may produce movement but never motivation.

What most executives fail to recognize is that Herzberg's observation is equally true of rewards. Punishment and rewards are two sides of the same coin. Rewards have a punitive effect because they, like out-right punishment, are manipulative. "Do this and you'll get that" is not really very different from "Do this or here's what will happen to you." In the case of incentives, the reward itself may be highly desired; but by making that bonus contingent on certain behaviors, managers manipulate their subordinates, and that experience of being controlled is likely to assume a punitive quality over time.

Further, not receiving a reward one had expected to receive is also indistinguishable from being punished. Whether the incentive is withheld or withdrawn deliberately, or simply not received by someone who had hoped to get it, the effect is identical. And the more desirable the reward, the more demoralizing it is to miss out.

The new school, which exhorts us to catch people doing something right and reward them for it, is not very different from the old school, which advised us to catch people doing something wrong and threaten to punish them if they ever do it again. What is essentially taking place in both approaches is that a lot of people are getting caught. Managers are creating a workplace in which people feel controlled, not an environment conducive to exploration, learning, and progress.

REWARDS RUPTURE RELATIONSHIPS Relationships among employees are often casualties of the scramble for rewards. As leaders of the Total Quality Management movement have emphasized, incentive programs, and the performance appraisal systems that accompany them, reduce the possibilities for cooperation. Peter R. Scholtes, senior management consultant at Joiner Associates Inc., put it starkly, "Everyone is pressuring the system for individual gain. No one is improving the system for collective gain. The system will inevitably crash." Without teamwork, in other words, there can be no quality.

The surest way to destroy cooperation and, therefore, organizational excellence, is to force people to compete for rewards or recognition or to rank them against each other. For each person who wins, there are many others who carry with them the feeling of having lost. And the more these awards are publicized through the use of memos, newsletters, and awards banquets, the more detrimental their impact can be. Furthermore, when employees compete for a limited number of incentives, they will most likely begin to see each other as obstacles to their own success. But the same result can occur with any use of rewards; introducing competition just makes a bad thing worse.

Relationships between supervisors and subordinates can also collapse under the weight of incentives. Of course, the supervisor who punishes is about as welcome to employees as a glimpse of a police car in their rearview mirrors. But even the supervisor who rewards can produce some damaging reactions. For instance, employees may be tempted to conceal any problems they might be having and present themselves as infinitely competent to the manager in control of the money. Rather than ask for help—a prerequisite for optimal performance—they might opt instead for flattery, attempting to convince the manager that they have everything under control. Very few things threaten an organization as much as a hoard of incentive-driven individuals trying to curry favor with the incentive dispenser.

4. REWARDS IGNORE REASONS   In order to solve problems in the workplace, managers must understand what caused them. Are employees inadequately prepared for the demands of their jobs? Is long-term growth being sacrificed to maximize short-term return? Are workers unable to collaborate effectively? Is the organization so rigidly hierarchical that employees are intimidated about making recommendations and feel powerless and burned out? Each of these situations calls for a different response. But relying on incentives to boost productivity does nothing to address possible underlying problems and bring about meaningful change.

Moreover, managers often use incentive systems as a substitute for giving workers what they need to do a good job. Treating workers well—providing useful feedback, social support, and the room for self-determination—is the essence of good management. On the other hand, dangling a bonus in front of employees and waiting for the results requires much less effort. Indeed, some evidence suggests that productive managerial strategies are less likely to be used in organizations that lean on pay-for-performance plans. In his study of welders' performance, Rothe noted that supervisors tended to "demonstrate relatively less leadership" when incentives were in place. Likewise, author Carla O'Dell reports in *People, Performance, and Pay* that a survey of 1,600 organizations by the American Productivity Center discovered little in the way of active employee involvement in organizations that used small-group incentive plans. As Jone L. Pearce, associate professor at the Graduate School of Management, University of California at Irvine, wrote in "Why Merit Pay Doesn't Work: Implications from Organization Theory," pay for performance actually "impedes the ability of managers to manage."

5. REWARDS DISCOURAGE RISK-TAKING   "People will do precisely what they are asked to do if the reward is significant," enthused Monroe J. Haegele, a proponent of pay-for-performance programs, in "The New Performance Measures." And here is the root of the problem. Whenever people are encouraged to think about what they will get for engaging in a task, they become less inclined to take risks or explore possibilities, to play hunches or to consider incidental stimuli. In a word, the number one casualty of rewards is creativity.

Excellence pulls in one direction; rewards pull in another. Tell people that their income will depend on their productivity or performance rating, and they will focus on the numbers. Sometimes they will manipulate the schedule for completing tasks or even engage in patently unethical and illegal behavior. As Thane S. Pittman, professor and chair of the psychology department at Gettysburg College, and his colleagues point out, when we are motivated by incentives, "features such as predictability and simplicity are desirable, since the primary focus associated with this orientation is to get through the task expediently in order to reach the desired goal." The late Cornell University professor, John Condry, was more succinct: rewards, he said, are the "enemies of exploration."

Consider the findings of organizational psychologist Edwin A. Locke. When Locke paid subjects on a piece-rate basis for their work, he noticed that they tended to choose easier tasks as the payment for success increased. A number of other studies have also found that people working for a reward generally try to minimize challenge. It isn't that human beings are naturally lazy or that it is unwise to give employees a voice in determining the standards to be used. Rather, people tend to lower their sights when they are encouraged to think about what they are going to get for their efforts. "Do this and you'll get that," in other words, focuses attention on the "that" instead of the "this." Emphasizing large bonuses is the last strategy we should use if we care about innovation. Do rewards motivate people? Absolutely. They motivate people to get rewards.

6. REWARDS UNDERMINE INTEREST   If our goal is excellence, no artificial incentive can ever match the power of intrinsic motivation. People who do exceptional work may be glad to be paid and even more glad to be well paid, but they do not work to collect a paycheck. They work because they love what they do.

Few will be shocked by the news that extrinsic motivators are a poor substitute for genuine interest in one's job. What is far more surprising is that rewards, like punishment, may actually undermine the intrinsic motivation that results in optimal performance. The more a manager stresses what an employee can earn for good work, the less interested that employee will be in the work itself.

The first studies to establish the effect of rewards on intrinsic motivation were conducted in the early 1970s by Edward Deci, professor and chairman of the psychology department at the University of Rochester. By now, scores of experiments across the country have replicated the finding. As Deci and his colleague Richard Ryan, senior vice president of investment and training manager at Robert W. Baird and Co., Inc., wrote in their 1985 book, *Intrinsic Motivation and Self-Determination in Human Behavior,* "the research has consistently shown that any contingent payment system tends to undermine intrinsic motivation." The basic effect is the same for a variety of rewards and tasks, although extrinsic motivators are particularly destructive when tied to interesting or complicated tasks.

Deci and Ryan argue that receiving a reward for a particular behavior sends a certain message about what we have done and controls, or attempts to control, our future behavior. The more we experience being controlled, the more we will tend to lose interest in what we are doing. If we go to work thinking about the possibility of getting a bonus, we come to feel that our work is not self-directed. Rather, it is the reward that drives our behavior.

Other theorists favor a more simple explanation for the negative effect rewards have on intrinsic motivation: anything presented as a prerequisite for something else—that is, as a means toward another end—comes to be seen as less desirable. The recipient of the reward assumes, "If they have to bribe me to do it, it must be something I wouldn't want to do." In fact, a series of studies, published in 1992 by psychology professor Jonathan L. Freedman and his colleagues at the University of Toronto, confirmed that the larger the incentive we are offered, the more negatively we will view the activity for which the bonus was received. (The activities themselves don't seem to matter; in this study, they ranged from participating in a medical experiment to eating unfamiliar food.) Whatever the reason for the effect, however, any incentive or pay-for-performance system tends to make people less enthusiastic about their work and therefore less likely to approach it with a commitment to excellence.

❖ DANGEROUS ASSUMPTIONS

Outside of psychology departments, few people distinguish between intrinsic and extrinsic motivation. Those who do assume that the two concepts can simply be added together for best effect. Motivation comes in two flavors, the logic goes, and both together must be better than either alone. But studies show that the real world works differently.

Some managers insist that the only problem with incentive programs is that they don't reward the right things. But these managers fail to understand the psychological factors involved and, consequently, the risks of sticking with the status quo.

Contrary to conventional wisdom, the use of rewards is not a response to the extrinsic orientation exhibited by many workers. Rather, incentives help create this focus on financial considerations. When an organization uses a Skinnerian management or compensation system, people are likely to become less interested in their work, requiring extrinsic incentives before expending effort. Then supervisors shake their heads and say, "You see? If you don't offer them a reward, they won't do anything." It is a classic self-fulfilling prophecy. Swarthmore College psychology professor Barry Schwartz has conceded that behavior theory may seem to provide us with a useful way of describing what goes on in U.S. workplaces. However, "It does this not because work is a natural exemplification of behavior theory principles but because behavior theory principles . . . had a significant hand in transforming work into an exemplification of behavior theory principles."

Managers who insist that the job won't get done right without rewards have failed to offer a convincing argument for behavioral manipulation. Promising a reward to someone who appears unmotivated is a bit like offering salt water to someone who is thirsty. Bribes in the workplace simply can't work.

READING 2

Bringing Out the Best in People

Aubrey C. Daniels
Summary prepared by Gayle Porter

Gayle Porter is an Assistant Professor of Management at Rutgers University, School of Business–Camden. Her research focus is employee development, including aspects of team training, motivational reward systems, and individual differences that inhibit development efforts. Her previous experience includes positions as Director of Curriculum Development for a human resource management degree program; Consultant on training programs, financial operations, and computer applications; Financial Manager for an oil and gas production company; and Financial Specialist for NCR Corporation.

Because behavior of people is at the center of every business decision, the science of human behavior offers a great deal to managers. Drawing from a body of knowledge referred to as behavior analysis, *performance management* applies those findings to the workplace. The central idea is *to create the right environment and conditions to bring out the best in people.*

Management is often approached as a matter of personal style, as common sense, or as an "art." In addition, when one company experiences success following the implementation of some new program, other managers too easily accept that intervention as the cause for success, which creates a cycle of fads in management theory. Performance management differs from style approaches and fads because it is precise and data oriented. It offers scientifically based management methods that will solve problems permanently. To understand people, you need only to witness their behavior and observe the consequences of that behavior. From that information, performance management is the means for managers to change behavior.

Managers can influence behavior by doing something before or after the behavior occurs. The actions before behavior are called *antecedents;* these set the stage for a behavior to occur. Effective antecedents are necessary to initiate performance, but are not sufficient to sustain it. Memos, training, policies, mission statements, slogans, posters, and buttons are all antecedents. These antecedents can get people going, but consequences keep people going. *Consequences* alter the probability that behavior will recur—whether the behavior

Aubrey C. Daniels, *Bringing Out the Best in People.* New York: McGraw-Hill, 1993.

occurs more or less often in the future. No matter how strong an antecedent is, it will have a long-lasting effect only if it is consistently paired with a meaningful consequence. *Behavior is a function of its consequences.*

❖ REINFORCEMENT AS THE FOUNDATION OF PERFORMANCE MANAGEMENT

The reality of human behavior is that everything people do relates to what is being reinforced. When experiencing poor outcomes, you have to identify the behaviors causing the outcome, and arrange consequences that will stop these behaviors; identify behaviors that will produce the desirable outcomes and arrange consequences that will positively reinforce them.

There are four types of behavioral consequences. Two are used to increase behavior; these are positive reinforcement and negative reinforcement. Two are used to decrease behavior; these are punishment and extinction. *Extinction* occurs when the performer does something and nothing happens, so the behavior stops. For example, going above and beyond the requirements of the job is not rewarded, so people stop doing it. This is important to understand. Management changes behavior by inaction, as well as by action. *Punishment* is a consequence that causes behavior to stop. We can only define something as punishment by observing the effect on behavior, because positive and negative aspects of a consequence are defined by the person who receives it. Punishment never solves a problem, it only stops a behavior. There is no assurance that a positive or productive behavior will take its place.

Negative reinforcement is the process by which demonstration of a desired behavior serves to avoid a punishment. Reliance on negative reinforcement is still the dominant management style. The result from this approach is that people perform as instructed only to avoid undesirable outcomes of not doing so. We see evidence of this style: when performance shows a sharp rise just before the deadline or goes flat after reaching the goal; when there is no celebration of accomplishment, completion of a project leads only to starting the next one; or when performance drops as soon as a specified requirement is removed. Although managers will agree that it is better to manage with positive reinforcement than with negative, few understand the difference. Negative reinforcement generates just enough behavior to get by. It works, when all we need is compliance or minimum performance. But negative reinforcement requires a continual push that is punishing for both the employees and their management. It is only effective in the short term, it can never sustain high levels of performance.

Positive reinforcement is any consequence that follows a behavior and increases its frequency in the future. It occurs any time there is a favorable change in the environment. Only positive reinforcement generates more behavior than is minimally required, and this *discretionary effort* in the workplace is the only way an organization can maximize performance. Again, whether or not a reinforcer is positive depends on the perception of the performer. If performance is not improving, reinforcement is not occurring, in spite of management intentions to provide rewards.

Because the reinforcement value of anything is highly individualistic, it is important to establish what people want. One direct approach is to ask them, but people may not know or want to tell you. If they are suspicious of your motives, they may say what they think you want to hear. There is also danger that the question itself may set up expectations. A better variation is to try something and then ask people what they did or didn't like about it. When you try to provide positive reinforcers, people find even the attempt itself to be reinforcing; they tend to be forgiving, if you make a mistake in this effort. *The best way to determine positive reinforcers (what people want) is to observe*. What do people talk about and how do they spend their time when they have a choice?

Positive reinforcement may be work related, peer related, or management related. Work-related refers to the task itself. This was the basis of job-enrichment initiatives, and these have failed to show long-term improvement. Other sources of reinforcement are needed along with work related. Peer-related reinforcement is the most effective source of reinforcement at work and the most under-utilized. Peers are in a position to observe performance more closely and more often than a supervisor or manager, but employees have never learned that it is their responsibility to give reinforcement to co-workers. Unfortunately, employees are rarely reinforced by management for providing peer reinforcement. Management-related reinforcement is the opportunity for managers to capture and enjoy the benefits of discretionary effort. The manager must realize that responsibility for performance includes responsibility for coordinating reinforcement. Managers do not provide all reinforcement, but they must ensure that reinforcement occurs for the right behavior, at necessary frequency, and from all sources available.

Effective use of reinforcement involves providing it as close in time to the behavior as possible, preferably while the behavior is occurring. Greater frequency of reinforcement strengthens this time connection. *The performer must perceive a clear and contingent relationship between the behavior and the consequence*. Also, everyone who earns reinforcement should receive it, regardless of who else is being reinforced. When there is too little reinforcement to go around, people will compete for it. Competition generates political behaviors and sabotage, which are incompatible with the team-oriented work environment most organizations are trying to promote.

❖ A SCIENTIFIC APPROACH TO LEADERSHIP

No longer is it sufficient to manage strictly by results. Even when things are working, understanding *why* is important. When circumstances change, that information will be needed to fix new problems. Even inappropriate behaviors may lead to desired results in the short term, and tolerating those behaviors will eventually cause problems. It is critical to know what results you want and what behaviors are required to achieve that result. Don't assume, for example, that zero defects equates to quality-oriented behavior. Both aspects are important, but begin with identification of desired results, and don't initiate process changes without linking them to needed results. To test whether specified behaviors actually lead to the desired results, always evaluate changes in behavior against changes in results. Use actual observation and solid evidence, not intuition.

Pinpointing involves specifying results and the behaviors required to achieve them. Pinpoints are real, tangible results and behaviors, not beliefs, attitudes, or anything else internal, subjective, or abstract. Pinpointing requires precise description of results and behaviors that are observable, measurable (in terms of frequency or duration), and reliable. The reliability aspect means that two or more people observing a behavior or result will come up with the same count or measure. This usually must be refined over a period of time.

Many people find it difficult, at first, to differentiate between results and behavior, but there are cues in common language that help. For example, behaviors are usually expressed in present tense, with verbs ending in "ing." Results tend to be expressed in past tense or describe something you see after people have stopped working.

It is critical to pinpoint in terms of behavior that is under the performer's control. No one has complete control, but the performer should have more control than other people. Correlating changes in behavior with changes in results is a means to check whether they are properly identified.

People have learned to avoid measurement whenever possible, because of the way organizations have used it. Based on measurement, we typically identify poor performers and take a negative action to correct that problem. If measurement instead is used to help people do better, and those improvements are positively reinforced, people will seek out or even create measurement opportunities.

Performance is measurable through either counting or judging. Counting is preferable, because it is objective. Judging is more subjective, but it is useful when counting is not a possibility. To avoid the appearance of arbitrary judgments, establish specific criteria that can be reliably be observed by two or more people. *Behaviorally Anchored Rating Scales* (BARS) is one approach. Ranking is not effective, because it sets one employee against another. With established criteria, everyone can be a top performer. Whatever measurement is used, it is important to validate the behavioral measures by comparing against results. If the behavior is good but not the results, you have the wrong pinpoints. Overall, measurement helps to identify small, incremental changes and, thus, provides opportunities to reward improvements. This brings out the best in people.

Performance data does not necessarily tell a person what to do to improve performance. Feedback is information about performance that allows the individual to adjust. It clarifies where current performance is in relation to past performance and against some goal. Learning requires information about how behavior is affecting the environment, so there is no learning without feedback. However, feedback is an antecedent and, as such, will not sustain behavior change. How performers choose to respond to the antecedent depends on the consequences they experience. When people know positive reinforcement is consistently paired with improved performance, a feedback trend may also become a source of reinforcement. *Feedback and positive reinforcement form the most powerful combination of techniques to bring out the best in people.*

The elements discussed here must be applied in a systematic format:

1. Pinpoint
2. Measure
3. Feedback
4. Reinforce
5. Evaluate

Use of pinpointing alone won't induce a lasting change; measurement alone does not solve performance problems; feedback without reinforcement can't sustain improvement. Even reinforcement alone is dangerous, due to the likelihood of reinforcing the wrong behavior at the wrong time. Companies often think this model is too simple for their complex problems, but there are no exceptions to its applicability. The model works on all performance problems and any aspect of business and lends itself to scientific analysis.

❖ WHAT ABOUT OTHER APPROACHES AND EXISTING SYSTEMS?

A number of strategies or techniques have gained popularity in the past few years, although many companies have not been entirely satisfied with outcomes. The principles of performance management offer some explanations for why their good intentions do not always result in higher performance.

◆ Goal setting has been extremely popular in organizations, in spite of the fact that it consumes a great deal of management time, and there is no agreement on how to set goals and document their value to business. Goals may limit performance, because people capable of more will stop when they achieve the goal. Goals are antecedents. The purpose of setting goals should be to increase the opportunities for positive reinforcement, and this will accelerate the rate of improvement. A key aspect in shaping behavior is to break down the task into small steps, supply incremental reinforcers for gradual improvement, and then celebrate achievement of the final goal.

◆ Quality-improvement programs also emphasize features such as training, policies, and meetings, which are antecedents. Often they are based on implementing dozens of new practices simultaneously, with very little connection between behaviors and results. A quality system may or may not result in improving the product or service. The real test is whether a company can accelerate the rate of improvement in order to outdo competitors. This acceleration effect happens only with precise and effective use of positive reinforcement.

◆ Teams and employee empowerment are desirable based on both common sense and theory, but there is not consistent evidence of success. The benefits of teamwork have been translated into a need for formal team structures, which takes tremendous effort from both the individual and the organization. One problem is that the process may consume more focus than the results. Another issue is that, too often, people are pushed into forming teams and given empowerment noncontingently. Teams progress at different rates and should be rewarded with empowerment gradually and systematically. In other words, people must earn empowerment. Unfortunately, one of the most important benefits of teams is almost entirely overlooked. The use of teams dramatically increases the opportunities for receiving reinforcement. Every team member is a potential source of reinforcement for other members.

◆ Downsizing has been used as a primary method to give shareholders a higher return on investment. At best it is a stop-gap measure, used because companies are unable to solve fundamental problems. If management is reinforcing the wrong things, reducing the work force or putting these people into different jobs will not cause them to suddenly do anything differently. The aftermath of a layoff is often that those left behind feel punished or afraid they will be next. Needed people may decide to leave, possibly joining the competition. The job of management during downsizing is to develop a system of reinforcement—one that ensures the right consequences for progressive behaviors; behaviors that allow the organization to do more with less.

◆ Recognition ceremonies are removed in time from behaviors and celebrate the accomplishments of a few; those who miss by a close margin are put in the position of losers. The larger the prizes awarded, the more they encourage behaviors to win (lie, cheat, sabotage) rather than to perform. Similar problems exist with the use of suggestion systems. Managers judge whether to implement a new idea based on dollar savings and totally ignore the motivational value of employees seeing their ideas put to use. Someone reinforced for a suggestion worth very little now may submit another one in the future that results in great savings. But without reinforcement, that person will not continue to make suggestions.

◆ Traditional compensation systems are primarily noncontingent. How hard you work today will not affect your next paycheck. Pay raises are competitive due to finite resources, so any gain is someone else's loss. To alleviate competition many companies have moved toward across-the-board increases, which is demotivating. Benefit plans—even the popular "cafeteria" plans—give as much total benefit to poor performers. Gainsharing is more closely aligned with controllable outcomes than straight profit sharing, but the usual plan is based on some formula to divide the benefit equally among all participants. There is no individual performance contingency. Annual performance appraisals are too far removed in time from performance demonstration. Forced-ranking or forced-distribution systems are demotivating; a company hires the best people possible and then forces them into a system that labels all but a few as average. In most cases, managers do not have enough flexibility to make pay and benefit plans contingent, but performance management offers suggestions on how to bring out the best in people in spite of traditional systems.

❖ PERFORMANCE MANAGEMENT TO REVITALIZE THE WORKPLACE

To executives who understand human behavior, changing business conditions don't present problems, just additional opportunities to exercise their skills. Those who don't understand will not survive, and they put their companies at financial risk. Executives establish the guiding principles and values of the organization, which lead to definition of desired results and the behaviors that will be reinforced to obtain them. Lack of success often results from saying one thing but rewarding another, so the executives must establish clear guidelines. It is also important to define limits of reinforcement that managers and supervisors have at their discretion. Managers and supervisors must be reinforced for their use of reinforcement with employees, rather than for short-term results that may be obtained through unwanted behaviors. Remember that all behavior is choice behavior, and people will engage in a particular behavior in direct proportion to the amount of reinforcement received.

Changes now occur so rapidly that on-the-job training is not practical, and we must do a better job of training people before they enter their jobs. The focus should be on achieving an advanced level of performance, called *fluency*. Repeated practice with feedback and reinforcement leads to fluency. The result is high retention, and people need less concentration and energy to perform, so they are able to stay on task longer and perform even under duress or when distracted.

People should be active participants in recognizing achievement, not just recipients of the company's benevolence. Rather than simply praising their accomplishments, engage them in telling the story of how they achieved their success. This becomes a true celebration for that person and may be an antecedent for other employees to try similar things. Whatever the number of employees in the company, each individual has that many possible sources of positive reinforcement. Imagine being excited to go to work every morning and working for a company where everyone else is, too!

Performance management is built around certain values: honesty, integrity, equality and respect, justice, self-esteem and personal growth, peace of mind, and the golden rule. These are demonstrated through making desired outcomes known to all; assuming that all people can be better than they are now, with support from their environment; and reducing stress by clarifying behavior/reinforcement connections and diminishing threats and punishment. Performance management is a precise scientific approach that works without gimmicks, because the laws of behavior are the same for all people.

EMPOWERMENT AND PARTICIPATION

$\mathbf{F}$or several decades there have been a small number of highly visible advocates of participative approaches to the practice of management. During the early 1960s, University of California-Berkeley management professor Raymond Miles, for example, built upon the earlier work of many behavioral management theorists as he advanced the human resource model. This model argues that through employee involvement, organizational performance will increase. Increases in performance (accomplishments) are satisfying to employees, and this satisfaction breeds the motivation and commitment for deeper involvement.

In spite of such claims, different participative management approaches (e.g., Management by Objectives, job enlargement, and job enrichment) are not widely practiced in American organizations. The classical (hierarchical, Theory X, top-down) approach continues to dominate the practice of management. The Japanese challenge, continued decline of American productivity and product quality, and other forces are causing many U.S. organizations to reexamine, adopt, and integrate participation into their management philosophies and practices.

In Part Seven several themes related to employee involvement and participation will be addressed. Each of the readings looks at the *empowerment* of the employee.

James Belasco and Ralph Stayer, authors of the *Flight of the Buffalo,* discuss their views on organizational leadership and the need for a new leadership paradigm in their article "Why Empowerment Doesn't Empower: The Bankruptcy of Current Paradigms." According to Belasco and Stayer, the current command and control paradigm, with its emphasis on placing leaders into roles where they plan, organize, command, coordinate, and control places responsibility for other people's performance on the shoulders of the leader. *This system guarantees organizational failure.* The authors argue that in high-performance organizations leaders have made it their job to make people responsible for their own performance—reasoning that the best person to be responsible for the job is the person doing the job because that person is the "expert in that job." This theme is similar to that presented by William Glasser in *The Control Theory Managers.*

James Belasco is a Professor of Management at San Diego State University and Ralph Stayer is the CEO of Johnsonville Foods in Johnsonville, Wisconsin. Mr. Stayer's management philosophy was presented in an interesting article published in the *Harvard Business Review* (1990, November/December, pp. 66–75, 80, 82).

Through a modern-day fable, William C. Byham focuses on ways to improve productivity, quality, and employee satisfaction in his book *Zapp! The Lightning of Empowerment.* The author argues that for organizations to be competitive during this, the latter part of the twentieth century, it is essential that the organization's human resources be used in such a way that their energies are focused on ways of making improvements in the organization's quality, output, sales, and customer satisfaction.

Through the empowerment of people, the organization's workforce will take on responsibility, experience a sense of ownership, gain satisfaction from accomplishment, and acquire power over the ways things are done. Through this process they will come to know that they are important to the organization, and the organization will have strong, enthusiastic, dedicated employees working toward improved quality and productivity.

Dr. William C. Byham is President and Founder of Development Dimensions International, a human resource training and development company. He is also the author, with Jeff Cox, of the book *Heroz: Empower Yourself, Your Co-workers, Your Company.*

Charles C. Manz and Henry P. Sims Jr. present a unique model of the leader of the future in their book *SuperLeadership: Leading Others to Lead Themselves.* They suggest that excellent leaders must not only be able to engage in self-leadership and self-control, but they must also be able to inspire their followers to do the same. *The superleader must create an organizational environment that facilitates the development and the exercise of self-leadership in others,* and this process represents a unique form of participative management.

Professors Manz and Sims are Professors of Management at Arizona State University and the University of Maryland respectively. Both have consulted, researched, and written extensively about organizations. They are the coauthors of *Business Without Bosses.*

READING 1

Flight of the Buffalo

James A. Belasco and Ralph C. Stayer

The president shifted nervously in his big chair. His youngish face—belying his 50ish age—was creased with worry. His was a most admired company. Mentioned frequently in business magazines, his stock sold at healthy profit-to-earnings multiples. With his Ivy League training he was a leading spokesperson for American business. Yet now his eruditeness had deserted him.

He rose, strode to the window, and peered out at the bucolic setting. "Not on my watch," he said to the huge oak outside his window. "This can't happen on my watch." After an eternity of shuffling his feet and clasping and unclasping his hands, he whirled and faced me, steel flashing in his eyes. "I've got five years to retirement. What can I do to make these five years count?"

The challenge was daunting. The company, despite its favorable press, was failing badly. It had lost market share in every single phase of its business. It was significantly late in several new product launches. Its cash cow was under attack by the Japanese. Despite its cash hoard and dominant market position, the company was in serious trouble. He saw with crystal clarity the potential danger if the business did not change—radically—now. The unthinkable could happen on his watch—and he did not know what to do. Nothing in his previous experience or training had prepared him to deal with this situation.

This president's problem is all too familiar. Though he sat in the CEO's chair, he was powerless to accomplish the changes he knew had to be made. He saw clearly what had to be done. The management mantra of the 1990s was familiar: teamwork, better quality, improved service, faster time to market. He knew them well. He preached them to anyone who would listen. Yet he was unable to make any of these vital outcomes occur in his organization.

It was not for lack of trying. In the last six years he had instituted programs designed to stimulate quality, customer service, and teamwork. He had slimmed down the organization, reorganized functional groups into product/customer focused units, and reduced the number of management layers. Yet he continued to lose market share, competitors continued to beat him to the market, and he had lost 50 percent of his market value. He just couldn't make his people do what he knew had to be done.

The leader presumably sits at the pinnacle of power. At least that's what we are led to believe. The corner office is the symbol of authority in America. Yet read the business press and feel the pain and anguish of so many executives as they are unable to make people produce the changes they know are essential to their organization's survival.

We know how it feels. We've been there through the long sleepless nights. One CEO said, "It's a cruel joke. I work a whole lifetime to make it to the top. 'Now,' I say to myself, 'I can finally do things the way I want them done.' Only now I discover that I have less ability to do things than in any other position I've ever held. It's a cruel joke." The power vacuum in the corner office is an epidemic. It undermines ability to compete in world markets. It deepens recession and flattens growth. In the long run, it is fatal.

Why does this power vacuum exist at the pinnacle of power? The single biggest reason is the obsolete leadership paradigm that robs leaders of their effectiveness. Under the current paradigm leaders are responsible for the performance of their people. They fix problems—including people problems. They answer questions. They make decisions. They do things to the organization and the people in it.

You've probably read it and heard it a million times. Leaders plan, organize, command, coordinate, and control. That's the current command and control paradigm. It's found in every management textbook, taught in every college classroom and seminar room. You see it practiced in almost every organization. It is "conventional wisdom."

Take vision, for instance. Leaders are responsible for crafting a vision, implementing it, and empowering their people to use it. It is this paradigm of leader responsibility for other people's performance that, given today's circumstances, guarantees organizational failure.

Our experiences in researching high performance organizations, running our own companies, and helping other people run theirs demonstrate that the leader's job is to make people responsible for their own performance. Kotter and Heskett (1992) report a significant relationship between economic performance and culture that emphasizes personal accountability to customers. Leonard-Barton (1992) cites the experience of Chaparrel Steel in managing so that individuals own the responsibility to solve production problems. Osborne and Gaebler (1992) argue that government can be reinvented by making people assume responsibility for their own performance serving their citizen-customers. Much of the work of Lawler (1992) leads in the same direction of self-management; Ouchi (1978) and Walton (1985) have presented a similar argument. There is considerable evidence to support this new approach to leadership. One of the consequences of this revised leadership paradigm is that it significantly alters the behavior of everyone in the organization.

An example will clarify the differences in leadership paradigms. We were visiting the president of a $6 billion company. As we walked with him out of his office one day we passed a groundskeeper raking leaves. She was using a rake that, when it was new, had thirty-one teeth; now it was very old with only five teeth, and wasn't raking up many leaves. We stopped and asked her, "What are you doing?"

"Raking the leaves," she replied.

"Why are you using that rake?" we asked. "You're not picking up many leaves."

"Because that's what they gave me to use," she replied.

"Why didn't you get a better rake?" we asked.

"That's not my job," she said.

As we walked away the president was visibly angry. "We have a backlog big enough to choke a horse," he said, working hard to restrain the level of his voice, "and it's growing every day. We're way behind on two large development projects that are draining us of cash. We're behind in both production lines and bleeding cash there too. This incident is a perfect example of what is wrong. People are constantly complaining because they don't have the right tools, parts, drawings, and God knows what. This just caps it for me. It's a perfect example of the lack of a sense of urgency I talked to you about. How are we ever going to make it if we can't even give someone a decent rake? I've got to find her supervisor and make sure she gets a better rake."

"Are you certain the supervisor is responsible?" we asked.

"Absolutely!" he almost yelled. Gaining his composure, he continued, "His job is to make certain his people have the right tools."

"Are you sure?" we asked.

"Well," he replied hesitantly, "If I'm going to be a hands-on leader—if I'm going to demonstrate a personal sense of urgency—if I'm going to live the vision—I guess I'll lead by example and go and get the rake myself." He turned and headed in the direction of the storeroom.

Who is the only person who can get the right tools? Obviously the person doing the job. Yet, hear the old paradigm at work: "It's the supervisor's responsibility to get the right tools. . . . I'll go and get the rake myself." This man had been working fourteen hours per day, seven days a week, and getting farther and farther behind—all because he had defined his role according to the old paradigm. He could chase rakes all day and not put his development projects back on time or his production lines back on schedule. As long as he sees his role as solving problems, people will bring him problems to solve. They won't be responsible for solving their parts shortage or inappropriate tool problems themselves, because he's there to solve them for them.

❖ THE EVOLUTION OF MANAGEMENT PARADIGMS

A little history puts the absolute necessity of this paradigm shift in perspective. Karl Marx was right: the owners of the tools of production determine economic structure. When Marx looked around in the middle of the nineteenth century he saw that capitalists owned the equipment and machinery, which were the tools of production. Therefore, capitalists, who set up the economic system, wielded the power and made the decisions. This system arose because in the mid-nineteenth century markets were local or national, communication took days or weeks, work was unskilled and manual, workers were uneducated, and stability was the rule.

Capital was the critical scarce resource. People were plentiful, being driven in droves from the farms by the agriculture revolution. The Scottish businessman and early management writer-philosopher Robert Owens wrote in the early 1830s, "A good horse is worth five pounds a day. A good man is worth two pounds." Guess who was treated better, the man or the horse?

Early entrepreneurs accumulated capital and risked it to build factories, buy equipment, and produce goods in advance of payment for those goods. All this required high risk, for which there was great return. Jobs, on the other hand, were rudimentary and mechanical. Factory jobs demanded little of the then typical craftsman skill.

Leadership paradigms emerged that reflected these economic conditions. The best examples were the German army and the French coal mines of the late nineteenth century. Henri Fayol wrote his *Principles of Administration* almost 100 years ago. In that book, based upon his experience running the French coal mines, he outlined the functions of management as planning, organizing, commanding, coordinating, and controlling. Max Weber, studying the German army of approximately the same time, came to very similar conclusions. Our present leadership paradigm methods are based on their model—even though our circumstances are far different from what they were then.

Times changed, however. In the mid-1930s another historian, James Burnham, realized that professional managers effectively controlled corporations, which were the tools of production. In his book *The Managerial Revolution* (1941), he argued that power had passed from the shareholder owners of the major corporations to professional managers. He realized that because professional managers set up the system, they wielded power and made the decisions.

Adolph Berle and Gardener Means came to the same conclusion in their book, *The Modern Corporation and Private Property* (1932). They clearly understood the separation between managers, who effectively ran the corporation, and owners, who had little or nothing to say about the disposition of their "property."

In his recent book, *Short-Term America: The Causes and Cures of our Business Myopia* (1991), Michael Jacobs updates and validates the Berle and Means and Burnham observations. He argues that the short-term myopia that plagues American business is the result of the separation of management from ownership and the ascendancy of management to the seat of power.

This transfer of power occurred because the brainpower capital supplied by professional managers became more important than the financial capital supplied by the shareholders. The critical capital resource needed for survival changed from such tangible physical assets as plant, equipment, and money to the brainpower capital supplied by managers. Capital had been transformed from a physical to an intellectual form. Karl Marx was right again: the owners of the tools of production become the dominant power in the economic landscape. But Marx could not have envisioned the day human brainpower would be more important than tangible assets.

Today circumstances have changed again. The principle tools of production today are not machinery and equipment, but the ideas and talents of the people. Today, the intellectual capital of the scientist, the machinist, and the programmer is the critical resource, so the possessors of the intellectual tools of production—people—will come to exercise effective power. Markets are now global, electronic highways enable instant communication and rapid competitive responses, work involves the creation, transmission, and manipulation of information and knowledge, and workers are highly educated.

◆ CADAVERS OF LEADERSHIP PARADIGMS: 100 YEARS AND STILL STINKING

Unfortunately, leadership practice hasn't caught up with this new reality. The leadership systems currently in use are designed to control relatively uneducated, mostly untrustworthy people in an environment of very slow change. In our free and democratic society, employees park their rights—along with their brains—at the door. Companies today are the last remaining feudal enclave. Too many people in organizations are subjected to authoritarian—and what they believe to be unreasonable—treatment. This is why there is so little effort to excel in authoritarian firms.

Several authors have written about the negative impacts of low trust and commitment, particularly Cook and Wall (1982), Wilkins (1989), and Kotter and Heskett (1992). The current popular management literature is also filled with examples of the negative impact of declining trust and commitment. Recent articles report employees' lack of commitment and loyalty, as well as the fear that cost cutting has gone too far and may be the precipitating cause of corporate disasters ranging from Exxon's string of spills and explosions to IBM's chronic underperformance.

The following anecdote highlights leaders' feudal thinking. A mid-level supervisor in a large, publicly traded company asked her secretary to wash and detail her car. Her instructions were not to do it if they didn't take her credit card because she didn't have enough money in her checking account to cover any cash expenditures. The secretary took the car down during working hours. When the car wash didn't take the credit card, she paid for the wash and detail herself, telling her boss, "Pay me back when you have the money, no problem." The boss was furious and fired the secretary on the spot.

Notice several assumptions. The boss thought nothing of asking the secretary to run a personal errand for her during working hours—or to terminate her at will when she was displeased with the performance. After all, the secretary "worked" for her. Notice the master-slave concept in action. So much of the early thinking about the employment relationship was based upon that concept. The vestiges of that thinking still exist. It didn't even occur to the boss that her request was inappropriate or her termination action likely illegal.

Notice also the boss's assumption that she could take care of her personal business during working hours and use company resources to do so. Hear the assumption, "I'm the boss and I'm in control of these resources to use as I see fit." This is managerial capitalism at its best. Hear how the property rights of the boss take precedence over the civil rights of the employee. Furthermore, the stockholders in this publicly traded company must be exceedingly angry with the boss for breaching her fiduciary responsibility to them—the owners of the resources she so freely uses for her own personal use.

The payoff was the immediate dramatic fall in her department's productivity. She couldn't figure out why, but it is clear to us. The people in the department were withholding their intellectual capital. In many departments in many companies across the world this same soap opera is being played out—to the detriment of everyone.

We both were thoroughly caught up in the old paradigm. We believed it, practiced it, taught it—even wrote about it (Belasco, Price, and Hampton 1978). We spent long sleepless nights wondering why it didn't work. The old paradigm was so logical. It was "proven." We loved being the drivers of things in our organizations. No matter how hard we tried, though, we couldn't make the old planning and control paradigm work. Out of our frustration came the search for a new, more effective model.

❖ THE INTELLECTUAL CAPITALISM PARADIGM

We have all grown up learning to follow authority: parents, teachers, bosses. The first and probably most often reinforced lesson we learn is: "Do as you are told by the person in charge." Now, however, the "person in charge" is the person who formally reports to you. In this topsy-turvy world as a leader you actually work for the people who work for you.

In the past, leaders planned products, budgets, facilities—the concrete financial aspects of the business. The assumption was that people would go along with the plan. Many authors have examined the relationship between strategic planning and its execution. The assumption in all this work has been that it is management's task to craft strategic plans and the worker's task to execute them. That assumption is no longer safe. Leaders must plan for the mind-sets and mentalities of the people if they want the financial plan to work.

Leadership tools have not changed significantly. The focus of their use has changed. The primary purpose of strategic planning is not to plan strategically for the future—although that is an important purpose of the exercise. It is primarily to develop the strategic management mindset in every person in the organization. The purpose is not only to produce a plan; it is to produce a plan that will be owned and understood by the people who have to execute it.

Leaders in the era of intellectual capitalism have a new set of responsibilities. At every level in the organization leaders must (1) transfer ownership for work to those who execute the work, and (2) create an environment for ownership in which each person wants to be responsible for his or her own performance. This can be accomplished by the following acts:

◆ Paint a clear picture of great performance for the organization and each person.

◆ Focus individuals on the few factors that create great performance.

◆ Develop the desire for each person to own—be responsible—for his or her own great performance.

◆ Align organization systems and structures to send a clear message as to what is necessary for great performance for the individual and the organization.

◆ Engage individuals—their hearts and minds as well as their hands—in the business of the business.

◆ Energize people around the focus of the business.

Leaders also must (3) coach the development of individual capability and competence, and (4) learn faster by learning themselves, and by creating the conditions under which every person in the organization is challenged to continually learn faster as well. Let's examine each of these leadership functions in turn.

◆ THE LEADERSHIP FUNCTION: TRANSFER OF OWNERSHIP

Early in our leadership careers we became grounded in employee involvement. We read a lot about it, and it sounded good. The human relations movement dominated the academic literature when we were undergraduate students. We used textbooks authored by the classic human relations writers Mayo (1933), Maslow (1943), and McGregor (1960).

We began by holding employee meetings to solicit employee participation. We wanted them to share in a two-way exchange of information and, hopefully, some problem solving as well. It rapidly deteriorated, however, into a bitch session. Employees kept bringing up situations that needed fixing. We made long lists of things to fix and worked hard to fix everything before the next meeting. But this turned out to be a full-time job. We told ourselves, "You have to demonstrate good faith. It will take time. Eventually they'll run out of things to fix and you can get on with solving the plant's real problems." Fixing their problems, after all, was part of our leadership responsibility. Eighteen months later, we were still receiving long lists to fix at every meeting. We ran out of patience before they ran out of lists.

In retrospect, the problem is clear to us. We were owning all the responsibility for fixing the problems. The employees' job was to identify what needed to be fixed; they were dedicated to doing that job well. They worked hard to keep us working hard; and we worked hard solving their problems. The plant continued to flounder. Our "fix them" leadership paradigm was failing.

We graduated from the university too soon. While we were discovering the inappropriateness of the simplistic employee participation notions of the human relations school in the 1960s and 1970s, a whole body of new research emerged to validate our experiential conclusions. Clayton Alderfer (1972) proposed a variation on Maslow's hierarchy. Frederick Herzberg (1959) revealed a different approach to motivation that challenged many of the original human relations assumptions about people's behavior. Many popular management books of the 1980s—including Peters and Waterman's *In Search of Excellence* (1982) and William Ouchi's *Theory Z* (1981)—echoed our experience.

Some time in the early 1980s after we had read "newer" research, we encountered a quality problem in one plant. Vowing to learn from the new data and avoid taking responsibility for the problem, we called a meeting of the employees involved and asked them for their input on fixing the problem. This time, however, we insisted that they had to be responsible for implementing any solution they suggested. The discussion took a very different tack.

The first suggestion was to change the equipment. When we revealed that the cost of such a change would be $1.5 million, they were shocked. Next, they suggested that we talk the customer into taking a lesser quality product. We arranged for a group of them to visit customers and discuss the problem in person. The group returned from the visit with higher quality standards, not lower ones. "Whew!" one member of the group told us. "This is hard work."

As the group struggled with what to do, several members complained. "This is management work," they said. "We are not paid to do this. This is your job. Stop imposing it on us." We were stunned and hurt by the comment. Writers told us that everyone wants to be self-actualized. People really love to be responsible, they wrote. We asked ourselves, "Why is it that our people don't? What are we doing, or not doing, that causes our people to not want to assume responsibility?" We then realized that we had trained them to be dependent upon us. We liked their doing whatever we told them to do. When we wanted them to be flexible, they had no model or training in how to share leadership.

We asked them if they would rather have us make the decision. They mumbled, "Well, no. But it isn't supposed to be so hard." We asked, "Haven't we been making all the decisions? Do you really think it's working out better? What do you need to do to make the decision easier, and to make a better decision? How can we help you make the decision?" The stewing and shuffling of feet convinced us that we were on the right track.

We got a few requests, but it was clear that the people were wrestling with what to do. After what seemed an eternity (but was only four days) the group came back with a plan to redo several of the procedures and learn a new process. The quality problem was solved. Total cost: less than $10,000. The group tried one last time to hand us the problem. "Here it is," they proudly said, "Now go fix it." We said, "Whoa, that wasn't the deal. How are you going to make it work?"

The sheepish grins told us we had successfully transferred the responsibility. "Here's the plan," they said. "We're ready to roll." Without looking at the papers thrust in front of us, we said "Go for it." It took a lot of restraint not to respond to our old leadership instincts and rush in to "help." Their answer was not as good as our own—or so we told ourselves. It took maximum control to keep from reading their proposal and "improving" it. Our restraint paid big dividends. Their execution of their own plan was flawless. The problem was solved and never came back. It was a win-win outcome. Gradually, we learned to transfer responsibility for solving other similar problems to the rightful owner.

We learned that the best person to be responsible for the job is the person doing the job. Because that person is the expert in that job, he or she should be the one to make the decision about how the work can best be done. The job design movement is based on this premise. Recent popular literature reports many successful examples of this approach. Theoretical literature leads to a similar conclusion. In the intellectual capitalism model, people with the knowledge about the immediate responsibilities have the ultimate power.

We resolved to stop providing answers and start asking questions. We learned to ask questions such as the following:

◆ What do you think?

◆ Why do you think that will or won't work?

◆ What else might you do?

◆ What prevents you from doing that?

◆ How can you overcome that obstacle?

These questions caused consternation. Because we were no longer providing a specific set of answers, people had to find their own answers. That was difficult for some.

Several employees informed us that there was a drug problem on the second and third shifts. Our first reaction was to order drug testing and hire undercover people to catch the users. Then, remembering our commitment to transferring ownership, we chose another route.

We passed on the information to the Quality of Work Life Pride Team, composed of people from all levels. They found that drug use was indeed a problem. After meeting with people throughout the company, they got together with us and set a goal of a drug-free plant. They announced a treatment program for anyone who needed help. They also promised that people who refused help would be asked to leave.

The program was very successful. The incidence of drug usage now is negligible. The program worked because the right people—fellow workers—owned the problem.

Resolve is never sufficient. Old leadership habits die hard. It takes much practice to rid ourselves of them. Leaders frequently fall back into the problem-solving trap. Our academic background taught us that leaders have powerful tools to institutionalize the transfer of ownership. Systems and structures could be modified to create the ownership environment.

Our focus on systems and structures stems from our academic experience. Much of the original thought in management by Weber, Fayol, and Marx was based on the implication that structure shaped behavior. The entire field of organizational theory is based on the same hypothesis. Much of Peter Drucker's writings are based on the similar premise that organizational attributes, similar to systems and structures, shape behavior. Rensis Likert (1961) and the Michigan study of leadership reflects the same presumption that organizational context controls behavior. Studies of organizational culture reaffirm the dominant place of structures and systems in shaping people's behavior within firms. The close relationship between organizational structure characteristics and organizational performance was demonstrated in at least three empirical studies. We therefore modified several systems and structures.

◆ The Leadership Function: Create the Ownership Environment

A team in our company sold software to government units in one local geographic region. Initially, the first team of employees sold, installed, and supported all the systems because they were the only people in the company. Everyone assumed that pattern would change as soon as the company grew sufficiently. After all, it is standard in our industry to separate selling, installation, and support. There is an assumption that salespeople are not good programmers and good programmers are not good salespeople, and good support people are different from both. That assumption, however, did not prove true.

The team quickly sold out its local market. To grow, it either had to seek out smaller customers within its geographic area, which meant changing its product, or move into new geographic areas. Sensing an opportunity for people to assume increased responsibility, we posed the following question to the group: "What can you do to ensure that each customer receives the best service and at the same time ensure that you personally continue to learn and grow?" Rather than our deciding what to do, we turned the decision over to the people who had to make the decision work.

The people decided to hire new people to both sell to smaller customers in their original geographic area and move into new geographic areas. They set up a rotation system within the teams so that everyone learned all the skills. They set up an internal monitoring system to keep the skills current. They assumed ownership for training and monitoring themselves—and for assuring superior service to their customers. One of the team members offered to start the new team for the smaller customers. Another offered to relocate temporarily to start up a new operation in a new geographic area.

Today there are more than seven hundred people in the company, organized into thirty-seven semi-autonomous teams stretching from Singapore to Moscow. These team members are responsible for hiring, training, and maintaining superior levels of service to customers. The team members themselves have assumed responsibility for delivering great performance to their customers. Getting people to own the responsibility for making crucial strategic decisions is leadership in the intellectual capitalism age.

As the company grew, so did complaints about performance discrepancies among teams. We tried several different tactics to deal with the discrepancies—all to no avail. Eventually we realized this was another opportunity to transfer ownership. At the next all-employee meeting we asked, "How can we assure consistent high performance across all teams? What can we do to be certain that we are all equally proud of the work of each person in the company?"

The employees wrestled with the problem for an entire day. Eventually they decided that each team would meet every week and set individual and team goals. These goals would be validated by customers and would expect measurable, responsible action from each member. The goals would be entered on the e-mail system along with daily progress. Team members agreed to help other team members—in their own team as well as in others—set realistic but challenging goals and then support each other in attaining them.

Today each team member inputs individual and team goals every week, reviews and comments on others' goals, and reports daily progress. There is a lively e-mail exchange about goals and performance among most people in the company. And goal attainment averages more than 99 percent every week. A system of goal planning, designed by the people, helped create the environment wherein the people assumed ownership for their results.

We have an extensive full-cost, real-time cost accounting system that uses "activity based costing." Everyone charges time, expenses, and materials directly to a project, customer, or program. These costs are collected daily and a real-cost, 30-day rolling average is computed for every product for every team. This real-time, full-cost data bank gives teams the opportunity to make such business decisions as pricing and delivery. It enables them to accept responsibility for making profitable bids.

Our decision to use the information system to shape behavior is supported by extensive research. The idea that controlling the information premises in an organization shapes individual behavior was most clearly articulated by Nobel laureate Herbert Simon (1945). Much of Edward Lawler's work leads to the similar conclusion that information is a powerful influencer of behavior in organizations. Much of the financial control literature is also based on the same premise that information is the central ingredient in control. Research in the 1980s demonstrated that access to information is a way of building commitment. The Management of the 1990s Research Program at MIT's Sloan School of Management empirically demonstrated how information technology shapes organizational behavior.

Initially we reviewed and approved each bid. We were concerned that bid prices wouldn't be high enough and they weren't. We found ourselves continually raising bids, and realized that we had to change the situation or else be forever reviewing bids—not exactly the future we had envisioned for ourselves. So we changed another critical system—the reward system.

Again, research offered good guidance in choosing a focus for leadership behavior. The works of Edward Lawler articulate the premise that you get what you pay for. In addition, Luthans and Kreitner (1985) support the linkage between reward (in its broadest sense, not just compensation) and performance.

In the first year, each person was paid a bonus based on a percentage of overall company profit and determined by the executive committee. In the beginning the bonuses were not very large, because start-up costs ate into profits and we needed to conserve cash. This caused considerable discontent. Eventually, after much fruitless discussion, we realized we had yet another opportunity to transfer ownership.

At the next quarterly all-employee meeting we asked, "What is a fair and equitable bonus system? What would make you feel like a winner and still leave a return to our shareholders and enough capital to grow the business? What bonus system would reward people on the basis of their contribution?" As a trigger to the discussion we suggested a 50/50 split of net profits before tax to be allocated on the basis of team performance.

The group took some time to decide. Eventually, the group chose to use the 50/50 split as a framework but added certain provisions. They decided that teams would allocate the bonus among team members, ensuring that everyone received a reward based upon his or her contribution. Eligibility for the bonus pool initially was restricted to individuals who met their weekly individual and team goals 90 percent of the time and received a rating of 8 or better (out of a possible 10) on the monthly customer satisfaction survey. The group has continually raised the standard for admission into the bonus pool. Today it has established 100 percent goal achievement and a perfect score of 10 on the customer survey as the eligibility standards.

Almost immediately bid prices and margins rose, as did the preoccupation with supplying superior products and services to create additional value. Further, after the initial excitement caused by the distribution of big monthly team bonus checks, the focus shifted to the weekly performance management reports. E-mail notes flew back and forth challenging, supporting, and sharing information relevant to attaining individual and team goals.

Over the period of a few months we withdrew from approving bids. The teams now had full responsibility to bid jobs and deliver a superior product. This delighted customers and earned the company a profit. They accepted the ownership for running their business. They had the intellectual capital. They were in control.

While we had been changing so dramatically internally, the market was changing as well. Our technology base changed four times in four years. Our programming language changed several times in the same four years. Our customer base shifted five times. All our leadership efforts directed toward transferring ownership paid off. Despite the external chaos, the people were able to remain focused on delivering great performance for their customers. By shaping the systems and structures we created the ownership environment. Nevertheless, leadership is a one-on-one phenomenon as well.

◆ THE LEADERSHIP FUNCTION: COACHING PERSONAL COMPETENCE

Coaching is frequently listed as an important leadership task. One of the first major writers to explore the coaching rather than directing role of a leader was Chris Argyris (1957, 1964). Tom Peters and Nancy Austin (1985) specify five coaching roles: educating, sponsoring, coaching, counseling, and confronting; they then cite numerous examples of successful coaching. Noel Tichy and Mary Anne Devanna (1986) visualize the leader as the coach of the change process. Edgar Schein (1983, 1985) makes the coaching role pivotal as the preferred change process. Stephen Covey (1990) uses coaching as the principal organizational leadership activity.

What does coaching mean? What does a world-class coach do? How does one measure whether one is a world-class coach or not? These are not easy questions, particularly because most of us have been raised in the old command-and-control leadership style: asking questions and not giving answers.

Initially we believed that great coaches helped other people find their own answers. So we concentrated on asking questions. We became experts in the "grunt and pause" methodology. That frustrated many people. It was certainly not a style they had come to expect. They believed we should tell them what to do, not ask them what they thought should be done. It came as a big shock. Many never recovered. Moreover, because we had been providing them with answers, they had difficulty finding their own. We had trained their incapacity.

We missed several significant business opportunities because senior people didn't know what to do. We learned that great coaches did more than ask questions and not give answers. Great coaches had to provide guidance so people could find the "right" answer.

Seeking to provide more guidance, we engaged each person in continuing conversations about identifying and measuring great performance for individual jobs. We still asked questions and worked to not provide answers, but this time we focused conversations on great performance. This improved performance but still left many people feeling insecure and unclear about what constituted great performance. We didn't want to provide the answers. We needed a better set of questions to provide more focus.

One day it finally hit us. The real experts in great performance are customers. Everything begins with delighting customers. That's why every one of our job descriptions begins with the statement, "The things I do to get and keep customers are. . . ."

The situation improved when we modified our focus to the following question: "From the customer's point of view, what is great performance?" The employees finally had a way to receive answers to their questions from true experts in what they had to do. As such, they felt more focused and secure.

There is risk in making people too secure, however. Coaches help people see beyond where they are now. Coaches help people see what they *can be*, which is usually much more than what they are now. The view of the tomorrow that *must be* creates discomfort. Nevertheless, discomfort leads to learning and growth. Hear the discomfort and learning that happened in the following anecdote.

A president worked in a very competitive industry. The firm had had a particularly difficult time in recent years and had averaged less than 1 percent net profit margin on sales over the past three years. Last year it averaged 0.5 percent. The CEO had established the goal for this year as a 0.7 percent return on sales.

We asked him if he was satisfied with this return. "Well," he said, "that's not bad. Competition's tough. We've come back from a very bad period. I think that's all we can achieve."

We asked, "Is that really great performance?"

"Well," he replied hesitantly, "maybe we could be a little better than that. Industry average is about 1.1 percent. We even did 1.2 percent once. So maybe 1.3 percent would be great performance."

"Maybe," we replied. "What do the best locations in your industry make?"

"We have locations in our company that make 2.26 percent, 2.08 percent, and several that make between 1.75 and 2.00 percent. One of our competitors has a location that makes a little better than 3 percent. When I think about it, I guess we can do better than 0.7 percent. Now that I think about it, 1.1 percent would be great performance for this year, and 2 percent plus next year would be fantastic."

"That will bring you closer to the best in your business," we responded, "but is that *great* performance? Is that as much margin as you can make? Look, how much do credits cost?" (Credits are returned merchandise, almost always because of shipping or order packing errors.)

After some time searching through papers he replied, "They run about 4 percent."

"How would your margin look if you eliminated all the credits?" we asked.

After some calculation he responded, "3.1 percent."

"So, if you could have zero credits, you could be the best in your industry, right? Why can't you do that?" we asked.

"I don't know why we can't," he said. "In fact. I'm sure we can. We just never thought about it before. We've assumed that credits were a 'normal' part of business."

Listen to how this CEO's low level of expectation yields a low level of return: "The best we can achieve is 0.7 percent; 1.1 percent is great performance; 2.0 percent is fantastic." Yet achieving zero defects in his packing and shipping departments alone could give multiples of that return. How much more money he could make by improving other areas of his operation remain unknown. Coaching questions helped him raise his expectations so he could become more of what he could be, which was far greater than he ever imagined. When you set the high-jump bar at five feet, your performance is average. When you set that bar at eight feet, you put in a gold-medal-winning performance. Moreover, you'd better be able to clear eight feet, one inch, because that's where the record probably will be next year. As one athlete put it, "They keep raising the bar all the time." As a coach you help people raise their expectations high enough to encourage great performance today and even greater performance tomorrow.

◆ **The Leadership Function: Learning**

Leaders learn fast and keep on learning. The world changes so quickly that we need to keep learning new things just so we can cope. Success is a valuable teacher, provided it does not lull us into complacency. Whatever put us where we are will not take us where we need to go. Circumstances change; leaders must change also, or be left behind. The skills learned to be a good supervisor will not help anyone be a good president. Continued learning is crucial to continued success.

Most armies are perfectly designed to fight the last war, especially if they were victorious in that war. The English destroyed the French nobility at Agincourt in one of the most lopsided victories ever recorded. The French wore armor that made them slow-moving targets for the English, who had longbows powerful enough to pierce it. While the French were forced to fight on the plain, the English fought safely from the hills.

The French knights liked their armor. It gave them status. They knew about the longbow, but they didn't want to change. The longbow transformed their armor—their source of safety and status—into a shiny coffin. One can imagine them discussing the topic before the battle. It probably went something like this:

> GENERAL: Men, we're fighting the English tomorrow. They'll be tough but we're the finest knights in the world. *We will prevail.*
>
> YOUNG KNIGHT: But Sir, the English have longbows. Their arrows can go right through this tin foil.
>
> GENERAL: Nonsense! My father fought in armor. My grandfather fought in armor. My family has fought in armor for 15 generations.
>
> YOUNG KNIGHT: But, sir, times have changed. . . .
>
> GENERAL: Quiet! Don't say another word. That's an order. I've been fighting like this for thirty years and if I haven't learned anything else, I've learned one thing: *If it ain't broke, don't fix it.*

The general was trapped. He had become a general by fighting a certain way. He couldn't change the ideas that had made him successful all his life.

England went on to develop a great empire; success, with the accompanying complacency, became its biggest enemy. In World War I, the English had the chance to pull the same trick again, this time in reverse. The English invented the tank in 1915. Its armor would have protected them against the German guns. Employed in strength, it would have breached the German lines, ended the war quickly, and saved many lives. But the English generals would have nothing to do with the tank. They had enjoyed unprecedented success for two-hundred years. They loved their heritage. They had lost what had put them there: the will to change and adapt to new circumstances. Without that will, they lost their empire.

Johnsonville Foods experienced the same "success malaise." One of us had become a national hero, lecturing around the world on how Johnsonville "did it." Sales grew, margins rose, and profit sharing bonuses increased. Then it happened. People took a deep breath and started to "tweak." Sales continued to rise but margins didn't; bonuses fell. The final blow came when Johnsonville sausage finished out of the running in a taste test in its local area. That experience awakened members to start learning again.

The mentality of "If it ain't broke, don't fix it" focuses on the present rather than the future. The present becomes the past overnight, and the future becomes the present all too soon. Success is the greatest enemy. We must keep learning new leadership skills, new leadership techniques, new leadership approaches, and new leadership paradigms.

We discovered the only way to change our leadership behavior was to learn how to lead differently. We thought we could just "turn on" the new behavior like you "turn on" a light bulb. If only it were that simple.

We hired a consultant to help us. His conclusion was devastating: "You are the problem," he told us. "You prevent people from really doing their jobs. You dominate meetings. You give your own solutions—sometimes even before the problem is raised. You finish other people's sentences. You state your opinions first. Who's going to argue with you? You cut people off. You change agendas during the meeting, raising issues no one else is prepared to discuss. People leave meetings feeling discouraged rather than energized. You insist on making every decision. No wonder people don't take responsibility. You won't let them."

We were stunned, particularly after we listened to several tape recordings of our meetings. But the consultant was right! We saw that our leadership behavior was counter-productive. So we said, "We'll change."

At the next meeting we tried to remain quiet. That lasted about three minutes. We tried to stop providing answers. That lasted about as long. It was tough being different. It was too easy for us to slip back into old leadership patterns. The staff, as much as they complained about the old us, liked the comfort of knowing what we were going to do. That helped them figure out what they needed to do. We all were trapped in this "death dance" of hating what we were doing but hating more the task of changing it.

To change our leadership behavior took conscious effort. First, we changed our mental picture of the leadership job. We stopped being the decision makers and micromanagers. We stopped deciding production schedules and fixing sales problems. Instead, we insisted that others handle those situations.

We needed new leadership skills to support this new leadership job definition. We inventoried what we needed to learn—and went to work to learn it. We worked on people development skills, such as asking questions rather than giving answers. Moreover, we extracted ourselves out of the decision-making and answer-providing loops. By deliberately scheduling ourselves out of production scheduling meetings and sales reviews, we encouraged people to decide those issues without us. Knowing that if we had the information about daily shortages, supplier problems, and such, we'd ask questions about it, we also stopped collecting detailed data about production and sales performance.

It wasn't easy for us to unlearn old leadership habits. We were afraid we'd have no real function to perform. Consultants and writers can talk glibly about coaching and question asking as the "new" leadership responsibilities. We were afraid that people wouldn't respect us if we didn't have quick, good answers. Asking questions looks impish. We still catch ourselves making decisions, telling people how to solve their problems. After all these years we still keep learning that we need to keep learning.

We don't know how to chart a course there. We just know we have to go. When we decided that we absolutely had to alter our management style we didn't know in detail how it would work. We knew we had to change. "How do we change?" and "What would the final change look like?" were questions to which we didn't have good answers. We knew that if we didn't start we'd never finish. If we waited until we had all the answers we'd be old and gray—and probably out of business.

When the head of Johnsonville Foods first stopped tasting the sausage, he didn't have a clear picture of what would happen next. He didn't know that the people would jump in and ask for production and quality data. He didn't know that they'd seize the opportunity to take more control over their work lives. He knew he had to change his style. His ceasing to taste the sausage was an opportunity for him to learn how to manage in a different way.

We did something when we started changing ourselves and the company that made it easier. We told our customers and people what we were trying to do and what it would mean for them. We told them we didn't know how to go there, but doing something was so important we were going to get started anyway. We said this meant we would probably make many mistakes, but nothing would be irreversible. We would make mistakes together and the minute a mistake became apparent we would fix it together. We gave ourselves and everyone else permission not to be perfect. Customers and the people saw our sense of urgency to improve. They knew it would no longer be business as usual.

Karl Marx had it right: those who hold capital exercise power. Today intellectual capital is the scarce resource, so the holders of that capital exert control. Henri Fayol is also correct. Managers plan, organize, command, coordinate, and control. Only now the managers who perform these functions are the holders of the intellectual capital. Leaders now perform the very different functions of transferring ownership, creating the ownership environment, coaching, and learning.

In this upside-down world, leaders lead and employees manage. Leaders who recognize this phenomenon and change their behavior will accrue power. Those who don't will pass from the scene.

READING 2

Zapp! The Lightning of Empowerment

William C. Byham with Jeff Cox
Summary prepared by Constance Campbell

Constance Campbell is an Assistant Professor of Management at Georgia Southern University and teaches in the areas of Management and Organizational Behavior. Her research interests include learned helplessness, attribution theory, creativity, and intrinsic motivation. Her research has been published in *Psychological Reports*, the *Journal of Social Behavior and Personality*, and the *Proceedings of the Decision Sciences Institute*. Dr. Campbell received her Ph.D. from Florida State University. She is active in the Academy of Management, the Southern Management Association, and the Decision Sciences Institute.

Zapp! The Lightning of Empowerment is aimed at improving quality, productivity, and employee satisfaction. It is a story about *empowerment* (employee feelings of ownership and personal interest in their jobs) written in the form of a fable containing dragons, trolls, Ralpholators, Sapps, Zapps, and (most importantly) Joe Mode's notebook.

Empowerment involves helping employees take ownership of their jobs. When this happens, they are more likely to take personal interest in improving the organization's performance. The book describes realistic and practical ways to empower people and uses the format of a fable to present its message.

The first part of the book, "Situation Normal," describes a typical organizational setting in which the workers are apathetic, the managers are antagonistic toward the workers, and productivity is marginal at best. However, one of the supervisors, Joe Mode, decides to try to improve the situation, with the help of one of the employees. "The Zapping of Dept. N" describes how Joe Mode empowers the people in his department. In Part Three, "Super-Charged Zapp," Joe Mode learns about the collective energy that is generated when groups are empowered to work together. Finally, in Part Four, "The Zapped Company," Joe Mode and his friends spread their empowerment ideas to the rest of the company. Contrary to the scenario in many fables, however, the characters in this fable do not ride off into the sunset and live happily ever af-

William C. Byham & Jeff Cox, *Zapp! The Lightning of Empowerment*. New York: Harmony Books, 1988.

186

ter. Instead, it becomes clear that empowerment is never a finished process. Throughout all of the sections, key ideas regarding empowerment are highlighted in part of Joe Mode's notebook. Each of these sections, including Joe Mode's discoveries, is described in more detail below.

❖ PART ONE: SITUATION NORMAL

In Part One, several characters are introduced who work in the Normal Company, a manufacturer of normalators, in Normalburg, USA. For example, Ralph Rosco, an employee in Normal Company, has been working on developing a revolutionary product, a Ralpholator. Ralph is trying to present his idea to his supervisor, Joe Mode, only to be rebuffed with three reasons that the Ralpholator is not a good idea:

1. It is not what Joe is supposed to be working on.
2. It is not the Normal way to do things.
3. If it really were a good idea, R & D would have already developed it.

Actually, Joe did not have time to worry about Ralph's invention, because Joe had enough problems of his own. With too much to do and not enough time to do it, Joe had been berated by his boss, Mary Ellen Krabofski, for not getting enough work done. Mary Ellen instructs Joe, in no uncertain terms, that he needs to crack the whip harder over his people to get more work out of them.

At the end of this trying day, Joe Mode goes back to his office to contemplate the events of the day and to record his thoughts in his notebook, as is his habit. This day he made entries about the problems he encountered in his job, ending with the lament that his employees rarely do more than the bare minimum. They never get excited about their work, and the results of his motivational efforts are short-lived. Joe could see no viable solution to his problems.

This is the state of life in Normal Company early in the fable: workers who are discouraged and supervisors who want to give up. But soon, things begin to change—due, in large part, to the fact that Ralph decides not to give up on his new idea. He continues working on it during all of his spare time and even some of his work time. Finally, Ralph's machine, the Ralpholator, is complete. With no one around to observe, Ralph decides to test his machine, sits down in the chair, flips a few switches, . . . and disappears. Later that same day, Joe Mode goes back to Ralph's work area and stumbles, literally, onto the Ralpholator, accidentally zapping himself to the same place that Ralph had gone, the twelfth dimension.

The 12th dimension is a place with fog and lightning, dragons and trolls, and fire and ice. As it turns out, as Ralph explains it to Joe, in the twelfth dimension one can see things "that we can't see in the normal world . . . like how people feel, what's going on in their minds, what it's like for them on the inside." With these kinds of visual abilities, Ralph and Joe discover that the people in their department, Dept. N, look pretty dark and dismal.

Joe begins to feel pretty dismal himself about the whole picture, until Ralph takes Joe to visit Dept. Z, where the people are glowing and happy. Ralph and Joe watch in amazement as one woman in the department grabs lightning bolts and ZAPPS the people in the department with them. When they are ZAPPed, Joe and Ralph are surprised to see that the Zapp not only doesn't hurt, but it actually increases the light in the people in the Department. It seems to give them added energy.

Naturally, Ralph and Joe are curious about this lightning, but before they have a chance to figure it out, Mary Ellen Krabofski, who is wandering around looking for Joe in Dept. N, manages to trip over the Ralpholator's extension cord and disconnect it from its power source. To their chagrin, this causes Ralph and Joe to become visible again, and they materialize right in the midst of Dept. Z. Standing there in the department, being very visible now, they are greeted by the woman who was Zapping people with lightning in the twelfth dimension, who asks if she can help them. After some fancy footwork (a.k.a. lying) by Joe, the woman, who is Lucy Storm, supervisor of the department, takes them on a tour of the department. During the tour they note that the workers in Dept. Z are productive and content, even though they are in jobs that do not appear to be very challenging at all.

Before Ralph and Joe can solve this puzzle, the tour of Dept. Z ends, and Ralph and Joe go back to their own department, where they find a stark contrast in attitudes from the place they had just seen. Mary Ellen Krabofski is still there, angry about her stumbling encounter with the Ralpholator, and just waiting to take it out on Joe and Ralph. As it happens, she mainly takes it out on Ralph, giving him a three-day suspension from work. Meanwhile, Joe goes back to his office to pick up his notebook once again. In trying to discern what the Zapp of lightning is that he saw flowing into people in the twelfth dimension, he decides to give the lightning a name, calling it *Zapp*, and describes it as "**a force that energizes people**" (p. 38).

Joe's next step is to try to find out how to Zapp people in his department. Of course, asking Lucy Storm for help might have been the easiest way to do it, but Joe had a rule against asking people for help, so Joe tried all sorts of things to Zapp people: Mr. Nice Guy, Mr. Mean Guy, and even Quality Circles. None of them worked. In fact, in looking over the long list of things that had been tried in his department and others, Joe found that they always worked in Lucy Storm's department, but there wasn't much consistency anywhere else. Joe concludes that Zapp is essential for the success of new ideas and programs, for they work with Zapp and they fail without it.

After his suspension time is over, Ralph comes back to work—not too happy to be there—until Joe convinces him to reassemble the Ralpholator so they can both learn about the Zapps. After reassembling the machine, Ralph disappears into the twelfth dimension. What he notices this time is not a Zapp, but a *Sapp*—a force that drains energy instead of giving it. From the twelfth dimension, Ralph watches Joe Sapp his people when he did not listen to them, when he took their problems away from them to solve them himself, and when he made decisions for them.

After further exploration, Ralph learns that Joe is not the only one Sapping people; others are doing it as well. Ralph tries to explain Sapps to Joe, but Joe does not believe it until he sees it himself. After his own trip into the twelfth dimension to observe Sapps, Joe identifies a list of *what Sapps people:*

◆ lack of trust

◆ not being listened to

◆ not enough feedback to judge one's success/failure

◆ overly-simplified jobs

When Joe and Ralph really think about this list, they realize that Zapp and Sapp are opposite sides of the same coin; that Zapp! gives power and Sapp!; takes it away. In contrasting Zapp and Sapp, Joe writes in his notebook items that people include: teams, recognition for ideas, support (approval, coaching, feedback, encouragement), and flexible controls. Joe decides to try to make his department more Zapped than Sapped.

❖ PART TWO: THE ZAPPING OF DEPT. N

Joe's first real effort at Zapping is to gather everyone and tell them that they are henceforth in control of their own jobs, will be making their own decisions, and should act like they own their jobs. Unfortunately, no one really understands what he means. However, they try it, with some deciding to take a break for the day. The abysmal failure of this approach causes Joe to conclude in his notebook that "**It is easy to Sapp. It is hard to Zapp**" (p. 66).

Ralph comes to Joe's rescue again, though, when he calls in constant reports from his newly-invented Ralphone in the twelfth dimension, and tells Joe that maintaining people's self-esteem is important. Joe decides to try it. Just like everything else he tries, Joe's first efforts at building self-esteem are clumsy at best, but he learns fairly quickly with practice and with help from Ralph that comments designed to built self-esteem must be sincere. It was an important discovery, learning the importance of people's self-esteem, so Joe wrote it in large letters in his notebook:

First Step of Zapp: Maintain Self-Esteem (p. 70).

But there were still other important ideas to learn. The next day, Ralph called on the Ralphone to report that he had discovered that Lucy Storm could Zapp people just by listening to them and then repeating back to the person a short summary of what had been said. Joe decided to try it in Dept. N. As usual, his first effort at listening was not a rousing success, but at least he did keep trying. With practice, he improved.

However, as Ralph and Joe were working on a problem one day, they discovered that merely listening was not enough. In addition to listening, it was important to respond with empathy, showing that the feeling behind the words was noted as well as the message. With that, Joe had discovered the second step of Zapp, which he wrote in large letters in his notebook:

Second Step of Zapp: Listen and Respond with Empathy (p. 78).

At this point, things were going well for Joe and Dept. N. Ralph could observe many more Zapps in the department during his times in the twelfth dimension. But then, one day, a huge dragon appeared. It was wiping out computer data, it was breaking important machines, and it was starting small fires all around the department. People in the department picked up a hose to extinguish the blazes started by the dragon, but, before they knew what happened, Joe Mode appeared on the scene, grabbed the fire hose himself, and took over the fight. Meanwhile, the employees, who no longer were in on the fight, went back to their routine or simply watched Joe practicing his heroics. Needless to say, the fires weren't extinguished effectively.

At the end of the day, a very tired and frustrated Joe approaches Ralph for some twelfth dimension help on how to deal with this situation. In answer, Ralph takes Joe to the twelfth dimension, where the dragon is wreaking havoc all around the company . . . until they arrive in Dept. Z, Lucy Storm's department. As you might have guessed, things were different there. Instead of fighting all of the fires herself, Lucy Storm was asking her people to pitch in and fight the fires together. This led Joe to a new realization, which he wrote in his notebook:

Third Step of Zapp: Ask for Help in Solving Problems (Seek ideas, suggestions, and information) (p. 89).

And so, of course, Joe tried it, although he got it only partly right. He enlisted people's help in coming up with some great solutions, but he took the projects away when it came to implementing the solutions. After thinking about it for a while, Joe realized that he had been taking away from people the responsibility for carrying out the plans. With some practice, he began to learn, and in his thinking process he was able to make a key discovery and record it in his notebook:

The Soul of Zapp! Offer Help Without Taking Responsibility (p. 97).

With everyone in Dept. N now getting Zapped on a regular basis, things were going rather smoothly. Except for one thing: Joe Mode was unhappy. He was worried about what people would do now that they were making the decisions. He knew that he would catch the heat from Mary Ellen Krabofski if something went wrong in the department. He began to realize that there still needed to be some control . . . but how? After several crises erupt in the department, Joe realizes that there is an appropriate amount of control to use, involving the proper balance between delegation and checking on how people are doing. He decides to tailor the amount of control to the situation.

Even then, all of the problems in Dept. N are not conquered. Another problem appears. People are enthusiastic in the department, they are Zapped, and they are working on projects. Unfortunately, though, they are working on the *wrong* projects. People are charged, but are not necessarily moving in the right direction. After thinking about it, Joe realizes that his department has no clear goals; people have been given no direction. So Joe decides to work on it. The goals that he developed had three parts:

1. "Key Result Area—The direction we want to go;"
2. "Measurement—A way to know we're moving in the right direction;"
3 "Goal—Something to tell us if we're there yet."

Once he got started, Joe had each person develop personal goals, which led to the accomplishment of departmental goals, which led to the accomplishment of company goals. This allowed everyone to see where they fit into the big picture. Soon Joe had initiated the use of feedback charts that kept track of progress toward goals. He even had people keeping track of their own feedback charts.

All was not perfect in Normalburg yet. Joe still had a problem with one of his employees, Mrs. Estello, who went on making mistake after mistake day after day, oblivious to the need to improve the quality of her work. When Joe's pleas for improvement fell on deaf ears, he finally realized that he should be more like a coach with her and less like a boss. He would go through the process of explaining why the job was important and how to do it, demonstrating how to do it, and then watching as Mrs. Estello did it to give her feedback on her performance. Finally, he would express confidence in her ability and agree on follow-up actions. After he took these steps, Mrs. Estello began to improve. All the while, Joe was making sure to notice when she did something right.

By this time, people were getting Zapped right and left in Joe Mode's department, and Joe realized one day that the nature of his job had changed dramatically. Instead of telling people what they should do, his role had become more of a facilitator. He discovered that he provided four things to his department: Direction, as in goals; Knowledge, as in training; Resources, as in facilities; and Support, as in encouragement. After reflecting on this, Joe realized that he was more of a Group Leader than a Supervisor. It was time to move on, time to move to Part Three.

❖ PART THREE: SUPER-CHARGED ZAPP!

It was time for Joe to go back to the Ralpholator and see what things looked like now in the twelfth dimension. When he arrived at Ralph's work station, he discovered that Ralph was already in the twelfth, so Joe took off, too, looking for Ralph. He found Ralph, with Lucy Storm, standing outside of the company observing how the company looked from the twelfth dimension. The company looked like a large imposing tower, but their own departments were fluid shapes that were in a process of continual transformation.

After a bit of discussion about this new finding, the three parted and went back to their areas, and time passed. Then one day Joe and Ralph discovered a new business area in Dept. Z, so they went to check on it. Instead of bolts of lightning, they were surprised to see wheels of lightning. The wheels did not just go from the supervisor to the employee, but they were generated by the group and went around the work group. After discussions with Lucy Storm,

Joe discovered that the key to generating these wheels of lightning was having people work in *semiautonomous teams,* where small groups of employees managed their own work affairs.

Joe decided to try it in his area. He used some of the same group leader skills with the teams that he had used to Zapp individuals. He provided direction, knowledge, resources, and support. Part of the knowledge he found that he needed to give people was in the form of training in "people skills," such as how to solve conflicts in the group, since they were working in teams instead of alone. Joe also found that he needed to train people in technology at the appropriate time but just before they needed it, not a long time before they needed it. After some initial rough spots, the groups became effective for the department, enZapping each other in the process of their work. Some of the functions the groups served were to deal with absenteeism and performance issues, schedule vacations, and improve quality and productivity.

With these groups working together and being supercharged in Dept. N, the next move was to focus on the total organization.

❖ PART FOUR: THE ZAPPED COMPANY

Things were going quite well in Depts. N and Z. In fact, from outside of the company in the twelfth dimension, their towers in the company castle looked more like starships prepared to fly away on some lofty errand. But, alas, they were being held to the ground by their attachment to the weighty gray castle that was the rest of the Normal Company.

A look inside the company showed a dismal situation. There were managers running around taking responsibility away from workers, Sapping them right and left. Mary Ellen Krabofski was especially busy driving around in the executive fire truck, taking away firehoses from people and putting out fires herself all around the company. A look at the customer service area indicated that the people there didn't seem to know how to service customers, and, furthermore, didn't seem to care.

After observing these scenes and other interactions around the company, Joe Mode, with the help of Ralph, made an interesting discovery. They discovered that the person's direct boss has the most influence over how Zapped an individual is. The next greatest amount of influence is held by the other people who affect the person's job, followed by top management, and then by the organization and its systems. Joe and Lucy had worked on number one, the direct boss part, but there was not much that they could do in their positions about other people, top management, and the organization. Except . . . talk to Mary Ellen Krabofski.

Now, by this time, everyone in Normal Company had noticed the improvements in Depts. Z and N. So it didn't take long to convince Mary Ellen to let them present their views. Joe and Lucy asked the Zapp teams to prepare a presentation. Their presentations were given with such enthusiasm that Mary

Ellen, being a rather intelligent person after all, decided to begin using the first three steps of Zapp herself:

1. Maintain self-esteem.
2. Listen and respond with empathy.
3. Ask for help in solving problems.

After some success with these three steps, she went straight to the soul of Zapp—offer help without taking responsibility. Since Mary Ellen was near the top of the company, she also realized that she needed to develop an environment where all people in the company could practice Zapp. Like Joe, she had to try and fail a few times, but she eventually became much better at Zapping.

As part of enZapping people, she encouraged under-utilized workers to form teams trying to develop new products for the business. She encouraged work teams to select their own members with guidance and assistance from Personnel, rather than having Personnel do the job completely. The customer service department even received training in how to Zapp the customers. Even old Ralph got to develop his Ralpholator for new product markets! In short, the whole place became Zapped, with lightning flowing everywhere.

Time goes by. A few years later, a rookie manager, Dave, shows up at Joe's office and wants to find out from Joe how to Zapp people. Dave reports that he has heard that Zapp is a source of energy that enables employees to seek and obtain continuous improvement in their jobs. In the process of showing Dave around, Joe let Dave know that this is not a "happily ever after" fable, because Zapp is not a destination (i.e., not a finished process) but a continuous journey. Joe suggests to Dave that he can start using Zapp by reading the notebook containing all of the main ideas, by seeking training in how to Zapp people, and by seeking continually to learn, grow, and improve.

READING 3

SuperLeadership: Leading Others to Lead Themselves

Charles C. Manz and Henry P. Sims Jr.
Summary prepared by Charles C. Manz and Henry P. Sims Jr.

Charles C. Manz is an Associate Professor of Strategic Management and Organization in the College of Business at Arizona State University. He holds a Ph.D. in organizational behavior from Pennsylvania State University. His professional publications and presentations concern topics such as self-leadership, vicarious learning, self-managing work groups, leadership, and group processes. He is the author of *The Art of Self-Leadership,* and coauthor of *SuperLeadership.*

Henry P. Sims Jr. is a Professor of Organizational Behavior at the University of Maryland. He has published in a variety of organization and management journals, and has been an active member of the Academy of Management. Professor Sims is the coauthor of *The Thinking Organization* (with Dennis Gioia) and *SuperLeadership* (with Charles C. Manz).

This review has two unique features. First, the authors are summarizing their own book, and there are some advantages to this unusual approach. Since the reviews in *The Manager's Bookshelf* are intended to provide an informative summary of contemporary management literature rather than a critical evaluation, the authors may be most qualified to do this. Nevertheless, "caveat emptor"—the reader is advised to look elsewhere for critical analyses.

A second notable feature is that the topic of the book—superleadership—is on the cutting edge of the most current thinking about modern organizations. At all levels of organizations and societies, leadership has become a critical issue.

Charles C. Manz and Henry P. Sims, Jr., *SuperLeadership: Leading Others to Lead Themselves.* New York: Prentice-Hall Press, 1989.

❖ PRIMARY LEADERSHIP PHILOSOPHY AND THEMES OF THE BOOK

When most of us think of leadership, we think of one person doing something to another person. This is "influence," and a leader is one who has the capability to influence another. A classic leader is sometimes described as "charismatic" or "heroic." The word "leader" itself conjures up visions of a striking figure on a rearing white horse, crying, "Follow me!" The leader is the one who has either power or authority to command others.

Many historical figures fit this mold: Alexander, Caesar, Napoleon, George Washington, and Churchill. Even today, Lee Iacocca's turnaround of Chrysler Corporation might be thought of as an act of heroic leadership. It is not difficult to think of Iacocca astride his white horse, and he is frequently thought of as "charismatic."

But is this heroic figure of the leader the most appropriate image of the organizational leader of today? Is there another model? We believe there is. We believe that in many modern situations, *the most appropriate leader is one who can lead others to lead themselves.*

Our viewpoint represents a departure from the dominant and, we think, incomplete view of leadership. Our position is that true leadership comes mainly from within a person, not from outside. At its best, external leadership provides a spark and supports the flame of the true inner leadership that dwells within each person. At its worst, it disrupts this internal process, causing damage to the person and the constituencies served by the leader.

Our focus is on a new form of leadership—one designed to facilitate the self-leadership energy within each person. This perspective suggests a new measure of a leader's strength—the ability to maximize the contributions of others through recognition of their right to guide their own destiny, rather than the ability to bend the will of others to one's own. Leading others to lead themselves means bringing out the best, but mainly in others, not just in oneself. This form of leadership brings out the best that lies within those that surround the leader.

Many organizations do not seem to understand how to go about bringing out the wealth of talent that each employee possesses. Many are still operating under a quasi-military model that encourages conformity and adherence, rather than emphasizing how leaders can lead others to lead themselves.

SuperLeadership presents a wide range of behavioral and cognitive strategies designed to lead others to lead themselves to excellence. Some representative themes of the process include the following:

◆ An important way to measure your own success is through the success of others.

◆ What makes you successful at one level can be counterproductive at a higher level.

◆ "This transition is even more difficult for me than other people—I started to realize that I better let some other people do some things and I better start looking at the big picture a little more."—Joseph Vincent Paterno.

◆ The strength of a leader is measured by the ability to facilitate the self-leadership of others—not the ability to bend the will of others to one's own.

◆ If you want to lead somebody, first lead yourself.

◆ The best of all leaders is the one who helps people so that, eventually, they don't need him or her.

◆ Give people a fish, and they will be fed for a day; teach them to fish, and they will be fed for a lifetime.

❖ A PRIMER ON SELF-LEADERSHIP

The primary focus of *SuperLeadership* is on facilitating the self-leadership of others. That is, the vehicle for exercising effective leadership is the facilitation of the inner leadership potential of followers. A primary premise is that everyone is a self-leader but not everyone is currently effective at the process. To achieve optimal success—to become a SuperLeader—the self-leadership of every person needs to be harnessed and enhanced.

Self-leadership can be defined as the influence we exert upon ourselves to achieve the self-motivation and the self-direction we need to perform. The self-leadership process consists of an array of behavioral and cognitive strategies for enhancing our own personal effectiveness. The SuperLeadership process in turn consists of a set of strategies for assisting followers in the development and practice of their own personal self-leadership skills.

Behavioral focused self-leadership strategies are specially designed to help individuals behave more effectively. Specifically, they include self-observation, self-goal setting, the management of cues, self-reward, self-punishment, and rehearsal. Each of these strategies, when practiced consistently and effectively, has been found to be related significantly to higher performance—except self-punishment. While self-punishment (e.g., guilt and self-criticism) can at times serve a useful purpose (we all need to have a conscience), it tends to have a demoralizing and destructive impact when overused. On the other hand, strategies such as setting challenging but achievable performance goals and rewarding ourselves (e.g., with self-praise) when we reach them tend to have a favorable impact on our performance. Also, observing and collecting useful information about our important behaviors and rehearsing (practicing) our planned performances before doing them "for keeps" can contribute to our effectiveness.

Nevertheless, even if we do achieve more effective behavior we cannot become optimally effective without establishing effective patterns of thinking. Consequently, self-leadership strategies also include methods for creating orientations toward work that facilitate a natural motivation to perform. That is, self-leaders can both physically and mentally redesign their own tasks to make them more naturally motivating. Other cognitive strategies are designed to assist us in analyzing and managing the assumptions we make about work-related issues. They also address approaches for harnessing the power of imagery and self-talk.

Part of the SuperLeadership approach is designed to assist and guide followers in the development of constructive patterns of thinking by helping them to master these *cognitive focused strategies*. Too often individuals can develop the habit of negative thinking, for example, that causes them to shrink in the face of potential obstacles because of inaccurate assumptions and dysfunctional self-talk and imaging that exaggerates potential risks and problems. Through the development of cognitive self-leadership skills we can learn to keep risks in better perspective and to experience more naturally motivating and positive work situations. A summary of the primary self-leadership strategies addressed in the book is provided in Figure 1.

❖ STRATEGIES OF SUPERLEADERSHIP

A major focus of this book is on tapping the potential of subordinates. From a SuperLeadership point of view every subordinate is viewed as a valuable resource and as a potentially effective self-leader. However, effective self-leadership consists of an extensive array of self-influence skills and strategies. While the perspective of the book is that everyone is already a self-leader—we all make choices that have an impact on our own behavior and effectiveness by the personal standards we set, the way we evaluate and react to our own performance, and so forth—not everyone is by nature an *effective* self-leader. On the contrary, most individuals have significant shortcomings in the way they influence themselves. And this is precisely why SuperLeadership (leading others to lead themselves effectively) is so important.

SuperLeadership consists of a practical set of strategies designed to bring out and develop the self-leadership potential of subordinates. The first strategy is to set a positive self-leadership *model* or example for subordinates. This means that the first step toward becoming a SuperLeader is to become an effective self-leader and then to display one's own effective self-leadership as a learning example for others. The effectiveness of this modeling process is enhanced to the extent that people can establish themselves as credible persons worthy of emulation. Also, the specific self-leadership skills should be displayed in a vivid and detailed manner.

A focus on *goals* is also an important part of the process. Subordinates need to develop skills in setting their own performance goals that are realistic and achievable. These goal-setting skills can be applied to developing self-leadership effectiveness. That is, goals to increase and improve self-leadership

FIGURE 1

SELF-LEADERSHIP STRATEGIES

❖ BEHAVIORAL FOCUSED STRATEGIES

Self-observation—observing and gathering information about specific behaviors that you have targeted for change

Self-set Goals—setting goals for your own work efforts

Management of Cues—arranging and altering cues in the work environment to facilitate your desired personal behaviors

Rehearsal—physical or mental practice of work activities before you actually perform them

Self-reward—providing yourself with personally valued rewards for completing desirable behaviors

Self-punishment—administering punishments to oneself for behaving in undesirable ways

❖ COGNITIVE FOCUSED STRATEGIES

Building Natural Rewards into Tasks—self-redesign of where and how you do your work to increase the level of natural rewards in your job. Natural rewards that are part of rather than separate from the work (i.e., the work, like a hobby, becomes the reward): result from activities that cause you to feel:

◆ a sense of competence
◆ a sense of self-control
◆ a sense of purpose

Focusing Thinking on Natural Rewards—purposely focusing your thinking on the naturally rewarding features of your work

Establishment of Effective Thought Patterns—establishing constructive and effective habits or patterns in your thinking (e.g., a tendency to search for opportunities rather than obstacles embedded in challenges) by managing your:

◆ beliefs and assumptions
◆ mental imagery
◆ internal self-talk

activity, in addition to personal performance goals, can be set. A subordinate in sales, for example, might set a goal to develop a self-leadership plan for increasing the motivation to prospect for new clients. The plan itself might consist of a monthly goal for the number of sales calls made, and the establishment of a reward (e.g., eating at a favorite restaurant) to be self-administered each time the goal is reached.

SuperLeadership also involves providing *encouragement* and *guidance* for subordinate self-leadership effectiveness. Through verbal encouragement and support for subordinate initiative and use of self-leadership strategies, the leader can generally stimulate subordinate self-leadership practice. In addition, the SuperLeader is an important source of guidance as these skills are developed. In part, the SuperLeader can accomplish this by practical explanation and instruction on self-leadership strategies. More often, however, this process is less direct. For example, a particularly effective technique is the use of questions that stimulate the follower to think about self-leadership. "What goal are you shooting for?" "How well do you feel you are doing?" "Wow, you sure did a great job on this assignment, are you going to celebrate?" or "How are you going to reward yourself?" and "Have you thought about how you might make your job more naturally motivating by changing the way you do your work?" are all examples of questions that will tend to stimulate thinking about self-leadership. Questions such as these can help indirectly guide subordinates' self-leadership thinking and development and also help them to design a customized approach to their own self-leadership.

Then, when subordinates display self-leadership, the SuperLeader will *reinforce* this desired behavior through praise or other available rewards. The key point here is that the focus of the reward process shifts to a particular focus on self-leadership behavior rather than just on higher performance. The reprimand process for undesired behavior, on the other hand, is left primarily to the subordinate. That is, a shift toward employee self-leadership requires a large degree of tolerance on the part of the leader to allow for subordinate mistakes and small failures that are an inevitable part of the development process. And when criticism does occur it should primarily come from the subordinate, though this too should not be excessive. Clearly, the available evidence indicates that the most effective behavior management approach is to reward successes and attempts to improve, rather than reprimand failures.

Finally, the SuperLeadership process involves the development of *self-leadership cultures* and *sociotechnical systems* that support subordinate growth and initiative. Much of this transition will occur naturally as the leader models, encourages, facilitates goals, guides, and reinforces subordinate self-leadership. Eventually, self-leadership is recognized by subordinates as something that is not only accepted but is expected within the work unit. And subordinates can come to serve as important sources of support for one another. In advanced self-leadership systems, for example, subordinates are often organized into teams that possess significant autonomy for managing themselves on a day-to-day basis. As the supporting values, beliefs, and system components that support self-leadership become more established, the

SuperLeadership process is greatly supported. The SuperLeader in turn is then especially able to enjoy the benefits of having dynamic, innovative self-leading subordinates.

❖ EXAMPLES OF SUPERLEADERSHIP IN PRACTICE: SOME CASES

Another feature of the book is the provision of real life cases—"Profiles in SuperLeadership"—that illustrate how SuperLeadership behaviors have been used by real leaders. Further, the text is enriched by the inclusion of many mini-cases and examples. Here is a sampling from three of the profiles: Joseph Paterno, William McKnight, and Dwight Eisenhower.

◆ JOSEPH VINCENT PATERNO

Joe Paterno is one of the winningest college football coaches in history. With a winning percentage of over eighty percent, his accomplishments as a football coach are strikingly impressive. He was honored as Coach of the Year after his team won college football's national championship in 1983, and Sportsman of the Year after the 1987 national championship. But Paterno is equally respected for his philosophy and opinions. Sometimes he seems more proud of the graduation rate of his players than he does of his own winning percentage.

In many ways Paterno's leadership style has demonstrated in real life the philosophy of SuperLeadership. In talking with Paterno we learned several things about the man that helped us better to understand his approach. First, Paterno's thoughts on coaching:

> A coach must be able to develop three things in an athlete; pride, poise, and confidence in himself. . . . The coach has to aim high, think big, and then make sure that the players aspire to the highest goals they can achieve. A coach has to be able to get people to reach up. As Browning wrote, "A man's reach should exceed his grasp, or what's a heaven for?"

Later, Paterno talked about allowing his assistants room for failure: "You can't grow (if you don't make mistakes). . . . I've got to give them a chance to do some things (on their own)." Paterno went on to reflect on some of the opportunities he was allowed to have to fail in his early coaching days, and how important they were. But then he also pointed out that there are limits to this strategy, depending on the severity of the consequences: "Ordinarily, a guy comes in and wants to try something. . . . you let him do it . . . but, [in] a big game, if he wants to try something you know won't work . . . I can't afford that kind of luxury."

Perhaps the most interesting aspect of Paterno's views on leadership is his natural inclination to *want* to control every aspect of the coaching process. Intellectually, however, he recognizes that this approach simply will not work, and so he discussed some internal struggles he has had in the past, and his evolution toward a more participatory style: "I can't tell you when it happened, but I started to realize that I better let some other people do some things and I better start looking at the big picture a little more. I've done it, and I've done more and more of it." As Paterno talked, it was apparent that this transition had been difficult. Those highly capable executives who (like Paterno) have been able to succeed in the past largely on their own abilities can easily find letting go of some control a difficult process. Yet, this transition is necessary, especially at higher levels of the organization. Paterno reflected that making this change in his style was probably more difficult for him than for others, but he nevertheless recognized that it needed to take place. The style that he has subsequently evolved in many ways is a model of SuperLeadership in action.

◆ William L. McKnight

3M Company is generally viewed as a model organization. It has been named to popular lists—"Excellent companies," "Best companies to work for," "Best-managed companies." Much of its success can be attributed to its style of management, which emphasizes autonomy and entrepreneurship in creating new ideas and developing them into useful, high-quality, and profitable products. A logical question that follows is, "How did this organization come to operate the way that it does?" The answer appears to lie largely in its history of leadership. And many say that it all began with William L. McKnight, one of 3M's earliest leaders.

3M employees point out that it all started with McKnight's faith in people; he gave his subordinates freedom early in their careers—a practice that is still followed. Among other things, today that translates into a chance for young entrepreneurs to make mistakes on the way to tomorrow's great discoveries. Indeed, McKnight's exemplary leadership style seems to stand for achieving excellence through the unleashing of the vast capabilities of employees. To understand better his leadership views, some of McKnight's comments over the years are particularly instructive. McKnight on delegation and initiative:

> As our business grows it becomes increasingly necessary to delegate responsibility and to encourage men and women to exercise their initiative. . . . Those men and women to whom we delegate authority and responsibility, if they are good people, are going to want to do their jobs in their own way. These are characteristics we want and should be encouraged. . . . Management that is destructively critical when mistakes are made kills initiative and it's essential that we have many people with initiative if we're to continue to grow.[1]

From a study of William McKnight's leadership style and philosophies, it is apparent that he had an underlying belief in the value and worth of every individual. He seemed to view each person as a valuable resource, and throughout his career he sought the input of employees, customers, and suppliers. In his early days in sales and eventually as national sales manager, for example, he advocated going beyond the front office and onto the shop floor. He reasoned that the workers that actually used 3M's products would be the most capable of providing information about their needs. This overarching philosophy carried over into his dealings with his employees as he moved through management to the helm of 3M.

Perhaps this overall belief in the integrity and potential in people is what caused him to place such a high value on initiative and self-reliance. In reflecting back regarding his career at 3M, McKnight would eventually comment, "We lose something valuable if we uproot all notion of personal self-reliance and the dignity of work. . . . To continue our progress and service to America and the world, we need a healthy appreciation of those who exercise the free man's option for excellence. . . ."[2] With these words and with his overall attitude and approach to dealing with people, McKnight epitomized a leader who believed in leading others to lead themselves to excellence.

◆ DWIGHT D. EISENHOWER

Dwight Eisenhower, hero of World War II, is considered by many historians as one of the greatest military leaders in history. His style, unlike that of the prototypical military leader who takes complete charge and commands and manipulates military units as though they were pieces on a chess board, was again powerfully indirect. He based his success on consistently encouraging, developing, and benefiting from the effectiveness of others. He gave much of the credit for his learned approach to leadership to leaders he served under early in his career. In particular, he singled out General George C. Marshall as an especially influential model. As an example, when Eisenhower proposed a Philippine strategy, Marshall praised his initiative. "Eisenhower, the department is filled with able men who analyze their problems well but feel compelled always to bring them to me for final solution. I must have assistants who will solve their own problems and tell me later what they have done."[3]

Throughout his career Eisenhower demonstrated this same familiar effective theme of believing in people, providing them with significant freedom, and helping them to develop and exercise their abilities. In 1967 he wrote,

> In our Army, it was thought that every private had at least a Second Lieutenant's gold bars somewhere in him and he was helped and encouraged to earn them. . . . I am inclined by nature to be optimistic about the capacity of a person to rise higher than he or she has thought possible once interest and ambition are aroused.[4]

With these words Eisenhower perhaps captured best the spirit of SuperLeadership.

❖ SUMMARY AND CONCLUSIONS

SuperLeadership provides a framework, a process, and a set of specific strategies to achieve people excellence in organizations. It is believed to be the most practical and effective means for reaching this objective within modern organizations. In a nutshell, it says that those managers and executives who want to become SuperLeaders can choose no better strategy than to facilitate and unleash the self-leadership potential of their subordinates. The authors believe that it is time to transcend the notion of leaders as heroes and instead *focus on leaders as hero-makers.* Leaders need first to learn to lead themselves and then to help others to do the same. In the process they will create an environment in which subordinates can achieve excellence and can themselves become SuperLeaders.

❖ NOTES

1. Minnesota Mining and Manufacturing Company, *Our Story so Far: Notes from the First 75 Years of 3M Company.* St. Paul, MN: Minnesota Mining and Manufacturing Company, 1977, p. 12.
2. Ibid., p. 130.
3. Stephen E. Ambrose, *The Supreme Commander: The War Years of General Dwight D. Eisenhower.* New York: Doubleday & Co., Inc., 1970, p. 134.
4. Dwight D. Eisenhower, *At Ease: Stories I Tell to Friends.* New York: Doubleday & Co., Inc., 1967, pp. 141–142.

8

TEAMS AND TEAMWORK

As organizations attempt to move forward in an increasingly hostile and competitive environment, more and more organizations are experimenting with and hoping to realize synergies associated with teamwork. Many organizations, influenced by the Japanese, have ventured into the use of employee involvement systems with problem-solving teams, such as quality control circles. Other organizations have made radical changes in their technologies, and some have organized around organizational processes by employing self-directed work teams. Butler Manufacturing, for example, has a team assembling an entire grain dryer; and at Hallmark a team of artists, writers, accountants, marketing, and lithographic personnel work together producing next year's Mother's Day cards, while another team works on cards for Father's Day.

Two readings in this section focus their attention on teams. The first, co-authored by Jon Katzenbach and Douglas Smith, is entitled *The Wisdom of Teams*. The second, *Empowered Teams*, was written by Richard S. Wellins, William C. Byham, and Jeanne M. Wilson.

In *The Wisdom of Teams*, Katzenbach and Smith argue that teams are the key to improving organizational performance. From a performance perspective teams are generally superior to individuals performing alone or in groups. As a consequence, they will be the building block of organizations in the future.

In their roles as senior consultants for McKinsey & Company, Katzenbach and Smith have worked on organizational performance practices. Drawing on their study of fifty different teams in thirty companies, the authors differentiate various levels of team performance, discuss where and how teams work best, and comment on how team effectiveness can be enhanced.

Many different approaches have been taken by organizations in their move toward the utilization of teams. Among them, it is common to hear about quality-control circles, quality-of-work-life programs, and joint labor-management teams. In *Empowered Teams*, Richard S. Wellins, William C. Byham, and Jeanne M. Wilson focus their attention on *self-directed work teams* (SDWT). SDWTs become empowered over time by taking on responsibilities that were once reserved for supervisors and their managers. SDWTs share management and leadership functions; plan, organize, direct, and control; work on improving their own production processes; set schedules; and hire replacement team members along with assuming the responsibility for a number of other human resource management functions. The authors discuss three basic themes: how teams work, how to prepare for teams, and how to build strong teams once they are in place.

Richard S. Wellins is Senior Vice President of Programs and Marketing for Development Dimensions International (DDI). William C. Byham is the President and CEO of DDI, a consulting firm providing human resource training programs and services. Jeanne M. Wilson is project manager for high-involvement clients at DDI. Wellins and Byham (with George Dixon) have also published *Inside Teams: How Twenty World-Class Organizations Are Winning Through Teamwork.*

READING 1

The Wisdom of Teams

Jon R. Katzenbach and Douglas K. Smith
Summary prepared by R. Warren Candy

R. Warren Candy is a Vice President of Minnesota Power, Duluth Minnesota, and General Manager of the Boswell Energy Center near Grand Rapids, Minnesota. He is responsible for implementing high-performance organizational improvements and change within the fast-changing utility marketplace. His areas of interest include teamwork, team building, high-performance leadership, and sociotechnical systems. He received his B.S. in Production Engineering from Swinburne College of Technology in Melbourne, Australia.

Fundamental change is needed in the way that managers and employees think about, and implement, performance improvements in the 1990s and beyond. Real teams hold the key to success. Real teams develop when groups of people work together with mutual support, joint accountability, trust-based relationships, and meaningful purpose with everyone being expected to think and grow.

❖ WHY ORGANIZATIONS NEED TEAMS

Teams outperform individuals acting alone or in large organizational groupings, especially when performance requires multiple skills, judgments, and experiences. Most people recognize the capabilities of teams, and most have the common sense to make teams work.

In exploring the use of teams, it becomes increasingly clear that the potential impact of single teams, as well as the collective impact of many teams, on the performance of large organizations is woefully underexploited. This is true despite the rapidly growing recognition of the need for what teams have to offer.

Jon R. Katzenbach & Douglas K. Smith, *The Wisdom of Teams*. Cambridge, MA: Harvard Business School, 1993.

Teams are more flexible than larger organizational groupings because they can be more quickly assembled, deployed, refocused, and disbanded, usually in ways that enhance rather than disrupt more permanent structures and processes. Teams are more productive than groups that have no clear performance objectives because their members are committed to delivering tangible performance results. Teams and performance are an unbeatable combination.

Most models of the organization of the future (e.g., networked, clustered, nonhierarchical, horizontal, are premised on the ability of *teams to surpass individuals as the primary performance unit in the company.* According to these predictions, when management seeks faster, better ways to best match resources to customer opportunity or competitive challenge, the critical building block will be at the team, not the individual, level.

Teams usually do outperform other groups and individuals. They represent one of the best ways to support the broad-based changes necessary for the high-performing organization. Executives who really believe that behaviorally based characteristics (such as quality, innovation, cost effectiveness, and customer service) will help build a sustainable competitive advantage will give their top priority to the development of team performance.

The good news is that there is a discipline to teams that, if rigorously followed, can transform reluctance into team performance. The bad news is that, like all disciplines, the price of success is strict adherence and practice. Very few people lose weight, quit smoking, or learn to play the piano or golf without constant practice and discipline.

❖ KEY LESSONS LEARNED ABOUT TEAMS AND TEAM PERFORMANCE

What do we know about teams? Eight lessons stand out:

◆ No team arises without a performance challenge that is meaningful to those involved.

◆ Performance is the crux of the matter for teams, including teams who recommend things, teams who make or do things, and teams who run or manage things.

◆ Organizational leaders can foster team performance best by building a strong performance ethic, rather than by establishing a team-promoting environment alone.

◆ Real teams are much more likely to flourish if leaders aim their sights on performance results rather than balance the needs of customers, employees, and shareholders. Clarity of purpose and goals have tremendous power in our ever more change-driven world.

◆ Most people at all organizational levels understand that job security depends on customer satisfaction and financial performance and are willing to be measured and rewarded accordingly. What is perhaps less appreciated, but equally true, is how the opportunity to meet clearly stated customer and financial needs enriches jobs and leads to performance growth.

◆ Biases toward individualism exist but need not get in the way of team performance.

◆ Teams are not opposed to individual performance. Real teams always find ways for individuals to contribute and thereby gain distinction. Indeed, when harnessed to a common team purpose and goal(s), our need to distinguish ourselves as individuals becomes a powerful engine for team performance.

◆ Discipline, both within the team and across the organization, creates the conditions for team performance. Any group seeking team performance for itself, like any leader seeking to build strong performance standards across the organization, must focus sharply on performance. For organizational leaders, this entails making clean and consistent demands that reflect the needs of customers, shareholders, and employees, and then holding themselves and the organization relentlessly accountable.

Several well-known phenomena explain why teams perform well. First, they bring together *complementary skills and experiences* that, by definition, exceed those of any individual on the team. This broader mix of skills and know-how enables teams to respond to multifaceted challenges like innovation, quality and customer service. Second, in jointly developing clear goals and approaches, teams establish *communications that support real-time problem solving and initiative*. Teams are flexible and responsive to changing events and demands. As a result, teams can adjust their approach to new information and challenges with greater speed, accuracy, and effectiveness than can individuals caught in the web of larger organizational connections. Third, teams provide a unique *social dimension* that enhances the economic and administrative aspects of work. Real teams do not develop until the people in them work hard to overcome barriers that stand in the way of collective performance. Finally, *teams have more fun*. This is not a trivial point, because the kind of fun they have is integral to their performance. People on real teams consistently and without prompting emphasize the fun aspects of their work together.

❖ WHAT IS A REAL TEAM AND HOW DOES IT DEVELOP?

A real team is a small number of people with complementary skills who are committed to a common purpose, performance goals, and working approach for which they hold themselves mutually accountable.

The team is a basic unit of performance for most organizations. It melds together the skills, experiences, and insights of several people. It is the natural complement to individual initiative and achievement because it engenders higher levels of commitment to common ends. Increasingly, we find management looking to teams throughout the organization to strengthen performance capabilities. A "team" is *not* a group of people working together. Unlike teams, working groups rely on the sum of "individual bests" for their performance. They pursue no collective work products requiring joint effort.

New teams evolve in five transition stages from "working group" to "high-performing team." In the early stages of development, performance often suffers before significant gains occur and stabilize.

1. *Working group* This is a group for which there is *no significant incremental performance need* or opportunity that would require it to become a team. The members interact primarily to share information, best practices, or perspectives, and to make decisions to help each individual perform within their area of responsibility. Beyond that, there is no realistic or truly desired "small group" common purpose, incremental performance goals, or joint work-products that call for either a team approach or mutual accountability.

2. *Pseudo-team* This is a group for which there could be a significant, incremental performance need or opportunity, but *it has not focused on collective performance and is not really trying to achieve it.* It has no interest in shaping a common purpose or set of performance goals, even though it may call itself a team. Pseudo-teams are the weakest of all groups in terms of performance impact. They almost always contribute less to company performance needs than working groups because their interactions detract from each member's individual performance, without delivering any joint benefit. In pseudo-teams, the sum of the whole is less than the potential of the individual parts.

3. *Potential team* This is a group for which a significant, incremental performance need exists and *that is trying to improve its performance impact.* Typically, however, it requires more clarity about purpose, goals, or work-products; more discipline in hammering out a common working approach, and collective accountability.

4. *Real team* This is a small number of people with complementary skills who *are equally committed to a common purpose, goal(s), and working approach for which they hold themselves mutually accountable.* Real teams are a basic unit of performance.

5. *High-performance team* This is a group that meets all the conditions of real teams and has *members who are also deeply committed to one another's personal growth and success.* That commitment usually transcends the team. The high-performance team significantly outperforms all other like teams and outperforms all reasonable expectations given its membership.

❖ TEAMS AND TEAM PERFORMANCE

A number of factors characterize "real teams." Some of these factors are intuitively known, while others are less obvious. Commonsense findings:

- A demanding performance challenge tends to create a team.
- The disciplined application of "team basics" is often overlooked.
- Team performance opportunities exist in all parts of the organization.
- Teams at the top are the most difficult to create.
- Most organizations intrinsically prefer individual over group (team) accountability.

Uncommon findings:

- Companies with strong performance standards seem to spawn more "real teams" than companies that promote teams *per se.*
- High-performance teams are extremely rare.
- Hierarchy and teams go together almost as well as teams and performance.
- Teams naturally integrate performance and learning.
- Teams are the primary unit of performance for more and more organizations.

❖ COMMON APPROACHES TO BUILDING TEAM PERFORMANCE

Teams can be created, developed, and maintained as long as a number of key ingredients are present:

1. *Urgency and direction are established.* Team members must believe the team has an urgent and worthwhile purpose; team members want to know what is expected of them.
2. *Members are selected based on skills and skill potential, not personalities.* The team members must have the complementary skills needed to do their jobs.
3. *Particular attention is paid to first meetings and actions.* Initial impressions are important.
4. *Clear rules of behaviors are established.* All real teams develop rules of conduct to help them achieve their purpose and performance goals.
5. *Immediate, performance-oriented tasks and goals are established.* Most teams trace their advancement to key performance-oriented events that forge them together.
6. *The group is regularly challenged with fresh facts and information.* New information causes a team to redefine and enrich its understanding of the performance challenge.
7. *Time is spent together.* Teams must spend a lot of time together, especially at the beginning.
8. *The power of positive feedback, recognition, and reward are exploited.* Positive reinforcement works as well in a team context as elsewhere.

❖ CONCLUSION

At the heart of the definition of *team* lies a fundamental premise that teams and performance are inextricably connected. Truly committed teams are the most productive performance-improvement technique that management has at its disposal—*provided there are specific results for which the team is collectively responsible and accountable, and provided the performance ethic of the company demands those results.* Within an organization, no single factor is more critical to the generation of effective teams than the clarity and consistency of the company's overall performance standards, or "performance ethic."

Within a team, nothing is more important than each team member's commitment to a common purpose and set of related performance goals for which the group holds itself accountable. Each member must believe the team's purpose is important to the success of the company, and they must collectively keep each other honest in assessing their results relative to that purpose. It is insufficient just to put "the monkey on the back" of each individual member; the *same* monkey must be put on their backs as a whole.

Specific performance goals are an integral part of this process. Transforming broad directives into specific and measurable performance goals is the surest first step for a team trying to shape a common purpose meaningful to its members. Specific goals provide clear and tangible footholds for teams while creating the measurement system for team accountability

At its core, team accountability is about the sincere promises that we make to ourselves and others. These promises underpin two critical aspects of teams: commitment and trust. By promising to hold ourselves accountable to the team's goals, members each earn the right to express their views about all aspects of the team's effort and to have others' views also receive a fair and constructive hearing.

Real teams are deeply committed to their purpose, to their goals, and to their approach. Team members are very committed to one another, and all understand that the wisdom of teams comes with a focus on collective work products, personal growth, and performance-oriented results. These all come from pursuing demanding performance challenges. When you observe a group of people who are truly committed, accountable for joint results, share a strong team purpose, and have embraced a common problem-solving approach, you know that you are seeing a "real team" in action.

READING 2

Empowered Teams

Richard S. Wellins, William C. Byham, and
Jeanne M. Wilson
Summary prepared by Cathy Hanson

Cathy Hanson is an MBA student at the University of Southern California; she has worked for over seven years in human resources. This experience included assisting with the start-up of two team-based manufacturing plants for Kraft General Foods.

What are self-directed work teams? Why are many of today's organizations moving toward teams? How do organizations implement teams? What are the roles of management, administration, and subordinates in a self-directed work team? These are some of the questions addressed here.

The buzzword in many organizations today is self-directed work teams. Many organizations realize that a distinct business advantage accompanies empowering their employees through teams. For organizations just starting this journey or those who are well on their way, many questions arise, and the search for answers can be overwhelming. Managers need to know how teams work, how to prepare for them, and how to build strong teams once they are in place. The information shared in this book comes from a variety of sources: a national survey, research, review of literature, and experience the authors have gained by working with teams.

❖ HOW TEAMS WORK

A self-directed work team (SDWT) is an intact group of employees who are responsible for a whole work process or segment that delivers a product or service to an internal or external customer. Some characteristics that differentiate SDWTs from other work teams include the following: SDWTs share

Richard S. Wellins, William C. Byham, and Jeanne M. Wilson, *Empowered Teams*. San Francisco: Jossey-Bass, 1991.

management and leadership functions; they plan, control, and improve their work processes; they set their own schedules; and they hire replacements for their team.

Organizations are moving toward teams for a variety of reasons. Many organizations report improved quality of products and service; greater flexibility; reduced operating costs; faster response to technological change; and the ability to attract and retain quality employees.

Self-directed work teams become empowered over time by taking on additional responsibilities that were once reserved for supervisors or managers. There are four levels of responsibility/authority that over time increase as the teams become more mature and able to handle greater responsibilities. At level one, the teams may take on the responsibility for administering and training fellow team members. At level four, the teams may be conducting performance appraisals, budgeting, and working on product development and modification.

The journey to SDWTs does not happen overnight. Many organizations report that SDWTs take between two and five years to develop, with many bumps along the way.

The term *self-direction* may imply that organizations with teams are organizations without leadership. This idea is simply not true. SDWT organizations share leadership responsibility with the teams. The amount of responsibility teams have varies from organization to organization. Another assumption is that these organizations have fewer people. This idea is not necessarily true; these organizations may have fewer managers and supervisors but the number of people may remain the same. Managers and supervisors can support the team by becoming trainers, team facilitators, and technical experts.

Redesigning an organization into teams is neither simple nor easy to explain, and there is no such thing as a typical team. Teams vary from organization-to-organization and sometimes across departments. Several key issues focus on how SDWT's work in redesigned organizations. The following discussion addresses a few of these questions and issues.

◆ NUMBER OF PEOPLE IN SDWTs

One of the questions often asked concerns how many people in an organization work in SDWTs. According to the authors' survey, 26 percent of organizations use teams. However, only a small percent of the workforce in these organizations is functioning in teams. Of the companies surveyed, teams were found mostly in manufacturing (80 percent). However, some organizations are organizing their white-collar workforce into teams as well.

◆ TITLES

What's in a title? In organizations that are moving toward teams, titles signify the change. Titles such as *employee* and *subordinate* are replaced with *team member* and *associate*. Supervisors' titles also change to *coach, team leader,* and *communicator*.

◆ SIZE

Team size varies; our survey indicated that the ideal size is from six to twelve people. Size is determined by the work process (with positions and functions fit together logically); research says that it is better to keep teams on the small side.

◆ MULTISKILLING

Many team organizations embrace *multiskilling* and job rotation. The advantages to the organization of having multiskilled team members and members who rotate jobs include greater flexibility and team members who understand the challenges faced by others on the team. Team members also have a better understanding of the total process and how each job contributes to the whole.

◆ SUPPORT

Support functions in the team environment have the philosophy of "we serve the team" and often work with coordinators in the team who take the expertise supplied by the functions back to the team. Teams may also integrate the functions into the work teams.

◆ COMMITTEES

Team members may participate on company-wide committees. The decisions these committees make, such as choosing training programs and preparing the annual business plans, affect all teams. Usually, one person from each team serves on the company-wide team.

Other nontraditional activities in which team members may participate include performance appraisals of fellow team members, interviewing new team members, and addressing performance and discipline issues.

❖ PREPARING FOR TEAMS

Deciding to implement teams is no small task; it requires involvement and commitment at all levels of the organization. Senior management must first work on implementing a new vision. The team concept must fit into the overall organizational structure and overall business objectives.

Three groups make strategic decisions when implementing teams. These include senior management, the steering committee, and the design team. After senior management has determined that the team concept fits into its goals and objectives, they play a key role in initiating the implementation.

Senior management is responsible for articulating the vision, deciding whether teams should be studied further, and providing the steering committee and design team with guidance. Senior management must also assess the long-term business needs and define the role of teams within the overall organization, determine if the organization's vision and values are compatible with the team, and determine the membership and responsibilities of the steering committee.

The *steering committee* is usually composed of upper and middle management, union representatives, team leaders, and in some cases prospective team members. This group takes the vision and direction provided by senior management and oversees the design effort. They often develop a team charter, provide the link between the teams and the organization, and protect the design process from negative influences.

The *design team* may be composed of members of the steering team, but will also include supervisors, human resource personnel, union officials, team members, and other functional representatives. This team plans the implementation strategy and acts as the champion of the team concept effort. This group will bring the details to the SDWT plan.

If the design team chooses, it may use the *sociotechnical analysis process*. This process involves four steps:

1. *Technical analysis*—looks at who works with the organization (customers, suppliers, etc.) and their expectations; this analysis also includes the process and technology that will be used.

2. *Social analysis*—looks at the roles, responsibilities, and tasks that need to be performed in order to produce the product or provide the service. The analysis is then used to create jobs with meaningful content. This analysis also includes how supervisor and manager roles can be transferred to the team.

3. *Joint optimization*—the information obtained in the technical and social analysis is compiled to optimize both the technical and social systems.

4. *Agreement on process and result measures*—conclusions are reached within the design team as to what will be measured and how it will be measured. These measures should be implemented at the start of the SDWT process.

SDWTs can be implemented in an organization in the following three ways:

◆ Create a pilot area where a single SDWT is started and evaluated.
◆ Phase-in teams by developing a plan to roll them out sequentially.
◆ Total immersion, wherein the organization/plant as a whole implements teams; this is often the approach in new plant start-ups.

Each approach has advantages and disadvantages associated with it. The approach an organization chooses depends on the organization's needs.

During the implementation of the team concept, supervisors and managers often wonder how their roles will change and whether or not there will be places for them. Many organizations are changing the roles of supervisors and managers by replacing responsibilities that are transferred to the team with new ones that were formally held by upper management. The supervisors may also take on coaching more teams as the teams absorb some of the supervisors' responsibilities.

◆ SELECTION

A critical step in the success of SDWTs is selection of team players, or identifying individuals who can work well together. The selection system in team-based organizations often differs from that of a traditional organization in many ways. In a team-based organization, team members often participate in the selection of other team members and support staff. Also, different criteria may be used in a team-based organization. Emphasis on how well the person works with others when solving a problem, technical *aptitude,* and desire to work in a team environment are examples of the criteria applied. Sometime during the selection process the candidate is given a realistic picture of the job and what it's like to work in a team environment. Since the criteria tend to be more extensive than in a traditional system, the selection ratio in a start-up operation is often as large as 20 to 1.

When an organization is developing the selection system, the first place to start is by conducting a detailed job analysis. This analysis will give the organization a list of behaviors, skills, and knowledge (dimensions) that an incumbent must possess in order to be successful in that position. (This analysis is also the basis for many human resource systems besides selection, such as performance appraisal and training.)

There are many tools to help organizations select team members. One tool, popular when selecting supervisors and managers, is the *assessment center.* This method consists of three types of simulations:

1. *Problem-solving simulation* An applicant is posed with a problem (production or service related) and asked to gather relevant information and make a decision regarding this problem in a given time period.
2. *Manufacturing simulation* Applicants are given a situation typically found in a manufacturing environment and asked to simulate the situation as if they were in this environment. This activity can provide opportunities to demonstrate teamwork, problem-solving ability, learning ability, and work pace.
3. *Group-discussion simulation* Short case studies are given to small leaderless groups of applicants; they are instructed to develop a solution by consensus. No roles are assigned in the group.

Another tool used in team selection is *video orientation.* Through a videotape, applicants are given a realistic job preview, showing what the various jobs are like and what it's like to work in the team environment. Ideally, people who would not like to work in this environment self select themselves out of the process. This method also allows an organization to begin building excitement for those who like this environment and to let them know what to expect in the selection process.

The *self-report inventory* requires applicants to answer questions regarding their preferences toward the work environment. These inventories show the applicant's desire to work in a team and the organizational environment that goes along with teams.

Cognitive ability tests can also play a critical role in team selection. These tests assess the applicant's ability to learn the technical aspects of the job. *Technical skills tests* are usually conducted in two parts. The first part is a paper-and-pencil test and the second part is observing the applicant perform technically. These tests assess the applicant's technical skills.

The interviewing technique often used by team organizations differs from traditional interviewing in several ways. The most obvious difference is that team-based organizations often call their interviewing system "targeted interviewing." As the name implies, *targeted interviewing* focuses on gathering facts versus theoretical information about the applicant. The questions in targeted interviewing focus on behavior by asking applicants how they have handled similar situations in the past. The underlying premise is that past behavior predicts future behavior.

When developing the selection system in team-based organizations, a combination of these methods may be used. From the job analysis, dimensions are developed, and each selection method evaluates one or more dimensions. Two different methods may assess the same dimension.

◆ TRAINING

Training the new teams can be quite an undertaking. However, the lack of training is the number one barrier to successful team implementation. Most training can be organized into three categories: job skills, team/interactive skills, and quality action skills. These categories have a multiplicative effect on one another. So, increasing the team skills in one area by even a little can increase the team's effectiveness substantially. When planning training for team members, the focus should be on two areas:

1. The core set of skills that must be provided to all team members: team/interactive skills, quality action training, and job-specific skills. Examples of team/interactive skills include training on handling conflict and on how to teach job skills to other team members. Examples of quality action training include identifying improvement opportunities and developing and selecting solutions. Job-skills training focuses on the specifics of performing the job.

2. Ongoing training that occurs at the "teachable moment." The *teachable moment* is the moment when the trainee is most apt to understand, internalize, and apply the learnings. Training is also needed for team leaders as

well as for support staff. Team-leader training can focus on such areas as coaching skills to prepare the leaders for their changing role.

◆ BUILDING STRONG TEAMS

Team development can be measured by a comparison of the team with the following key factors of effective teams:

- *Commitment* Team members identify themselves with the team and are committed to team goals over their personal goals.
- *Trust* Team members believe in each other and are willing to uphold their commitments to the team.
- *Purpose* Team members see how they fit into the organization and believe they can make a difference.
- *Communication* Team members communicate among themselves as well as with others outside the team.
- *Involvement* Each team member has a role on the team. The team reaches decisions through consensus.
- *Process orientation* The team has several tools, such as problem-solving and planning techniques, to help them attain their goals.

Teams go through four stages as they develop into self-directed work teams. Each stage can be measured in terms of the key factors.

STAGE ONE: **GETTING STARTED**   At this stage the team is not yet a team. Members don't know what to expect and are cautious about buying into the SDWT concept.

Key factors at stage one:

- *Commitment* Members are not yet fully committed to the team. They are cautious and not fully participating within the team.
- *Trust* Members are "feeling each other out." They have a wait-and-see attitude.
- *Purpose* While the team understands its purpose and mission, the mission is not a "living document."
- *Communication* The communication goes from leader to members and back again in the form of questions and answers.
- *Involvement* There are varying degrees of involvement. Assertive members may dominate.
- *Process orientation* The process is new and unfamiliar.

Helping the teams through stage one involves helping them to develop the team's identity and a sense of "teamness." This is usually done by having the team write a charter or mission statement.

***Stage Two:* Going in Circles**   At this stage the "honeymoon" is over, and the team struggles with "who does what?" and tends to pull apart. Managers struggle at this stage with how much responsibility to relinquish to the team. Key factors at stage two:

◆ *Commitment* Subgroup commitment exists but not to the team as a whole.

◆ *Trust* Members trust some and not others.

◆ *Purpose* Members are developing a purpose but still need guidance from others.

◆ *Communication* Conflicts may arise as individuals express their concerns.

◆ *Involvement* Domination by some members.

◆ *Process orientation* Some awkwardness in the use of a group's "standard" processes.

Helping the team through this stage involves letting the individuals know ahead of time what to expect. Reassurance that the team will work through stage two is important.

***Stage Three:* Getting on Course**   The team at this stage is more goal focused, and team members accept the diversity that is needed within the group to get the job done. The members may at this stage put the team and its members above others in the organization. Key factors at stage three:

◆ *Commitment* Team members are committed to getting the job done.

◆ *Trust* Faith in other members begins to solidify.

◆ *Purpose* Focus is on the achievement of team and performance goals.

◆ *Communication* Communication within the team is focused on tasks; the team begins to develop relationships with support groups.

◆ *Involvement* Team members are comfortable with their roles in the team.

◆ *Process orientation* Team members feel comfortable with the process.

Helping the team through stage three involves broadening the team's focus. This can be done by training in interdisciplinary groups, encouraging more customer/supplier contact, and setting up opportunities for the team to work with other levels within the organization.

***Stage Four:* Full Speed Ahead**   After several years of working together, the team may reach stage four. At this stage the team develops expectations about their "rights," such as being consulted on decisions that affect them. Key factors at stage four:

◆ *Commitment* Team members are committed to the team and to the organization.

◆ *Trust* Members trust each other.

◆ *Purpose* The team has a clear vision and mission; the team is able to change according to business demands.

◆ *Communication* Communication is complex and adjusted as needed.

◆ *Involvement* All individuals are highly involved; previously reluctant members are participating.

◆ *Process orientation* Team processes have become second nature.

Helping the team stay at this level can be even harder than helping the team through the earlier stages. The teams at this level need to learn more about the business through training. Teams at this stage may be interviewing new team members, hiring, or dealing with performance/disciplinary issues. One of the best ways to help the team stay at this level is to let the team serve as a mentor to other less-advanced teams.

Organizations wishing to implement teams should design careful, thoughtful, and well-planned implementations; set realistic goals; provide appropriate training; make teams part of an overall business strategy; and always look back and see where the team has been and recognize the accomplishments they have made.

9

◆   ◆   ◆

LEADERSHIP

$\mathbf{T}$his is the "decade of the leader." Nationally we seem to be looking for the hero who can turn us around, establish a new direction, and pull us through. Organizations are searching for visionary leaders—people who by the strength of their personalities can bring about a major organizational transformation. We hear calls for charismatic, transformational, and transactional leadership. A myriad of individuals charge that the problems with the American economy, declining organizational productivity, and lost ground in worldwide competitive markets are largely a function of poor management and the lack of good organizational leadership.

John Gardner, former U.S. Secretary of Health, Education, and Welfare, and currently the Miriam and Peter Haas Centennial Professor at Stanford Business School, is the author of *On Leadership*. In his book Gardner suggests that one of the biggest problems and challenges facing America today is one of leadership and the "issues behind the issues" of leadership (e.g., shared values, institutional renewal, and motivation). Gardner argues that the large-scale and complex organizations that dominate society tend to stifle those who enact roles within these social systems. Not only does Gardner highlight many of the grave problems challenging us, but he also provides insight into how we can make these organizations flexible and adaptive systems—much of which can be achieved through leadership.

Jay A. Conger is an Associate Professor of Organizational Behavior at the Faculty of Management, McGill University. His book *The Charismatic Leader: Behind the Mystique of Exceptional Leadership* provides illustrations of individuals like Steve Jobs, Lee Iacocca, Mary Kay Ash, John DeLorean, and Ross Perot to define the characteristics of the charismatic leader. Vision, articulation skills, empowerment, unconventionality, and risk-taking are attributes that Conger suggests set apart the charismatic from the noncharismatic leader. He details how the charismatic leader motivates others to act in a self-assured manner and to be willing to take risk. Conger has also published the books *Learning to Lead* and *Charismatic Leadership*.

Burt Nanus contends that the great leaders—individuals like Abraham Lincoln, Martin Luther King Jr., Alfred P. Sloan—are those who were able to develop a unique vision that attracted the commitment of others, inspired people, revitalized organizations, and mobilized the resources that were needed to make their visions a reality. *Vision,* according to Nanus, *is the key to leadership,* and it serves as the central theme of this work.

Burt Nanus is Professor of Management in the School of Business Administration at the University of Southern California. He is the Director of Research at USC's Leadership Institute and the author or coauthor of several other books focusing on leadership, including *The Leader's Edge* and *Leaders* (with Warren Bennis).

Peter Block, in his book *Stewardship,* argues that the environment confronting organizations today requires the replacement of traditional concepts of leadership and management with new ideas of stewardship. *Stewardship means empowering people to be accountable for their own actions,* rather than being dependent on leaders and managers. Stewardship is predicated on the notion that people in organizations are willing to choose service over self-interest.

In order to move toward the stewardship model, Block notes that the traditional pillars of management (i.e., an emphasis on control, consistency, and predictability) must be replaced, partnership must be created between employees and top management, and a new governance system and structure that integrates managing and doing the work must be created. Consistent with Manz and Sims' (see Part Seven) work on superleadership, and Wellins, Byham, and Wilson's focus on self-directed work teams, stewardship-based organizations stress a major role placed upon *self-management.*

Peter Block is a founding partner of Designed Learning, Inc., a training firm, and the consulting firm of Block Petrella Weisbord, Inc. A consultant to businesses, schools, and governments, he focuses on changing organizations. He is the author of *The Empowered Manager* and *Flawless Consulting.*

A wide array of other books on leadership have appeared. Alternative perspectives can be found in Tichy and Devanna's *The Transformational Leader;* Covey's *The Seven Habits of Highly Effective People* and his follow-up book, *Principle-Centered Leadership;* Koestenbaum's *Leadership: The Inner Side of Greatness;,* and Conger's *Learning to Lead: The Art of Transforming Managers into Leaders.*

READING 1

On Leadership

John W. Gardner
Summary prepared by James R. Meindl

James R. Meindl is an Associate Professor of Organization at the State University of New York at Buffalo, where he teaches and conducts research on organizational behavior, leadership, power, and justice. He received his M.A. and Ph.D. in social psychology from the University of Waterloo. He has served on the editorial boards of *Administrative Science Quarterly, Academy of Management Journal,* and *Academy of Management Review.*

On Leadership is the result of an intensive five-year field study of organizations and interviews with hundreds of contemporary leaders. Gardner attempts to illuminate aspects of leadership that may be useful as society faces many tough social, ecological, and economic problems. More frightening than the problems themselves are the questions they raise concerning our capacity to meet them. The institutions which have served us so well in the past have lost much of their capacity to focus our energies and to sustain our commitments to resolve tough problems. The fragmentation and divisiveness in American life have made it difficult for people to channel their efforts to any worthy common purpose. When motivation and confidence in our institutions slip too far, the efforts of leaders are gravely diminished. *The great challenge of leadership in America today*—in corporations, labor unions, schools, government agencies, and so forth—*is to renew and reinvigorate our human institutions,* with matters of motivation, values, social cohesion, and reawakening a sense of community as the real "issues behind the issues."

The book contains three major themes. The first few chapters describe and analyze what leadership is and is not. The middle chapters present ideas about the tasks, attributes, and morality of leadership within difficult social and institutional contexts. The last few chapters focus on leadership development.

John W. Gardner, *On Leadership.* New York: Free Press, 1989.

❖ THE NATURE AND TASKS OF LEADERSHIP

The concept of leadership too often carries near-mystical connotations. Thinking clearly about the topic requires a demystification of it. *Leadership* is a process by which an individual (or leadership team) induces a group to pursue objectives held by the leader or shared by the leader and his or her followers. Leadership ought not be confused with status, power, and official authority. High-ranking bureaucrats are not necessarily selected for their leadership skills; dictators can coerce their subjects; and officials have subordinates who often are not their followers.

◆ LEADERS VS. MANAGERS

The commonly used distinction between leaders and managers is misleading. First-class managers are often likely to possess a good measure of leadership as well. These leader/managers distinguish themselves from run-of-the-mill managers in that the former think in the longer term, they grasp how their unit fits within a larger system, they are able to influence others beyond their jurisdictions and thus can integrate fragmented constituencies, they emphasize intangibles such as vision, values, and intuition, they have good political skills in coping with conflict, and they think in terms of renewal, seeking to revise and improve the status quo. Such qualities, however, do not lead to a single profile or image of an idealized leader. There are many kinds of leaders with unique constellations of personal strengths and attributes, and their effectiveness often represents the matching of strengths with historical contexts and the particular contemporary settings in which they act.

◆ LEADERSHIP FUNCTIONS

There are at least ten significant functions of leadership, and leaders differ strikingly in terms of how well they perform them. The ten functions are: envisioning goals, affirming and regenerating important group values, motivating others toward collective goals, managing the processes through which collective goals can be reached, achieving unity of effort within a context of pluralism and diversity, creating an atmosphere of mutual trust, explaining and teaching, serving as a symbol of the group's identity, representing the group's interests to outside parties, and renewing and adapting the organization to a changing world.

The various tasks of leadership are intermingled in the complex interplay between leaders and their followers. In this relationship, leaders are never as much in command and followers never as submissive as one might imagine. Leaders and followers must shape each other. In such a process, two-way communication is extremely important, as is mutual trust. It is also true that failures of leadership are often also failures of followership; qualities such as apathy, passivity, and cynicism invite the abuse of power by the leader. The purposes of the group are best served when the leader enables followers to build their own initiative.

❖ THE CONTEXTS AND ATTRIBUTES OF LEADERSHIP

The interaction between leaders and followers does not take place in a vacuum, but it is located in a historic and cultural context, within some institutional setting. These contexts affect the nature of the interaction and the leadership attributes that are effective. Great leaders emerge because their attributes match the contexts in which they operate. In a contemporary world, the context is increasingly one of interdependence.

◆ LEADERSHIP ATTRIBUTES

Despite the interplay between contexts and personal attributes, there are some attributes which seem to be linked with higher probabilities that a leader in one situation could also lead in another. These include

1. Physical vitality and stamina
2. Intelligence and action-oriented judgment
3. Eagerness to accept responsibility
4. Task competence
5. Understanding of followers and their needs
6. Skill in dealing with people
7. Need for achievement
8. Capacity to motivate people
9. Courage and resolution
10. Trustworthiness
11. Decisiveness
12. Self-confidence
13. Assertiveness
14. Adaptability/flexibility

◆ LEADERSHIP AND POWER

Effective leaders must be willing to use the power available to them. Much leadership talent is lost because so many young people abhor the image of power as exemplified by leadership roles. If we are to attract more young people to leadership roles, we must show them more positive aspects of the leader's task. Power is, after all, ethically neutral.

Leaders and their exercise of power are ultimately judged within a moral framework of values. In the contemporary U.S., morally acceptable leaders can be defined in terms of their objectives with respect to the group and the individuals who comprise it. These include the release of human energy and talent, balancing individual interests and communal needs, adherence to a moral order, and active involvement of followers in the pursuit of group goals.

An important characteristic of contemporary leadership is the necessity for the leader to work with and through extremely complex organizations and institutions. The sheer size of organizations can create problems for a leader interested in creativity and change. Getting rid of turf fights, overcoming communication barriers, appropriate decentralization schemes with the proper allocation of functions, and maintaining high levels of motivation and initiative are a few of the problems that need to be resolved. Leaders need to take advantage of their strategic centrality, their agenda-setting powers, and their capacity to mobilize lower-level leaders to overcome the problems of large-scale organizational systems.

❖ COMMONWEAL INTERESTS AND RENEWAL

We live in a fragmented, rather than a tightly knit society. A central problem in a fragmented society is the war which takes place between narrow, parochial interests, and those of the common good. Pluralism places a special burden on leadership. The task for leaders is not just to work across boundaries to achieve the goals of their own groups, but to act in a way which supports commonweal interests. Networking, conflict resolution, coalition building, and political compromises are important to commonweal concerns.

◆ COMMUNITY-BUILDING SKILLS

Failures of leadership today are often traceable to a breakdown of community: a disintegration of coherence, continuity, and allegiance in American life. Skill in building and rebuilding a community is one of the highest and most essential skills a contemporary leader can command. Such skills must be aimed at creating the conditions which foster the development of community. These include:

1. Wholeness which incorporates diversity
2. Shared norms and values
3. Good internal communication among community groups
4. Attitudes of caring, trust, and teamwork
5. Institutionalized provisions for governance
6. Sharing of leadership tasks
7. Development of young people
8. Permeable boundaries to the outside world.

The effective contemporary leader lives with the idea of renewal, and overcomes the "trance of nonrenewal." Measures must be taken to enhance the possibility of renewal: enabling young leaders to move into positions where they can do the most good; periodically reassigning talented leaders; surrounding oneself with people who can motivate; creating a climate of experimentation and risk-taking; freeing-up communication; renewing self; and paying attention to the culture. Above all else, leaders must see their primary renewal task as the release of human energy and talent.

How can we define the role of leaders in a way that most effectively releases the creative energies of followers in the pursuit of shared purposes? The answer is that *leadership must be shared.* This begins with the notion of leadership teams, a circle of close advisors, but ought to extend down through all levels of an organization and to the farthest reaches of the system. It is important, though, even when leadership is distributed throughout a system, that power be held accountable. *The task is to design more empowering systems, but in a way that ensures accountability.*

❖ DEVELOPING LEADERS AND RELEASING THE HUMAN POTENTIAL

Where have all the great leaders gone? The Jeffersons and Lincolns of today *are* among us. There are many unawakened leaders who have neither felt an overpowering call to lead nor are yet aware of their own potential. These individuals require leadership development. Leadership can be taught and it can be learned. But most human talent along these lines remains undeveloped. As a result, our society faces a severely diminished supply of leaders today. Common obstacles include

1. Slowly developing crises as opposed to explosive ones which seem to call forth leadership talents.
2. The suppressive effects of large and complex organizations and communities.
3. The prestige of specialist, professional training.
4. An educational system which places too much emphasis on individual performance.
5. Negative publicity often associated with public office.

The leaders of today must nurture the development of tomorrow's potential leaders. Leadership development is a lifelong process. Traditional selection and recruiting are often incapable of identifying leadership potential. Organizational cultures also have invisible selection processes which may select out those with deep commitments to the group in favor of opportunistic careerists. Schools and colleges in particular need to take a more active role.

Higher education typically removes most young people from the mainstream of the American experience, at a time when they should be brought closer to it. More opportunities are needed to develop and test skills, as well as more role models and mentors to observe and from whom to learn.

In order to develop others, leaders must be motivators. Motivation by coercion is inherently imperfect because it offers too many ways for group members to frustrate group purposes, and it stunts growth. It's not enough that leaders are committed; they must also develop commitment in others. The task is to help people see how both personal and group needs can be met by shared action. The chances of doing that are enhanced by recognizing the needs of followers, building a system of shared values, regenerating a sound moral order, getting others to see interdependencies between group and individual interests, and committing people to visions of a better future and for things which extend beyond themselves. Leadership entails the obligations and duties without which freedom and liberty cannot be sustained.

The development of human potential is often held in check by negative attitudes toward the future, by over-aversion to risk taking, and undue discouragement in the face of hardships. In order to develop others, leaders must themselves maintain their morale and optimism. There must be a sense of confidence in others and in the future, expectations of success and a breaking away from attitudes of defeat and discouragement, and a commitment to human nature and its potential for greatness. The will to act cannot be maintained without the conviction that, however negative the outward appearances, everyone has the leadership potential to help build civilizations. It simply must be released, developed, and appropriately used.

READING 2

The Charismatic Leader

Jay A. Conger
Summary prepared by Jim Laumeyer

Jim Laumeyer has an MBA from the University of Minnesota, Duluth. He is the Director of Administration for the Minnesota Department of Transportation. He also serves as an instructor at the University of Minnesota, Duluth, and is a member of the Society for Human Resource Management's National Employee and Labor Relations Committee.

❖ IDENTIFYING THE CHARISMATIC LEADER

Archie J. McGill (AT&T), Dee Hock (Visa), Lee Iacocca (Chrysler), and Steve Jobs (Apple) are individuals who are frequently identified as examples of charismatic leadership. All of these individuals found themselves in organizations that were poised at a crossroad leading either to crisis or to regeneration dependent upon the organization's next move. Their organizations elected to take a risk and commission a new type of leader. Each firm needed an individual who would embark on a mission designed to bring about a major organization change. Unfortunately, the organizations were not always eager and totally willing to embrace either the leader or the change sought by the leader.

This demonstrates that although charismatic leaders sometimes do wonderful things, they are not always appreciated or cherished by all the other individuals in their organization. Not only do they typically impact others negatively on a personal basis, but their accomplishments sometimes also result in them becoming ostracized by forces within the organization.

Perception plays a powerful role in the definition of the charismatic leader. Comparisons of various charismatic leaders, such as Adolf Hitler and Franklin D. Roosevelt, often reveal very different personalities. If there were a single and simple charismatic personality, America would have perceived Hitler as charismatic, just as many Germans did. Instead, the charismatic phenomenon is quite complex in nature.

Jay A. Conger, *The Charismatic Leaders*. New York: Jossey-Bass, 1988.

The basic dilemma lies in the apparent ambiguity of the term. It has commonly been used to describe a number of leaders with very different personalities operating under a variety of conditions. There is, however, a valid criterion for discerning and defining the charismatic leader—a behavior model for organizational transformation that accents the charismatic person's ability to induce quantum change in organizations. A *charismatic leader* builds one's trust in self and senses unexplained opportunities, formulates and communicates an idealized vision and support for the vision, and provides the means for achieving it. There are four stages in the development of charismatic leadership.

◆ STAGE ONE: SENSING OPPORTUNITY AND FORMULATING A VISION

Research suggests that charismatic leaders possess two skills that often set them apart from other leaders. The first is a sensitivity to their constituents' needs (both employees and customers). The second quality is an unusual ability to see the deficiencies of the existing situation as well as the untapped opportunities. Once this is done, an idealized vision (a challenging and desirable future state) must be formulated.

◆ STAGE TWO: ARTICULATING THE VISION

Charismatic leaders tend to be different from others because of their goals and the way in which they communicate these goals. Charismatic leaders usually have a profound sense of strategic vision and a remarkable capacity to convey the essence and viability of that to a broad group of people.

◆ STAGE THREE: BUILDING TRUST IN THE VISION

For the leader to be effective, it is often important that subordinates must desire and support the goals the leader proposes. Commitment by coercion or edict is not likely to provide sufficient motivational energy for long-term success. Thus the leader must build exceptional trust among subordinates—trust in the leader and trust in the viability of the goals to be sought. The charismatic leader does this through personal risk taking, unconventional expertise, and self-sacrifice.

◆ STAGE FOUR: ACHIEVING THE VISION

In the final stage, charismatic leaders generally differ from others because of their extensive use of personal example and role modeling, their reliance on unconventional tactics, and their use of empowerment practices to demonstrate how their vision can be achieved.

❖ SEEING BEYOND CURRENT REALITIES

A very critical impetus for the desired transformation of an organization, which is the mission of every charismatic leader, is the leader's vision. The vision is essential not only for the leader, but also for the individuals that the leader must enlist and/or influence in order to be successful. The *vision* is a mental image or a dream of a highly desirable future state for the organization. The leader and others must find the vision desirable enough so that they will commit substantial energy to make this vision a reality. In essence, the vision must become the "Piped Piper's" tune, launching the leader and the followers on their mission.

These dreams or visions must be perceived as exciting, but yet they must be realistic, reasonable, and attainable. In essence, the vision must become the common cause for the leader and supporters if it is to become the basis for the desired organizational transformation.

To this end, visions must be both strategic and compatible with the organization's purpose. While compatible, the vision must create broader parameters so that all individuals perceive more authority, develop a broader mindset, and perceive more value in their personal contributions. Accordingly, a paradox for visions is that they must fit the organization's purpose and mission, while providing an impetus for a significant cultural shift relative to how the organization will serve that purpose. The charismatic leader not only seeks to keep the organization's purpose constant, but tries to change dramatically the way the organization operates to serve its mission. Visions, therefore, enlist commitment and mobilize the group to achieve the organization's purpose.

Visions may be categorized along two dimensions—focus (broad or narrow) and orientation (internal v. external). These differences create four major types of visions:

1. Product/service innovation (narrow and external).
2. Contribution to society (broad and external).
3. Organizational transformation (narrow and internal).
4. Contribution to the workforce (broad and internal).

❖ BUILDING IMPRESSIONS OF TRUSTWORTHINESS AND EXPERTISE

Even with the best vision, the charismatic leader would accomplish nothing without involving others. The mission of charismatic leaders is to bring about organizational transformations. For this to occur, followers must place trust in the leader and believe that the mission will be successful. Accordingly, they must perceive the charismatic leader as unique, extraordinary, and almost bigger than life.

In order to determine whether leaders who may have charisma are real and trustworthy, their expertise and commitment must be assessed. Leaders must demonstrate that they know what they are talking about, since this is a critical factor in the development of employee perceptions that they can accomplish this mission successfully.

Similarly, the mission to transform an organization requires risk and commitment from each individual. Followers are not inclined to make that commitment unless they believe that the leader is totally committed.

❖ EMPOWERING OTHERS TO ACHIEVE THE DREAM

After establishing the appropriate trust level, charismatic leaders must motivate their subordinates to accomplish the improbable. Not only must they motivate their subordinates to great heights, but they must also be able to sustain that level of motivation for the often prolonged and difficult period of time necessary to bring about the organizational change. Successful charismatic leaders use any number of techniques for empowering others. Charismatic leaders generate power through their accomplishments, verbal persuasion, emotional arousal, and vicarious experience.

❖ A TRIP TO THE DARK SIDE

There is, however, a somewhat negative element to the charismatic leadership phenomenon. While sometimes helping organizations achieve near-miracles, charismatic leaders can also be seen as agents of destruction. These disastrous outcomes may stem from the self-righteous mission of the leader or from other problems such as a faulty vision, assumption of excessive risk, inaccurate perceptions of market environment, failure to recognize or be informed about flaws, and disintegration of managerial functions.

❖ DEVELOPING EXCEPTIONAL LEADERSHIP

Increasingly, organizations are discovering that they need to initiate major transformations. To achieve this magnitude of change, they will likely need charismatic leaders. Several actions can help bring this about. First, they need to recruit and develop men and women who show potential for charismatic leadership. Second, organizations must widely champion examples of effective behavior demonstrated by its core of charismatic leaders. Finally, organizations must realize that this new commitment to leadership will require a significant culture change and shift in attitudes and processes in order for it to succeed. For example, decentralization, more tolerant supervisory styles, and more (charismatic) leadership skill training will be necessary. In addition, organizations need to recognize that the management of a charismatic leader requires a more flexible approach than previously used. Charismatic leaders—especially if they are infused at all levels of the organization—will require more freedom to operate in unique ways. They will also likely be more comfortable with, and challenged by, environments featured by ambiguity, risk, and even crises.

There is a sense of urgency for American business to embrace and develop charismatic leadership. Organizations and their members need to be prepared to respond productively to such leadership when it appears. The key lies in eliciting appropriate leader and follower behaviors in the same organization at the same time.

READING 3

Visionary Leadership

Burt Nanus
Summary prepared by Gayle Baugh

Gayle Baugh is an Assistant Professor of Management at the University of West Florida. She received her Ph.D. in Management in 1992 from the University of Cincinnati. Her research interests include leadership and team development, organizational attitudes, and gender issues in the workplace. She has published in these areas and presented numerous conference papers at academic meetings. She is a member of the Academy of Management, the American Psychological Association, and the Southern Management Association.

A good vision, widely shared, can help an organization on its path to excellence and renewal. *Visionary leadership* is the ability to develop and implement an engaging image of what the organization can become, and the ability to set up systems to make that vision a reality. Visionary leadership is less about interactions between leaders and followers (a focal point for many leadership models) and more about interactions between leaders and groups, or leaders and systems.

Although it is easy to talk about great vision, it is much harder to develop and implement it. Practical guidelines are necessary in order to know what steps to take in order to develop and implement a vision for an organization's future. Information from leaders of many sorts, from the private sector and public agencies, and from published literature in the areas of leadership and strategic management, provides a basis for practical instructions for the development of visionary leadership.

❖ DEFINING VISION AND VISIONARY LEADERSHIP

Vision is an engaging picture of what the organization could be like in the future. The vision must, however, be realistic enough to attract the organization's stakeholders, especially employees, to invest time and energy in it.

Burt Nanus, *Visionary Leadership*. San Francisco: Jossey-Bass, 1992.

Although vision is not verifiable in any factual sense, it must be based on a realistic assessment of the challenges and opportunities that the organization will face in the future.

Vision is not, however, synonymous with the organization's mission. The *mission* provides the purpose for the business (why it exists), but the vision indicates the direction in which it is moving (what it will become). Vision is also not the same as *objectives* or *plans*, although both will be necessary in order to pursue the vision. Objectives and plans are much more specific in terms of expected outcomes and how to achieve them than is an organizational vision.

Vision results in several positive outcomes for a business or organization. It attracts commitment and energy. Vision infuses employees' work with meaning, and helps persuade them that their activities are significant to the direction that the organization is taking. Vision also sets standards of excellence, so that progress toward a desirable future can be evaluated. Finally, vision provides a bridge between the present and the future, showing where investment of resources, including time and energy, are most likely to be effective.

An effective vision for an organization has several characteristics. It must

◆ capitalize on the organization's unique strengths and fit with the organization's current external environment.

◆ be lofty and inspire followers.

◆ provide a clear, engaging direction that is easily grasped by followers.

◆ be challenging in order to command greater performance.

Thus, a vision is not just an endpoint toward which to strive, but instead it provides a clear direction for the organization to take.

Managers can look for several indicators in order to determine if a new vision is necessary. A definite indicator is a sense of uncertainty about purpose or a feeling among employees of being "stalled." Loss of customers or loss of status would suggest the need for a new vision, as would a sense that the organization is somehow out of touch with its surrounding environment. Other indicators include a lack of pride in work or the unwillingness to take risks. Excessive gossip or rumors within the company suggest that workers do not know which direction the company is taking. If managers sense some of these symptoms, then the need for a new vision is apparent.

❖ DEVELOPING THE ORGANIZATIONAL VISION

The first step in developing a vision is to determine exactly what business the organization is in. The definition of the core or *essential business* will influence the future directions available. It is important to determine what the current mission of the organization is and what value it provides to society. In addition, determining the unique position of the organization within its industry is essential in order to create a vision that is consistent with organizational capabilities. Managers need to speculate on what capabilities or strengths will be necessary to succeed in the marketplace of the future.

While these issues involve the organization's position in the external environment, the internal environment must also be addressed. The organization's vision must fit with the *culture*, which is the underlying structure of key beliefs and values that are held in common within the workplace and taught to new members. The vision must capitalize on current operating strengths, whereas weaknesses must be acknowledged in order to avoid stumbling in those areas. An internal assessment of culture, strengths, and weaknesses will provide some clues as to a workable vision for the company.

Organizational vision may be limited in terms of geography and social constraints, depending on the organization in question. The vision may also be limited in terms of its time horizon. The ideal time horizon is that period of time over which major changes can be accomplished, but which is still relevant to the current managerial workforce. One must look beyond that time period, however, in order to measure the success of the vision, because the returns on the investments of resources will probably not be forthcoming until a decade beyond the implementation of the vision.

As a result, the outcome measures for determining success must be contemplated over this longer time horizon. The vision must support the organization's future success, which means that measures of success must be defined. Because there are numerous operational measures of "success," the five or six criteria of success essential to survival must be identified. Then attention can be directed toward the alternative visions (possible futures) that are available to promote success on these essential criteria.

❖ DEVELOPING FUTURE SCENARIOS

Guessing at what will occur in the future is never easy. But in order to develop vision, leaders need not *predict* the future; they need only assess likely future events and how these events would affect the organization. Specific future events can be integrated into *scenarios* that describe sets of possible (and relevant) futures. Flexibility to accommodate the most likely scenarios can then be built into the vision.

Visionary leaders must determine which dimensions of future changes can affect the organization's vision, and what can potentially happen in each of these dimensions. For most organizations, the relevant concerns include changes in the wants and desires of the major market, changes in the desires of the major stakeholders in the organization, and changes in the social, political, economic, and technological environments.

After listing possible changes, some predictions must be made about which are most likely to occur. Then, these probable events must be integrated into scenarios of future states of the world. Usually four to six scenarios are sufficient to accommodate most of the possible states of the future. The scenarios must be internally consistent and must appear to be possible, even likely, to an outside observer. Then the implications of each scenario for the organization in question can be evaluated. The firm must determine how it would position itself to achieve success (as previously defined) under each scenario.

It is easiest to make predictions and develop scenarios when there are multiple perspectives brought to bear on these questions. Thus, *vision is probably best developed by a multidisciplinary team,* wherein speculation is encouraged and synergy is possible. Further, when it comes time to implement the vision, employee commitment to it is much more likely when they have felt involved in the vision from its inception.

Vision is, above all else, innovative. It requires looking at the well-known facts of an organization's situation and putting them together in new and innovative ways. Whereas the process of developing a vision requires some amount of inspiration, insight will most likely occur as a result of deep thinking about the question. Structuring the process of thinking about the future will facilitate visioning.

❖ EVALUATING ALTERNATIVE VISIONS

First, it is helpful to review all of the information about the organization's current situation and anticipated future. A mental map or a schematic model increases the ability to think systematically about the current situation. A schematic can be developed by placing all competitors in the current market on a graph defined by the two key identifying dimensions to which the market responds. Or a mental map can result from listing the distinctive competencies of the business and identifying market niches that use the largest number of them.

Vision, or more appropriately, multiple possible visions, will begin to develop at this point in the process. A series of vision statements should be elaborated, but judgments about practicality or feasibility must be withheld. Once a number of vision statements are generated, the evaluation process will require that the most feasible among them be tested against the qualities of a good vision: consistency with the values and culture of the organization, congruence with its strengths and weaknesses, consistency with possible future scen-arios, and the likelihood of success on outcome measures identified earlier.

The most attractive among the vision statements must be evaluated. Alternative visions can be rated according to the degree that they

- ◆ Are future-oriented.
- ◆ Are based on high principles.
- ◆ Clarify purpose and direction.
- ◆ Will generate deep commitment.

◆ Fit with the organization's strengths, weaknesses, and culture.

◆ Reflect the organization's distinctive competencies.

◆ Are challenging.

These ratings can be totaled for each vision, providing an indication of how well each vision statement meets the criteria for a good vision. The same process can be used to evaluate the five or six essential criteria for measuring a vision's success and to evaluate its fit with organizational factors. Based on these totals, one vision is likely to emerge as more appropriate than the others.

Two or three alternative visions may emerge that are highly rated in all three areas. These should be examined more closely. Some of the alternative vision statements may be combined, producing a stronger overall vision statement. With some additional experimentation, a vision statement that is focused, exciting, and inspirational can be generated.

The final part of the process is to implement the vision, which is not necessarily straightforward. It is, however, essential if the organization is to move into the future.

❖ IMPLEMENTING THE VISION

Once the vision has been developed and communicated throughout the organization, the remaining task is to make the vision a reality. Although leaders are not generally involved in the day-to-day tasks of accomplishing the work of the organization, there are many things that leaders must do in order to ensure effective implementation of the vision. Three roles are important to the implementation process.

First, the leader must be the *spokesperson* for the vision. The vision must be communicated to others both inside and outside the organization in such a way that it inspires action. Communicating the vision involves networking with major stakeholders in order to ensure that the vision is accepted and that actions congruent with the vision are given the highest priority.

As a spokesperson, the leader must also personify the vision, or "live the dream." Thus, the leader speaks with actions, not just words. How the leader follows through on commitments, what issues and which individuals attract the leader's attention, when and how actions are taken by the leader, and the leader's formal and informal statements are all scrutinized to determine the leader's real desires and commitment to the vision.

The second role the leader takes in the implementation process is as *change agent*. The strongest influence the leader can have as a change agent is through the power to control resources and to direct them to areas crucial to the implementation of the vision. The leader has direct influence on the implementation process through resource allocation, staffing, changing the organizational structure, directing information flows, and changing organizational processes. Indirect influence is exercised through consultation, persuasion, participation, inspiration, and motivation.

The third role the leader takes in the implementation process is as *coach*. For the most part, the leader will not have time to engage in one-on-one coaching, but instead will be involved with work units and groups within the organization. By carefully controlling assignments to groups and tasks, especially the assignment of group leaders, the leader can exert great influence on the implementation process. Further, the design of jobs, the resources and support services made available, the design of the reward system, and the goals and expectations with work units all affect the implementation of the vision. *Leaders must ensure that the vision as implemented is consonant with the vision as communicated.*

❖ RE-VISIONING

The story is not over when the vision is implemented. No vision, no matter how innovative, will be appropriate for an organization for all times. As a result, the leader must look for clues internally and externally that a new vision is needed.

Monitoring the vision internally will ensure that the vision still fits the organization. The leader wants to see that the vision has been adopted by employees at all levels, that influential managers are using their power to enhance implementation, that employees are cooperating in realizing the vision, and that the organization's goals, priorities, structures, and processes are all consistent with the vision.

In addition, *tracking* the vision—gathering information about its effectiveness—through the external environment will ensure that it is appropriate for the current situation. For example, the major stakeholders should all understand and accept the vision, and the organization should be performing well according to the measures of success identified in the visioning process. The situation should be tracked so that if changes occur in the markets or in other facets of the external environment that affect the organization's vision, the organization can adapt to those changes quickly. Competitors, too, should be tracked to ensure that their actions do not endanger achievement of the organization's vision.

The easiest time to make changes is when the organization is running smoothly, not when the company is already under competitive or regulatory pressure. It is important, therefore, to focus on both the internal and external environments to anticipate changes that will affect the organization's vision before they become major threats. Monitoring and tracking the vision will facilitate constant organizational renewal.

While leadership at the highest levels of the organization has been emphasized, *visionary leaders are needed at all levels within organizations.* If managers at all levels are encouraged to be true leaders, to develop vision for their work units that is consistent with the organization's overall vision, and to imbue their own work units with enthusiasm and energy for pursuing that vision, the organization will thrive. With leaders at all levels seeking to understand the internal and external environment, it is much less likely that important changes in either will pass unnoticed. One of the most important tasks of visionary leaders is to *develop a climate where more visionary leaders are encouraged and developed.*

READING 4

Stewardship

Peter Block
Summary prepared by Robert C. Ford

Robert C. Ford is a Professor and Chair of the Department of Hospitality Management at the University of Central Florida. Bob holds a Ph.D. in Management from Arizona State University. In addition to publishing texts in principles of management and organizational theory, he has authored, or co-authored, a number of articles on applied managerial practices, human resources management, and social responsibility in both applied and academic journals. He is an active member of the Academy of Management, serving as chairperson for the Management Education and Development Division, the Management History Division, and Placement. In addition, he has served as President of the Southern Management Association and is Chairperson of the Accreditation Commission for Programs in Hospitality Administration.

We live in a world of change. Organizations, like people, are confronting the economic impact of those changes, and this has led to a major reassessment of how organizations are governed, led, and structured. The modern organization promises little and asks a lot of its members. Gone is the security and implied social contract of earlier days when an employee could expect that he or she would be rewarded with loyalty, job security, and an ever-increasing salary as the payment for organizational commitment, hard work, and enthusiastic support for the organizational mission and goals. The new social contract guarantees nothing as organizations are forced to quickly adapt to the changing forces in the market place and a new emphasis on customer responsiveness.

In this new environment, the dominant managerial style must change from the traditional concept of leadership to the new ideas of stewardship. Traditionally, leadership meant that managers are somehow responsible for their subordinates who look to the leader for guidance, direction, reward, evaluation, and protection. A manager and an organization committed to stewardship operate in a very different way. *Stewardship is predicated on the*

Peter Block, *Stewardship*. San Francisco: Barrett-Koehler, 1993.

idea that people in communities and in organizations are willing to choose ser-vice over self-interest. They are prepared to take responsibility for the larger community without needing to control it. *Stewardship* means empowering people to be accountable for their own actions rather than asking them to be dependent upon the managers. This is the essence of how a free and demo-cratic people govern themselves and take stewardship for their own lives within that society. It is the antithesis of the managerial practices typically found in most organizations.

❖ THE TRADITIONAL PILLARS OF MANAGEMENT

Choosing stewardship means renouncing three pillars of the traditional orga-nization's managerial practices. These are control, consistency, and pre-dictability. *Control* is achieved through the classic reliance on lines of author-ity. Top management makes all the important decisions, sets the overall organizational mission, defines its vision, and structures the reward system to encourage everyone to go along and punishes those who don't. People at lower levels are responsible for executing those decisions and implementing the vi-sion. Organizations want *consistency* to ensure they have standardized ways of dealing with policies and people. The need for consistency leads to the cre-ation of staff support people who develop training strategies to make sure everyone does what they do in the same way, oversee the consistent execution of policies and procedures, and audit the results. Organizations seek *pre-dictability* to ensure that events are going to come out the way they want them to come out. Managers set goals and measure progress toward those goals. They do not like or want surprises and therefore design mechanisms to elimi-nate surprises.

These three pillars of traditional management practice lead to a patriar-chal system where leaders are viewed as parents of the organization and the rest of the members are children looking for structure, guidance, direction, praise, and an appropriate allowance (salary) for performing what the leaders want. The problem with reliance on control, consistency, and predictability is that ownership and responsibility for solving the modern challenges of cost reduction, customer satisfaction, and employee commitment are vested in the patriarch and not in the members. If the organization needs a strong sense of ownership, commitment, and responsibility for customer satisfaction from the employees on the firing line, this traditional approach to managing won't work.

❖ CREATING PARTNERSHIPS

Partnerships must be created between employees and top managers in the stewardship-based organization. Each partner has the responsibility for help-ing the larger community or organization succeed in the face of a dynamic and changing market place. In effect, both have a stewardship role to play whereby they individually take on the responsibility for the organization's success. Partnership changes the balance of power between the top managers and the core employees—those who actually meet the customers, make the product, and deliver the service.

A partnership has four requirements. The first is that *the parties have to define for themselves their own purpose within the organization.* Historically, the organization's top management defines the organizational purpose and sends it down the hierarchy to lower-level employees. A partnership requires dialogue between the partners to give every organizational level and unit the opportunity to define the purpose that makes sense for it. If the departments have no participation in the definition of that purpose then it becomes merely an echo of top management thinking and beliefs rather than providing the necessary ownership that each unit has to have. *Partnership means that everyone at every level is responsible for defining the vision and values for their unit.* Partnership gets defined through dialogue, and everyone, including customers, suppliers, and other stakeholders, needs to be a part of the discussion.

The second requirement for a true partnership is *to give everyone the right to say no.* When organizations take away the right to say no, they take away the individual's sovereignty and sense of personal responsibility for the ultimate outcome of a decision. Although the leadership of every community and every organization has the ultimate authority to say yes or no, this should not detract from individuals' rights to say no for themselves. Like a voter in a democratic government, partnership doesn't mean you always get what you want, but it does mean that you never lose your voice in the ultimate outcome.

The third cornerstone of partnership is *joint accountability by the partners.* Each person has an individual responsibility for both the organizational outcomes and their own current situation. Managers are no longer responsible for the morale or career of their subordinates. Partners are not caretakers of each other. Partnership offers individual organizational members freedom but the price of that freedom is personal accountability for results. The fourth requirement for partnership is *absolute honesty* between the partners.

No organizational partnership can ever be a true fifty-fifty relationship. Organizations, like entire social communities, will always continue to have bosses and leaders. The partnership should be as close to this split in responsibility as possible to move toward a stewardship-based organization. Practicing stewardship and partnership is not inconsistent with being a boss. *Stewardship is the willingness to hold power without using reward, punishment and direct command to get the necessary things done.* Instead, stewardship relies on empowered employees who can and do take the responsibility for themselves and their unit's success.

Stewardship is a difficult thing for most employees to accept. It requires them to choose adventure and freedom over safety and job security. Organizations, especially bureaucratic organizations, have traditionally been safe. Indeed, bureaucracy is patriarchy in the extreme because it provides the ultimate in caution, risk aversion, predictability, and exercising control over others. When employees join such organizations, they collude with the principles of the traditional managerial system and acknowledge the organization's right to control their behavior. Employees accept the dependency relationship as a condition of the job. In return for giving up their individual freedom, however, they then feel entitled to a sense of job safety and security. Empowering employees takes away this entitlement. If the organization gives its people freedom instead of security and safety, it must also have the right to require accountability for the use of that freedom. *While empowerment means that every person has the right and responsibility to define for themselves what kind of organization they work in, it also creates an obligation for employees to commit themselves and become emotionally involved with the organization.* In effect, if the organization empowers its employees, it must also teach them that the only reliable leadership for monitoring costs, ensuring quality, and providing real service is themselves. Indeed, it is even a responsibility of the employees to teach those above them the concepts of empowerment, stewardship, and service.

❖ DEVELOPING A GOVERNANCE STRATEGY FOR STEWARDSHIP

The concepts of empowerment, stewardship, and service require eliminating the traditional distinctions between managers and workers. Traditional managerial practices created a managerial class separate from those who do the work. Managers were responsible for planning the work and workers were responsible for doing it the way management planned. This leads to two major problems. First, it is expensive, and second, it creates an organizational class system that gets in the way of producing the service, quality, and flexibility the customers and the organization need in a volatile marketplace. If we need an employee who is able and willing to respond correctly to the customers' needs, make the product correctly the first time, and discover new efficiencies in production, then having a class-based organization where one group is responsible for planning, organizing, and controlling the work while the other is responsible only for producing the product or delivering the service is doomed to fail. Real stewardship requires a governance system and structure that completely integrates managing the work with doing the work. Six points capture this idea.

◆ The organization must affirm the spirit of stewardship. Everyone wants to do something that matters and is important and for which they have responsibility.

◆ The members of the organization, both core employees and top managers, must confront and successfully resolve the power struggle between a patriarchy form of organization and a partnership forum. Our collective organizational experiences and traditional managerial theory lead everyone to believe that control, consistency, and predictability are essential for organizational success. Partnership substitutes a balancing of power and accountability throughout the organization.

◆ Each person takes responsibility for creating the organization's culture, delivering outcomes to the customer, and ensuring the quality of their own organizational experience.

◆ The management of work and the doing of work must be integrated. Otherwise, there is a class system in the organization that leads to patriarchy.

◆ Organizations can't legislate partnership, stewardship, and service. One can't order someone to care about their job, themselves, the customer, or the organization. Developing a sense of stewardship is a gradual reeducation process for both employees and management.

◆ Most existing organizational practices, policies, and procedures, are designed to reinforce and maintain the traditional concepts of control, predictability, and consistency. These must all be carefully reviewed, rethought, and redesigned if they are to lead to partnership instead of patriarchy.

Once the strategy has been set to move toward an organization driven by stewardship, partnership, and service, the next step is to understand the impact this will have on existing organizational governance and authority relationships. Stewardship creates a governance system that dramatically rearranges social and power relationships between the organizational leadership and the core employees. Such a governance system should rest on the following principles:

◆ Decision-making authority and responsibility must be maximized for those closest to the work. Core employees need to have the training, ability, and freedom to act for the customer.

◆ Everyone must do work that translates into value in the marketplace, and everyone should do some of the core work of the organization some of the time. No one should think of themselves as above the work done by those who are the primary deliverers of the organization's value to the customer. Even top managers should serve the customer now and then to reinforce the value of the core work of the organization as well as ensuring that they too stay close to the customer.

◆ Measurements should be developed by those who are going to be measured. The organization should eliminate any measures that have nothing to do with what the person being measured is responsible for.

◆ Consistency across the organization should be sacrificed in favor of developing local solutions to local problems. One organizational policy or procedure doesn't fit all organizational situations or departments. Those who know the local problems should develop the local answers.

◆ Service is the key to everyone's job. Whether this is service to a customer, service to a co-worker, or service to the entire organization, everyone is accountable and stewards to those they serve.

◆ Minimize staff management. Redefine the role of staff to be a service to the core employees rather than an extension of top management's effort to maintain control, consistency, and predictability. In essence, staff should be valued for what they add to the core employees' output. If the people directly responsible for producing the product or delivering the service don't want the product staff offers because it yields no value to them, or the core people can get the product better somewhere else, then they should be able to do so. This redefines the relationship between the traditional line and the staff support groups as staff must now prove its worth to the line or line will ignore them.

◆ End secrecy, and give truthful information to anyone who needs and wants it. This creates literacy in the business across the entire organization. Only when people have the necessary and accurate information they need to completely assess the impact of their decisions are they truly empowered.

◆ Demand commitment to the organization as a whole as the price for individual empowerment and freedom. If one is to be a free partner in an empowered organization, the price is making a commitment to delivering results.

◆ Redistribute the rewards across the organization. By eliminating the class system through this system of organizational governance, there should be a concomitant elimination of differentials in both the amount of organizational rewards and the reward system among the levels in the organization. The very high salaries of very senior executives in comparison with the core employees must be eliminated. Further, the evaluation system needs to be reworked to ensure that the same premises about employee loyalty, commitment, and individual effort are built into the evaluations for both top management and core workers. Finally, the reward system must also recognize contributions to a group and collective effort. Individual rewards promote self-interest and work against partnership and stewardship.

❖ THE STEWARDSHIP CONTRACT

This system of governance is implemented through the *stewardship contract.* This becomes the new social contract governing the relationships and behaviors of people inside the organization. Each unit creates a stewardship contract to define and limit what is to be controlled, the boundaries and limitations of the partnership, and the relationship between employees and the organizations. The contract has five key elements:

◆ The core mission of each organizational unit and its key customers.

◆ Financial accountability and the results expected. Every boss has the right to define the required outcomes, and the contract spells them out clearly in a way that holds people accountable without controlling them.

◆ A basic structure that fits the tasks and mission of the organization. It includes what the organization can't permit as well as what it does allow.

◆ The basic governance strategy.

◆ What specifically needs to be done to make stewardship work.

The stewardship contract defines and details the ground rules for employees to participate in the new governance structure. It makes each employee responsible for the institution's well-being and asks them to be clear about their mission, know completely the customers they serve, and the product that they make or produce. Further, it clearly defines the results that are required, the constraints within which they must live, and the changes that will be made toward greater empowerment, partnership, and service. If people cannot commit to the contract, then the time to find out is at the start of creating the empowered organizations that are committed to stewardship.

❖ TRADITIONAL VERSUS PARTNERSHIP ORGANIZATIONS

Organizations that practice stewardship are different from the traditional organizational focus on control, consistency, and predictability. They promote different values, beliefs and managerial practices. Consequently, they are different in the way they are structured, the roles defined from their managers and their staff groups, and their reward system. Traditional organizations tend to be functional in structure. This makes it relatively easy to supervise people doing like jobs and to structure career paths for functionally trained and oriented people. Accountants can easily see accounting opportunities in a functionally structured organization. *The marketplace demands a customer-focused structure.* Successful organizations in today's highly competitive environment don't switch customers from one function to another until the customer's problem is solved or the service is provided. Further, these organizations are flattened to ensure that the organization is more flexibly responsive to the needs of a rapidly changing marketplace. These two trends put new challenges on core employees who must know more about the product to respond to a broad range of customer needs and about the organization in order to identify how these needs can be best served. Employees must be empowered to respond with service.

Bosses also need to change the way they manage. As the employee at the core level takes on new responsibilities, the boss becomes more of a banker and broker and less of a traditional leader. As a banker, the boss is responsible for securing funds for the unit, communicating the results of the unit to others throughout the organization, and ascertaining the financial requirements that will assure the continuing effective operation of the unit. As a broker, the boss maintains liaisons with other parts of the organization that have services the unit needs or require the services of the unit the boss manages. The boss adds value to the unit by ensuring that the unit has the resources it needs from others, communicates the output value to other parts of the organization, and seeks to ensure the continuing availability of resources the unit needs to continue its role. Beyond that, it is the unit membership's responsibility to articulate the purpose and mission, define the measures of performance, and ensure that the primary product or service that unit produces meets the market test. This is a very different role for the traditional manager because the supervisory roles of training, teaching, and overseeing are now placed in new organizational locations.

The role of staff also changes in the organization that seeks to empower its employees by adopting the concepts of stewardship. The individual operating unit now has the right to use or not use the services that staff offers. If staff can't defend the value these services add, then the core employees can choose not to use them. This means that staff now has the same market test applied to them that production units have always had. This changes the alignment of staff from being a service to top management to being a service for the core employees. As long as top management was the primary client for staff, they rightfully defined their role as policing, auditing, and acting as the corporate conscience. *The stewardship alternative requires staff to operate as authentic service units.* They must add capability to the core units or they will cease to have function. If the core doesn't want or need the training programs, expert advice, or other staff policing, inspection, and caretaking type functions that they have traditionally provided in organizations, then the core units can choose not to pay for them. Staff soon learn by their ability to gain billings from the operating departments who and what adds value.

The stewardship-based organization stresses self-control as a substitute for bosses and staff oversight. This means that the financial practices have to change to support this idea, presenting its financial data in a format that promotes self-management, self-auditing, and self-control. This also means that the traditional human resource management practices have to be rethought in order to promote the organization's commitment to partnership, service, and stewardship. Most traditional human resource policies and practices reinforce the traditional patriarchal system of management in how it hires, fires, pays, promotes, and trains employees. Human resources, like financial reporting staff and other staff support operations, should redefine who its customers are.

Finally, the compensation system needs to be redesigned in order to eliminate the class systems now in place in most organizations. Traditional compensation systems are predicated on the idea that organizations can buy the individual behavior they require, and they communicate the message that the customer for employees is the boss and not the marketplace. The stewardship-based organization seeks to use performance criteria that are linked to the market results of the unit, shares the wealth more equitably across the organization, and ends secrecy about who got what and why. The evaluation of all employees is predicated on trust and self-control and not on the basis that only core employees have to add value while the overhead is a naturally occurring outcome and efficient organizational cost. Thus, *partnership organizations design pay systems that value interdependence, teamwork, and success in the creation of products, customer satisfaction, and other factors that really mat-*

ter. There is a price for this new type of organizational governance. The old pay and performance systems disappear. The old promise that employee pay should keep up with inflation, that employees are not responsible for the bad results of the organization, and that rank does not necessarily have its pay and privileges are all at risk in this new organizational orientation.

Stewardship has to be accepted on faith as a governing principle for organizational membership. There is little proof, no handy "how to" books on implementation, and no guarantee that it will succeed at all levels and in all organizations. Yet, the logic of instituting a governance system inside the organization that is congruent with the larger society's democratic principles and practices and that has proven to be a successful way to govern social relationships is compelling. Just as Eastern European countries have concluded that autocratic and patriarchal regimes are ineffective and inappropriate for managing the affairs of entire economic systems, so, too, are the traditional organizational practices that rely on control, consistency, and predictability inappropriate for managing the modern organization. It is inconsistent to have a patriarchal organization management system in a free society. The principle of stewardship, of being individually responsible for the greater community and for ourselves within that community, is the underlying concept that makes democracy work.

◆ ◆ ◆

10

MANAGING DIVERSITY

$\mathbf{A}$ wide range of biases (such as racism and sexism) are still entrenched in our society and—too frequently—exhibited in its organizations. Despite powerful federal and state laws and potent corporate policy statements, both public and private organizations still have a limited number of female upper-level managers. The discrimination is not limited just to women. There are a number of different groups within our society who find themselves singled out and subjected to discriminatory treatment.

Several interesting books and reports have been written on the changing demographics in the United States and the implications for businesses and organizations. The popular press reminds us almost daily that diversity in the workplace will become increasingly common as we move into the twenty-first century. As a consequence of these dramatic demographic trends and the need for constructive response, Part Ten will highlight the issues of diversity and its management in the workplace.

Marilyn Loden (author of *Feminine Leadership*) and Judy B. Rosener wrote *Workforce America! Managing Employee Diversity as a Vital Resource,* in which they explore the rapidly changing demographic nature of the American workforce. They remind us that in just a few years, less than 40 percent of the total American workforce will be characterized by the white male, because women and people of color will fill 75 percent of the new jobs created in the United States.

Loden and Rosener focus on three themes. First, they define diversity and discuss its institutional impact (such as increased creativity, innovation, and enhanced productivity). Second, they examine the problems and challenges to be encountered when organizations employ diverse populations. Finally, the authors articulate a specific set of strategies that can be implemented to change organizational culture so that it values diversity. Loden is a San Francisco-based organization change consultant, and Rosener is a professor at the University of California-Irvine Graduate School of Management.

Pat Barrentine, in *When the Canary Stops Singing,* applies the miner's canary as a warning of danger to the world of work. She warns that the traditional practices have created a toxic environment for many women, and their dissatisfaction is a harbinger of danger to others and a call for action. This book, a collection of essays by fifteen authors, suggests that the use of feminine ways of relating to others (through the use of love, nurture, and compassion) can enrich the workplace for all employees. Managers are urged to get in touch with their feelings, truly listen to others, seek to establish spiritual havens for workers, and strive toward balance in their thinking and behaviors. Barrentine is the owner of an information packaging and communications company and former editor of *World Business Academy Perspectives*.

READING 1

Workforce America! Managing Employee Diversity as a Vital Resource

Marilyn Loden and Judy B. Rosener
Summary prepared by Linda E. Parry

Linda E. Parry is an Assistant Professor of Organizational Studies in the Management Studies Department at the University of Minnesota, Duluth, where she teaches strategic management. She received her Ph.D. from the State University of New York at Albany. Her research interests are in the areas of macro-organizational theory, organizational responsiveness, and organization culture.

The face of the American workforce is rapidly changing. The traditional picture of the white, middle-aged male worker is being replaced by a medley of different faces representing a variety of ages, ethnic groups, and races. By the twenty-first century, white men will account for less than forty percent of the total American workforce. At the same time, women and people of color will fill seventy-five percent of the new jobs created in the United States. This dramatic shift in demographics provides the foundation for Marilyn Loden and Judy B. Rosener's book *Workforce America! Managing Employee Diversity as a Vital Resource.*

Based on observations both from their research and professional experience, Loden and Rosener contend that diversity can be an asset to organizations. *Workforce America!* is divided into three parts. Part One, "Raising Awareness," defines diversity and focuses on its impact on institutions. Part Two, "Managing Key Issues," examines the problems and challenges often encountered when employing diverse populations. Part Three, "Diversity and Organization Change," gives specific strategies that can be implemented to change organizational culture so that it values employee diversity.

Marilyn Loden & Judy B. Rosener, *Workforce America! Managing Employee Diversity as a Vital Resource*. Burr Ridge, IL: Irwin Professional Publishing, 1990.

❖ PART ONE: RAISING AWARENESS

Everyone is made up of several dimensions. *Primary dimensions* are those characteristics that are inborn or immutable. They comprise such factors as age, ethnicity, gender, race, physical characteristics, and sexual/affectional orientation. *Secondary dimensions* are acquired and encompass such characteristics as educational background, geographic location, income, and marital status. Although each dimension can be examined separately, the interconnectedness of these dimensions really shapes identities, values, and perceptions. For example, a young black male lawyer would in all likelihood have different priorities and perceptions than an elderly black boxer, although both people are the same race and gender.

Diversity is the result of these dimensions and the multiple ways in which they can be combined. In the past, organizations ignored the impact that diversity had on the attitudes and behaviors of employees. After all, most Americans lived in homogeneous communities where they worked and associated with others of similar backgrounds. Diversity simply was not an issue. However, twenty-five years of political, social, and legal change brought new groups of employees into the workplace. These others were different from the dominant group along several dimensions of age, ethnicity, gender, race, sexual orientation, and so on. At first, organizations attempted to handle these others through assimilation. People were expected to "fit in." Equal treatment in the workplace meant the same treatment for each employee. Ignoring individual differences became the norm. As a result, assimilation often resulted in pressure to conform, exclusion and isolation, and reinforcement of the dominant group values. This problem became compounded as the number of diverse groups within organizations increased and the number of white men, who traditionally made up the workforce, declined. The stage was set for a change in the ways in which American corporations handled diversity.

❖ PART TWO: MANAGING KEY ISSUES

The American worker has often been portrayed as a rugged individual (e.g., the "Marlboro Man" or Lee Iacocca). These are plain-talking, risk-taking adventurers. They are also white, Protestant, male, heterosexual, and in excellent health. When others enter the workforce who do not fit this image, people attempt to place them into categories. Often these classifications are based on stereotypes which reinforce underlying prejudices about others.

Prejudices foster ageism, racism, heterosexism, sexism, and so on. Moreover, when combined with institutional power, prejudices can be systematically used to disadvantage others. Ignoring prejudices is not the solution. Those institutions that chose to do "business as usual" have been plagued with a high turnover among non-traditional employees, low morale within the organization, underutilization of employee skills, numerous intergroup conflicts, low productivity, and an inability to attract new workers.

Prejudices should not only be recognized but also managed. A five step process includes

1. Accepting responsibility for the problem;
2. Identifying problem behaviors;
3. Assessing the impact of problem behavior on others;
4. Modifying negative behavior;
5. Obtaining feedback from others.

For example, in the past some male managers pretended not to notice the small number of qualified women employees who were being promoted into senior management positions. They hoped that as the number of women increased, the problem would simply go away. Unfortunately, this did not happen. Although the number of women in the workforce has increased, the U.S. Department of Labor reports that there are still barriers to senior management for women. Consequently, corporations that want to retain women and benefit from their contributions have initiated programs to identify, mentor, and place women employees in responsible positions.

In order to be successful in managing diversity, three key issues must be confronted. These are issues of communication, group dynamics, and cultural class. If people are going to interact proactively with others, communication needs to be straightforward and clear. Often people are unaware of how the nuances and innuendoes of the words they use can lead to garbled communication. For example, the term *minority* is often used to describe people of color. This term is numerically incorrect since there are far more people of color than there are white people in the world. Also, the term is inappropriate because it implies less power as in "majority versus minority." The term *handicapped* is also frequently used. However, it is a term which focuses on a problem rather than on the total person. A less ambiguous term is *differently abled* which focuses on abilities while acknowledging physical and/or developmental differences. Unfortunately, there is no complete lexicon of words that can be used in communicating inoffensively with others. Nevertheless, some terms are currently considered appropriate when communicating with such diverse groups as older adults, Native Americans, women, and black people.

◆ COMMUNICATION

The preferred emphasis is not to focus on rules but rather to improve the quality of communication. Four key variables should be recognized when evaluating the impact of one's style on others. These variables include identifying one's own communication style, continually testing one's own assumptions, acknowledging one's style when communicating with others, and being aware of differences in cultural context. For instance, most Americans are accustomed to giving explicit messages in which the actual words carry most of the meaning. In Asian cultures, by contrast, words carry only a small part of the message. The rest is implicit in the context of the communication. Consequently, communicating with Asians can be frustrating for Americans who place a great weight on words and miss the contextual message. By understanding cultural differences in communication, the risk of garbled communication can be reduced.

◆ GROUP DYNAMICS

Group dynamics is another key issue. Since *group dynamics* by definition refers to the pattern of interaction that occurs within groups, they can help or hinder the accomplishment of tasks. When groups are formed in an atmosphere of cooperation and respect, disputes are aired and open communication encouraged. When groups are formed along primary and secondary dimensions of diversity, they can consciously or unconsciously reinforce stereotypic attitudes, behaviors, and norms. Cliques develop and soon subgroups find themselves competing for a limited supply of resources. Clique members seldom go against the group norms since doing so risks alienation and ostracism.

In research of major corporations, four factors are particularly important for the effective functioning of groups:

◆ There needs to be open membership in which all individuals feel accepted without restriction.

◆ There needs to be an atmosphere of shared influence in which all the group members feel that they have an opportunity to have input in decisions that affect goal-setting and the establishment of group priorities.

◆ There needs to be mutual respect among the group members so that core differences are realized and viewed as having value to the group.

◆ There needs to be candor within the group so that members feel free to raise issues, challenge others, and disclose personal opinions and feelings.

◆ CULTURE CLASH

Cultural clash is also a key issue when discussing diversity in the workplace. *Culture clash* is conflict over basic values that occurs between groups of different core identities. It usually occurs when the values, attitudes, and behaviors of the dominant group are questioned by others. Culture clash can be threatening, confusing, or enhancing. In the first two conditions, it can be an impediment to an organization. Consider the case of the Los Angeles City Fire Department, where the mayor attempted to institute a policy of desegregation in 1953. The initial reaction by the department included avoidance, defensiveness, denial, and hostility. Although there were 1,700 fire fighters in the department, only fifty-five were black. These black fire fighters were all assigned to two stations in predominantly black neighborhoods. Although eighty percent of the men requested transfers, the Chief routinely turned them down to avoid potential culture clash between black and white employees.

When culture clash is enhanced, it can improve the effectiveness of an organization. Another example from the Los Angeles Fire Department illustrates the point. This time it was 1982 and the commissioner mandated that the department institute a program to prepare women to enter the service. A gym, an outreach program, and several informational programs resulted in seventy-seven women fire fighters and paramedics. Such an approach added diversity to the department without compromising the professionalism or downgrading standards.

The differences between the positive and negative effects of culture clash appear to be in perceptions of the dominant group. If the dominant group perceives that the inclusion of others has little value to them or the organization, the likelihood of negativism is high. In instances where the dominant group recognizes the "value added" that the group brings to the task, the likelihood of developing creative solutions is high. The rewards for diversity in work groups are clear. According to the Los Angeles Fire Chief, Donald Manning, "There is strength in heterogeneity. When there is inbreeding or homogeneity in an organization, it loses its ability to be objective—to meet the needs of a diverse community" (p. 131).

❖ PART THREE: DIVERSITY AND ORGANIZATION CHANGE

Today, many organizations are involved in efforts to manage employee diversity. The most successful of these organizations share some common characteristics. First, there is a commitment by senior management to the value of diversity. For instance, at Levi Strauss & Company, senior managers not only attend classes on "valuing diversity," but they also participate in team building sessions designed to encourage open communication with employees. Second, the operating philosophy endorses "different but equal." Managers recognize the critical difference between equal treatment and the same treatment. They respect the varied perspectives and communication styles of employees. Third, there is an effort to reward people on their ability to contribute to the organization's goals and not just on their ability to maintain the status quo.

Organizations that value diversity also have pluralistic, rather than participative, leadership. *Participative leadership* assumes that something can be learned from employees. It emphasizes empowerment and increased employee input in decision making. *Pluralistic leadership* not only emphasizes empowerment and increased employee input, but goes further and assumes that organizational culture must change for diversity to happen. Such culture change mandates that everyone in the organization be consulted. A pluralistic leader proactively provides the vision, inspires ethical commitment to fairness, is aware of the primary and secondary dimensions of diversity, and provides a model for organizational change.

Leading-edge organizations have adopted several practices that have helped them institutionalize the value of diversity. One practice links the concept of diversity to the organization's strategic vision. For example, Stanford

University, after being criticized for its lack of diversity, entirely revamped its curriculum to reflect the teachings of diverse cultures and is "now committed to building an interactive, pluralistic community of students, faculty, and staff" (p. 167).

Since managers are ultimately responsible for coaching and developing employees, another practice is to involve managers in all efforts to change the culture. To insure that managers can perform these tasks, successful organizations train managers as facilitators of change and reward appropriate performance.

However, training and appropriate reward systems are not just for managers. Successful companies make sure that everyone within the organization has the opportunity to learn about the importance and value of diversity. For instance, within US West, employees at all levels are included in diversity training. Currently, the program offers two programs to its more than 70,000 employees. A one-day workshop addresses the problem of stereotyping. A three-day seminar explains the relationship between effective leadership and employee diversity. Rewards are then distributed to employees on the basis of performance results and not just on style.

For those organizations that truly value diversity, certain assumptions begin to emerge among employees. One assumption is that employee diversity is a competitive advantage and valuable in the marketplace. The principle behind this belief is straightforward. Basically, the company that values diversity can attract a larger and better pool of applicants than companies which limit themselves to a traditional workforce. Another assumption is that the process of accepting diversity has made the organization and its members more flexible. This ability to adapt is critical in a rapidly changing world. The third assumption is that organization culture can change (not just people). Unlike traditional times when people were forced into fitting into the mainstream, managers recognize the need to accommodate the culture to fit the people. Although this may require additional effort, it forces managers to look for core reasons for problems rather than just blaming individuals.

The blueprint for creating an organization that values diversity is a three-phase approach. In Phase One, the organization acknowledges that there is a difference between equal employment opportunity and valuing diversity, and it articulates a vision for pluralism. In Phase Two, the organization implements an educational and change agenda. Awareness training is supplied, support is solicited from everyone within the organization, structures are created to support change, and reward systems are put into place that reflect diverse employee priorities. Phase Three involves monitoring the recruitment, hiring, development, and training operations within the organization so that valuing diversity in the workplace becomes an ongoing activity and not just a quick fix for temporary problems.

Clearly, the American work place is at a crossroads. Organizations can continue to follow their traditional path of hiring or they can follow a new path which values diversity in the workplace. Recent shifts in demographics indicate that following traditional paths may lead to high turnover, low morale, and lagging productivity whereas the advantages for embracing diversity include full utilization of human resources, enhanced working relationships, greater innovation, and improved productivity. If the American workplace is to be competitive for the year 2000, organizational cultures must be changed to value diversity.

READING 3

When the Canary Stops Singing: Women's Perspectives on Transforming Business

Edited by Pat Barrentine
Summary prepared by Scott L. Newstrom

Scott L. Newstrom is a graduate of Grinnell College, Iowa, where he majored in English. He has done research at the Newberry Library, Chicago, and at Oxford University, and was a recipient of a 1993 National Endowment for the Humanities Grant. He is currently pursuing a graduate degree at Harvard University.

Early coal miners would guard against potential air poisoning by keeping canaries in the mining shafts with them, because these birds are more sensitive to changes in air quality than people are. Acting as a natural indicator of toxic gases, the canary would warn the miners of impending danger by stopping its singing. Analogously, *many women are currently leaving high levels of corporations to work elsewhere because of the similarly "toxic," stifling, and oppressive business environments they encounter.* Their dissatisfaction with existing corporate structures can serve as a warning to others that corporate structures must be transformed in multiple ways. In particular, *feminine notions of relating to others and the world can enrich and renew American businesses today.* As a consequence, it is desirable to explore the various responses women have and the different values they bring to business today, both of which can lead to constructive change.

The word *feminine* does not imply qualities or emotions that are unique to women, although they may be more prevalent in women than in men. Rather, *feminine* is applied as psychoanalyst Carl Jung defined the term, emphasizing the characteristics of compassion, loving, and nurturing, which can be found in men as well as women. Thus the application of feminine ideas and methods to the workplace does not exclude businessmen. Both men and women can benefit from business environments that encourage and utilize both feminine and masculine qualities. However, masculine structures have been present for so long that an integration and evaluation of feminine structures is necessary and will produce a positive impact upon business.

Pat Barrentine, *When the Canary Stops Singing*. San Francisco: Barrett-Koehler, 1993.

Today's world is marked by accelerating change, and, therefore, the older ways of doing business can become dysfunctional as time progresses. But organizational renewal through a transformation in business practices can produce valuable results. As business becomes an increasingly powerful and prevalent institution throughout the world, it also needs to take responsibility beyond its traditional economic concerns. Business should be a provider of moral and ethical support at work as well as a major catalyst for change in the world. In addition to simply providing employment, business needs to look at how it affects individuals, communities, entire cultures, and nations. This transition will be difficult, yet necessary if we are to triumph over the problems facing business and the world today. By valuing integrity rather than simply money, *business can begin to adopt a new tradition of taking responsibility for the whole of the world and its people.*

❖ ALTERNATIVE MODELS

If women are harbingers of a toxic environment that calls for change in business, what kinds of change do they recommend? One major change involves examining existing organizational hierarchies. While hierarchies provide a structural solidity for organizing business, they also can become ineffective as a result of their slow rate of change. Hierarchical business architecture is rooted in a *dominator* model of social organization. Like a hierarchy, the dominator model has a vertical structure in which power means power over people. While a dominator model is not uniquely masculine, historically it emerges as a male's power to control others. Dominator models, in old societies, functioned through fear that was backed by force. A system of vertical ranking can lead to domination and conquest. The modern, hierarchical workplace is based on a ranking, vertical system like a dominator model.

In contrast to a dominator model, a *partnership* model is decidedly non-hierarchical. This model of social organization is more supportive and productive than a dominator model. Our economy, as well as our society, would benefit from redesigning the workplace to be more similar to a partnership model. By compartmentalizing responsibilities and capabilities in a narrowly defined, pyramid-like organizational structure, hierarchies encourage workers to ignore the larger problems of a business and instead focus on their specified assignment. By limiting the scope of their job, hierarchies discourage creativity. Since partnership models encourage thinking about the business as a whole and communicating with others, creativity finds a nurturing environment. A diagram of a partnership model of business would look more like an flat circle than a pyramid. Because of the lack of ranking in this newer model, workers relate to each other as equals rather than as subordinates to superiors.

Another diagram of a partnership model could look like a web of relationships, as opposed to a generally more linear hierarchy. It is appropriate that such a model should be espoused by women, since the theory of female moral development articulated in Carol Gilligan's *In A Different Voice* asserts that women tend to focus on their responsibilities within existing webs of relationships. People can learn the values of interdependence from women business leaders who utilize these kinds of organizational webs in structuring their corporations. While converting from a hierarchical business structure to a web or circle structure may involve extensive transformations in the way people think about business, a more difficult transformation is involved in the creation of *community*. As employees work through changes in the workplace environment, a sense of community as true partnership can significantly reduce the fear and confusion surrounding these changes.

❖ STAGES IN COMMUNITY DEVELOPMENT

Sometimes managers may believe that their business has aspects of a community, when in reality this is simply a *pseudo-community* that projects the surface elements yet lacks the content of true communal spirit. When superficial kindness and respect disintegrate and reveal the hollowness of the pseudo-community, organizations often find themselves in a *chaos* mode, where individual differences prevail. Crisis management takes place here, for without such management little would be accomplished. Many organizations seem to be permanently lodged in this mode, never reaching the important *emptying* stage, in which individuals develop a critical self-awareness. This differs from the chaos mode in that rather than simply being aware of diversity and differences in others, workers recognize their own weaknesses and strengths. The final stage is a true *community* mode, in which people feel comfortable about straightforwardly expressing their ideas on both an interpersonal and group level.

Before community acquires form and structure, it first requires an attitude or feeling. While business tends to ignore this, *getting and staying in touch with feelings is crucial for all human development*. Drives toward consciousness and love are essential, which is why some employees become frustrated at work when they lack a deep, communal, loving connection with colleagues. When employees can feel communal love at work (not in a sexual or amorous way but in a caring, supportive sense) they can achieve more. Because of the connections they create and feel with others, they also become conscious of the responsibilities of business leadership that extend beyond the office into the world. Community, love, and consciousness all have roots in a social organizational model of partnership rather than in domination. Partnership emphasizes collaboration rather than cooperation, and affirms the value of differences rather than enforcing conformity and similarity.

❖ THE ORGANIC METAPHOR

Another model that helps to portray interdependence of life and business is an *organic metaphor*. For example, when conducting a job search, a person can help their own search by creating a tree-like chart that connects everyone they know. Main branches indicate groups of people (such as friends, colleagues, family), and smaller branches and leaves become more specific as they decrease in size. By charting their acquaintances this way, they can graphically recognize the numerous sources they have for job information and opportunities. Such a "tree" also reminds them of the way relationships grow from one another, rather than sprouting completely independently.

An organic metaphor can apply to businesses as well, for an organization can be viewed as a garden and management as similar to gardening. Life in organizations requires planting of ideas and values, attention, and sensitive nurturing, similar to how gardeners care for a garden. Weeding out destructive forces from organizations is also necessary in order to allow favored concepts and people to flourish. As a final parallel, organizations eventually enjoy the fruits of their harvest, whether through new products, increased employee productivity, improved workplace morale, or anything that they have taken the time to plant and nurture. This reflects the biblical invocation "As you sow, so shall you reap." Like gardens, organizations that lack carefully planned nurturing can become dysfunctional and sterile. A gardener/manager must also confront the lack of resources and support and the differences that always exist between an ideal plan and the reality of the workplace situation. *Organizational gardening* can be another organic metaphor for a business paradigm.

❖ WHOLE-PERSON DEVELOPMENT

Gardening teaches that there is a direct relationship between the amount of attention given to a plant and the success of the plant's development. This is analogous to how people flourish in organizations. Business needs to recognize that its employees can only reach their greatest potential through whole-person development. Among other things, this means being able to feel love in their work and appreciate community as discussed previously. Developing a person also includes an awareness that people are all part of a larger whole (i.e., they live in an interconnected world). Love, community, and wholeness all can find expression through creativity in the workplace. One way to overcome the apathy and self-doubt that often pervade the workplace is through generating the passion that is the primary source of employee creativity. This personal passion stems from the ability to value uniqueness in oneself as well as in others, and to accept the creative tension that arises from the mixture of one's masculine and feminine qualities. Too often the workplace unconsciously stifles creativity, but organizations need to learn that every worker has huge creative potential which can benefit both the individual and the community. Individuals must also remember that the greatest creativity is inspired by limitations, which encourage creative methods and ideas to surpass these limitations. Finally, creativity grows when personal concerns can be integrated in the workplace, rather than being ignored or even repressed.

Developing a whole person also requires developing vision, both in the individual and in the corporation. By creating new visionary realities people can begin to achieve new possibilities. Too often workers accept their surroundings as they are rather than imagine and work toward what they can be. Tolerating one's own unhappiness unfortunately can lead to a forced resignation rather than inspiring work toward change. The vision that is needed to overcome problematic circumstances is in many senses a spiritual vision. Increasingly, people are looking for greater fulfillment through their work by uniting the spiritual and logical aspects of their lives. This is important, because spiritual poverty at the workplace can leave employees as diminished as physical poverty does. When employees lack spiritual authenticity at work, they may experience grief and even despair. This can drain employees of energy that could be exerted on more valuable projects. Sometimes such a spiritual emergency may require temporary relief, such as having an outside consultant come in and examine what ails the business. In order to build community, people at this stage may need to go through the process of self-reflection involved in emptying so that community can be formed with spirituality.

Spiritual crises could be averted if organizations were to set up *spiritual havens* for employees. As people feel the need to develop themselves wholly and fully, business could provide a program of support and education for them during periods of transition. While programs would vary from business to business, all should include flexibility, solitude, safety, and simplicity. This may mean providing leaves of absence for those who need time for spiritual development, or discussion groups that could provide a dialogue for those who desire to share their experiences. People seek meaning and purpose at work, and providing spiritual havens could encourage employees when they need to turn inward. Because spiritual support is usually absent in today's workplace, a radical shift in values would be required.

Getting in touch with your spiritual side could also include the practical aspect of recognizing the importance of personal intuition. There are times when people need to make a choice based on something beyond their logical capabilities. Intuition gives them this type of insight for important decisions and is actually a skill that can be practiced and improved. One way to improve is through a process of relaxation and meditation called *grounding*. Basically, an individual must relax alone and visualize a grounding cord attached to the base of the spine, where one's intuition will be centered. By using this technique consistently and slowly, trained persons soon will be able to visualize such a grounding cord in stressful situations, which will allow them to check their intuition for the particular situation. If used properly, this relationship with the subconscious can become a useful tool for creative leadership. Proper use includes assessing and questioning the ethical dimensions of intuition, such as confirming that others will not be hurt by personal decisions, making sure that actions are not manipulating others for personal gain, and checking one's intuition against common sense.

Learning to use intuition means learning to listen to the subconscious. Employees also need to re-learn to listen to their colleagues. Since every business must operate through communication, listening and understanding are critical to enabling communication. Yet too often co-workers engage in *automatic listening*, where they don't actually attempt to hear what someone has to say, but rather only affirm their own unexamined assumptions. Within seconds of beginning a conversation, some people react as they always do to a certain person or idea. Automatic listening acts as a filter, only allowing people to hear what they already believe. In a sense, during every conversation each party is "voting" whether they agree with the other's ideas or not. An organization that wishes to maximize its abilities must learn to recognize the automatic listening that is too often present in communication.

Managers need to acknowledge that all of these goals—listening, interdependence, intuition, and so on—can be better understood not as goals that end in completion ("We now have community in our workplace") but rather as processes ("We are creating community"). Much like the garden that needs continued effort, contemplation, and nurturing, all of these goals are ongoing developments that require energy, thought, and time. Thinking of them as ongoing processes also encourages flexibility in planning; unexpected events don't prevent the goals from being met, they merely add to the development of the process in which the organization is engaging.

As organizations become involved in these progressing processes, they also need to be aware of the values that are created and perpetuated through business. The search for meaning and purpose finds its expression through these values. As business's influence becomes more pervasive in the global marketplace, managers need to scrutinize and transform traditional ways of thinking. The challenge is to support those values (e.g., ecological balance, social responsibility, economic transformation, political participation, global spirituality, and world peace without armed conflict) that will both promote business development as well as improve life—not just for those involved in the business but for people everywhere.

❖ CONCLUSION

Essentially, what is most critical to emphasize is *the importance of balance,* from the local level (workplace) to the global level (world market). Like the strength that arises from the equal and complementary status of *yin* and *yang* in Chinese philosophy, individuals, businesses, and nations can all benefit from a balance in all aspects of life. Feminine traits have historically been overshadowed by masculine traits, and there is a need for a more balanced (yet dynamic) equilibrium. In particular, *managers should work toward balance between short- and long-term thinking, local and global perspectives, the individual and the community, action and contemplation, listening and speaking, rationality and spirituality.* Similarities and diversity need to coexist as well. It is time to listen to others, to listen to oneself, and to challenge the imbalances existing today.

11

◆ ◆ ◆

ORGANIZATIONAL CHANGE AND RENEWAL

A philosopher once noted that a person never steps into the same river twice, for the flowing current is always changing. Contemporary organizations have their own "river"—a turbulent environment around them. Consequently, managers of today's organizations are being called on to integrate their operations with a rapidly changing external environment. To do this, they must often adapt their organization's internal structure, processes, and strategies to meet these environmental challenges. The ability to manage change is far different from the ability to manage and cope with the ongoing and routine side of the organization.

Experts frequently advise American managers to invest in research and development (R & D) to keep their product mix current. Some companies (e.g., 3M Corporation) derive as much as 25 percent of their revenues from products introduced in the past five years. Nevertheless, many critics charge that one of the reasons for the decline in the competitiveness of U.S. industry revolves around its failure to innovate at sufficiently high levels. Clearly, organizations need to manage change, stimulate renewal, and seek to convert themselves into continuously learning organizations.

James Belasco, Professor of Management at San Diego State University, wrote *Teaching the Elephant to Dance* (and later, with Ralph Stayer, *Flight of the Buffalo*). Belasco focuses attention on five problems that can hinder change initiatives (time, exaggerated expectations, carping skeptics, procrastination, and imperfection), and identifies four ideas (nichemanship, focus, efficiency, and customer service) that can help overcome organizational resistance to change. He proceeds to offer some insightful ideas on how to devise and implement an organizational vision.

Rosabeth Moss Kanter, in her book *When Giants Learn to Dance*, uses the metaphor of "global corporate olympics" to set the stage for her discussion of the challenges and management strategies that will be necessary for the remainder of the 1990s and beyond. She suggests that leaner organizations must learn to "do more with less" through restructuring and synergy-creation. Winners of the corporate olympics will be those who are focused, able to redeploy resources quickly, friendly toward allies and employees, and flexible in responding to challenges. Kanter discusses six ingredients of effective partnerships, the need for newstreams of products and services, and the emergence of entrepreneurial career paths. Kanter has also written the award-winning *A Tale of O* and, with coauthors Barry Stein and Todd Jick, *The Challenge of Organizational Change: How Companies Experience It and Leaders Guide It.*

Tom Peters is a prolific author, dynamic speaker, and highly sought consultant. He has written or coauthored *In Search of Excellence, A Passion for Excellence, Thriving on Chaos, Liberation Management,* and *The Pursuit of WOW!.* A man who thrives on being provocative, Peters suggest that not just change, but a total transformation of business is underway, marked by revolution, disorganization, entrepreneurizing of jobs, independent mindsets, virtual organizations, leveraging of knowledge, the encouragement of curiosity, and competitive improvements on a firm's existing products. He bravely urges firms to be willing to abandon everything they are now doing and to reinvent themselves.

Michael Beer and Russell Eisenstadt (Professors of Business Administration at Harvard Business School) and Bert Spector (on the faculty at Northeastern University) have focused their recent energies on the management of corporate revitalization. In *The Critical Path to Corporate Renewal,* Beer and his colleagues present a comprehensive theory of corporate revitalization. Their research on six successfully revitalized companies found several key elements featured in each. They encourage the attainment of *task alignment* through actions involving vision, consensus, consolidating changes, and continuous monitoring and strategizing. Key to the renewal process are *revitalization leaders*—high-level executives who use their persuasive powers, articulation skills, and personal actions to stimulate change.

READING 1

Teaching the Elephant to Dance

James Belasco
Summary prepared by Kim A. Stewart

Kim A. Stewart is an Assistant Professor of Management at the University of Denver. She holds a Ph.D. in management from the University of Houston, and teaches courses in strategic management and organizational behavior. Her research interests focus on the post-acquisition integration of acquired firms, and entrepreneurship.

Today's competitive and environmental conditions demand that organizations change to become more efficient, effective, and competitive. However, although the pressures for change are ongoing and often enormous, many organizations are surprisingly resistant to change. One view suggests that organizations resist change because they are like shackled elephants. Although it has the strength to "pull the stake and move beyond," the organization/elephant stands still, bound by earlier conditioned restraints such as past learning or success, or the standard "We've always done it this way." *Teaching the Elephant to Dance* presents a multi-point strategy for organizations to break free of such conditioned constraints and achieve effective change through a strategy that is driven by a vision for the organization.

❖ GET READY FOR THE CHANGE

Preparing for change requires building an urgency for change by convincing employees of the need to change. This can be done by first obtaining "symptoms" of inadequate performance such as customer complaint letters, field sales reports, or competitors' comparisons and then communicating these symptoms to employees via mechanisms such as newsletters, competitor comparison displays in the plant, employee letters, or meetings. Management must also create the clear path of change on which employees will travel and communicate a simple-to-understand destination (the vision). Behaviors that are vital to change (e.g., active listening, quickly handling customer complaints)

James Belasco, *Teaching the Elephant to Dance: The Manager's Guide to Empowering Change.* New York: Plume, 1990.

should be identified, communicated to employees, and reinforced and rewarded when they occur.

❖ ANTICIPATE OBSTACLES

Five potential problems can beset major change initiatives:

1. **Time** Effective change always takes much more time to achieve than people expect. New behaviors are slowly learned and easily forgotten. As a result, leaders must recognize the substantial time requirements and make sure they're committed to spend the time necessary to realize lasting change. They must also report a continual stream of short-term progress produced by the change effort to employees so people don't lose interest in the change vision.

2. **Exaggerated expectations** Once people are actively on the change bandwagon, most want results—now. Unfortunately, results are rarely immediately forthcoming, and worse, inevitable mistakes occur which leave people questioning the wisdom of continuing the change effort. This obstacle can be combatted by clarifying the relationship between the organization's biggest problems and the change effort/vision, by empowering employees to take responsibility for implementing the vision, and by being honest about the problems in implementing the change.

3. **Carping Skeptics** In every organization, some individuals loudly and persistently point out the negatives in any situation or change effort. They can be ignored (which usually works in the short run). However, a better strategy is to confront the critics and their concerns early and directly. Change leaders should show personal interest in skeptics' concerns, and enlist their aid and support in the change effort. The enthusiasm of other employees and the progress measured to date can also be effectively used to convert skeptics.

4. **Procrastination** Given employees' workload and the intangibles of change efforts that many managers like to avoid (e.g., customer attitudes and employee motivations), it's easy for people to postpone vision-supporting activities. Procrastination can be dealt with by breaking change-supporting actions into small, more doable steps, by keeping up a steady but reasonable pressure for change behaviors, and by emphasizing the successes in an immediate and dramatic way.

5. **Imperfection** Mistakes are made and failures occur in all major change initiatives. However, organizations must strive for continual improvement in the change effort rather than explicit perfection. Mistakes should be seen positively—as learning experiences and as an opportunity to refocus efforts on the change vision.

❖ BUILD A NEW ORGANIZATIONAL STRATEGY

Major internal changes often require a new internal strategy. Four strategies (*nichemanship, focus, efficiency,* and *customer service*) merit the attention of changing organizations that are striving to build a better product or service. Companies that purse a *nichemanship* strategy fulfill a segment of unmet demand in a larger market. For example, Von's Supermarket moved from fourth place to the top spot among grocery store chains in southern California by identifying and fulfilling specific niches. This included Spanish neighborhoods in Fresno, California, where Von's introduced into its stores a wider selection of Hispanic foods, new lighting and displays, and a black-and-red colored decor. Success at nichemanship requires that companies dominate the niche, stay on top of customer needs, find upscale applications for commodity products, use advertising to enhance the company's niche image, stay flexible, avoid direct competition with major players, and avoid dependence on a small number of suppliers and customers.

The *focus* strategy involves getting back to the basics—focusing on those things that are essential to the company's success, such as customer needs. The *efficiency* strategy focuses on achieving long-term efficiencies often via the use of automated equipment to cut manufacturing/distribution costs. The *customer service* strategy seeks to enhance service via highly selective recruiting and extensive training of employees, measuring service levels continuously, and consistently rewarding top-service performers.

❖ FOCUS RESOURCES ON THE CHANGE EFFORT

Strategy alone does not achieve the change vision; people and funds are essential tools in realizing the "new tomorrow." Effectively addressing the people factor in change involves identifying the "leverage positions"—those jobs which have the most impact on achieving change and realizing the vision (e.g., R&D staff in a new product development strategy). For each leverage job, the skills, knowledge, attitudes, and behaviors needed to do the job well should be identified, and the individual who best matches this "ideal profile" should be hired. Two major tasks concern resources. The first involves reducing spending on the nonessential activities. The second entails lowering the costs of essential activities by such strategies as simplifying operations (reducing steps in manufacturing, eliminating decision-making and layers of management), tapping employee creativity, and improving quality that reduces the costs of product rework, scrap, and warranties.

❖ CREATE A VISION

The vision drives major organizational change. The vision should be:

- ◆ "a short, simple statement . . .
- ◆ "of some value-adding and marketplace-advantage factors . . .
- ◆ "which positively distinguishes the organization in the minds of everyone with whom the organization interacts (customers, employees, suppliers) . . .
- ◆ "and provides clear, inspiring criteria for decision making."

Honda Motors' vision, for example, is one that meets these criteria. It accents (1) "Quality in all jobs—learn, think, analyze, evaluate, and prove; (2) reliable products—on time, with excellence and consistency; and (3) better communication—listen, ask, and speak up."

In crafting a vision, the major change initiators should be sure that the vision is practical and is consistent with their personal values. The vision statement should be reviewed with people from all areas and levels of the organization to be sure it is clearly understood (as people can only be empowered by a vision they understand).

❖ EMPOWER PEOPLE TO USE THE VISION

Actions that lead to employee empowerment to use and realize the vision can take many forms. Initially it is essential that the CEO or change initiator identify the behaviors and actions that reflect the vision and then personally demonstrate these behaviors in highly visible situations. For example, CEO J. W. Marriott, Jr., believes that Marriott guests value the little touches that distinguish between average and great service. So he spends much of his time touring Marriott's hotels, personally inspecting those little things and making sure that hotel employees see him doing it.

The CEO must also continually remind people that the vision is working, in part by identifying behaviors that are key to realizing the vision, and keeping a very public charting of those behaviors. For example, in the employee cafeteria at Springfield Remanufacturing Company, a large electronic board flashes the plant's hourly results of activities (e.g., labor usage) that are critical to the company's profitability.

The CEO should use employee meetings to discuss the vision and report change progress. The CEO can utilize group management meetings in efforts to empower managers to accept and use the vision. The CEO should work on getting managers to understand the vision by discussing specific action steps that support the vision, and developing short-term action plans that managers can more easily implement.

❖ DEVELOP EXPECTATIONS AND MEASURES

Once the vision is established, it should be translated into specific quantitative measures by which employee behavior and performance will be evaluated. The measures should be simple and limited to those activities that support the new vision (a long list of measures can be confusing and diffuse employee efforts). Clear, quantitative, and short-term expectations should be clearly communicated to employees. People should receive direct and fast feedback concerning the behaviors needed and desired.

❖ USE THE PERSONNEL SYSTEM TO EMPOWER CHANGE

Concerning the recruitment element of the personnel system, a selection profile should be developed that includes characteristics that support the vision. Interviewers and those who make hiring decisions should be trained to use the profile, looking for the right knowledge, skills, and attitudes. (Indeed, these individuals should reflect the vision.) Orientation programs are an excellent opportunity to communicate the vision. Immediate supervisors can also develop a specific orientation program concerning how the vision is used in the particular department. Training programs can be used to reinforce the vision. For example, at United Parcel Service over eighty percent of the full-time work force attend voluntary workshops held after work that focus on the company's competitive challenges. These workshops support the UPS vision: boosting efficiency and customer service. Some part of every training program can also focus on how a particular tool or information can be applied to support and reinforce the vision.

Behaviors that are essential to the vision should be included in the performance appraisal system. The organization's compensation system should reward vision-related performance. Rewards can be group-based or individual (for example, Genentech Company provides instant bonus "Genenchecks" of $1,000 for employees who develop new research applications). Recognition is also a powerful motivation tool. For example, at Transco Energy in Houston, quarterly "bragging sessions" are held where individuals tell all attending employees about what they've done to boost customer services and cut operational costs. According to CEO George Slocum, these sessions have helped to save over $18 million.

❖ DEVELOP A VISION-BASED CULTURE

If the vision is new, a new culture that supports the vision must be created, and the old vision (and culture supporting it) must be laid to rest. A ritual of passage is essential to mark this transition. In this meeting with all employees, the CEO should recall the best of the organization's past (which can be contrasted with the present which is less positive), and point to a better future. The actual risks and challenges of implementing the new vision should be addressed. Once the organization is on the path to the new vision, this transition-in-the-making should be celebrated.

Beyond this passage ritual which launches the transition to the new vision, the new culture can be further developed by building work activities that support and reflect the vision. For example, Hewlett-Packard's long-held vision of product innovation was for years encultured by the company's tradition of the "next desk." Here, engineers were encouraged to leave their work on their desk so others could look it over and contribute their own ideas to its development.

Shared social activities and special events can also be created to develop the culture. Again at H-P, Friday afternoon beer busts are held which the company believes enhance the values of individual respect and communication. A vision-supporting culture can be developed by crafting phrases that aptly convey the vision and repeating them frequently in company media, and by communicating stories about "heroes" (individuals whose actions exemplify the new vision). AT&T, for example, has a number of heroes that populate its rich history. Among the most aptly remembered heroines was a telephone operator who remained at her station amidst a raging fire so that she could maintain crucial telephone connections.

❖ EMPOWER INDIVIDUAL CHANGE AGENTS

This task involves bringing the vision and the change process down to the gut level for each and every individual in the organization. Doing so involves first developing for each business unit or department *strategic business issues* (SBIs)—those issues which are critical to the unit's performance and success. The vision should be linked to the resolution of the issues. These linkages should be communicated to the unit's employees, to enhance the commitment of employees to the vision. It is also useful to encourage all employees to identify their own contributions to the unit's strategic business issues, to focus efforts on those issues and vision-relevant behaviors.

Another way to empower individual change agents is to identify, within each unit, each individual's suppliers and customers. (For a production control manager at a metal fabrication plant, for example, a supplier is a purchasing agent who provides the materials the manager needs; a customer is the manager of the plant's second shift who uses the first manager's finished parts). Then, employees should regularly meet with their suppliers and customers to establish and update "contracts" which specify how each party helps the other in the performance of their jobs. These contracts should be linked to the department's SBIs and the organizational vision, and the contracts should focus on "specific, quantifiable, short-stroke deliverables."

READING 2

When Giants Learn to Dance

Rosabeth Moss Kanter
Summary prepared by Robert C. Ford

Robert C. Ford is at the University of Central Florida. He holds a Ph.D. in management from Arizona State University. In addition to publishing texts on principles of management and organization theory, he has authored or coauthored articles on applied management practices, human resource management, and social responsibility in both practitioner and academic journals. He is an active member of the Academy of Management, the Southern Management Association, and the Society for Human Resource Management.

Are organizations ready for the Global Olympics? Can corporate giants (organizational elephants) learn to dance with the grace and nimbleness of the practiced ballerina or even, for that matter, the untrained kid at the prom? This is the question that Rosabeth Moss Kanter seeks to answer by reviewing the lessons learned on her multiple-year journey through the organizational experiences of her clients at Goodmeasure and her research investigations as a scholar in the Harvard Business School. Her answer is maybe. But first there must be a sea of change in the corporate culture and managerial style for those organizations who seek to compete successfully in the rapidly changing and highly competitive world arena. Kanter details the strategies that organizations can adopt to meet these changes as well as the reasons why the "old answers" simply don't work any more.

❖ COMPETING IN THE CORPORATE OLYMPICS

Corporations are competing in a worldwide arena in which the rules of the game are not unlike the croquet game in *Alice in Wonderland* where everything is alive, changing, unpredictable, and moving. The whole field of competition is in motion, and the old rules, the expectation of some consistency in the game, and the availability of clearly defined goals to guide strategy and decision-making have become anachronisms. American businesses, once the

Rosabeth Moss Kanter, *When Giants Learn to Dance*. New York: Simon & Schuster, 1989.

proud exemplar of modern management, are now trying to adjust to a new world of contradictions. Now they seek to find ways of becoming lean and mean, a great company to work for, competitive in a global marketplace, and able to do more with fewer resources.

These are not only competing demands; they are increasingly important challenges for those firms that wish to compete successfully in the "Corporate Olympics." The solution can be found in the rise of the post-entrepreneurial organization. This relatively new form of organization is somewhere between the classical and too-familiar bureaucratic form of a Kodak, a PacTel, or a General Electric that Kanter terms a "Corpocracy" and the highly individualist, young, highly entrepreneurial form of organization of an Apple Computer that she labels "Cowboy." As the bureaucratic Kodak struggled to become more entrepreneurial and the cowboy Apple struggled to be less individualistic, they both gravitated towards a middle ground by adopting the strategies which characterize the post-entrepreneurial organization.

This form of organization is one that effectively implements three strategies:

1. Restructuring to create synergistic relationship;
2. Creating strategic alliances with key stakeholders (e.g. suppliers, customers, and venture partners);
3. Developing specific programs to nurture, encourage, and support entrepreneurial activity within their organizations.

While different organizations may implement these strategies differently, those who are set on winning will find a way of doing so. The next two sections explain how to implement these strategies, and the consequences for the corporation, the employees, and society as a whole.

❖ DOING MORE WITH LESS

◆ RESTRUCTURING

Too many efforts to restructure organizations have failed to solve the people and economic problems that such corporate upheavals create. Therefore, they miss achieving the gains expected through synergy. This failure leads to discontinuity, disorder, and distraction. *Discontinuity* is caused by moving from the old to the new (restructured) organization. Whether the restructuring is a result of downsizing, merger, or buy-out, the uncertainty to the participants is the same, as they attempt to bury the old and create something different: new structures, cultures, and interpersonal relationships. *Disorder* arises from the confusion created as the restructured organization builds new channels of information, loses key resources and people, and redefines new corporate values and job expectations. *Distraction* results from management's inevitable shift of focus and energy away from the process of running the business to the more immediate problems created by the restructuring. Restructuring can, therefore, create an enormous vulnerability to problems at precisely the same time that everyone's attention, energy, and focus are distracted. This very point in time the organization desperately needs the recommitment, rededication, and reinvigoration of its employees so that it can gain the expected benefits of its restructuring, yet it is most at risk to lose them all. Since reorganization leads to uncertainty and insecurity, and employee commitment requires certainty and security, the successful post-entrepreneurial organization must strike a balance between these competing forces.

◆ OBTAINING SYNERGY

This balance can be achieved by restructuring in ways that create a new whole that is greater than the sum of its previous parts. This search for *synergy* has two levels. At one level is the search for organizational gains that can be obtained by finding good combinations of parts and avoiding bad combinations. This can be done through a "value-added" test. At the other level are the people gains obtained by restructuring the intellectual content and personal responsibility. This can be done through various strategies of empowerment.

Finding good combinations of organizational parts is a result of thoughtful consideration of what each part contributes to the entire organizational purpose. The idea of "value-added" forces those considering a restructuring to think through whether or not any new organization units will in fact allow them to gain the efficiencies of economies of scale, fill out a product line, access new management or technical expertise, attract better people through better career opportunities, enhance access to competitive information or previously unavailable markets, and reaffirm a shared value structure with a commitment to performance. Using this "value-added" test forces a reassessment of every part of the organization, to see what that part actually contributes and whether or not there might be a better way to obtain that contribution. In short, the post-entrepreneurial organization thinks of itself as a central information and command center for all of its component elements, constantly evaluating each organizational component to decide what it wants to do itself and what it is better off letting someone else do for it. No part of the organization should be immune from this "value-added" test.

Those organizations which actually gain these synergies have three characteristics in common. First, top management leads the way. Senior executives show their commitment to finding the synergies by creating the methods and developing the managers who identify them. Second, the organization shifts its incentives and reward programs to focus everyone's attention on cooperating with each other in pursuit of the corporate well-being instead of competing against each other in pursuit of their individual goals. The third characteristic is the existence of a culture of cooperation, which leads to good interpersonal and interdepartmental relationships and information sharing. These characteristics allow the post-entrepreneurial organization to respond flexibly and effectively to the changing environment.

◆ CREATING STRATEGIC ALLIANCES

It is not enough, however, to improve the cooperation and communication only within the organization. The post-entrepreneurial organization recognizes the need to build the same quality of communication and cooperative relationships with those upon whom its effectiveness depends. It recognizes the importance of the extended "economic family" and finds ways to keep these relationships healthy.

There are three basic strategies for accomplishing these ends. They are "(P)ooling," "(A)llying," and "(L)inking." *Pooling* refers to a method by which the organization shares resources with another. *Allying* refers to the formation of temporary corsortia or joint ventures. *Linking* is the process whereby the organization forms a partnership to link together specific parts of itself with another organization. All three strategies have as their goal the creation of organizational "PALs" which replace the traditional adversarial relationship between those inside and those outside the firm with a collaborative and cooperative one: strategic alliance.

These new forms of relationships created by PAL strategies are not only important to improving the post-entrepreneurial organization's ability to respond flexibly and efficiently in the rapidly changing world market place, but they also have significant and important impact inside the organization as well. When management seeks to build cooperative linkages *between* organizations, this causes further disruptions inside the organization itself. PALs, for example, challenge the traditional hierarchical power relationships by shifting managerial authority orientation from control to collaborative. Managers must now learn how to manage a network of collaborative, cooperative relationships rather than merely controlling people. Problems can include overmanagement, undermanagement, conflicts over scope, and hedging on resource allocations by one or all of the partners.

◆ THE SIX "I"s

There are six ingredients (six "I"s) which must be in place for a partnership to be successful. These are:

1. The relationship must be **I**mportant to all partners.
2. There is an agreement for a long term **I**nvestment which balances the rewards over time.
3. The partners have thoroughly defined their **I**nterdependence to balance the power relationships.
4. The partners have built into their organizations points of **I**ntegration to ensure smooth communication and cooperation.
5. Each keeps the other **I**nformed about its plans and expectations.
6. The partnership is somehow **I**nstitutionalized through both formal legal documents and informal social ties and shared cultures which can maintain mutual trust.

◆ NEWSTREAMS

Besides the use of PALs which permit flexible response to changing market demands by organizations, there are internal strategies as well. These are based on managers being able to develop newstreams of products and services, while not neglecting their mainstream. Mainstream products and services are closely associated with the past and present organizational survival and profitability. *Newstream* reflects future products and services, and they present management with an entirely different set of concerns. Newstream differs from mainstream in the type of performance criteria used to measure success, the amount of uncertainty associated with dealing with untested ideas, and in the impact that the newstream may have on the existing structure, people, and power relationships. Since the potential payoffs are so great, the requirements for organizational commitment to newstreams are likewise great.

Newstreams are important to the post-entrepreneurial organization not only because they represent the future products and services necessary to compete in the Corporate Olympics, but also because of what they represent in defining the culture. The message that emphasis on newstream sends throughout the organization is one of commitment to innovation in all aspects of the organization. This emphasis does, however, create some dilemmas. One is that newstream efforts require personnel to be effective change agents. Newstream projects need autonomy, but not so much that they lose their linkages to the mainstream organization. Newstream peoples' efforts are driven on by an entrepreneurial energy, but the fruits of these efforts must be captured or shared by the organization. This raises some interesting problems for the post-entrepreneurial organization. How can it allow some elements of its organization to have the thrill, rewards, and energizing experience of discovering newstream products and services without at the same time finding similar rewards and experiences for its mainstream people? If newstream people can be trusted to be creative and entrepreneurial, why can't the mainstream? Management can't allow the organization to separate into "haves" and "have-nots" without compromising its ability to secure commitment and effort from all of its people in the face of continuing uncertainty and change. This raises the question of how it can ensure that all the members are included in the "haves" category.

❖ JOBS, PEOPLE, MONEY

◆ CONSEQUENCES OF THE POST-ENTREPRENEURIAL REVOLUTION

As the post-entrepreneurial organization comes to grips with the need for PALs and the Newstream ventures also come to grips with their impacts on traditional personnel policies, management must rethink its reward systems. The hierarchy upon which the traditional organization depended as a means for assigning power, status, and money is increasingly challenged in an organization driven by the power of new and creative ideas and people. Increasingly, people expect pay to reflect contribution and not just longevity or position in the chain of command. The pressure on organizations to encourage the needed entrepreneurial activity which leads to newstreams means that they must reshape their traditional pay plans to encourage and reward fairly this type of employee behavior.

◆ NEW PAY PLANS

The response has been to develop gainsharing systems, pay for skills, pay for performance, profit sharing, and merit pay that is meaningful. Managing pay plans in the post-entrepreneurial organization is a delicate balancing act as the organization seeks a reward system which fairly balances recognition of individual contributions (to reward individual effort) with recognition of the group (to maintain the necessary interdependencies of all individuals), the unit accomplishments with overall organizational achievements, and the traditional internal pay structure and external market forces with individual contributions. The post-entrepreneurial organization is likely to discover that the pay scheme it finds most workable is one that incorporates recognition of all these diverse elements.

The post-entrepreneurial organization is not only finding the need to discover new pay schemes, but it is also confronting new types of jobs and the pressures on its employees that go with them. These jobs are rich with challenge and opportunity. They are exciting, and people become committed to them, think about them intensely, and take time away from family and outside activities to pursue them. This leads to information overload and job-related stress. The very nature of entrepreneurial activity creates more time commitments. Time is required to ensure that the necessary communications partnerships and interactions develop. Time is required to handle the inevitable stream of new tasks and activities that change creates. And time is required to respond to the flatter, more fluid, organizations that allow a variety of people to initiate ideas to which someone has to listen and respond.

Post-entrepreneurial organizations have an important and often unrecognized role to play here. Successful organizations do three things to help. First, they delegate the authority to go along with the expanded responsibilities to eliminate the need to spend time checking with the boss. Second, they minimize the number of changes occurring simultaneously by prioritizing the important and less important issues and not trying to implement everything at the same time. Finally, they simplify by constantly rethinking the systems, procedures, rules, and regulations so there is not any unnecessary burden on their people. In addition, managers need to recognize a legitimate role for life outside the firm. Also, for these people, most work is done in cycles of intense effort followed by lulls. The lulls could be used to allow mini-sabbaticals, vacations, and time away from the job, which help people to regroup and get revitalized.

◆ CAREERS

The last major impact on the individual from the creation of post-entrepreneurial organizations is a redefinition of the individual career. Traditionally, people have thought of a career as something that takes place in one organization where a person progresses up some functional career ladder. Thus, marketing trainees work their way up the corporate ladder, perhaps rising to senior marketing positions, as they enter the twilight of their "corporatic" careers. There is a strong attachment to the organization and weak attachment to the task or work group. The organization rewards loyalty and seniority by gradual promotion up the hierarchy. Room is made for these promotions by expanding growth and narrowing spans of control to allow more senior-level positions to become available.

◆ TWO CAREER PATHS

This idyllic scenario will be less and less true in the emerging post-entrepreneurial organization. The hierarchy is getting flatter while organizations are downsizing and eliminating opportunities for career growth in the traditional way. Instead, there will be two new paths for individuals to follow. One is the professional career where people make a career out of seeking excellence in their own areas of functional expertise, moving from one task and organization to another, continuously seeking new opportunities to display that expertise as well as adding to their professional reputation.

The second new path is the entrepreneurial career. Here individuals leave the corpocracy behind and strike out on their own. These people are ready and willing to take the risk of gaining the freedom, independence, and control over their own economic and personal life that owning their own business can bring. Further, they give business and the economy more flexibility by being available to supplement the efforts of the traditional organization on an "as-needed," value-added basis. These career professionals and the entrepreneurs are critical in helping the giant to dance with grace and nimbleness in the global market-place.

❖ CONCLUSION

Corporations that hoped to succeed in the Corporate Olympics need to use the four "Fs":

1. Focused on what they're doing.
2. Fast in redeploying their resources to meet the changing environment.
3. Friendly toward their PALs and own employees.
4. Flexible in responding to the changing environmental circumstances they face.

This means that their leaders will also need to learn seven new skills to gain the value-added synergies available through new alliances and newstreams, while maintaining a dynamic, committed, and motivated work force energetically seeking new ideas. First, these new leaders must learn to manage without relying on the traditional authority of the hierarchy. Instead, they need to learn how to exercise personal influence and interpersonal skills to get things done. Second, these leaders must learn how to compete in a way that promotes healthy cooperation to achieve excellence instead of an unhealthy quest for devastating the competition. Third, these leaders must be ethical to retain the trust necessary to make these cooperative relationships work. Fourth, they must be humble enough to listen to other ideas and receptive to learning new ways of doing things. Fifth, they need to develop a respect for the process of how things are done rather than focusing solely on what is done. Sixth, these new leaders need to be flexible enough to seek out and build new relationships within and outside the organization when they can add value, and be able to cut them loose when they don't. Finally, these new business leaders must find satisfaction in performance instead of status and in attaining results instead of promotions. This portrays a new type of manager for a new type of organization managing a new type of employee with new types of relationships to the organization and to the work itself. While the challenge is considerable, the rewards for those giants that do learn to dance are equally great.

READING 3

The Tom Peters Seminar

Tom Peters
Summary prepared by Jane Giacobbe-Miller

Jane Giacobbe-Miller is an Associate Professor of Management at the University of Massachusetts at Amherst. She received a Ph.D. from Cornell University. She conducts research in team-based management, labor mobility, and organizational justice. She teaches in the fields of human resource management, labor relations, and employment law. She has also consulted for organizations regarding the implementation of teams, empowerment programs, and Total Quality Management initiatives.

The rapidly-changing world and its associated challenges to the ways in which business is conducted should cause all managers to reexamine their previously held beliefs about management. Preservation of the U.S. position in the world economy will come from innovation and the creation/dissemination of knowledge. The emergence of Third World countries as ready sources of low-paid labor will continue to erode the manufacturing base in the United States. Organizational assets will no longer be valued primarily (if at all) on equipment, machinery, or facilities. Increasingly, "human imagination" will become the primary organizational asset.

"Beyond empowerment," "beyond TQM," "beyond continuous improvement"—the future look and feel of organizations is well "beyond" the button-down corporate world as we know it. The concept of corporations with headquarters, with an established and permanent workforce, with hierarchical structures and systems to support them are revolutionized in the new, innovative, knowledge-based economy. The organizational transformation is well underway, and it is marked by nine major phenomena.

❖ 1. NOT CHANGE . . . REVOLUTION

In order to prepare for the knowledge-based economy, managers must be prepared to *abandon everything*. Change, continuous improvement, and incremental steps towards implementation of a strategic plan need to be scrapped.

Tom Peters, *The Tom Peters Seminar*. New York: Random House, 1994.

Today's emerging economy requires unbounded thinking and quick reactions to customer needs. We are in a period of rapid acceleration, pedal to the metal. The organization that stays in the slow lane will be run down by the competition. The U.S. organization that thrives, or even survives, will do so by selling its knowledge, its creativity, its magic. Physical products will be of declining importance, particularly if their production is routine, requiring little skill. How does the manager begin the dismantling of the old organization? It begins with . . .

❖ 2. *DISORGANIZATION*

The old, formal, bureaucratic organization has got to go. Up the chain of command, down the chain of command. How many ideas get buried, lost, diluted, or become obsolete by the time they clear all of the hurdles? The new, rapid-response organization has few, if any, layers. Small-scale units, even within large enterprises, are called for in the new, knowledge- and innovation-based economy. Modeled after the "Mom and Pop" corner store, these small-scale units are close to the customer and close to the edge. Their survival is dependent on the goodwill of a handful of customers. Their relationships with their customers are close, intimate, seamless as they work together at all stages of product development and delivery. *Beyond decentralization, what is called for is a new federalism where power is vested in the periphery and shared only sparingly with the center.* The concerns of the center are to support the periphery with information and paperwork.

Titeflex, a company in Springfield, Massachusetts, embodies the new concept of small companies within larger ones. Business-development teams were created out of a larger workforce of 500 employees. Beyond contemporary notions of empowerment, these teams deal directly with customers, generate sales, and engage in capital spending. Without bureaucracies and layers, the teams can respond creatively, and quickly, to the needs of their customers. All of this requires nerves of steel, as managers abandon strategies and relinquish control to the small business unit. Beyond business-development teams, organizations should empower employees more deeply and more meaningfully than ever before.

❖ 3. *ENTREPRENEURIZING EVERY JOB*

How can average employees tap the limits of their imagination when they are told to think no further than their job description? Most employees can do far more than they are currently trusted to do. In their private lives they make mortgage decisions worth hundreds of thousands of dollars. Employees make decisions about cars, insurance, major household purchases and often even run businesses on the side! Yet they are frequently not trusted to make financial decisions at work or even to exercise sound judgments about what they need to make their jobs more efficient or effective. *Employees should be given complete ownership over their jobs.* Employees acquire ownership by having (a) complete knowledge obtained through cross-training in all relevant skills; (b) personal budgets to be expended as they deem necessary to better serve the customer; (c) mechanisms and processes for quality assurance; (d) access to internal and external expertise; (e) their own customers, to whom their service is limited only by their imagination; (f) an unlimited travel budget; and (g) the authority to make final decisions. Period. Beyond entrepreneurship, employees must have . . .

❖ 4. *THE MINDSET OF AN INDEPENDENT CONTRACTOR*

The emerging jobs of today, the good jobs of tomorrow, are lacking in definition. They defy description. They are the products of joint ventures between organizations and customers. The incumbents of these jobs must learn to live and flourish with ambiguity. The only performance appraisal will come in the form of endorsements from customers. Established processes and procedures will be abandoned, to be replaced by blank pages and blank checks, "whatever it takes," constrained only by law, ethics, and the imagination. Career paths within organizations will disappear. Job security comes from investing in oneself, building one's portfolio, increasing the investment in one's human capital. The casual approach to continued learning, attendance at the occasional seminar or two-day training sessions, will no longer be enough to ensure marketability. Introductory courses and passing familiarity will give way to true mastery of cutting-edge research. *Mastery of the ability to acquire knowledge, not just knowledge itself, will be paramount.* Navigating the informational highway at breakneck speed will be a prerequisite to success.

Employees' futures will be secured by their skills inventory, their personal resume, and their network of business contacts. Everything that is done today should be done not only for the business, but also for personal growth and development. Outcomes that can be displayed, identified by customers, and provide testimony to the unique abilities of the employee will replace the references of today. The resume should tell a story of continuous personal improvement. Taking these steps now will prepare employees for the new, boundaryless organization.

❖ 5. *ORGANIZATIONS CREATED BY ROLODEXES*

Imagine an organization without a headquarters, where employees have laptop computers instead of desks. Imagine a continuous cycle of creating loosely woven organizations in response to specific customer needs and then disassembling them when the job is complete. The temporary "organization" encompasses a collection of the best talent for the particular project, who may never be reassembled in precisely this way again. Imagine projects that are not done vertically, from inception of an idea to completion of a product. Rather, projects are done horizontally, as specialists are called upon to tackle the problem from all perspectives, at all stages, simultaneously. Anything that can be done vertically can be done faster and cheaper horizontally, by a network of specialists. Pedal to the metal.

The new virtual organization will be without boundaries. It will be edgeless, with fluid forms and shifting configurations. The concept of employees will be replaced by independent contractors, who *sign on* for a project and then *move on* when the project is complete. Mutual trust will hold it all together.

But what do organizations do? What is the role of management? *The most important thing management can do in the new organization is to facilitate the acquisition and dissemination of knowledge.*

❖ 6. *LEVERAGING OF KNOWLEDGE*

The organization that learns to leverage knowledge will be most likely to survive, perhaps even thrive, in the new economy. Yet, leveraging knowledge requires organizations to persuade individuals to change old habits. The hierarchial organization rewarded those who possessed information. Information was power. Information was security. In order to leverage knowledge, the new organization must change the basis for power. *The most powerful person in the new organization will be the one who not only acquires knowledge, but shares it freely throughout the organization.* The recognition and reward structure must be changed to support the desired outcome. Those who hoard information will find themselves out of a job.

McKinsey & Co. may serve as an example of the possibilities. The company has established thirty "practice centers" that serve as storehouses of corporate knowledge in specialty areas. The goal is to use electronic network capabilities to share the collective knowledge of the organization with each consultant. Consultants may direct questions to any of the practice centers. Consultant-specialists provide rapid responses using state-of-the-art company practices. This allows general consultants or consultants from different specialties to draw on the best practices the company has in its repertoire. But how does one expand the repertoire of practices, the breadth of company knowledge? Besides encouraging employees to become entrepreneurs and independent contractors, their imaginations must be nurtured.

❖ 7. *THE CURIOUS CORPORATION*

Most companies today are dull, lethargic, stiff, barely breathing. To create a curious corporation, the organization should hire lively, curious people. These are people with gaps in their resume who have done extraordinary, or extraordinarily weird, things. These unlikely applicants in today's corporate world will show a propensity to follow the road least traveled, if there is any sense of a road or direction at all. Once hired, the organization should foster their creativity. Have contests for the most unusual, the most wacky idea. Banish the idea that "looking busy" is important. Allow for people to explore the depths of their imaginations by letting them do what works for them, whether it's a dart game, working at night and sleeping in the day, or taking extended sabbaticals and vacations. Some of the most creative ideas happen when people are at leisure.

Encourage curiosity by teaching the art of brainstorming and problem solving. Allow employees to clutter their desks and their minds with uncontrolled thinking. Alter the physical environment so that everyone can be self-expressive. Allow for ample open space for sharing of ideas, information or simply building a comfort level so that idea sharing will come easily. Make the workplace comfortable, one that is conducive to dreaming.

Think beyond the one-dimensional measure of excellence. Rather than determining success by the profit margin, stockholder dividends, or customer satisfaction, measure success by the answer to the following question. *Would you want your son or daughter to work here?*

Unleashing creative energies, establishing loose networks of knowledge and information specialists, competition for the craziest idea—where's it all heading? Our nation's corporations have worked so hard to get control, to embrace the concept of continuous improvement, to record what we do so that our processes and outcomes are dependable. All of that was important in the past, but continuous improvement isn't enough. We have to move beyond TQM.

❖ 8. BEYOND TQM AND TGW TO TGR AND WOW!

After the quality coup of the 1980s, most U.S. products that survived can today pass the quality test. They have mastered the ability to detect and correct the TGW (things gone wrong). But quality is not enough to ensure a leading position in today's product markets. Flawless products are not a rarity, in domestic or global markets. In order to be a stand-out today, products must pass the "Wow!" test. They have to capture the imagination, rise above the mundane, dazzle the customer. They have to shift their focus to TGR (things gone right).

It all begins with the premise that anything, *anything*, can be made special. Take as an example the cab driver who, besides taking the most direct route and delivering the passenger safely, offers snacks, newspapers, and a choice of music. Then there's the example of the "counterfeit mailbag." In reality, it's an imitation, old-fashioned mail bag. But it's promoted as a national treasure, as the bag that carried the "ideas and feelings" of an entire nation.

Innovation and success brings with it the risk—no, the *promise*—that the product will be copied. Once innovation meets with success, continuous improvement to old ideas won't be enough. The competition will be focusing on ways to improve the idea, too. The companies who flourish in the new product markets will offer a continuous wave of new, vastly different products.

What are the sources of these new ideas? Some will come through collaboration with customers. But if a company listens only to its current customers it limits its own imagination to theirs. If the organization has done what was suggested earlier—hiring curious people and transforming employees into entrepreneurs—the successful organization will have to go beyond meeting its customer's needs in new and creative ways. It will also have to set its people free to *create* customer needs (invention is the mother of necessity).

Before one reaches the conclusion that wild and wacky products and symbiotic relationships with the customer is enough, don't forget the importance of process. *Customers are influenced at least as much by the process as they are by the outcomes.* How they are sold a product or treated by the designer will be at least as important as their satisfaction with the product itself. Beyond the "Wow" will be the "Woo."

❖ 9. *PERPETUAL REVOLUTION*

The biggest handicap in today's corporation is conservative thinking, cautious behavior. Ironically, companies should be more afraid of doing nothing, or doing something insignificant, than of doing something that fails. Fear of failure creates paralysis, and paralysis will cause death in the new economy.

To break out of the mold of conservative, "small steps" thinking, *companies must abandon everything.* They must continuously and completely reinvent their products, their standards, their reward structures, and senior management behavior. There should be a continuous turnover of old ideas (an idea is "old" as soon as it reaches the market), or turnover of people if they can't break away from old-pattern thinking.

The new economy is not for the weak of heart. Forget courage. What's needed is well beyond courage. The new economy requires us all to throw caution to the wind.

READING 4

The Critical Path to Corporate Renewal

Michael Beer, Russell A. Eisenstat, and Bert Spector
Summary prepared by Warren Candy

A native of Australia, **Warren Candy** received his B.S. in Production Engineering from Swinburne College of Technology in Melbourne, Australia. His career in the United States has been in industrial engineering, and as the Leader of the Organizational Development Team at Minnesota Power, an investor-owned utility in northern Minnesota. He currently is the Director of the Clay Boswell power generation facility with the utility and is active within several industrial engineering and organizational innovation associations.

In the battle to reclaim competitiveness, a powerful approach that is being used by an increasing number of American companies is that of organizational revitalization. Leaders in these companies look beyond the need to manage financial assets wisely by recognizing that competitiveness is inexorably linked to the abilities and effectiveness of their employees.

Six large corporations engaged in a conscious effort to make fundamental change in their patterns of management were studied. The companies were selected on a number of criteria: the need for a variety of industries, for representation in the manufacturing and service sectors, for inclusion of both single and multibusiness firms, and their willingness to provide open research access. The companies' sales ranged from $4 billion to $10 billion. Five were in the manufacturing sector, and one was a large international bank. Although the companies and individuals in the study are real, all names used are fictitious. They are referred to as Continental Glass and Container, General Products, Fairweather Corporation, Livingston Electronics, Scranton Steel, and U.S. Financial.

A comprehensive theory of corporate revitalization is presented that will help managers develop an adaptive organization. In these firms, organizational members understand all the plans and strategies, know and anticipate one another's roles and responsibilities, and are eager to work together by looking at the success of the business, rather than their own function or job.

Michael Beer, Russell A. Eisenstat, & Bert Spector, *The Critical Path to Corporate Renewal*. Cambridge, MA: Harvard Business School, 1990.

❖ THE CHALLENGE OF REVITALIZATION

Revitalization involves enhancing the abilities of, and contributions made by, managers, workers, and the organization as a whole to cope with an increasingly competitive environment. Revitalized corporations reduce their exclusive reliance on the authority of management, on rules and procedures, and on a strict and narrow division of work. Instead, employees at all levels are involved in decision-making; teamwork is encouraged among functions, business units, union and management; information concerning performance and the competitive environment is shared and communicated throughout the corporation; and responsibility and accountability are pushed far down the hierarchy.

The degree to which an organization can achieve cost, quality, and innovation is affected by the extent to which it has the necessary level of coordination through teamwork, commitment through motivation and competence in business knowledge, and analytical and interpersonal skills required to solve problems as a team. These human resource attributes are in turn determined by elements of the organization's design: structure, people, roles/responsibilities/relationships, and systems.

❖ SUCCESSFUL REVITALIZATION: AN OVERVIEW

The results of the six-company research established that, at both the company and the unit level, several key elements were identified that characterize the successful organizations, and were absent in the "lagging" organizations.

Specifically, it was found that:

◆ Change efforts that begin by creating corporate programs to alter the culture or the management of people in the firm are inherently flawed, even when supported by top management.

◆ Formal organizational structure and systems are the *last* things an organization should change when seeking renewal—not the first, as many managers assumed.

◆ Effective changes in the way an organization manages people do *not* occur by changing the organization's human resource policies and systems.

◆ Starting corporate renewal at the very top is a high-risk revitalization strategy *not* employed by the most successful companies.

◆ Organizations should start corporate revitalization by targeting small, isolated, peripheral operations, not large, central, core operations.

◆ It is not essential that top management consistently practice what it preaches in the early stages of renewal, although such action is undoubtedly helpful.

For the task-driven organization to function effectively, far higher levels of coordination and teamwork—across functions, borders, business units, organizational levels, as well as between management and union—will be needed. To achieve that coordination, higher levels of employee commitment and competence will be required at all levels of the organization. Successful unit-level renewal occurs only when units directly align a call for new employee behaviors and skills with an urgent response to the unit's central competitive challenge.

While renewal can be achieved by mandating changes in formal systems and structure, that approach reduces commitment and fails to develop the competence people need to function effectively within the newly-aligned organization. The *Critical Path* identifies a sequence of interventions, which creates task alignment in a way that increases coordination as well as commitment and competence.

❖ THE TASK-DRIVEN ORGANIZATION

The new competitive environment requires a flexible and adaptive organization, as well as a different pattern of work behavior. Managers and workers must be aware of what the customer wants and what competitors are doing. They must translate this knowledge into effective decisions about improvements in product, service, quality, and cost, and they must implement these decisions at all levels. The competitive environment requires using the skills and abilities of a much larger number of employees than ever before.

Managers are becoming aware that it is impossible to respond rapidly to changing customer demands and meet lower cost and higher quality requirements without radically improving coordination and teamwork.

This kind of quick responsiveness and adaptability are possible because the task, rather than the hierarchy, is the basis for assigning roles and responsibilities. Knowledge replaces formal authority as the basis for influence. A firm that uses this approach is called a *task-driven organization.*

In virtually all cases of successful revitalization, management focused on the business' central competitive challenges as the means for motivating change and developing new behaviors and skills. This is called *task alignment,* and it involves a redefinition of work roles, responsibilities, and relationships within a unit in a way that will enhance the coordination required to accomplish the tasks critical to the success of the business.

By changing how people work together around core tasks, without changing the organizational chart, a commonly understood and legitimated ad hoc team organization emerges. Because it focuses on the most important problem facing a business, task alignment occurs within units small enough for a group of individuals to have responsibility for a common goal, not within a large and diverse corporation as a whole.

❖ THE CRITICAL PATH TO RENEWAL

Revitalization efforts in twenty-six plants and business units across the six companies revealed that effective renewal occurred not when managers chose one alternative course of action or the other. Instead, effective revitalization occurred when managers followed a *critical path* that obtains the benefits of top-down as well as bottom-up change efforts, while minimizing their disadvantages.

The critical path is a general manager-led process that implements task alignment at the unit level by following six steps:

1. Mobilizing energy for change among all stakeholders in the organization by involving them in a diagnosis of the problems blocking competitiveness.

2. Developing a task-aligned vision of how to organize and manage for competitiveness. Without a vision, employees do not have an understanding of how the organization will function in the future or a clear rationale for the changes in roles, responsibilities, and relationships they are being asked to make.

3. Fostering consensus that the new vision is "right," developing competence to enact it, and creating cohesion to move the change along.

4. Spreading revitalization to all departments of the unit in a way that avoids the perception that a program is being pushed from the top, but at the same time ensures consistency with the organizational changes already under way.

5. Consolidating changes through formal policies, systems, and structures that institutionalize revitalization to ensure the long-term success of a revitalization effort, particularly given the inevitability that managers will move on to other jobs.

6. Continually monitoring and strategizing in response to predictable problems in the revitalization process.

The experience of revitalization uncovers strengths and weaknesses in an organization. Since organizations are interdependent systems, changes in one part of an organization lead to stresses and strains in other parts. These problems are not signs of failure. Rather, they represent dilemmas to be addressed and managed.

❖ REVITALIZATION LEADERS

Corporate renewal is not an impersonal process unfolding of its own accord. It is possible only when individual managers at the unit and corporate level have sufficient commitment and skill.

The research indicated that leaders at the unit level had to be willing to break traditions of management and labor relations that may have existed for

many years. To do this, they raised dissatisfaction with the status quo by articulating with some urgency the core tasks (improving quality, decreasing cost,
and/or increasing product innovation) that their organizations had to perform
to compete successfully. They then managed a participative change effort that
aligned the organization and management process with the business' core
task. All this required commitment to renewal as well as conceptual and con-
sensus-building skills.

❖ WHO WERE THE REVITALIZATION LEADERS?

Who were the members of the small group capable of running with the baton
of revitalization? Surprising as it may seem, this group of corporate leaders
did not necessarily include the very top executive. However, the key leaders
were at high levels, including an executive vice president of a major business
group, a vice president of manufacturing, and the chief operating officer. They
had responsibility for sufficiently large company segments to get revitalization started, and they typically exerted influence over other parts of their companies by their persuasive powers and, often, through their transfer from one
segment to another.

For revitalization to succeed at the unit level it was essential that the general manager be actively engaged as its leader. Perhaps because of the smaller
size and relative homogeneity, no examples of successful unit-level revitalization were seen that were not led by the general manager. Conversely, many
failures occurred where general management leadership was lacking.

Although revitalization leaders functioned at all levels of the organization,
it was found that they generally shared a common set of attributes. At the unit
level, three attributes were found that distinguished those managers who were
most successful in leading revitalization:

1. *A persistent belief that revitalization is key to competitiveness* Effective
   revitalization leaders shared a common conviction. They believed that fundamental changes in organizing and managing people would have a significant impact on the bottom line of their organizations.

2. *The capacity to articulate this conviction in the form of a credible and
   compelling vision* Effective revitalization at any level cannot occur without a vision of the future state of the organization, a vision that aligns new
   patterns of management with the performance of the organization's core
   task. Effective leaders also had the capacity to present their visions in a
   way that appealed to their constituents. That appeal allowed employees to
   commit to change emotionally, not just intellectually.

3. *The ability to implement this vision through a consistent pattern of
   words and behaviors* Revitalization leaders communicated values and intentions not only through words, but also through actions.

❖ WHERE AND HOW TO START A REVITALIZATION EFFORT

Corporate revitalization rests on the capacity of leaders to develop an organizational context that will influence people—managers, workers, and union leaders alike—to change behavior and attitudes. However, each change leader's capacity to begin and sustain revitalization is also a function of the environment within which he or she operates. The unit manager's ability to manage change is affected by the many policies and practices handed down from headquarters and the support for revitalization provided by top management. Top management's ability to manage and sustain renewal is in turn affected not only by business conditions and capital markets that shape the economic environment of the corporation, but also by the response of its board to external factors.

A manager's efforts to revitalize, while a function of personal conviction and skills, is also a function of a corporate environment that can be influenced, but not controlled. Given this reality, it is easy for a manager to conclude that there is nothing that can be done to start revitalizing the organization. This is far too pessimistic an attitude and is self-defeating.

American corporations will become more competitive only when individuals at every level take the initiative to create a favorable environment for renewal in the domain over which they have some control. A good-faith effort to work cooperatively with the next level up to shape the environment so that it supports revitalization initiatives is also desired.

❖ A PARTNERSHIP OF CHANGE LEADERS

Any one of a number of people can begin the process of revitalization, whether it be the unit general manager, corporate human resource manager, union leader, or top management, so long as that person recognizes the unique role each plays and what each can or cannot do. Thus, simply beginning the process is the most important step.

The transformation of a large corporation requires that change leaders work as a team. Each has a different and valuable perspective. Each commands the respect and loyalty of a different constituency. Each is able to influence some, but not all, of the many conditions for company-wide learning. Each requires help and support from others. Together, they can succeed in creating the task-driven corporate organization that can survive and prosper in the hotly contested global markets of the 1990s and beyond.

12

MANAGING QUALITY IN CUSTOMER-DRIVEN ORGANIZATIONS

Quality, customer service, total quality management, and continuous improvement have become organizational buzzwords in the past decade. One of the leaders in developing strategies for building quality into manufacturing processes was the late W. Edwards Deming. During the 1950s, Deming went to Japan to teach statistical control, where his ideas received a very warm reception. The Japanese built on Deming's ideas and moved the responsibility for quality from the ranks of middle management down to the shop floor level. Deming's ideas on quality control soon became an integral feature in Japanese management. Deming has been called by his admirers both the "prophet of quality" and the "man of the century."

Total quality control (TQC) means that responsibility for quality is a part of every employee's job. Deming's *Out of the Crisis* calls for long-term organizational transformation through the implementation of a fourteen-step plan of action focusing on leadership, constant innovation, and removal of barriers to performance. Interested readers may also wish to examine other books about Deming and his influence in *The World of W. Edwards Deming*, *The Deming Dimension*, *Thinking About Quality*, and *Deming's Road to Continual Improvement*.

Many noted authors, such as Joe Juran (*Juran on Leadership for Quality*) and Phil Crosby (*Quality is Free*) have written about their approaches to quality, while others such as Karl Albrecht (*The Service Advantage*) and Ron Zemke (*The Service Edge*) have focused on creating organizations with outstanding customer treatment. Other follow-up books, such as Kathleen Ryan and Daniel Oestreich's *Driving Fear Out of the Workplace*, have expanded on one of Deming's specific points.

Creating value for customers as a path to organizational success has also received attention. This is the theme of William A. Band's *Creating Value for Customers*. Band describes techniques for value creation, while providing anecdotes about their successful application in North American and international firms. The result is a compendium of strategic initiatives that managers can employ in order to increase the value delivered to their customers.

The idea of benchmarking has been added to the manager's vocabulary in recent years as another path to quality. *Benchmarking* is the process of monitoring and learning the methods, practices, and performance measures of one's best competitors so as to create exceptional performance. As portrayed by Gregory Watson in *Strategic Benchmarking,* it is a tool for identifying and upgrading customer satisfaction. Watson discusses four types of benchmarking (internal, competitive, functional, and generic) as ways to gain a (short-term) competitive advantage over one's competitors.

READING 1

Out of the Crisis

W. Edwards Deming
Summary prepared by William B. Gartner and M. James Naughton

William B. Gartner is a Professor at Georgetown University.
M. James Naughton is the owner of Expert-Knowledge Systems, Inc.

Deming provides an ambitious objective for his book when he begins by saying:

> The aim of this book is transformation of the style of American management. Transformation of American style of management is not a job of reconstruction, nor is it revision. It requires a whole new structure, from foundation upward. *Mutation* might be the word, except that *mutation* implies unordered spontaneity. Transformation must take place with directed effort.

Few individuals have had as much positive impact on the world economy as Dr. W. Edwards Deming. With the broadcast of the NBC white paper, "If Japan Can, Why Can't We?" on June 24, 1980, Dr. Deming gained national exposure as the man responsible for the managerial theory that has governed Japan's transformation into a nation of world leaders in the production of high quality goods. This transformation did not happen overnight. Since 1950, when Dr. Deming first spoke to Japan's top managers on the improvement of quality, Japanese organizations have pioneered in the adaptation of Dr. Deming's ideas.

As a result of his seminars, Japan has had an annual national competition for quality improvement (the Deming Prize) since 1951. Japan has numerous journals and books devoted to exploring and furthering the implications of Deming's theory. However, it has only been within the last few years that a number of books have been published in the United States on "the Deming Theory of Management." An overview of the ideas that underlie Deming's theory, which cut across all major topical areas in management, will be provided here.

W. Edwards Deming, *Out of the Crisis*. Cambridge, MA: MIT Press, 1986.

❖ DISEASES AND OBSTACLES

Deming's book is not merely about productivity and quality control; it is a broad vision of the nature of organizations and how organizations should be changed. Deming identifies a set of chronic ailments that can plague any organization and limit its success. These, which he calls "deadly diseases," include an overemphasis on short-term profits, human resource practices that encourage both managers and employees to be mobile and not organizationally loyal, merit ratings and review systems that are based on fear of one's supervisor, an absence of a single driving purpose, and management that is based on visible figures alone.

The reason that managers are not as effective as they could be is that they are the prisoners of some structural characteristics and personal assumptions that prevent their success. Among the obstacles that Deming discusses are the insulation of top management from the other employees in the organization, lack of adequate technical knowledge, a long history of total reliance on final inspection as a way of assuring a quality product, the managerial belief that all problems originate within the work force, a reliance on meeting specifications, and the failure to synthesize human operators with computer systems for control.

❖ THE CONCEPT OF VARIABILITY

The basis for Deming's theory is the observation that variability exists everywhere in everything. Only through the study and analysis of variability, using statistics, can a phenomenon be understood well enough to manipulate and change it. In many respects, using statistics is not very radical. Statistics are fundamental to nearly all academic research. But Deming asks that the right kind of statistics (analytical) be applied to our everyday lives as well. And that is the rub. To recognize the pervasiveness of variability and to function so that the sources of this variability can be defined and measured is radical. In Deming's world, the use of statistical thinking is not an academic game; it is a way of life.

The concept of variability is to management theory and practice what the concept of the germ theory of disease was to the development of modern medicine. Medicine had been "successfully" practiced without the knowledge of germs. In a pre-germ theory paradigm, some patients got better, some got worse, and some stayed the same; in each case, some rationale could be used to explain the outcome. With the emergence of germ theory, all medical phenomena took on new meanings. Medical procedures thought to be good practice, such as physicians attending women in birth, turned out to be causes of disease because of the septic condition of the physicians' hands. Instead of rendering improved health care, the physicians' germ-laden hands achieved the opposite result. One can imagine the first proponents of the germ theory telling their colleagues who were still ignorant of the theory to wash their hands between patients. The pioneers must have sounded crazy. In the same vein, managers and academics who do not have a thorough understanding of variability will fail to grasp the radical change in thought that Deming envisions. Deming's propositions may seem as simplistic as "wash your hands!" rather than an entirely new paradigm of profound challenges to present-day managerial thinking and behaviors.

An illustration of variability that is widely cited in the books on Deming's theory is the "red bead experiment." Dr. Deming, at his four-day seminar, asks for 10 volunteers from the attendees. Six of the students become workers, two become inspectors of the workers' production, one becomes the inspector of the inspectors' work, and one becomes the recorder. Dr. Deming mixes together 3000 white beads and 750 red beads in a large box. He instructs the workers to scoop out beads from the box with a beveled paddle that scoops out 50 beads at a time. Each scoop of the paddle is treated as a day's production. Only white beads are acceptable. Red beads are defects. After each worker scoops a paddle of beads from the box, the two inspectors count the defects, the inspector of the inspectors inspects the inspectors' count, and the recorder writes down the inspectors' agreed-upon number of defects. Invariably, each worker's scoop contains some red beads. Deming plays the role of the manager by exhorting the workers to produce no defects. When a worker scoops few red beads he may be praised. Scooping many red beads brings criticism and an exhortation to do better, otherwise "we will go out of business." The manager reacts to each scoop of beads as if it had meaning in itself rather than as part of a pattern. Figure 1 shows the number of defective beads each worker produced for four days of work.

Dr. Deming's statistical analysis of the workers' production indicates that the process of producing white beads is in statistical control; that is, the variability of this production system is stable. The near-term prediction about the *pattern*, but not the individual draws, of the system's performance can be made. Near-future draws will yield about an average, over many experiments, of 9.9 red beads. Any one draw may range between one and 18 red beads. In other words, the actual number of red beads scooped by each worker is out of that worker's control. The worker, as Dr. Deming says, "is only delivering the defects." Management, which controls the system, has caused the defects through design of the system. There are a number of insights people draw from this experiment. Walton lists the following:

◆ Variation is part of any process.

◆ Planning requires prediction of how things and people will perform. Tests and experiments of past performance can be useful, but not definitive.

◆ Workers work within a system that—try as they might—is beyond their control. It is the system, not their individual skills, that determines how they perform.

◆ Only management can change the system.

◆ Some workers will always be above average, some below.[1]

Name	Day 1	2	3	4	All 4
Neil	3	13	8	9	33
Tace	6	9	8	10	33
Tim	13	12	7	10	42
Mike	11	8	10	15	44
Tony	9	13	8	11	41
Richard	12	11	7	15	45
All 6	54	66	48	70	238
Cum $\bar{x}$	9.0	10.0	9.3	9.92	9.92

$$\bar{x} = \frac{238}{6 \times 4} = 9.92$$

$$\bar{p} = \frac{238}{6 \times 4 \times 50} = 198$$

$$\left. \begin{array}{l} \text{UCL} \\ \text{LCL} \end{array} \right\} \begin{array}{l} = \bar{x} \pm 3\sqrt{\bar{x}(1 - \bar{p})} \\ = 9.9 \pm 3\sqrt{9.9 \times 802} \end{array}$$

$$= \left\{ \begin{array}{l} 18 \\ 1 \end{array} \right.$$

Adapted from Deming, p. 347.

FIGURE 1
Number of defective items by operator, by day.

The red bead experiment illustrates the behavior of systems of stable variability. In Deming's theory, a system is all of the aspects of the organization and environment—employees, managers, equipment, facilities, government, customers, suppliers, shareholders, and so forth—fitted together, with the aim of producing some type of output. Stability implies that the output has regularity to it, so that predictions regarding the output of the system can be made. But man-made systems are inherently unstable. Bringing a system into stability is one of the fundamental managerial activities in the Deming theory.

In Deming's theory, a stable system, that is, a system that shows signs of being in statistical control, behaves in a manner similar to the red bead experiment. In systems, a single datum point is of little use in understanding the causes that influenced the production of that point. It is necessary to withhold judgment about changes in the output of the system until sufficient evidence (additional data points) becomes available to suggest whether or not the system being examined is stable. Statistical theory provides tools to help evaluate the stability of systems. Once a system is stable, its productive capability can be determined; that is, the average output of the system and the spread of variability around that average can be described. This can be used to predict the near-term future behavior of the system.

The inefficiencies inherent in "not knowing what we are doing," that is, in working with systems not in statistical control, might not seem to be that great a competitive penalty if all organizations are similarly out of control. Yet we are beginning to realize that the quality of outputs from organizations that are managed using Deming's theory are many magnitudes beyond what non-Deming organizations have been producing. The differences in quality and productivity can be mind-boggling.

For example, both Scherkenbach[2] and Walton[3] reported that when the Ford Motor Company began using transmissions produced by the Japanese automobile manufacturer, Mazda, Ford found that customers overwhelmingly preferred cars with Mazda transmissions to cars with Ford-manufactured transmissions—because the warranty repairs were ten times lower, and the cars were quieter and shifted more smoothly. When Ford engineers compared their transmissions to the Mazda transmissions, they found that the piece-to-piece variation in the Mazda transmissions was nearly three times less than in the Ford pieces. Both Ford and Mazda conformed to the engineering standards specified by Ford, but Mazda transmissions were far more uniform. More uniform products also cost less to manufacture. With less variability there is less rework and less need for inspection. Only systems in statistical control can begin to reduce variability and thereby improve the quality and quantity of their output. Both authors reported that after Ford began to implement Deming's theory over the last five years, warranty repair frequencies dropped by forty-five percent and "things gone wrong" reports from customers dropped by fifty percent.

❖ FOURTEEN STEPS MANAGEMENT MUST TAKE

The task of transformation of an entire organization to use the Deming theory becomes an enormous burden for management, and Deming frequently suggests that this process is likely to take a minimum of ten years. The framework for transforming an organization is outlined in the fourteen points (pp. 23–24):

1. Create constancy of purpose toward improvement of product and service, aiming to become competitive, to stay in business, and to provide jobs.

2. Adopt the new philosophy. We are in a new economic age. Western management must awaken to the challenge, must learn their responsibilities, and must take on leadership in order to bring about change.

3. Cease dependence on inspection to achieve quality. Eliminate the need for inspection on a mass basis by building quality into the product in the first place.

4. End the practice of awarding business on the basis of the price tag. Instead, minimize total cost. Move toward a single supplier for any one time and develop long-term relationships of loyalty and trust with that supplier.

5. Improve constantly and forever the systems of production and service in order to improve quality and productivity. Thus, one constantly decreases costs.

6. Institute training on the job.

7. Institute leadership. Supervisors should be able to help people to do a better job, and they should use machines and gadgets wisely. Supervision of management and supervision of production workers need to be overhauled.

8. Drive out fear, so that everyone may work effectively for the company.

9. Break down barriers between departments. People in research, design, sales, and production must work as a team. They should foresee production problems and problems that could be encountered when using the product or service.

10. Eliminate slogans, exhortations, and targets that demand zero defects and new levels of productivity. These only create adversarial relationships because the many causes of low quality and low productivity are due to the system, and not the work force.

11a. Eliminate work standards (quotas) on the factory floor. Substitute leadership.

11b. Eliminate management by objectives. Eliminate management by numbers or numerical goals. Substitute leadership.

12a. Remove barriers that rob the hourly worker of his right to pride of workmanship. The responsibility of supervisors must be changed from sheer numbers to quality.

12b. Remove barriers that rob people in management and in engineering of their right to pride of workmanship. This means, inter alia, abolishing the annual or merit rating and management by objectives.

13. Institute a vigorous program of education and self-improvement.

14. Put everybody in the company to work to accomplish the transformation. The transformation is everybody's job.

As mentioned earlier, the fourteen points should not be treated as a list of aphorisms, nor can each of the fourteen points be treated separately without recognizing the interrelationships among them.

❖ CONCLUSIONS

Out of the Crisis is full of examples and ideas, and Deming calls for a radical revision of American management practice. To his credit, Deming constantly recognizes ideas and examples from individuals practicing various aspects of his theory. This constant recognition of other individuals provides a subtle indication that a body of practitioners exists who have had successful experiences applying his fourteen steps and other ideas.

A transformation in American management needs to occur, it can take place, and it has begun already in those firms applying Deming's theory. Deming offers a new paradigm for the practice of management that requires a dramatic rethinking and replacement of old methods by those trained in traditional management techniques. In conclusion, Deming recognizes that "it takes courage to admit that you have been doing something wrong, to admit that you have something to learn, that there is a better way" (Walton, 1986, p. 223).

❖ NOTES

1. William B. Gartner and M. James Naughton, "The Deming Theory of Man agement," *Academy of Management Review,* January 1988, pp. 138–142.
2. William W. Scherkenbach, *The Deming Route to Quality and Productivity: Roadmaps and Roadblocks,* Milwaukee, WI: ASQC, 1986.
3. Mary Walton, *The Deming Management Method,* New York: Dodd, Mead, & Company, 1986.

READING 2

Creating Value for Customers: Designing and Implementing a Total Corporate Strategy

William A. Band
Summary prepared by Susan Rawson Zacur

Susan Rawson Zacur is a Professor of Management in the Robert G. Merrick School of Business at the University of Baltimore where she teaches human resource management and organizational behavior. She received her D.B.A. from the University of Maryland. Dr. Zacur is a management consultant and author, and is active in the Academy of Management.

Contemporary organizations must create value for their customers. Further, they must demonstrate that their value is superior to that of their competitors. Creating value for customers leads to organizational success. To achieve this, organizations must make the transition from the *vision* of being a more customer-driven organization to the reality of continuous customer value improvement. Organizations must adopt a strategy of continually increasing value to customers as their primary focus. With this objective in mind, Band defines the concept of value creation, discusses how to create a value-driven culture, outlines value-creation strategies, and provides suggestions for value-creation improvement.

❖ VALUE CREATION

Value creation is an essential competitive strategy in today's global economy. It includes all the evolving tools and techniques for quality, service, and customer satisfaction that combine to produce real and perceived customer value. In this context, *customer service is a means while value creation is the end*. Value creation integrates the company's functional areas and focuses

Portions of this summary appeared in a review for *The Academy of Management Executive*, August, 1991, pp. 99–101, and are used with permission. William A. Band, *Creating Value for Customers: Designing and Implementing a Total Corporate Strategy*. New York: Wiley, 1991.

their efforts toward the common goal of creating and delivering value to customers. Being able to deliver sustainable value to customers profitably means being able to choose and understand the target customer so that the business can offer attractively priced, desired benefits that are, on balance, perceived as superior in value.

The need for value-creation strategic alternatives is supported by research studies that have attempted to quantify the costs of customer dissatisfaction. For example, one study found that sixty-eight percent of customers would change suppliers based upon the indifference of just one employee. Another study reported that the average business never hears from ninety-six percent of its unhappy customers. Of those customers who are unhappy, ninety percent will not buy again. Compounding the problem is the fact that the average customer who has had a problem with an organization tells nine other people about it. Clearly, dissatisfaction is a key issue for the company since lost customers may result from both direct contact with the firm and from "word of mouth" indictment by dissatisfied customers.

◆ KNOWING YOUR CUSTOMER AND YOURSELF

In value creation, the definition of the customer is important. The customer is more than just the end user of a product. For the purpose of value creation, the customer is also the distributor, employees, owners, and shareholders. Each of these constituencies will have a perception of value that will be their reality. Organizations must identify who their customers are and let them define what constitutes value. They will clarify what quality factors are important to them if their specific ideas and recommendations are sought. Research suggests that for manufactured items, these factors are likely to be performance, durability, ease of repair, service availability, warranty, ease of use, and price—in that order. Service quality factors include courtesy, promptness, a basic sense that one's needs are being satisfied, and a good attitude on the part of the service provider. Companies that do this kind of research and develop appropriate policies in response to the findings will create streamlined complaint procedures and warranty policies that deliver perceived value. They will work to understand the company's strengths and weaknesses in ability to meet customer desires and then target areas for improvement that will deliver improved value for customers.

❖ CREATING A VALUE-DRIVEN CULTURE

◆ THE VISION/MISSION STATEMENT

The first step in working toward a customer-value-driven organization is to develop a clear vision (or mission) statement. This will include all of the following: customer satisfaction as the main driving force, impossibly high standards of product and service quality, a long-run profit perspective, cross-functional teams (enabling people from different functional areas to contribute automatically to decision-making), and all employees staying close to the customer. The resulting vision statement must be in harmony with the company's own beliefs and values that influence management behavior. The company must treat its employees (internal customers) as well as it treats its external customers in order for all company representatives to believe in and espouse a customer-value-driven vision.

❖ VALUE CREATION STRATEGIES

◆ Marketing/Measuring Customer Satisfaction

Creating value for customers involves measuring and monitoring value perception. The scope of the traditional marketing research function should be expanded to include an emphasis on understanding the buyer-seller relationship over time with a focus on products as well as the company employees who interact with the customers concerning products. This expanded focus will result in a customer satisfaction research program. Before embarking on such a program, it is useful to define *customer satisfaction,* which is the degree to which customer needs, wants, and expectations are met or exceeded, resulting in repurchase and continuing loyalty. From the company's own working definition of customer satisfaction, various measurement initiatives can be derived. The ingredients for a customer satisfaction research program should include a list of important attributes to measure such as product quality, after-sales support, and aspects of the interaction between employees and customers. Sample research surveys for measuring customer satisfaction should be developed to examine customer needs and wants, previous experience with the company's output, messages received about the company's offering from peers, and advertising initiatives. Data-gathering techniques can range from mail surveys to in-person interviews. The choice of a research method will depend on cost, timing, and the type of data to be collected. *Benchmarking* (understanding what the best of the competition is doing) is a vital part of customer satisfaction research. By comparing their firm with the best of the competition, managers can learn which in-house programs and actions might be developed to close the gap between themselves and the industry leaders.

◆ Managing Customer Relationships

The method of analysis for managing all elements of the customer satisfaction process is *blueprinting,* which means looking at the basic systems and structures of the organization in order to understand better the process of creating satisfied customers. Three frameworks for blueprinting are:

◆ cycle of service analysis—examining how the customer experiences each point of contact with the organization;

- ◆ value-chain analysis—examining each step in the value-adding process, from production to service maintenance, to uncover opportunities to build customer satisfaction;

- ◆ story-boarding—examining the hypothetical scenes in which a customer comes in contact with the organization, improving on them, and then building the support processes necessary to make the improved scenes come alive.

Once the blueprinting analysis is completed, companies can choose from a host of techniques that range from frequent-patron programs to buyer risk-reduction programs. These eliminate roadblocks and help build lasting customer relationships and trust, based on high product quality and consistent service support.

◆ HIGH-QUALITY PERFORMANCE

Managers should strive to achieve high-quality performance by emphasizing compliance with customers' requirements. Corporate or company-wide quality control (CWQC) consists of managerial attention to quality, involvement of all functions and employees, a belief in continuous improvement, and a strong customer focus as the keys to high quality performance. CWQC is achieved through checklists for action, tools for quality control, problem-solving techniques, and quality function deployment (QFD). QFD is a system for designing a product or service based on customer demands and involving all members of the producer or supplier organization.

◆ PEOPLE AS VALUE CREATORS

Many firms attempt to treat their external customers with great care and respect. However, they sometimes fail to place the same value on their internal "customers"—their employees. Failure to do so significantly diminishes the success of any customer-value-improvement initiatives, since employees are likely to treat customers the way they are treated by the organization. Organizational audits should be used to monitor employee perceptions on the extent of their organization's customer orientation, understanding of the organization's goals and objectives, quality of intraorganization communication, effectiveness of conflict resolution procedures, and the extent to which employees feel that their ideas are solicited and valued by management. This information should help organization leaders understand corporate culture, plan for their own responsibilities in articulating a customer-focused vision, examine barriers to employee and customer emphasis, and develop strategies for building teamwork as the mechanism for employee commitment to a customer-value-driven mission. In building a customer-oriented work force, management should focus on selecting employees with a customer-oriented attitude and demonstrated ability to work in teams. They should develop job descriptions, training programs, and reward systems to reinforce the importance of a customer focus.

❖ IMPROVING VALUE CREATION

◆ ORGANIZATION DEVELOPMENT

Organization development helps a firm prepare for change by encouraging managers to develop an action plan, implement the plan, and evaluate results. In preparing for and implementing change, managers may take a number of steps to make the vision of excellence a reality. Some of the most important steps are to:

◆ measure the wants, needs, and expectations of customers

◆ translate customer requirements into company standards of operation

◆ develop a value-creation mission statement

◆ select an appropriate strategy for organization change and commit the necessary resources to the process

◆ establish a value-creation training program for employees

◆ change departments, product and/or service features, advertising and marketing strategies, product/service delivery systems as appropriate

◆ monitor customer feedback regularly

◆ tell customers to define standards by which they should judge your organization and its offerings in the future

◆ lock in continuous improvements by creating a recognition system, developing performance measures, and realigning incentive systems and human resource management policies

◆ track performance in order to ensure gradual, unending improvement over time

◆ develop a system of effective customer-complaint management

◆ continuously measure the organization's products, services, and practices against those of the toughest competitors or industry leaders

◆ create a customer satisfaction index (CSI) to measure the organization's performance against selected product or service attributes that customers judge to be critical to their satisfaction

◆ assess the effectiveness of the customer-value-improvement process by examining leadership, information and analysis, strategic quality planning, human resource utilization, quality assurance of products and services, and customer satisfaction

These steps help managers instill a value-driven customer focus by unfreezing their organizations, building vision, developing action plans, measuring progress, managing customer complaints, benchmarking, and monitoring organizational performance. Clearly, creating value for customers results in value for the delivering organization, as both internal and external constituencies are considered and accommodated.

READING 3

Strategic Benchmarking

Gregory H. Watson
Summary prepared by David A. Wyrick

Dave Wyrick is an Associate Professor in and Assistant Department Head of the Department of Industrial Engineering at the University of Minnesota, Duluth where he teaches courses in ethics and law for engineers, engineering management, production management, and capstone design. He received his Ph.D. in Engineering Management from the University of Missouri-Rolla in 1989. He worked for Atlantic Richfield Company in Texas and Alaska in various engineering assignments and also worked with IBM-Rochester as a project management engineer on ISO 9001 preparations. A registered professional engineer, Dr. Wyrick is active in numerous professional societies, including ASEE, ASEM, ASME, ASQC, IIE, NSPE, SME, and TIMS.

What should companies do to compete successfully? The successful company will have higher quality, introduce new technology earlier, and have costs lower than its competitors. To rate its performance, the company needs to "benchmark," that is, to continuously compare and measure its business processes against business leaders anywhere in the world in order to gain information that will help the organization take action to improve its performance.

The term *benchmarking* is relatively new. As a tool for quality improvement, it first became widely publicized in 1989 after Xerox won the Malcolm Baldrige National Quality Award. Several books and numerous articles and reports have addressed the various aspects of benchmarking, but *Strategic Benchmarking* is the first book to address how it can and should be used as an integral part of a company's strategic planning process.

❖ INTRODUCING BENCHMARKING

As a quality process, benchmarking is rapidly being adopted. It is similar to competitive analysis techniques managers have used in the past, and the per-

Gregory H. Watson, *Strategic Benchmarking: How to Rate Your Company's Performance Against the World's Best*. New York: Wiley, 1993.

sonal visibility arising from being part of a benchmarking team can be a good career move. Also, many people are comfortable with it because it does *not* have an acronym (such as TQM, SPC, and DOE).

Benchmarking is a measurement process and results in comparative performance measures. Just as importantly, benchmarking identifies and describes process enablers, the practices that lead to exceptional performance.

The basic process of benchmarking follows the Plan-Do-Check-Act (PDCA) cycle. The first step is to answer two fundamental questions: (1) What should we benchmark? and (2) whom should we benchmark? The second step is to conduct secondary and primary research; secondary research includes public or disclosed information, and primary information is gathered through direct contact with the company. The third step is to analyze the data to determine the magnitude of the *gaps* between the companies and to identify the process enablers that facilitated the performance improvements at the leading companies. The final step is to adapt, improve, and implement the appropriate enablers at the home company in order to improve its performance and quality.

The concept of benchmarking dates back almost a century to Frederick W. Taylor, who encouraged comparison of work processes. Today, benchmarking is viewed as a five-generation evolutionary process, beginning with (1) *reverse engineering*, and moving through (2) *competitive benchmarking*, (3) *process benchmarking*, (4) *strategic benchmarking*, up to (5) *global benchmarking*.

Benchmarking is important because it helps identify the level of customer satisfaction. Customers tend to be satisfied with innovative features even if the engineering is lackluster; for items that are offered by several companies, however, customer satisfaction is directly related to the degree of engineering excellence. Customers expect items with basic performance characteristics (such as UL registration for electrical appliances) to perform well, so even outstanding engineering performance is recognized only when the item fails. Product and process design must continually improve because the innovative item is soon imitated and improved, as was the case of the coffee cup holder originally introduced in the Ford *Taurus*.

While companies must be careful about sharing information regarding specific product design and trade secrets, the sharing of information on processes can be mutually beneficial. Benchmarking is not a form of industrial espionage because it is conducted in an open manner. To ensure that the needs of the participants are met, the Strategic Planning Institute of the American Productivity & Quality Center has developed a *Benchmarking Code of Conduct.*

Senior managers should understand that benchmarking topics and potential partners for benchmarking studies are strategic choices. The benchmarking studies should augment other information when considering company plans. Certain intellectual property must be protected and employees must understand the criteria for disclosure to other companies. Management should use benchmarking information to establish reasonable goals and to develop the change implementation strategies to achieve those goals.

❖ LINKING STRATEGIC PLANNING WITH BENCHMARKING

Strategy can be called the persistence of a vision. The vision and strategic goals are set by the corporate management team. Middle management teams are responsible for developing the strategy to achieve those goals. The subsequent actions are implemented by operational teams.

Understanding the strategic intent is important. Does the company have the commitment to global leadership over its arch rival? The company must do environmental scanning to guard against latent competitors—companies who are currently not competitors but who have the technology to be, such as Canon becoming a competitor of Xerox.

Companies should understand and develop their five or six core competencies. These provide potential access to a wide variety of markets, make a significant contribution to the perceived customer benefit of the product, and should be difficult for competitors to imitate. Similarly, companies have key business process capabilities that provide them with certain advantages.

Benchmarking becomes strategic when it is used to develop a better understanding of strategic business issues and may include long-term alliances with benchmarking partners. These issues may include building core competencies, targeting a specific shift in strategy, developing a new line of business, or creating an organization more capable of learning and responding to change. Strategic benchmarking should propel companies toward *world class* competition, where they are widely recognized as leading performers.

❖ UNDERSTANDING THE ESSENTIALS OF PROCESS BENCHMARKING

The appropriate acquisition and application of quality methods, combined with the pursuit of business knowledge, sets the foundation for successful benchmarking. An organization must continuously apply and develop key quality and decision tools to analyze both qualitative and quantitative practices. Benchmarking is an advanced quality practice; as such, it is *not* a tool to be used by companies just beginning the implementation of a quality culture.

The degree to which an organization should benchmark is determined by its level of quality maturity, of which there are four levels. In the inspection level, the focus is on quality assurance; teams should concentrate on process improvement rather than benchmarking. In the control level, the focus shifts toward problem prevention as all employees become aware of and begin to regularly use the quality tools, and ISO 9000 may be used as a tool for documenting processes; appropriate benchmarking may be in an industry-specific study or one of the company's key business practices. The third level of quality maturity is partnership, and the focus shifts to improving key processes; "internal customers" may expand to include other business units within the corporation and companies in the supply chain. Benchmarking at this level should move to the strategic level. The fourth level is called maturity; teams work in all areas of operation and all people consider quality issues in all aspects of the business system to insure customer satisfaction; benchmarking is a standard practice.

The benchmarking process is to identify the gap in performance for a given process, to identify the process enablers that allow that gap to exist, to learn from the analysis, and to modify and adapt those process enablers to improve one's own process.

The four basic principles of benchmarking are reciprocity, analogy, measurement, and validity. Reciprocity means that the companies participating in the exercise insure a win-win situation from the start. The processes to be benchmarked should be comparative or analogous. To facilitate analysis, hard data are needed to measure, monitor, and verify process performance. Data also must be valid, timely, and accurate to make sure management is indeed done by fact.

Benchmarking presents significant room for observing another company's proprietary information or intellectual property. Federal anti-trust laws impede inter-company cooperation and hamper American competitiveness and productivity, but must be obeyed. A Code of Conduct is available to industry to provide an accepted standard of behavior. The nine principles of the Code cover the following:

◆ Legality (all laws must be obeyed).

◆ Exchange (be open, honest, and don't take any information the partner does not want to release).

◆ Confidentiality (do not reveal data to nonparticipants).

◆ Use (only use the information to improve one's own processes).

◆ First-party contact (initiate benchmarking inquiries through proper channels).

◆ Third-party contact (do not release partners' names to a third party).

◆ Preparation (first do a self-analysis on processes, strengths, and weaknesses before contacting potential partners).

◆ Completion (make sure that results can be given to management and partners in a timely manner).

◆ Understanding and action (information to share, protocol, and guidelines should be agreed on from the start).

When preparing for a benchmarking study, several questions need to be addressed. What processes should be benchmarked? Who should be the benchmarking partner(s)? How does our own company perform this process? How do they perform this process? Because benchmarking is expensive and time consuming, care should be taken to insure the study addresses a key business process, the business practices used to perform that process, and their impact on critical success factors. Operational definitions are important in preparing the planned study. To understand one's own processes, typical measures include a first-pass yield (effectiveness), value-to-cost ratio (process economy), and cycle time (process efficiency); these metrics and process maps indicate how a process functions. The same measures and process mapping will assess how the partner performs the analogous process.

The process for benchmarking is to first plan the study by identifying the strategic intent, core competencies, key business processes, and critical success factors; the particular process to be benchmarked is documented and characterized; requirements for selecting a benchmarking partner are defined; preliminary questionnaires are prepared and tested (testing is a critical activity). The second step in the process is to collect the necessary data by applying quality tools, performing secondary research in the literature, and conducting the primary research of interviews, mailed questionnaires, or on-site observation of the partner's processes and practices; the data are then sorted and organized. The third step of the process consists of data analysis, data presentation, root cause analysis, results projection, and enabler identification (including evaluating the nature of the process enablers to determine their adaptability to the company culture). The fourth step is to drive selected improvements into the organization as a result of the benchmarking study (some improvements will be obvious from the self-inspection); management may set parity goals (to meet the partner's performance level) or stretch goals (to improve upon the partner's performance level). At the end of the benchmarking process, management should provide a proper celebration and recognition for the benchmarking team.

❖ APPLYING BENCHMARKING RESULTS FOR MAXIMUM UTILITY

Organizations need to evolve from a control-based management system to a learning-based management system. Benchmarking will facilitate this transition. It involves the networking of knowledgable companies and companies with needs or issues to resolve.

Dewey's learning theory cycle is similar to the Deming-Shewhart PDCA continuous improvement cycle. Dewey's Phase 1 is discovering new insights (plan a course of action); Phase 2 is inventing new possibilities (do a test); Phase 3 is producing the action (check to study the results); and Phase 4 is observing the consequences (act on the process based on the trial results). For an organization, learning must be targeted to better understand the customers' needs and expectations.

Organizations do not change quickly, especially if they have done well in the past. Corporate learning can be improved by communicating; program managers for Merck record their best and worst project development experiences in a "Book of Knowledge."

Corporate learning can occur in four basic types of benchmarking studies: internal, competitive, functional, and generic.

◆ *Internal benchmarking* targets partners within the same corporation and is the easiest to conduct.

◆ *Competitive benchmarking* evaluates competitors' products for performance, manufacturability, technology, operability, safety, and support.

◆ *Functional benchmarking* focuses on a particular operating activity or function; evaluation criteria should be established to provide assessments based on facts and data.

◆ *Generic benchmarking* does not involve an aspect of competitive advantage, but may be of interest in a given industry (such as training and education approaches for the electronics industry). External studies may be competitive or noncompetitive, and noncompetitive studies may be either functional or generic.

❖ DOING AN INTERNAL BENCHMARKING STUDY

Internal benchmarking is an approach to process benchmarking in which organizations learn from other operating units, divisions, or companies within the corporation. These often yield the most detailed information about process improvement potential because intercompany barriers are not present.

In 1986, Hewlett-Packard CEO John Young set a stretch goal of cutting development times in half by 1994. Corporate engineering spearheaded the effort by conducting a study within H-P to find the practices that contributed to success in terms of time to market. A company-wide productivity network in each of the firm's fifty-six R&D centers conducted best-practice analyses on recently completed projects; because of their autonomy, the project analyses were far from uniform. Corporate engineering analyzed the reports to identify the common causes of schedule slippage. The most frequent cause of scheduling delays was changing of specifications; moving products to market quickly could be improved by a common measure of time-based performance and a better focus on customer requirements.

Today, H-P provides personnel with software, instructions, and staff consultants on how to use the time-to-market measure. To systematically focus on customer requirements, H-P has adopted Quality Function Deployment; there is no need to change a design specification if it is responsive to the customers' needs. Time to market has been reduced dramatically, from four and a half years for the DeskWriter jet printer to twenty-two months. This project has reduced cycle time and order turnaround in other areas as well.

❖ CONDUCTING A COMPETITIVE BENCHMARKING STUDY

Competitive benchmarking studies target specific designs, process capabilities, or administrative methods used by a company's direct competitors. These studies are frequently conducted by a third party to report information that has been approved by the contributing company, among other reasons. It is much more difficult to share information one-on-one with a competitor because of potential concerns over antitrust violation and unfair trading practices.

In 1978, Ford recalled more U.S. models than it produced and lost $1.5 billion in 1980. The decision to develop the *Taurus* line was an opportunity for Ford to turn their fortunes around. Lew Veraldi was appointed the "heavyweight project manager" for Team Taurus; he could make things happen without seeking numerous approvals. He assembled a team to stay on the project from start to finish rather than a traditional "throw it over the wall" approach. The team first drew up a list of features that would seem important to the customer, and invited comments from many stakeholders, including auto body repair specialists; this took two years and resulted in 400 features to consider.

Taurus was intended to be "best in class" in each feature. To determine what was best, Team Taurus purchased fifty automobiles that catered to the middle-market car buyer; most of the cars were either U.S.-produced or foreign cars made for the American market. Each car was measured for its performance on the 400 selected features. This gave Ford the data to design a world-class car.

The *Taurus* was introduced in 1986 and became *Motor Trend*'s car of the year and helped restore Ford to financial health, surpassing General Motors in earnings for the first time in decades. The production car incorporated 77 percent of the 400 features benchmarked. The aerodynamic styling of the *Taurus*, employee participation, and quality initiatives also helped *Taurus* become a success. The experience taught Ford that competitive benchmarking can provide perspective and guidance on critical design and development issues and that the process is as important as the product.

❖ PERFORMING A FUNCTIONAL BENCHMARKING STUDY

Functional benchmarking investigates the performance of a particular function within an industry-wide application. This type of study offers a good opportunity to develop breakthrough results in terms of identifying and understanding process enablers. External consultants usually facilitate this type of study because of the need for logistical coordination and the need for "blinded" results.

Following the problems with the firm's "X" and "J" cars of the early 1980s, General Motors Corporate Quality & Reliability Department (Q&R) began working with Sandy Company consultants and 150 GM managers to study GM's larger quality issues, and to pinpoint matters of product quality, dependability, reliability, and performance that failed to match the expectations of customers. To achieve buy-in from defensive divisional managers, Q&R needed to be process-oriented and deal with quality issues from a strategic standpoint.

The study group identified ninety-two companies that were known for quality; this list was trimmed to twenty, of which eleven agreed to participate. The study was conducted unlike most benchmarking exercises. GM developed hypotheses on ten factors as distinguishing quality-competent companies and contributing to their success. GM teams visited the eleven host companies in the summer of 1983, spending three to five days at each site. A workshop consolidated the findings into a 136-page final report; the scores for each company conformed fairly well to the hypotheses. The report was useful to the team members and the host companies, but it was poorly received by GM management. Implementation did not occur, in part because of a massive reorganization of the company, although many of the people who helped conduct the study for GM have created change in daily activities outside the boundaries of official corporate programs.

❖ DEVELOPING A GENERIC BENCHMARKING STUDY

Generic benchmarking represents the broadest application of data collection to industry partners; it is confined only by the ability to develop an analogous process and understand how it translates across industries. This innovative approach can result in changed paradigms and reengineering of business processes.

A 1981 study revealed that Japanese producers held approximately a one-month inventory, compared to Xerox's 3.2 months of inventory, costing roughly $33 million per month. The order-picking operations at Xerox were typically small-sized orders. Xerox decided to benchmark generically high-quality order-picking operators. Trade journals, professional associations, and management consultants specializing in material handling were researched. One article in *Modern Materials Handling* described L.L. Bean's mail-order operation.

The Xerox team arranged a site visit and prepared a questionnaire. They gathered data on the process, the information system, workers, equipment, and scheduling. Upon analysis, L.L. Bean's productivity was roughly three times that of Xerox. The Xerox team discovered the process enablers and adapted and incorporated them in their warehouse operations. This study has become a classic story of benchmarking at Xerox.

❖ EXPANDING BENCHMARKING FOR BROADER APPLICATIONS

Benchmarking is the search for *best practices* that will lead to superior performance. It can be used in the service industry as well as in manufacturing. The International Facilities Management Association has organized a focus group to provide baseline information to its members on a number of operational parameters. Because associations cut across industry lines and include a diverse membership, they are natural repositories and potential clearinghouses for information on generic business functions.

Because of the rapid rise in health-care costs, providers have begun to examine their internal operations. The Health-care Forum is an international not-for-profit association of health-care individuals and organizations. It began a study on how hospitals admit patients, with assistance from the International Benchmarking Clearinghouse of the American Productivity and Quality Center. In March 1992, twenty-eight participating hospitals began benchmarking their admitting process for elective acute-care patients. The study is to identify best-practice candidates, determine measurements of the admitting processes, and identify the process enablers, inhibitors, and improvements to guide future action. Each hospital was evaluated for opportunities for improvement. A second phase of this study will go beyond the health-care industry to analogous practices in airlines, hotels, rental-car agencies, and insurance companies.

❖ CREATING A BENCHMARKING CAPABILITY

Benchmarking is a process. Like any process, it can be benchmarked—Hewlett-Packard did it in 1989, beginning with Xerox's process.

Pitfalls to avoid in benchmarking efforts are lack of management commitment (or worse, management disbelief), failure to learn from others' mistakes and failures, not factoring customer expectations into the study, lack of participation by the process owners, penalizing managers or employees for the current gap in performance observed during benchmarking, studying companies with a poor cultural fit, and too much informality in the method of benchmarking.

To help ensure that benchmarking succeeds, the Benchmarking Code of Conduct should be followed, management needs to be committed to the effort, the process cannot be rushed, team approaches are critical, and the study needs to be supportive of the company's strategy and vision.

Benefits of benchmarking include better understanding the needs of the customer and the dynamics of the industry, learning from the successes and failures of others, and providing a sense of urgency for continuously learning and improving.

Senior management must insure that benchmarking teams focus on strategic objectives and have sufficient resources to succeed. They must also review plans and progress and act accordingly. If an outside consultant is needed to conduct a study, management should allow the team to learn how to conduct the study so that learning takes place. Benchmarking can be likened to a heart transplant; it represents significant change and must be handled carefully.

Benchmarking studies are valid for a point in time. They are perishable and time-sensitive. Benchmarking must be continually updated for those key business practices that affect the competitiveness of the organization.

The recipe for successful benchmarking requires three basic ingredients: a supportive management team with a real problem that needs to be solved; access to prospective benchmarking partners who have previously solved this problem; and a knowledgable benchmarking team with the ability to use basic quality tools and research methods to investigate process problems to their root cause. Add a dash of perseverance and a bunch of patience.

13

ETHICS AND MANAGEMENT

Almost daily, newspaper and television reports appear that document unethical activities engaged in by organizations, their managers, and their employees. Simultaneously, the past several years have seen an increase in the number of schools of business that have introduced ethics courses into their curricula. A large number of organizations are discussing ethical behavior, developing codes of conduct or codes of ethics, and making statements about the core values of their organizations.

Earlier books (e.g., Kenneth Blanchard and Norman Vincent Peale's *The Power of Ethical Management,* and Edward Freeman and Daniel Gilbert's *Corporate Strategy and the Search for Ethics*) explored the ethical dilemmas that managers face, the core principles that guide ethical decision making, and the need for linking corporate strategy and ethical reasoning. However, there still seemed to be questions about which values ethical leaders should hold, and how those values could be conveyed to their employees. Two widely read books address the need for managers to be ethical and credible.

Stephen Covey has provided answers to the ethical question in his books *The Seven Habits of Highly Effective People* and *Principle-Centered Leadership.* He offers a series of nearly moralistic prescriptions to guide managers as they chart their own work (and life) courses in the turbulent times ahead. Drawn from his extensive review of the "success literature," Covey urges people to be proactive, identify their values, discipline themselves to work on high-priority items, seek win-win solutions, listen with empathy, synergize with others, and cultivate their whole character (physical, mental, social/emotional, and spiritual). Covey, a popular inspirational speaker, is also the author of *First Things First,* which urges people to manage their time and life well so as to achieve the goals consistent with their values.

James M. Kouzes and Barry Z. Posner surveyed 15,000 managers, analyzed 400 case studies, and interviewed 40 managers prior to writing *Credibility,* their second major book on leadership. (Their earlier work was *The Leadership Challenge*). They discovered that employees want their ideal leaders to be honest, forward-looking, inspiring, competent, and supportive. Most-admired leaders were highly principled, held clear and strong values, were optimistic and hopeful, and demonstrated their belief in the self-worth of others. Kouzes and Posner urge readers to strengthen their credibility through a continuous internal dialogue, staying in touch with their constituents, developing others' capacities, affirming shared values, and sustaining employee hopes. Kouzes is president of TPG/Learning Systems, and Barry Posner is professor of organizational behavior at Santa Clara University.

READING 1

Principle-Centered Leadership

Stephen R. Covey
Summary prepared by Stephen Rubenfeld

Stephen Rubenfeld is Professor of Human Resource Management in the School of Business and Economics at the University of Minnesota, Duluth. He received his Ph.D. from the University of Wisconsin, Madison, and was previously on the faculty of Texas Tech University. His professional publications and presentations have covered a wide range of human resource and labor relations topics, including job search behaviors, appeals procedures, employee staffing, and concessionary bargaining. He is a member of the Society for Human Resource Management, the Academy of Management, and the Industrial Relations Research Association.

In the quest to uncover the secrets of effective leadership, a rapidly expanding body of literature has profiled the successes and failures attributed to organizational leaders. But after decades of research and thousands of publications, a comprehensive understanding of the leadership phenomenon is missing. What are the attributes of effective leaders? Do the charismatic aspects of leadership behaviors make a more significant contribution than the managerial elements? Under what circumstances are leaders successful? The existing literature does offer answers to questions such as these, but the explanations are personalized, situation specific, and technique bound.

The existing literature provides descriptive portraits of what the leader *does* in the organization setting, but fails to shed much light on what the leader *brings* to the organizational setting. This is not merely an oversight, but a fundamental deficiency that limits both the insight and practical value of this literature. Principle-centered leadership approaches leadership from a distinctive perspective. Personal effectiveness and leadership successes are seen as anchored in universal "laws." These laws form the conceptual foundation for a view and practice of leadership that is based on widely held humanistic principles.

Stephen R. Covey, *Principle-Centered leadership: Strategies for Personal & Professional Effectiveness*. Bellevue: S&S Trade, 1992.

Principle-Centered Leadership is premised on the belief that effective people are guided both in everyday living and in work relationships by universal principles or "natural laws," whereas ineffective people tend to place their energies on finding situation-specific behavioral paths to success as they are confronted by an evolving set of challenges. A principle-centered leadership approach is a natural extension of these habits of effectiveness to interpersonal and organizational settings. In addition to enhancing the prospects for personal success, this approach to leadership is an essential ingredient in the pursuit of productivity, quality, profitability, and other contemporary organizational goals.

❖ THE NEW PARADIGM

Quick, simple, superficial solutions to organizational problems often fail because they overlook the proven principles that govern human existence. These guiding principles not only endure over time, but serve as the basis for the success of individuals, groups, organizations, and societies. In dealing with challenges and opportunities, we sometimes lose sight of the fact that it is not principles that change, but only their application. The new paradigm introduced by principle-centered leadership suggests that *people must simultaneously center their leadership behaviors and their lives around "true north" principles.*

These laws are believed to be self-evident and self-validating, and unlike values, they represent an objective reality. Like a compass, they always are there to point people in the right direction. In this view, leadership techniques, intricate structural adaptations, and homilies based on someone else's successes are relatively unimportant. They are of value only where they are consistent with, and help people apply, the guiding principles.

An understanding of the "why to do's" provides a necessary foundation for guiding a leader's decisions on the "what to do's." Principle-centered leaders must first be principle-centered people who have a clear vision of the interrelated roles of *wisdom* (perspective on life), *guidance* (direction, identity, conscience), *security* (self-esteem, identity, personal strength), and, *power* (capacity, courage, and the will to act). Carried through all facets of life, these four ingredients provide the underpinnings of effective leadership.

❖ CHARACTERISTICS OF PRINCIPLE-CENTERED LEADERS

Seven basic human attributes provide humans with the *capacity* to strive for, and to achieve, personal effectiveness:

◆ Self-awareness
◆ Imagination and conscience
◆ Willpower

◆ Abundance mentality

◆ Courage and consideration

◆ Creativity

◆ Self-renewal

However, not all people take full advantage of these capabilities in their leadership endeavors. Observation reveals eight behavioral characteristics of effective, principled leaders:

1. *Learn throughout life* Through observation, curiosity, careful listening, reading, and other forms of self-improvement, principle-centered leaders continually extend their knowledge and experience base.

2. *Place a priority on service* Principle-centered leaders view life as a mission of service; they give to others and take responsibility for improving society.

3. *Believe in others* They recognize individual differences, value diversity, and believe in the potential for all people to make meaningful contributions.

4. *Seek balance in life* In attitudes and actions they seek a balanced existence. Principle-centered leaders are neither workaholics nor unidimensional. They are active socially, physically, and intellectually.

5. *Radiate positive energy* They are optimistic, think positively, and are aware of the effects of their energy level and demeanor.

6. *See life as a challenge* Principle-centered leaders are open minded and flexible. They enjoy life and its challenges.

7. *Serve as catalysts* They are change agents and strive to improve any situation of which they are a part.

8. *Exercise for self-renewal* They consistently work to develop and enhance the physical, mental, emotional, and spiritual aspects of their lives.

❖ MASTER PRINCIPLES OF MANAGEMENT AND LEADERSHIP

While both management and leadership are essential in the organizational setting, it is important to understand the differences between these roles. The primary *management* activities involve implementation, setting up systems and structures to obtain desired results, control, and logistics. In exercising the management role, emphasis is placed on cost-effectiveness, quality measures, rules, procedures, and policies. *Leadership*, on the other hand, deals with bigger and at the same time less tangible issues. Leadership provides vision and direction but also inspires and motivates people to work in diverse ways to achieve a common purpose.

The leadership and management roles must function together effectively for the organization to achieve long-term and lasting success. Nevertheless, owing to emphases on short-term, quantifiable results, it is the management role that predominates in most organizations, while leadership development is neglected. A leader who possesses both strategic and motivational competencies can bring to the organization a sense of direction and purpose, while concurrently building work groups of inspired and motivated employees. Leaders and managers working in tandem represent the marriage of effectiveness and efficiency in the pursuit of organizational goals.

Principle-centered leadership must operate simultaneously at each of four levels:

◆ *Personal*—self awareness and comfort
◆ *Interpersonal*—relationships with others
◆ *Managerial*—responsibility to get the job done
◆ *Organizational*—need to organize people

At each level, fundamental principles guide behaviors and are the basis for leadership effectiveness. At the personal level, *trustworthiness* is determined by a combination of character and competence. Effectiveness at the interpersonal level requires a high level of *trust*, which grows out of trustworthiness. Trust is also a product of interpersonal experiences and a determinant of future interactions.

At the managerial level, *empowerment* is the desired operating principle. If the level of trust is low, formal control systems are typically required to assure that people do what needs to be done. If trust levels are high, direction based on rank or position can be supplanted by a more constructive system of self-governing work groups. Finally, at the organizational level, when there are trustworthiness, trust, and empowerment, the organization can be structured to reflect *alignment,* or fit. Under these conditions, a flat and flexible structure rather than a rigid, hierarchical system will facilitate the attainment of organizational goals.

❖ PRINCIPLE-CENTERED LEADERSHIP AND TOTAL QUALITY

The pursuit of "total quality" objectives is inextricably related to principle-centered leadership. As already noted, *principled leadership is an all-encompassing philosophy that calls for continuous improvement in the personal, interpersonal, managerial, and organizational domains.* In this respect, "total quality" relies on principles very much in concert with natural laws that provide the conceptual foundation for principle-centered leadership, as well as concepts such as the following:

◆ Consistency
◆ Predictability

- ◆ Continuous improvement
- ◆ Feedback
- ◆ Measurement
- ◆ Honest and ethical relationships

Without such principles, the techniques and methods of quality improvement are unlikely to provide long-lasting results.

Principle-centered leadership suggests that total quality and continuous system improvement cannot be attained without simultaneously striving to perfect interdependent and interpersonal relationships. When applied to quality initiatives, principle-centered leadership empowers people to pursue improvement in each of the four domains (personal, interpersonal, managerial, organizational), reinforces continuous quality improvement activities, and suggests systems to support quality improvement objectives.

Seven habits of personal effectiveness are applicable not only to principle-centered leadership, but also to the principles of total quality. The key habits are:

1. *Be proactive* Take the initiative; respond on the basis of principles rather than emotion or "gut feel."
2. *Begin with an end in mind* Have a long-term focus on people based on principles to achieve a sense of direction.
3. *Put first things first* Manage time and priorities around roles, while keeping in mind the desired ends.
4. *Think win-win solutions* Seek mutually beneficial, rather than competitive, outcomes.
5. *Seek to understand, then to be understood* Communications should be empathetic—encompassing a clear message, as well as recognizing feelings and emotions.
6. *Synergize* Develop and use appropriate management styles along with supportive systems and structures.
7. *Sharpen the saw* Personally and organizationally, create an environment of (and practice) continuous learning and improvement.

❖ IMPLICATIONS

The principled leader empowers people and their organizations in the pursuit of desired outcomes by extending the natural laws first introduced in *The Seven Habits of Highly Effective People* to the organizational setting. In order to succeed, these laws require complete acceptance of the new paradigm in life and work, along with perseverance and patience. Applied thoroughly and consistently, these principles offer the opportunity for personal and organizational transformation.

Principle-centered leadership is as much a philosophy of life as a guide to becoming an effective leader. While not directly answering the question of whether leaders are born or made, it is clear that one can't be an effective leader unless an appropriate set of personal beliefs and values is carried into the leadership realm. Adherence to these principles may provide the opportunity to *become* a more effective and successful leader.

The principle-centered leadership perspective helps people to confront change by providing the wisdom and skills to take advantage of opportunities. This perspective is similar to the adage that suggests:

"Give [people] fish and you feed [them] for a day.
Teach [people] to fish and you feed [them] for a lifetime."

READING 2

Credibility

James M. Kouzes and Barry Z. Posner
Summary prepared by Gregory R. Fox

Gregory R. Fox is the Vice Chancellor for Finance and Operations at the University of Minnesota, Duluth. He earned his master's degree at the University of Washington, and received a Bush Mid-Career Leadership Fellowship. He has developed instructional support materials for the Newstrom and Bittel book *Supervision: Managing for Results* (Glencoe, 1996).

Leadership is many things—a series of actions, an encounter between people, an intangible, a performing art. Leadership does not, and can not, exist independently, for it is a *reciprocal relationship* between those who choose to lead and those who decide to follow. There have been dramatic changes in the nature of the relationship between leader and subordinate (employer-employee) during the last decade. Most significant have been an increased awareness of the leader's need to serve others, to build seamless partnerships with others, and to build a community of individuals and teams at work. Wise leaders have become servers, supporters, partners, and providers, building their relationships on mutual obligations, commitments, and collaboration. This changing leader-follower relationship increasingly creates *servant leaders* who value the role of serving, and giving to, those with whom they work.

❖ KEY LEADERSHIP CHARACTERISTICS

In a survey, 15,000 managers were asked to identify their seven most admired leadership characteristics from a set of twenty qualities. The results of the survey, subsequent case studies, and in-depth interviews were remarkably consistent. The most desirable characteristics (those selected by more than half of the respondents) identified for leaders were honesty, forward-looking, inspiring, and competent. *Honesty appears to be essential to leadership,* with 87 percent of the respondents selecting that characteristic.

James M. Kouzes & Barry Z. Posner, *Credibility*. San Francisco: Jossey-Bass, 1993.

Results also suggest that *competence* (being capable, effective, challenging, and encouraging), while still widely cherished as a leader characteristic, *is valued somewhat less today than in the past.* This could be seen as a cause for concern if companies start being led by visionary and inspirational individuals who don't have the complex skills needed to implement their visions. In contrast to the decline in valuing competence, the leader quality that has increased most in value during the last ten years is *supportiveness.* This characteristic originally ranked eleventh, and now ranks sixth overall as an admired leadership attribute. This change reflects a strong societal trend toward empowerment, and indicates that people are searching for more understanding and encouragement from their leaders.

The qualities of honesty (trustworthiness), inspiration (dynamism), and competence (expertise) in combination are often referred to as source credibility. *Credibility is believed to be the primary foundation of future global leadership,* although it has often been overlooked in the past.

Studies done by Lou Harris, The Opinion Research Corporation, and others suggest that there is a significant gap between the value that constituents place on credibility and the likeliness it will occur in their place of work. The recent savings and loan and Wall Street scandals and religious fraud have led to a sense of betrayal and public disillusionment. Fueling this disillusionment have been recent reports of CEO compensation at up to 150 times the level of the average worker in manufacturing and service industries. When employees believe that management doesn't "walk their talk" a *credibility gap*—a strong sense of cynicism—occurs, which weakens the bond that is required for effective leadership.

Earning credibility is done one-to-one, a little at a time, through personal contact with constituents. Managers are encouraged to "Do what you say you will do"—and then substitute "we" for "you" in that motto to build a bond with those they are serving. Three critical elements for strengthening leader credibility are clarity, unity, and intensity. *Clarification* of values, visions, and aims helps others understand the guiding principles. *Unity* is the degree to which people understand, agree on, and support the clarified values and directions. *Intensity* is the strength of commitment to deeply held aims and aspirations.

When leaders demonstrate credibility through clarity, unity, and intensity, workers tend to feel enthusiastically motivated, challenged and inspired, capable and powerful, as well as respected, valued, and proud. The predictable employee outcomes of these feelings include pride in belonging, strong team spirit, congruence of personal and organizational values, organizational commitment, and sense of ownership. Credible leadership stimulates employees to contribute their time and talents toward a common purpose.

❖ THE SIX DISCIPLINES

Leaders earn credibility, respect, and loyalty when they demonstrate that they believe in the self-worth of others. Leaders must appreciate others, affirm others, and develop others. They must demonstrate these behaviors persistently and tenaciously. Through the study of leaders and leadership, six disciplines that underlie credibility emerge. They are as follows (see additional details in Table 1):

- ◆ Discovering yourself (clarifying your values)
- ◆ Appreciating constituents (talking and listening to them)
- ◆ Affirming shared values (striving for consensus and community)
- ◆ Developing constituents' capacity (constantly educating)
- ◆ Serving a purpose (becoming servant leaders)
- ◆ Sustaining hope (maintaining energy and optimism)

◆ SELF-DISCOVERY

A review of those individuals who are identified as the most admired leaders reveals that they are people who are highly principled, with strong beliefs. Their individual values clarify what they will or will not do, directly contributing to their credibility as a leader. In addition, strong personal values assist in resolving conflicts and serve to motivate others.

Those interested in leadership are encouraged to write their own personal leadership philosophy and then evaluate what has been written. This assessment is aimed at identifying the values that are expressed in this credo. Exercises like this make it possible for those interested in the study of leadership to assess what values are most evident in effective leaders.

Another important characteristic associated with self-discovery is developing confidence and self-efficacy. This requires identifying the skills, knowledge, and abilities that are necessary to represent the values you claim with moral force. Effective leaders identify the skills necessary for their job. They acquire competence (mastery) in each of these areas and then expand the skills they have to be more effective in a wide variety of circumstances. They observe successful role models, seek social support from others, and manage the stresses in their lives. Then they seek to exhibit optimal performance, or *flow*, through goal setting, becoming immersed in their roles, avoiding distraction through intense attention to the present, and learning to enjoy their current activities.

◆ APPRECIATING CONSTITUENTS

Effective leaders recognize that organizations (and individuals) are enriched through diversity. They seek to create cultures where each person values and affirms others, relationships are collaborative, co-workers develop a sense of shared history, and the whole person (work and family elements) is recognized. These leaders keep their minds open, appreciate the uniqueness in others, solicit and use feedback from others, trust others, and stimulate constructive controversy.

TABLE 1

THE SIX LEADERSHIP DISCIPLINES

Discovering Yourself	Developing Capacity
Leaders Should:	Leaders Should:
Keep a journal	Stop making decisions
Discover their life themes	Stop talking at staff meetings
Assess their values	Set up coaching opportunities
Audit their ability to succeed	Invite people to assume
Seek mastery experiences	responsibility
Ask for support or help	Give everyone a customer
Evaluate the five "Ps" of	Have an open house
personal mission:	Share the big picture
◆ Proficiency	Enrich people's jobs
◆ Product	Let constituents be the teachers
◆ People	Use modeling to develop
◆ Place	competencies
◆ Purpose	

Appreciating Constituents and Their Diversity	Serving a Purpose
Leaders Should:	Leaders Should:
Be accessible, even at home	Manage by storytelling
Listen everywhere and listen well	Create heroes
Learn your constituents' stories	Speak with confidence
Step outside your cultural experience	Reduce fear
Keep in touch with your constituents	Ask questions
Become an employee for a day	Hold yourself accountable

Table 1 (Continued)

Appreciating Constituents and Their Diversity	Serving a Purpose
Leaders Should:	Leaders Should:
Be the first to take a risk	Keep score
Know what bugs your constituents	Conduct a personal audit
Practice small wins	Conduct an organization audit
	Get everyone to champion values

Affirming Shared Value	Sustaining Hope
Leaders Should:	Leaders Should:
Get together to start drafting your group's credo	Exercise
	Write your vision for the future
Make sure there is an agreement around values	Set goals and make a plan
	Choose flexible optimism
Conduct a values survey	Suffer first
Connect values with reasons	Nurture optimism and passion
Structure cooperative goals	Go visiting
Make sure everyone knows the business	Dispute your negative beliefs
Be an enthusiastic spokesperson for shared values	Reclarify your values
Say "yes" frequently	
Go slow to go fast	
Establish a sunset statute for your credo	

◆ AFFIRMING SHARED VALUES

Leaders seek a common core of understanding—an identification of shared values and consensus around paradigms. They struggle to identify common ground, they advocate cooperative community of purpose, and they foster consensus around key issues. They create drafts of underlying creeds, and demonstrate flexibility as revisions are sought and made.

◆ DEVELOPING CAPACITY

Credible leaders believe in the abilities of others to grow and develop. They empower others through distributed leadership; they provide educational opportunities for building others' knowledge and skill; they encourage a sense of ownership in employees; and they inspire confidence in employee abilities to act responsibly and capably. They invite employees to accept mutual responsibility for results, and share information and feedback that allows others to grow.

◆ SERVING A PURPOSE

Leaders must have a strong sense of faith in what they are doing, and why. They recognize their servant leader role and set examples that others can follow. They are visibly "out front" demonstrating their priorities, staying in touch with their constituents, and making an impression on others through storytelling, utilizing the "teachable moment" when others are particularly susceptible to learning, and standing up for their beliefs. Perhaps most importantly, they create enduring organizational systems and structures that reinforce and support their values long after the leader has departed.

◆ SUSTAINING HOPE

People struggle. People get discouraged. People lose hope. These are moments when credible leaders need to be proactive, demonstrating that it is possible to regain internal control over external events. Leaders can inspire others to take initiative courageously, to balance hope and work for reasonable results, and to enjoy themselves along the path. And leaders are encouraged to demonstrate the acceptability of being caring, loving, and compassionate in the workplace so as to inspire others to do so, too.

❖ CONCLUSION

Currently, the work world is experiencing a fundamental restructuring. There are no guarantees that a perfectly executed leadership plan will result in a satisfying, successful worklife. Credible leaders, those most in touch with their constituents, feel the pain most strongly. Leaders seeking to establish their credibility are urged to develop understanding and learn to love the struggle. But a caveat is in order—*excessive emphasis on any one of the six disciplines can damage a leader's credibility.*

Leaders can strengthen their credibility by engaging in a dialogue about the fundamental tension between freedom and constraint. In nearly every workplace, more freedom is becoming commonplace; at the same time, institutions will continue to have some sharp constraints. The dialogue will focus on questions of how many, how much, and what type.

The success of leaders should be measured by whether or not they left their organization a better place than when they found it. To respond to the organizational struggle, credible leaders need to be optimistic, hopeful, and inspiring. They need to discover their own selves, appreciate the diversity of others, and recognize that renewing credibility is a continuous struggle. They need to take risks, accept the associated pain and excitement, and revel in the exhilaration of becoming continual learners about what it means to be leaders. In short, they need to be credible—to themselves and to others.

14

GLOBAL DIMENSIONS

"The world has become an international marketplace." Has anyone not heard this assertion in the past decade? Does anyone still deny the inevitability of the assertion? Nevertheless, the global arena is a new domain for many organizations, and there are key lessons to be learned. Furthermore, the dynamics generated by organizations doing business in the global arena are leading toward the creation of a "borderless world."

Several contemporary books focus our attention on global issues of managerial interest. Ouchi's *Theory Z* (see Part Three) was a forerunner to this interest, of course. Part Fourteen presents two recent books that address global aspects of organization and management.

Kenichi Ohmae challenges some of the ways that managers have historically viewed the world and the way that business has been conducted. Performance standards are being created by those who buy products in the global marketplace; these standards are no longer being created by those who manufacture or those who regulate the manufacturers. As a consequence, organizations need to adjust their structures so that they see and think globally, are focused on customers, and operate as "insiders" in countries around the globe as opposed to operating merely as exporters to these countries. Ohmae proposes that organizations rid themselves of a centralized "headquarters mentality" and their engrained *companyism* (seeking to beat their competition) and instead avoid competition where possible. He also advocates the adoption of a *China mentality*, wherein managers act with the confidence that they understand and can change key markets in the world.

Kenichi Ohmae is the Managing Director of McKinsey and Company, a large international consulting firm. He draws on his experiences with businesses and governments doing business in the emerging global economy to derive suggestions for how companies can win in the new global marketplace.

Many writers, such as Robert Quinn and coauthors Bolman and Deal (see Part Two) have urged managers to develop the capacity to see and handle paradoxes. John Naisbitt, in *Global Paradox*, points out the seeming contradiction (paradox) that *smaller* players will become increasingly powerful as the world economy gets larger. They are more flexible and agile, less burdened with bureaucracy, and able to react to changing marketplace needs more rapidly. The emergence of giant new markets (e.g., China, Asia, Latin America) and the blurring of nation-state boundaries (e.g., the European Community) will open up immense opportunities to be successful for both small firms and large firms who "act small."

Naisbitt achieved popularity with his early book *Megatrends,* which sold over six million copies. With Patricia Aburdene, he has also published *Megatrends 2000, Megatrends for Women,* and *Re-Inventing the Corporation.* Naisbitt and Aburdene are widely known for their reporting of key trends and their social forecasting that draws from extensive data-gathering of political, economic, technological, and social events.

READING 1

The Borderless World

Kenichi Ohmae
Summary prepared by Robert Wharton

Robert Wharton is an Assistant Professor of Management Studies at the University of Minnesota, Duluth, where he teaches courses in strategic management and business and society. He received his Ph.D. from Rutgers University and is a member of several professional associations, including the Academy of Management.

"An isle is emerging that is bigger than a continent—the Interlinked Economy (ILE) of the Triad (the United States, Europe, and Japan)" (p. xi). Joined by aggressive economies in Taiwan, Hong Kong, and Singapore, the ILE has grown so powerful that it is destroying the old national borders that once defined consumer groups and corporate identities.

The emergence of the ILE has resulted in a great deal of confusion, both for managers and for economic policy makers. Old theories that compared one nation against others simply do not work anymore. When the economy grows stronger, jobs are created abroad and not at home, disappointing the experts. If the government raises interest rates to control inflation, cheaper money rushes in from other countries in the ILE. Statistics on the balance of trade become meaningless when corporations spread their production and distribution functions throughout the ILE. Any managers or politicians who do not understand this new reality risk isolating their companies, or their citizens, from the dynamic economy of the borderless world.

The Borderless World is organized into three parts. First, the strategy and organization of companies operating in the new international environment are discussed. Second, government bureaucrats who are causing great problems for their citizens are attacked, even as these officials are becoming powerless and irrelevant. Finally, Ohmae's vision of the economic world into which we are moving is presented.

Kenichi Ohmae, *The Borderless World*. New York: Harper Business, 1990.

❖ STRATEGIES FOR INTERNATIONAL COMPANIES

◆ AN INSIDE-OUT VIEW OF MACROECONOMICS

In a borderless world, strategic managers need to understand, and master, five concerns in order to operate effectively in an interlinked economy. Striking the correct balance among these *five Cs* is essential to any successful business.

CUSTOMERS   Managers must understand the growing power of consumers around the globe. Customers throughout the Triad have few national allegiances; they are only interested in buying the products that offer them value—the best quality at the best price. Lack of allegiances gives consumers their power, and as news of product performance becomes harder to suppress, consumer power grows greater still. The critical objective for a company, therefore, is to find new ways to create new value for its customers.

COMPETITION   Products on the market today require so many different technologies, and the technologies change so rapidly, that no company can maintain a lead in all of them. Fifty years ago, General Motors could keep in house all the technology involved in building a car. But today, consider what has made the IBM Personal Computer such a success. Lotus, along with many other companies, wrote the application software for an operating system designed by Microsoft. Microsoft wrote the operating system for a microprocessor designed by Intel. Today, no single company can simultaneously master all of the technologies essential to making a product successful. And because companies are forced to cooperate, no technology stays secret for long. Therefore, operating globally means finding partners, some of whom may also be competitors.

COMPANY   A fundamental change has taken place in business over the last ten or fifteen years. Automation has nearly eliminated the labor component of manufacturing a product, so production is increasingly a fixed-cost activity. Because new technologies are so critical and change so rapidly, research and development (R&D) is also becoming a fixed-cost activity. And because maintaining brand recognition for powerful customers is essential, marketing and advertising become fixed costs as well. Managers can no longer boost profits by reducing wages or labor hours or other variable costs. For companies with large fixed costs, the only way to defray their investment is to find more customers and increase sales. This means rising fixed costs are driving companies toward globalization.

CURRENCY   In a borderless world, currency exchange rates are much more volatile than they were just a few years ago. In order to neutralize the effect of currency, managers of global companies are forced to become strong in all areas of the Triad. Then, if currency becomes a negative in one area, positives in another area cancel it out.

COUNTRY Companies move into a country as they seek to neutralize the impact of currency fluctuations. To serve them well, though, they have to move deeply into those countries to get as close to their customers as possible. Managers have to find a way for their companies to benefit from world-scale operations. But at the same time, they must know and serve their customers as well as any local company from the same country. Coca-Cola's success in Japan, for example, is partly a result of introducing unique products for Japanese consumers.

Changes in the five Cs have forced companies to spread out across national borders, but the changes have been so rapid that managers have not always been able to make the necessary adjustments in the way they organize their companies, in the way they think about strategy, or in their assumptions about how to do business.

◆ THE EQUIDISTANT MANAGER

Most managers are nearsighted, with their vision dominated by customers in their home countries. Too few try to plan and build companies as if all key customers were equidistant from the corporate headquarters. Honda, for example, has divisions throughout the Triad, but its managers do not act as if the company were divided into Japanese and overseas operations. In fact, the word "overseas" has no place at Honda. The first rule of equidistance is to *see and think globally.*

National boundaries may still be clear on a map, but for managers those boundaries have largely disappeared. With the persistent flow of information around the world, people quickly learn what products are available, and what level of quality they can expect. People have become genuinely global consumers. For managers, this flow of information puts a priority on learning to meet the demands of a borderless world.

This may mean becoming an *insider,* replicating a complete business in every country or key market in which your company does business. Managers cannot hope to run every business in every market around the world from corporate headquarters. They have to become a true *insider* in each market so they can respond to competitors and provide the value local consumers demand.

Managing effectively in the borderless world means paying central attention to delivering value to customers, and to developing an equidistant perspective on who they are and what they want. First and most important is the strategic need to *see your customers clearly.*

◆ GETTING BACK TO STRATEGY

For many managers, strategy still means beating the competition. It means doing what your competition does, only better. This belief is wrong, since strategy should first be a process of responding to the needs of customers and delivering value to those customers. Indeed, strategy should include an effort to *avoid* competition whenever possible.

Many Japanese managers have failed to learn this lesson. As these firms went global, they concentrated on differentiating their products from those of their competitors. Today, though, many find themselves trapped between competing customer needs. On the one hand, German companies, such as Mercedes or BMW in automobiles, command high prices by serving the quality end of the market. On the other hand, companies like Korea's Hyundai have tried to satisfy price-conscious consumers on the low end of the market. The result, for Japanese firms, is a painful squeeze caused by their focus on competitors, rather than on customer needs.

How should a manager respond to this squeeze? Consider the strategy of Yamaha, a Japanese maker of pianos. The piano market is in decline, as people simply are not buying many new pianos today, and most of the existing ones are sitting around gathering dust. Yamaha decided to take a hard look at its customers and the product. What they found was fewer and fewer people with the time to play the piano, or even to learn how to play the piano. How does one provide value for these customers? Yamaha worked hard on new electronic technology that could turn existing pianos into sophisticated player-pianos. Now, for $2,500, customers can turn their idle pianos into useful instruments. And instead of a dying market, Yamaha now has the prospect of a $2,500 sale to retrofit up to forty million old pianos.

Like Yamaha, many Japanese companies are talented value-adders. Many others are so intent on beating the competition that whole industries have suffered as a consequence. In the blind pursuit of *companyism* (the desire to beat the competition by *doing more better*), Japanese shipbuilders and producers of semiconductors, color TVs, and watches have relentlessly overbuilt and overproduced in an effort to beat their competitors. Now, these industries are flooded with overcapacity and all companies are robbed of an opportunity to make a profit.

Companyism is not entirely a bad thing, of course. Many American companies suffer from too little company orientation. Japanese firms build loyalty, in part, by nurturing a sense of equal participation throughout the company. In most firms, for example, the total compensation of most Japanese CEOs is no more than ten times that of a factory worker. By contrast, Lee Iacocca of Chrysler had an income that was roughly one thousand times greater than that of one of his factory workers.

What is critical, however, is that managers not be so blinded by company loyalty that they forget to ask whether the system needs to be the way it is. Managers in a borderless world need a certain mindset. They need the freedom to rethink their products and ask whether there is a better way to serve their customers. In a changeable world, very few solutions will work forever.

◆ THE CHINA MENTALITY

In product development, one remedy for companyism is to create multiple product teams, each with the same general direction, and then set these teams free to find their own approaches to a single problem. Managers will then not only have multiple solutions from which they may choose, but they will also be able to offer their customers several solutions to the same problem. At the same time, their companies keep churning out new or improved products at regular intervals. NEC, for example, introduces something new to the market every month. Its competitors do so only once every year or two.

What is necessary for world-class product development is the freedom to keep asking the question "Why?" when attempting to meet customer needs. Unfortunately, too many managers lack the *China Mentality* (China, literally translated, means "center of the universe"). Too many managers fail to believe they are the center of the universe, and hence lack the inner confidence that they can change the world. Lacking this confidence, managers do not allow themselves to be led to answers that deviate far from the company norm. For global players, however, confidence to act on their knowledge of key markets is the secret to success in a borderless world.

◆ GETTING RID OF THE HEADQUARTERS MENTALITY

Company headquarters often becomes another problem for managers as they begin the process of globalization. Overeager and overanxious corporate managers have frequently destroyed profitable businesses by trying to supervise from a distance. No company can operate globally by centralizing all key decisions at the corporate headquarters. Rather, *decomposing* the corporate center into several regional headquarters is becoming an essential ingredient in the strategy of effective global competitors.

The real challenge in decomposing the corporate center, what Akio Morita of Sony terms *global localization,* is not organizational. The real challenge is psychological, a matter of values. When the mother-country identity of the old corporate headquarters disappears, it must be replaced by a commitment to a single, unified global identity. When managers overcome their headquarters mentality, when they come to believe that they may work *in* different nations but they are *of* the global corporation, then the company will have taken the last step toward true global status. Managers will then be free to decide how best to run their business in their particular market.

◆ THE GLOBAL LOGIC OF STRATEGIC ALLIANCES

For most managers, management means control. Alliances, though, mean sharing control. So it's not surprising that managers have been slow to experiment with genuine strategic alliances. But in a borderless world, in a world of rapidly changing technologies and escalating fixed costs, true alliances become an essential component of strategy.

Glaxo, the British pharmaceutical company, did not want to establish an extensive sales and service network in every country in which it did business. It could not afford to, given its costly commitment to R&D. So Glaxo decided to develop alliances with major pharmaceutical companies in Japan, trade its best drugs with each partner, and focus its own resources on its base in Europe. Now, for each alliance, Glaxo has two profitable drugs to market without any increase in its fixed investment in R&D or marketing.

True alliances are marriages of equals. They avoid the problems of equity ownership and parental control that have plagued so many joint ventures. Instead, alliances help global companies address the common problem of fixed costs. Nissan distributes for Volkswagen in Japan, and Volkswagen reciprocates in Europe. Ford and Mazda swap cars throughout the Triad. Unless an organization is committed to building a fixed investment in every region of the world, it makes sense to cooperate with someone who already has that force in place.

❖ GOVERNMENTS AND BUREAUCRATS

◆ "LIES, DAMNED LIES, AND STATISTICS"

The charges are familiar. The United States has an enormous trade deficit, especially with Japan. And while the value of the dollar falls, selfish consumers save virtually none of their incomes. Worse, they insist on buying products manufactured abroad. The country is on an irresponsible binge, in the process of being destroyed by selfishness and short-term thinking.

The charges are familiar, but a different picture can be painted. The United States does not have a trade deficit. In fact, because dollars are the settlement currency in foreign trade, the United States does not have any "foreign" trade at all. Unlike Brazil or France, or even Japan, the United States never has to earn foreign currency to purchase something from abroad. All it has to do is expand its domestic economy across the borders of its trading partners. Because the money used to buy foreign goods is always in dollars, buying cars from Japan is no different than buying PCs from Texas or oranges from California.

Government trade statistics measure goods that cross the national border, but in a borderless world the figures they report are completely meaningless. We act as if they really mean something, when in fact they bear no relation to the real flows of economic activity in the world. Most American corporations have developed a local insider presence in countries around the world, and this is the biggest reason why United States exports have declined statistically. The products they sell to global markets are made in those markets. In fact, any goods they ship back home are recorded as Japanese or European exports to the United States.

The trade deficit is an illusion, created by a system that only measures goods crossing national borders. Consider that in 1985, Japanese purchases of American goods (regardless of where those goods were produced) averaged $580 per person. American per capita purchases of Japanese goods averaged just $298.

Americans also assume that the Japanese have a much higher savings rate. Yet these savings statistics are just as flawed and misleading. A closer examination of the assumptions behind these statistics suggests that there is little or no difference in the savings habits of American and Japanese consumers. In fact, if one looks at the assets we collect rather than the income we put away, Americans may actually be far *better* savers than the Japanese.

Americans worry that the United States has become a debtor nation, that we have mortgaged our future and put ourselves in debt to the rest of the world. But there is no reason to be concerned with most of these "liabilities." The United States is an attractive place for foreigners to invest their money, so foreign investment pours into the country. Most of these investments (the purchase of companies or real estate, for example) carry no interest charges, so the United States incurs no financial obligations. But most foreign investments are recorded at the national border as "external liabilities," so people worry.

◆ DEVELOPMENT IN A BORDERLESS WORLD

Politicians and policy makers, misled by official statistics and not fully understanding the nature of the borderless world, continue to intervene in the economy with disastrous results. Attempts are made to weaken the value of the dollar in order to make American goods more competitive. But officials succeed only in frightening new investments away. Governments try to "manage" the foreign exchange markets, but accomplish little more than to punish their own domestic companies and consumers.

Perhaps the most murderous effects of confused government policy result from the folly of protectionism. Nations that have been successful at development efforts have made the determination to open the door to the global economy. They have decided to become a part of the global marketplace. Those that fail still harbor the illusion that participation in the interlinked economy is not important.

In a borderless world, the role of a responsible government is to give its people as much choice as possible, and to keep its people well informed. The government of India does not do this. Their domestic auto industry is highly protected against foreign products. But cars in India are miserable vehicles, and the auto industry is still sick. Hong Kong, by contrast, has no natural resources and a tiny population. Yet, with a "free port" approach, the people of Hong Kong have achieved a per capita GNP that rivals Great Britain's.

❖ VISION OF THE FUTURE

We need to accept the fact that information and knowledge, not natural resources, are the key to wealth and economic growth. National borders mean little for the real flows of economic activity, and national governments no longer have the ability to produce economic wealth based on what's under the soil, or on what can be taxed, or on the strength of their military. Instead, *wealth emerges from the hard work of well-educated people.*

Given this new reality, what is the role of a modern government? It must educate its people, and guarantee them as much information and as much choice as possible. In the interlinked economy, it does not matter who builds this factory or who owns that office building. What is important is that the global corporations that do business in an area give people good work to do and an opportunity to buy the products they want.

It makes no sense for politicians and journalists to be concerned about national industrial competitiveness. Nations are no longer in competition. The only thing that matters is that IBM is in global competition with DEC and Fujitsu, or that Toyota competes worldwide with Honda and Ford. No government should be in the business of dictating choices for their citizens in order to protect domestic firms. In a borderless world, the best companies will be organized on a global scale. Companies that will not, or cannot, compete globally are simply not worth saving.

How close is the ILE to becoming a truly borderless world? Perhaps closer than we think. Certainly, there are still problems. Many companies still suffer from a headquarters mentality. Too few are ready to take advantage of genuine strategic alliances. National borders are still controlled, and domestic markets are still protected. But more and more corporations are now committed to globalization, and they have benefitted from that commitment. And daily, the information age makes consumers more knowledgeable and more demanding. As these trends continue, government leaders may soon realize that their role is not one of dictating choices to their citizens. Governments may provide guidance on such issues as safety and minimum levels of service. But they must step back and allow people the freedom to vote with their pocketbooks.

READING 2

Global Paradox

John Naisbitt
Summary prepared by Kelly Nelson

Kelly Nelson has been a Staff Supervisor of Employee Relations of U.S. Steel's Minnesota Ore Operations and is now employed at U.S. Steel's Mon Valley Works in Dravosburg, PA. She has a Bachelor of Business Administration from the University of Minnesota, Duluth, and is currently pursuing her MBA.

Although citizens of independent countries want to trade more freely with other countries of the world, they still desire political and cultural independence in their own countries. The *Maastricht Treaty*, calling for the political and economic unification of the European countries, is poised for failure. As countries surrender their currency and replace it with a common currency, a part of their heritage, culture, and independence is relinquished. Further, electronic networks make this loss unnecessary. Electronic networks today connect banks, businesses, and communities worldwide.

❖ THE GLOBAL PARADOX

Although an apparent contradiction, the statement "the bigger the world economy, the more powerful its smallest players" is actually a *paradox* (a statement that seems absurd but is actually valid or true). The expanding world economy makes it possible to study the smallest economic player, the entrepreneur, in an attempt to understand the economic workings of the largest economic entities.

Although large corporations created the American economy, this has changed in recent years. Now 90 percent of the goods exported from the United States come from small- and medium-sized companies. In fact, large U.S. corporations have had to decentralize and downsize in order to survive. By eliminating the bureaucracy, large corporations are becoming more flexible and able to react to the needs of the marketplace more efficiently. By practicing *subsidiarity* (retaining power at the lowest possible level within an orga-

John Naisbitt, *Global Paradox: The Bigger the World Economy, the More Powerful It's Smallest Players*. New York: Morrow, 1994.

nization), corporations are trying to recapture the entrepreneurial spirit of their employees. This results in smaller and stronger units within the organization. However, large corporations have not reached the level of subsidiarity found in small- and medium-sized companies. Because *small companies,* by their nature, retain power at the lowest possible level, they *are poised to dominate more and more of the world economy.*

Mergers and takeovers, once commonly viewed as a way to control the marketplace, are being replaced by strategic alliances in which corporations cooperate with their largest competitors. For instance, Nissan purchases automobile parts from Toyota. By creating strategic alliances, corporations take advantage of their competitor's assets, while avoiding the capital investment necessary to improve their own similar products. Strategic alliances fit the large organizations' need to avoid corporate growth and thereby enable small organizations to grow globally. Small corporations can also compete more easily in today's world economy through the removal of trade barriers, the increase in computer and telecommunications, the deregulation of financial markets, and the melding of consumer tastes. A metaphor for the movement from bureaucracies to small, autonomous units is the shift from mainframes to personal computers and then to personal computers networked together.

❖ THE NEW TRIBALISM

Tribalism is the belief in fidelity to one's own kind, defined by ethnicity, language, culture, religion, or profession. Tribalism is surging throughout the world, and a balance must be found between tribal identity and global competition. As the world's economies become more universal, the population begins to act more tribal in an effort to keep the norms it has known. As the world's population becomes more global, traditional nation-states are losing their importance, but the importance of tribalism is growing. The decline of the nation-state is evidenced daily by news reports of countries gaining their independence and the growth of democratic societies out of formerly communistic regimes. This is caused by the tribalistic feelings of citizens within countries, the efficiency created by smaller countries (similar to small corporations), and the revolution of telecommunications; it leads from hierarchical power to networking, from vertical to horizontal emphasis. The demise of the nation-state causes the Global Paradox to focus on smaller and smaller parts.

❖ POWERING THE PARADOX: THE TELECOMMUNICATIONS REVOLUTION

Telecommunications will provide the infrastructure on which the global economy will flourish. Through the maturation of telecommunications, technologies have combined, strategic alliances have been formed, global networks have been established, and personal computers have become available for virtually all citizens. The advancement of telecommunications has allowed each individual to become more empowered. Even ordinary citizens without computer programming knowledge can operate computers effectively; cellular phones are accessible and affordable for most; the fax allows individuals to communicate worldwide with virtually the touch of a button.

The progress made in telecommunications is paving the way for strategic alliances between cable, telephone, and computer companies. Telephone companies such as GTE Corp. are partnering with cable companies such as Daniels Cablevision (California) to provide educational, financial, shopping, and travel information on television screens, and Microsoft is developing operating systems for future televisions. The strategic alliances being developed are uniting corporations across nation-state borders. This is possible through deregulation, liberalization, and privatization of telecommunications corporations. Through privatization of formerly public-sector organizations, countries are realizing faster economic growth. Privatization is also encouraging the upgrading of telecommunications systems throughout countries of the former Soviet Union, Eastern Europe, and Asia. The upgrading of telecommunication infrastructure is paving the way for strategic alliances between multinational corporations in both the development and establishment of satellite systems.

The goal of the telecommunications networks, strategic alliances, and developments is to create a global, interconnected, compatible network of telecommunications. The networks will meet the individual's need to communicate in real time, whether across the street or across the world. Through digitalization, all communication—voice, text, image, and video—can be translated into the 1 and 0 language of microprocessors and transmitted via telephone lines around the world. The advancement of this technology will allow individuals to work "at the office" wherever they are, the language barrier will crumble (translation will be done via the terminal); time, distance, and language barriers will be eliminated. The transition to advanced telecommunications is happening now; already, less than half of telecommunications traffic within the United States is via voice. With the global communication possibilities, the pace of change is accelerating. The technology is rapidly changing to accommodate people instead of people accommodating the technology.

❖ TRAVEL: GLOBALIZATION OF THE WORLD'S LARGEST INDUSTRY

Today, travel occupations employ 10.6 percent of the global workforce, contribute 10.2 percent of the world's gross national product, and account for gross output of $3.4 trillion annually. With globalization, travel will grow even larger. As individuals become acquainted with other cultures through telecommunications, the desire to experience those cultures firsthand will grow. The travel industry is already responding to the changing needs of the global individual: deregulation, privatization of state-owned airlines, code-sharing, and co-promotions of airlines are all resulting in less work, worry, and expense for travelers; the travel infrastructure of countries, such as airports, bus lines, railways, and highways, is being built or renovated; and hotels are accommodating business travelers with in-room offices, fax machines, computers, and less-stress international phone calling ability.

Political activities within and between countries are also fueling the growth of global travel. Countries such as the former Soviet Union and the United States have ended the Cold War, and they are forming strategic alliances; China and South Korea have diplomatic relations; countries in the Middle East are pursuing unprecedented peace accords. Individuals are contributing to the increase of global travel as well. Baby boomers and retirees are traveling in ever increasing numbers, people are becoming more aware of the value of cultural differences, and the global interest in environmental issues fuels individuals' desires to see exotic landscapes and surroundings. As the world's economy integrates, the individual's desire for travel will be fueled, not dampened.

❖ NEW RULES: A UNIVERSAL CODE OF CONDUCT FOR THE TWENTY-FIRST CENTURY

As communication becomes faster and more global, individuals of all nations are insisting on a higher code of ethics for all countries. Through advanced communication, people have a new awareness of cultural diversity and its worth, the health of the environment and its importance to all, and the right of all humans to be treated with dignity. With this new awareness, individuals are holding corporations and governments accountable to a higher, universal code of ethics. Politicians worldwide are resigning under the threat of impeachment or prosecution for dealing in less than an ethical manner. Corporations are facing economic ruin as a result of unethical and environmentally irresponsible decisions. The universal code of ethics that is emerging calls for the respect of tribalism, while respecting the human rights of all. Further, the code of ethics calls for local management of environmental resources for the good of the global population. Corporations are responding to the universal code of ethics by acting in an environmentally responsible manner, by implementing policies that go beyond the letter of the law, and by encouraging other corporations and governments to do the same. Corporations will also see the benefit of these actions in their operations. By acting as responsible corporate citizens, corporations elicit the loyalty of their employees, resulting in higher productivity and better quality work. Corporations are also feeling the pressure from consumers to operate in a socially conscious manner and to deal with suppliers who assist them in creating a reputation for socially conscious operations. As the global paradox widens and the smallest players become more and more powerful, individuals will carry a greater share of the responsibility for an organization's social performance.

❖ THE DRAGON CENTURY: THE CHINESE COMMONWEALTH—GAINING POWER FROM ITS PARTS

The face of China and its place within the global economy is changing. China is in the process of changing its central economy to a "socialist market economy" and in doing so, is allowing its people to use their individual and collective imagination and enthusiasm to become entrepreneurs. Individuals are giving up government-assigned positions in state-owned enterprises, and they are entering private business. Entrepreneurship and making money are now considered respectable. The new Chinese entrepreneur is helping the Chinese economy grow as never before. This economy is also being decentralized, resulting in an increasing number of small players. The larger the Chinese economy becomes, the smaller and more powerful are its parts. By some estimates, almost one third of the 103 million government employees have given up their positions to start their own businesses. Entrepreneurs are also gaining political influence in China. Rong Yiren, one of China's most prominent entrepreneurs, was elected the country's vice president. The entrepreneurs share values, large numbers, and a quest for money. With money, they know, comes power.

Deng Xiaoping knew that by allowing citizens to become entrepreneurs, productivity would rise. By turning farmers into entrepreneurs, a source of capital for future industrial development was ensured. Throughout the 1980s, the productivity of the Chinese peasant increased more than that of any other workers in the world. By competing with the entrepreneurs, state-run facilities are also streamlining and improving productivity and quality. Further, state-run facilities have improved to better meet the needs of Chinese consumers who have increasing disposable income.

China is also in the process of improving the country's infrastructure to provide the basis for continued expansion. To improve the infrastructure, the Chinese government turned to foreigners for expertise. Improvements in China's airlines, airports, ground transportation, power capacity, and communication network are all underway.

The economic shift to entrepreneurs, the improving infrastructure, and the ever-increasing disposable income of the citizens have taken American businesses to China. Corporations such as Coca-Cola, Procter & Gamble, 7-Eleven, American Express, and Avon are all making inroads into the Chinese economy.

As the Chinese economy reforms, many ask how long it will take before the Chinese political system reforms. Changing from its communistic government is not part of the Chinese plan; communists are very much in power and plan to stay there. The economic reform happening today is not considered by Chinese communists to be outside the realm of communism.

The changes within the Chinese economy are not without downfalls: unemployment has risen, accompanied by increased corruption and serious inflation have increased, and there has been a lack of attention to the training of human resources. There is also a need for restructuring the financial and taxation relationship between the country-wide and provincial governments. These problems and others notwithstanding, the economic growth of China is a monumentous occasion.

❖ ASIA AND LATIN AMERICA: NEW AREAS OF OPPORTUNITY

For the rest of the 1990s and beyond, the new areas of great economic feasibility are in Asia and Latin America. Countries such as Vietnam, India, Argentina, Chile, Brazil, Uruguay, Paraguay, Bolivia, Colombia, Ecuador, Peru, Venezuela, and Mexico have all demonstrated the will to implement structural reforms necessary to promote free markets as well as to create capital markets and financial infrastructure. In most Latin American countries, private citizens are encouraged to participate in the reform process and it is generally accepted that the fruits of free-market economy must extend to all citizens and not just to a privileged few.

Asia and Latin America are promising newcomers in the Global Paradox, while Europe is not. The unification of Europe was heralded as the vehicle by which to make Europe an economic superpower. However, the reunification costs have been staggering, and Europe has suffered a recession. The reunification efforts are further compounded by ethnic tensions, the cost of corruption, and the sluggish economies of the European countries. Further, the countries are burdened by the welfare programs within them.

While Europe flounders, Asia and Latin American countries are replacing their leaders with young talented, and many times, American-educated bankers and economists. Their vision is to make deals, facilitate changes, and provide the means necessary for their country's economic growth. Countries in both areas of the world are cooperating with neighbors in a previously unseen manner. Nationalist sentiments are giving way to economic realities. This is evidenced by the *Mercorsor agreement* whose purpose is to accelerate economic growth by linking Argentina, Brazil, Paraguay, and Uruguay in a common market. Not only did it create Latin America's largest economic base, it also created Latin America's largest industrial base. By capitalizing on the strengths of each country, all countries benefit. By realizing the synergistic effect of such cooperation, these nations are also able to cooperate to facilitate political advantage.

Vietnam has encouraged foreign investment by revising its foreign-investment laws to make them some of the most attractive in the world. Companies from many countries worldwide are investing in Vietnam and are gaining power and income from that investment. Americans need to recover from the Vietnam War and to start looking at Vietnam as a country that offers Americans an economic opportunity.

The Asia Pacific Rim—bounded by Tokyo, Shanghai, Hong Kong, and Singapore—is destined to lead the global economy into the next century. The considerations shaping this global order are (1) the worldwide collapse of communism, (2) the revolution of telecommunications, and (3) the rise of the Asia Pacific region. The countries within this region are an excellent example of the Global Paradox. Not only are the more prosperous countries investing in the less-developed countries, but also the entrepreneurs are fueling the economies of their own countries as well as neighboring countries. The leaders of these countries must have a clear vision of their own future in order to assert worldwide leadership. A consensus of that vision may be difficult for the countries to attain, however.

❖ CONCLUSION

The end of the Cold War, the fall of communism, decentralization, and the growth of telecommunications are all revolutionizing the economic realities of the world. As nation-state boundaries blur, the Global Paradox is becoming real: The bigger the world economy, the more powerful its smallest players.

15

PREPARING FOR THE TWENTY-FIRST CENTURY

Each of the three perspectives provided in this section focuses attention in a unique, interesting, and thought-provoking way on the environment facing organizations in the years ahead and invites managers to explore alternatives ways of responding.

Twenty-first century capitalism is likely to be characterized by organizations operating as a loosely configured network seeking to operate across national borders as though they were part of a global economy and reflections of it. Robert B. Reich, in *The Work of Nations*, observes that money, technology, and ideas will flow across borders, and argues that jobs will ultimately go wherever they can be performed most efficiently. As corporations lose their national identities, the early and big winners will be those who become the generators and brokers of ideas—those who identify and solve problems and create the necessary connections to bring products and services to areas of need. He calls for *global enterprise webs* and foresees the rise of the *symbolic analyst* who can engage in abstract reasoning, systems thinking, experimentation, and collaboration.

Reich was formerly a member of the faculty of the John F. Kennedy School of Government at Harvard University, and more recently the U.S. Secretary of Labor during President Clinton's administration. His book focuses on what nations must do if their citizens are to prosper during the years ahead and identifies issues that need to be addressed at the national level. He believes that in the absence of major shifts in national, organizational, and labor policy, a significant portion of our society will fall further and further behind those who are becoming part of the global web.

Peter Vaill, in *Managing as a Performing Art*, attempts to challenge and revise some of the traditional thinking about management strategies for success. Addressing issues of leadership, organizational excellence, communication, teamwork, change, and ethics, Vaill argues that there is a need for dynamism, fluidity, complexity, and individuality in one's approach to management during times of "permanent white water." The management of organizations should be seen and approached as a performing art, with the manager acting as the conductor for a set of competent professionals.

The constants for managers and their organizations are change and the chaos that accompanies the uncertainty produced by change. Instead of presenting a set of "principles" for the practice of management, Vaill provides a number of ideas and concepts that need skillful application, such as working collectively, reflectively, and spiritually. Like several other authors represented in *The Manager's Bookshelf,* he argues that managers need to confront paradoxes, examine their underlying assumptions, and take on new roles of servant leadership. Dr. Vaill is a Professor of Human Systems at George Washington University's School of Government and Administration.

Soul, community, yielding, communion, family, compassion, spirituality— these and a host of other terms unfamiliar in business are becoming increasingly common parts of some managers' vocabularies, according to Martha Nichols in the concluding reading. She reviewed a number of New Age business books—including Tom Chappell's *The Soul of a Business,* Anita Roddick's *Body and Soul,* Bill Rosenzwieg's *The Republic of Tea,* and Charles Handy's *The Age of Paradox*—and found they paint a unique portrait of experimental work organizations. These are characterized by visionary leaders, self-directed employees, flexible schedules, ecology-friendly products, a continual search for meaning in work, and cultures that are open, expressive, and facilitative of meaningful connections with others. Is the world of work changing? Only time will tell if these organizations (e.g., Tom's of Maine, The Body Shop, Esprit) are the forerunners of a major trend, or another passing fad.

READING 1

The Work of Nations

Robert B. Reich
Summary prepared by Robert E. Heller

Robert E. Heller is an entrepreneur and the former Director of the Small Business Development Center and Small Business Institute, and a Lecturer in the School of Business and Economics at the University of Minnesota, Duluth. Prior to assuming this position, Mr. Heller practiced law, specializing in the areas of business, employment, and intellectual property law. He also served as general counsel of Jeno's, Inc., and general counsel and president of Paulucci Enterprises. Mr. Heller received his B.A. from DePauw University and his J.D. from the University of Michigan Law School.

"A nation's economic role is to improve its citizens' standard of living by enhancing the value of what they contribute to the world economy" (p. 301). This is the basic premise of Robert B. Reich's book, *The Work of Nations*, which is based on several years of research, interviews, and discussions. Our national economic leaders are caught up in viewing and planning the economy on the basis of "vestigial" (historic and outdated) understandings of the goals of economic achievement. A new picture of the world economy is needed in which future economic policies should be aimed at developing our nation into one composed of *symbolic analysts*. These are the people who will control and contribute to wealth in the twenty-first century economy.

Most nations' leaders direct their efforts toward the development of a national economy. These leaders assume that there *is* a national economy, and that the public interest is served by national economic growth. Economic independence is believed to provide the means to face the threat of foreign competition. However, this picture of a national economy is outdated.

These policies were once correct for a variety of reasons, but this is no longer true. First, corporations are no longer as profitable as they once were. Second, organized labor continues to contract. Third, many corporations are now owned by foreigners. At the same time, Americans' investment in foreign corporations has increased more rapidly than their investment in domestic corporations. Finally, the difference between executive and workers' compensation has grown. For example, in 1960, the typical chief executive officer

Robert B. Reich, *The Work of Nations*. New York: Alfred A. Knopf, 1991.

earned about forty times as much as the average factory worker. By 1989, the average chief executive officer earned ninety-three times the compensation of the average factory worker.

A new economic picture needs to be described in more detail, and recommendations for policies to prepare for twenty-first century capitalism need to be offered. The challenge is to prepare *symbolic analysts* who are capable of adding value to the global economy. The symbolic analysts will be paid the most compensation and thereby be able to achieve higher standards of living. Historically, national economic policy has frequently reduced the taxes of the wealthy in order to promote their investment in the national economy. As the global economy has gained in stature and dominance, the wealthy increasingly invest in the global economy. As a result, a nation's gross national product, national economic growth, and competitiveness are no longer important.

What *is* important is the economic welfare of a nation's people, as distinguished from the national economy per se. The challenge is whether high-income Americans, a minority, can sacrifice to help the majority participate in the new global economy. Does a nation's people still have concern for a national society and its economic well being, or has the idea of a "nation" become passé? These questions are addressed next, ending with some recommendations for dealing with the twenty-first century world economy.

❖ THE ECONOMIC NATION

"Economic Nationalism" during the last century meant producing what you need at home and exporting manufactured items. This typically resulted in accumulating wealth in the home economy. The goal was to improve the overall well-being of the nation's population. Patriotism was defined in terms of working for the good of the country, and therefore the good of its population. In turn, the nation, as a whole, supported the development of its industries. The historical rationale revolved around the beliefs that (1) a strong manufacturing base increased the nation's revenue and wealth, (2) opportunities for employment grew, (3) immigration was stimulated, (4) foreign capital was attracted, and (5) the nation became more independent and secure. Countries implemented protectionist policies, such as import tariffs and subsidies, which were thought to protect their businesses. In addition, countries spent money on internal improvements such as roads, bridges, and harbor construction.

◆ LARGE-VOLUME PRODUCERS

In the nineteenth century, inventions transformed production into large-volume or mass production. Transportation and communications improvements escalated the efficiencies of economic achievement. This resulted in production outstripping demand and drove nations to seek new markets. At the same time, nations increased tariff rates to protect their domestic markets. High-volume manufacturing caused a shift in population from rural areas to cities. By the start of the twentieth century, economic nationalism had taken root. It was nation against nation.

◆ MERGER ERA

In the next stage, production became consolidated in large national-based corporations. Citizens' well-being was linked to success of the national economy, which revolved around the success of giant corporations. The United States moved slowly in this direction. People remained somewhat skeptical, however, as corporations continued to buy up their competition and to consolidate vertically to avoid protected prices. Mergers proliferated. Consolidation, it was argued, was a necessary result of foreign competition.

◆ GROWING MIDDLE CLASS

At the same time, government agencies were created to police the large corporations, and national planning evolved. By the late 1950s free enterprise became the watchword, along with mass production and mass consumption. Large corporations led the economy and set industrial norms, prices, wages, and methods of high-volume production. Growth of the large corporations resulted in growth of a large middle class of skilled and semiskilled workers. Wealth was not based on rank or ownership. The corporate bureaucracy became military-like. National leaders came from the corporate world. Decisions made by these corporate leaders affected the nation as a whole. Even organized labor acquired the same type of bureaucratic structure.

As the 1960s dawned, less and less regulation of corporations emerged. Government developed policies that stimulated mass consumption: for example, offering low interest home loans and manipulating the money supply. Second, government fostered preparing children for gainful employment; therefore, even education became mass-produced. Third, national defense became an economic policy. All of these decisions and trends benefitted the large corporations. These policies resulted in the rise of a large middle class which would work for the general welfare. The prosperity of the middle class was premised on high-volume, standardized production of goods.

By the late sixties, foreign competition existed in mass-produced goods. The reaction of economic policy makers was once again based upon older views of a national economy. First, these policy makers sought to keep foreign goods out of the market through tariffs. This protectionist strategy provided only temporary relief. It actually resulted in the diminution of foreign markets and increased costs at home. Second, the policy was to cut costs at home to meet the foreign competition. If foreigners could produce goods cheaply, so could Americans. However, profits of these corporations continued to plummet no matter how much cost cutting went on. Third, economic policy makers further encouraged conglomerate mergers in order to promote efficiencies. This policy didn't work either. Profits still continued to decline.

The picture that these economists were using to set their policies was incorrect. There is no longer a national economy; U.S. industry is now part of a *global web*. The standard of living of a nation's people no longer depends on the success of large corporations, but on the worldwide demand for skills and insights.

❖ THE GLOBAL WEB

The evolution of a nation's economy into *global webs* has several features. Corporations are no longer high-volume producers, they are no longer American, and they are becoming high-value producers serving the unique needs of particular customers. This specialization leads to higher profits and results in less competition from high-volume producers. Corporate policies now focus on worldwide searches to achieve their goals. In order to be successful within these global webs, three skills are required. First, skills at solving problems are required in order to put things together in unique ways. Second, problem identification skills are required to develop new ways to use products and to persuade others of the correctness of these ways. Finally, strategic brokering skills are required to link the problem solvers with the problem identifiers. Every high-value enterprise can be described as being in the business of providing these skills. These skills include "the specialized research, engineering and design services necessary to solve problems; the specialized sales, marketing, and consulting services necessary to identify problems; and the specialized strategic, financial and management services for brokering the first two" (p. 85). The worldwide economy has evolved into one where the demand for these skills and insights is the basis for the picture of our global economy now and in the twenty-first century.

◆ ENTERPRISE WEBS

The old pyramidal structure of an organization is no longer appropriate in today's global economy. Problem solvers, problem identifiers, and strategic brokers work together to create a profit without the traditional bureaucratic structure. The new picture looks like a "spider's web." The strategic broker is at the center with all sorts of connections to problem solvers and problem identifiers. In these *enterprise webs*, stress is placed on rapid problem identification and problem solving.

Enterprise webs acquire a variety of shapes. First, there is the *independent profit center*, where middle-level managers are eliminated and product development is the goal. Second, in the *spin-off partnership*, strategic brokers form groups of problem solvers and problem identifiers to nurture ideas. These ideas are then sold off with part ownership retained. Third is the *spin-in partnership*. In this enterprise web, strategic brokers purchase ideas from groups of problem solvers and problem identifiers. An example is the computer software house. A fourth enterprise web is the *licensing web*. Brand names are licensed, with strategic brokers given the responsibility of putting together the licensing network and ensuring compliance. The final web is *pure brokering*, in which the strategic broker contracts out with problem solvers and problem identifiers, and for the production of components. All items produced and coming from elsewhere are then sold, with the proceeds going to the broker.

◆ HIGH-VALUE ASSETS

The ownership and control of a corporation is no longer as clear as it once was. The assets of a high-value corporation are the skills of the individuals involved in linking solutions to particular needs. The real power depends on the capacity of individuals to add value to the enterprise web. The result is that those persons who are the strategic brokers, problem solvers, and problem identifiers are the ones who are richly rewarded. Receiving less are the production workers and owners. In the high-value enterprise, the ability to identify problems, solve problems, and broker become the key assets, and through experience these assets take on greater value.

◆ GLOBAL WEBS

Enterprise webs are reaching across the globe. Corporations are no longer national corporations. Groups of problem solvers, problem identifiers, and strategic brokers are formed around the world. These *global webs* combine to create something of value for customers. They are bound together through threads such as computers, fax machines, and satellites. Many contemporary politicians, however, still try to inhibit this flow because of their vestigial view of a national economy. Old products have distinct nationalities, new products are individualistic, and nationality no longer matters. Even though nations create restrictions, global webs, through their problem solvers, problem identifiers, and strategic brokers, figure out ways or find loopholes to beat down the barriers. What nations' leaders have to ask is whose workers gain in the enterprise webs and what effect the restrictions have on nations' workers.

Corporations sell products created through global webs. Nationality of a firm has little to do with where a firm or its owners invest and with whom it contracts. Monies are spent around the world, so that the problem solver, problem identifiers, and strategic brokers may become part of the web. American and foreign corporations look more and more alike. Standardized production, no matter what nationality a corporation holds, occurs in the low-wage countries. Corporations look for high-value problem solving, problem identifying, and strategic brokering wherever they can be found. The high-value global enterprise evolves into an international partnership for combining the insights of skilled people. The enterprise then contracts with unskilled workers from around the world to produce standardized products in high volume.

◆ IMPLICATIONS OF GLOBAL WEBS

What are the implications of global webs? First, national savings will be invested wherever products can be produced the cheapest. Second, a nation's competitiveness is based on what its citizens can do. Third, United States trade imbalances are not due to foreign predators but to U.S.-owned firms making things abroad. As corporate executives are pushed to make a profit they will inevitably look to global webs for solving these problems. Cross-national ownership will continue to increase as electronic training networks link different areas of the world. Brokers will scour the globe to find good investments. Therefore, the total return to U.S. investors doesn't depend solely on the success of U.S. firms, but on the global network of enterprise webs.

The concern about foreign ownership should be forgotten. Foreigners invest in the United States to make use of United States assets and workers in order to make a profit. By investing in the United States they believe they can make better use of these assets and be more competitive. American investments in foreign companies are based on the same premise that they can make better use of the foreign assets and be more competitive. The key lies in having American problem solvers, problem identifiers, and brokers residing in the United States. The people in the web with the most valuable skills and insights will receive the largest rewards.

The perils of vestigial thought remain. Policy makers still want to restrict foreign ownership. This policy creates a barrier to the improvement of problem-solving, problem-identifying, and strategic brokering skills at home. As a result, Americans are losing out on the remuneration that might be paid for these services. National policy should encourage the development of these skills in the United States even through foreign investment. Policy makers continue to miss the picture that *the critical assets are embedded in the capabilities of Americans to be problem solvers, problem identifiers, and strategic brokers.* Once the policy makers realize that corporations are global webs rather than national entities, they will change their thinking from the profitability of U.S. corporations to encouraging improvement in skills that will add value to the world economy.

❖ THE RISE OF THE SYMBOLIC ANALYST

Classifications of twenty-first century workers are important for understanding that it is not the nationality of a company nor of its owners but the identification of the most valuable employees that is most important. Who are they? What skills do they possess?

◆ CLASSIFICATION OF WORKERS

Three broad categories of workers exist in the world economy. The first group of workers are the *routine producers*. These people perform routine jobs which are done over and over. They represent about twenty-five percent of the work force and might be compared to the old line workers. These types of people do repetitious jobs. An example might be a stuffer of computer circuit boards. Because companies seek to pay as little as possible for these workers, the number of them in United States has been declining over the past decade. For competitive reasons, companies increasingly have been locating routine production in other areas of the world.

The second category of worker is the *in-person server*. This group also performs tasks which are simple and repetitive; however, they perform services which are provided person-to-person. These services are not sold worldwide. In-person servers have direct contact with the ultimate beneficiaries of their work. In-person servers include waiters, waitresses, janitors, and taxi drivers. Thirty percent of the work force in 1991 was composed of in-person servers in the United States.

The third category of worker is the *symbolic analyst*. Symbolic analysts include the problem solvers, problem identifiers, and strategic brokers. Their work can be traded worldwide. They are the research scientists, engineers, lawyers, and some creative accountants. These people use analytic tools, are well-educated, and represent twenty percent of the U.S. job force. The other twenty-five percent of the work force are farmers, miners, or government employees, who are somewhat sheltered from global competition.

◆ THE PROBLEM DESCRIBED

Since the mid-seventies, the trend has been toward a growing disparity of income between the twenty percent who are classified as symbolic analysts and the rest of the workers, primarily the in-person servers and routine production workers. No longer is the middle class growing. Several reasons account for this trend. Taxes on the rich have decreased and taxes on the poor have increased as a percentage of income. The rich spend their money, not nationally, but globally. The social policies of the Reagan era caused a decrease in the amount of welfare, thereby making it harder for the less fortunate to move out of the routine producer or in-person server class into the strategic analyst class. The growth of the single-parent family has resulted in less opportunity to move from one type of worker classification to another. Also, the baby boomers have arrived in the job market. Based on the functions performed by workers within global webs, this disparity continues to increase. Symbolic analysts continue to receive more money because they can market their specialized skills worldwide. In the twenty-first century, they will be compensated most highly for their services, while routine producers and in-person servers will remain at a relatively low level of compensation.

◆ SKILLS OF THE SYMBOLIC ANALYST

Four basic skills are required for the symbolic analyst. The first skill, *abstraction*, is that of discovering patterns and meanings. The symbolic analyst is able to interpret and reinterpret information so that it can be understood and manipulated to the benefit of those for whom the symbolic analyst is working. Second, the symbolic analyst is capable of *system thinking*, which is the capacity to see the whole, and to understand how the processes are linked together. A strategic analyst looks at how the problem arises and connects it to other problems to look for different solutions. A third skill of the symbolic analyst is *experimentation*. Utilizing information, the symbolic analyst, through trial and error, develops the capacity to explore different paths emanating from the same set of data, to test the outcomes, and to draw conclusions from the tests. Through this process, symbolic analysts continue to learn and become more valuable. *Collaboration* is the fourth skill. Symbolic analysts do not work in isolation but rather work in teams or groups of teams. They must communicate in order to achieve an outcome.

Because of the nature of this work, *symbolic analytic zones* are created. These zones are areas in which symbolic analysts live, work, and learn with each other. An example of such a zone is Silicon Valley in California for computers, or Minneapolis for medical devices. As symbolic analysts gather together in zones, the disparity between them and other workers grows. The question emerges: "What can be done to stop this growing disparity?"

❖ THE MEANING OF NATION

Policies are needed that will promote the advancement and expansion of the symbolic analyst. The ultimate economic success of a country depends upon how well its citizens are able to live and whether their standards can be sustained and improved. The challenge to the symbolic analyst in America is to improve the living standards of the majority who are now routine producers and in-person servers. The critical factor is whether the symbolic analyst has the will to be a part of, and implement, solutions.

◆ THE QUESTION RESTATED

The question is whether the symbolic analyst is willing to make the sacrifices necessary to achieve the solutions. The wealthy must limit spending on themselves and must spend more for the benefit of the routine producers and in-person servers, so that they might be promoted to symbolic analysts.

◆ POSSIBLE SOLUTIONS

There are three possible solutions. First, tax loopholes should be closed, and a truly progressive income tax should be implemented. Second, any reasonably talented child should be able to be educated to become a symbolic analyst. Third, symbolic analysts need to play a role in increasing opportunities for routine producers and in-person servers to gain experience at symbolic analysis and thereby have a chance to become symbolic analysts. Three components of these solutions are (1) education and training, (2) nutrition, and (3) health care at all levels. Job training efforts, free day care, and remedial courses in reading, writing, math, and preschool programs are necessary. Methods of education must be improved, and the political infrastructure must have the will to implement these types of proposals.

Without appropriate infrastructure, the nation is doomed to becoming one of routine producers and in-person servers. To avoid this, governments must be willing to spend money on training symbolic analysts and providing for their development. They must reverse the trend of laissez-faire. They must stop forcing states and cities to spend for education and welfare. The current policy of doing so only fosters the development of symbolic analytic zones. Those communities that can afford to spend on education and training will continue to spend on education and training whereas those who can't will not be able to.

Positive economic nationalism is needed. This would encourage public spending to enhance the capacities of citizens to lead full and productive lives. Policy makers should limit competition with other areas of the world so that these areas can also develop. Enhancing global welfare is the ultimate goal. Subsidies to high-value-added production companies should be encouraged. Also needed is a common fund for worldwide retraining when overcapacity exists. Finally, international policies should promote the upgrading of workers in third world countries to symbolic analysts.

◆ RESULTS

If the policy makers, the rich, and symbolic analysts make the investment in developing a work force that is knowledgeable and skilled in dealing with complex issues, wealth will be spread to that work force. Global webs of enterprises will be developed and, in turn, will generate more jobs for symbolic analysts. As the skills of these symbolic analysts increase, the demand for them becomes greater, and more workers will enjoy better circumstances.

READING 2

Managing as a Performing Art

Peter B. Vaill
Summary prepared by Richard S. Blackburn

Richard S. Blackburn is an Associate Professor at the Kenan-Flagler Business School at the University of North Carolina at Chapel Hill. He earned his MBA and Ph.D. at the University of Wisconsin, Madison. He teaches in the undergraduate, MBA, doctoral, and executive programs at UNC. His research interests include creativity and innovation, causes and consequences of service quality in professional organizations, and the impact of corporate design and identity on corporate performance. His research work has been published in both professional and academic journals, and he has served on several editorial review boards. He is co-author of *Managing Organizational Behavior.*

Managing as a Performing Art provides managers with ideas for coping in chaotic environments. These ideas are organized around the twin themes of chaotic change and organizational action. Appropriate actions are seen as dynamic, fluid, extraordinarily complex, and fundamentally personal organizational action. The performing arts metaphor generates a fresh perspective on the managerial world.

❖ PERMANENT WHITE WATER

What metaphors do managers hold about their work environments? *Permanent white water* is one, and Chinese baseball (Siu, 1980) is a second. A manager rarely finds calm water, but lurches instead from one change to another as a raft through rough waters. Chinese baseball reflects this continuously changing context. The game is played like American baseball, but whenever the ball is in the air, the team in the field can move the bases anywhere they wish. Consider the strategies employed to play this game successfully. Would the most runs scored still be the best measure of success?

Peter B. Vaill, *Managing as a Performing Art.* San Francisco: Jossey-Bass, 1989.

To operate in chaotic environments, managers must "work smarter." Historically, this meant managers worked *harder* by working longer hours, worked *more intelligently* by learning to be better managers, or worked *more shrewdly* by playing politics to be more effective. Working smarter in these ways helped when management was about planning, organizing, and controlling in stable environments. Those days are over. One-time management principles are now myths: a single all-powerful manager/leader, managing a single, freestanding organization; a pyramidal chain of command; producing a product via the establishment of official goals and rational analysis without concern for people or culture.

New managerial jobs have emerged that replace these "myths" with the following characteristics:

1. More accountability
2. More need for leadership
3. More emphasis on teamwork
4. More intense involvement with people
5. Greater ambiguity of authority
6. Greater emphasis on one's individuality
7. More involvement of the whole person
8. More stress
9. A new mix of an intellectual and an action orientation

Today's managers must work smarter in new ways. They must work smarter *collectively* (developing supportive attachments to others), *reflectively* (reframing perspectives on organizational problems), and *spiritually* (attuning themselves to timeless truths).

❖ THE THEORY OF MANAGING IN THE MANAGERIAL COMPETENCY MOVEMENT

How do managers improve in times of continuing and complex changes? One school asserts that mastering certain competencies improves job performance. Researchers and educators subscribing to this competency perspective ask not "What do managers do?" but "What are the main factors in the manager's job?" By analyzing lists of factors gathered from experts and managers, a series of job functions is identified. Unfortunately, managers do not experience their jobs as a list, but in a variety of other ways. The competency movement (CM) makes a number of other equally dubious assumptions about management and the managerial environment:

CM Assumptions	Counter-Arguments
Competencies are distinct and independent.	Competencies exist in clusters.
Managers produce identifiable outputs from the exercise of various competencies.	Not all managers produce identifiable, physical outputs related to competencies.
Increased organizational effectiveness is greatly influenced by competencies.	Organizational effectiveness is affected by many more important factors than managerial competencies.
Managers create and/or restore order.	Managers must be innovators and creators of disorder.
Possessing a competency implies knowing when, where, and how to use it.	Perceptions distort judgments about when, where, and how to use competencies.
Competencies can be used regardless of the party who is the target of this use.	Interaction with others influences the effectiveness of competency usage.
No untoward effects of correct competency use on the system will occur. If they do, competencies to deal with these can be learned.	Even the correct use of competency can create systemic problems.

The increasingly precise definitions of managerial competencies may lead to undesirable specialization in management. Managers need to cling to their own definitions of being a whole person with unique purposes in a situation, while also recognizing that others will have their own objectives.

❖ WINNING IS ONLY THE THING YOU THINK WINNING IS

In organizations, managers can no longer view goals as etched in stone. Winning, success, or effectiveness must be defined as actions proceed, and differences about such definitions create a myriad of disagreements. Managers are quick to define what they see as "truth" while forgetting that others may define "truth" differently.

To minimize these problems, management engages in *purposing,* which is continuous leadership action to induce clarity, consensus, and commitment regarding the organization's basic purposes. This process demands ongoing efforts at *values clarification,* which is a highly critical task for managers, but one whose significance is often underestimated.

Values clarification requires a framework suggesting where value-related issues will arise in the future. The following categories of values reflect key stakeholder concerns in any definition of "winning" that the organization chooses to propose. These categories include:

1. Economic Values—reflecting what the firm's bottom line will be.
2. Technological Values—reflecting how the firm will do what it chooses to do.
3. Communal Values—reflecting the kind of "home" the firm will be for its employees.
4. Sociopolitical Values—reflecting the kind of neighbor the firm will be to external constituencies.
5. Transcendental Values—reflecting what the firm means at a deeper level to those same constituencies.

These five categories are not independent, and choices made in one category will have multiple effects in the other categories. What any firm must develop via this values clarification process is a value *system* to identify the purpose for the organization and those associated with it.

❖ THE PEAK PERFORMANCE CULT

Organizational excellence and peak performance have attained a certain cultishness, arising because: (1) excellence and peak performance are too "American" to be questioned; (2) the urgency for organizational revitalization prohibits these ideas of seemingly practical worth from being tinkered with; (3) the commercial value of peak performance packaging crystallizes ideas, thus discouraging changes in the packaging; and (4) excellence requires commitment in its presentation to others, reinforcing cultishness.

There are a variety of unsolved problems arising from this "process of excellence." We know little about how excellent organizations attain the clarity of purpose so often attributed to them. Does "burnout" sap the strength of those asked to provide peak performance over long periods of time? Can groupthink arise when high-performing firms are unwilling to accept different perspectives on certain issues? Since high-performing firms are attuned to their own uniqueness, how are boundary-spanning activities conducted? Can excellence and peak performance be sustained over long periods of time? If excellent organizations are unable adequately to explain how they got that way, is it even possible to design processes by which other organizations can achieve excellence? Finally, does the belief in the ultimate rightness of an excellent organization's strategy close its value system to examination and comment by external stake-holders?

These unanswered questions may lead the managers of excellent organizations to confront a basic paradox:

In order to become excellent, it (the organization) needs to conduct among its members and stakeholders a creative process of values clarification in all five of these (previously discussed values) categories, including their inter-relationships;

but the more excellent it becomes by its own values, the more it will feel that the need for continued discussion is not necessary, while its stakeholders will feel that the organization's growing potency (excellence) makes the need for such discussion more necessary than ever (p. 76).

❖ THE GRAND PARADOX OF MANAGEMENT

The education of managers tries to provide both an understanding of what is going on in the organization (comprehension) and ways in which these events can be controlled (control). Despite fifty years of education in schools and organizations, the grand paradox of management remains: organizations are simultaneously "mysterious, recalcitrant, intractable, unpredictable, paradoxical, absurd, and funny" (p. 77).

There are two other paradoxes management confronts. First, the more we develop comprehensive management models, the more likely we are to identify factors excluded by the models that nevertheless influence organizations. Second, the impact of a manager's actions on an organization can never be completely determined because the manager is part of the system.

Traditional management training views paradoxes as problems to solve. But paradoxes represent conflicts between apparent truths, waiting to be resolved. Contemplation of and reflection on paradoxes rather than attempts at their resolution frequently yield better comprehension and control. Firms are urged to develop corporate cultures that are friendly to paradox. To do so requires: (a) the realization that paradoxes abound in organizations; (b) more holistic thought about situations; (c) more dynamic views of the world; (d) a willingness to drop cherished truths; and (e) that rather than thinking of the present as the means and the future as the end, managers begin to think of the future as the means and the present as the end.

❖ REFLECTION AND THE TECHNOHOLIC

Technoholics solve problems with cookbook techniques. They despise the contingencies and reverse causal loops typifying organizational life. They live for the *technique*, believing that dogged adherence to the plan will yield desired solutions regardless of changes in the situational context. Technoholics suffer from "domino theory thinking," "reification," and a preference for "how-to-do-it" over "why-to-do-it."

The *domino theory* asserts that as long as some predetermined plan is followed, the steps of the plan will yield desired results despite changes in reality that made previous steps invalid. *Reification* involves "making a thing out of what is not a thing" (p. 90). So a plan becomes a thing, and the technoholic ignores or reinterprets events that do not fit into the plan. The "how" question is the technoholics' turf. They never ask, "*Why* are we doing this?"

Antidotes to technoholism arise by analyzing the assumptions that must hold for technology to work as intended. Assumptional grounds can be found in: (1) the amount, quality, and timing of the technology's inputs; (2) the impact of technology's operation and outputs on its human users; (3) the side effects of the technology; and (4) the fit between technology and existing norms and mores. Consideration of such assumptions forces the humanization of technology.

❖ SATCHMO'S PARADOX

Earlier, the concept of "purposing" was discussed. But how does a top manager communicate this purpose to key constituents when permanent white water forces changes in purpose or confusion about current purposes? Managers must overcome *Satchmo's Paradox*—a lament reflecting the late jazz man's helplessness at being unable to explain jazz to the lay person. (Satchmo once said, "Man, if you gotta ask [what jazz is] you'll never know.")

At issue is communicating information to the uninitiated about some managerial gestalt or "big picture" for the organization. Certain ideas only have meaning within these gestalts, but managers acquire these gestalts in unknown ways; the gestalt prevents these same managers from seeing their worlds in other ways, and the ideas are nearly impossible to communicate to others. For years, communicating this gestalt/vision was done by persistence, force, and/or coercion. But coercion can have deleterious side effects on commitment, creativity, and innovation levels of the coerced. What are some noncoercive alternatives for such communication?

This communication must occur in felicitous circumstances, suggesting an off-site location with a format less like a military briefing and more conversational and open-ended. Participants need not leave with specific deliverables nor with concrete plans. Discussions should involve key stakeholders and be open to examining the values underlying the communications. Practice at "gestalt passing" is useful as is use of a variety of media in communicating the gestalt.

❖ MANAGING AS A PERFORMING ART

The "list-of-functions" approach to management currently dominates management education. But *knowing* that managers perform discrete functions (planning, organizing, controlling, etc.) and actually *doing* these functions are not the same thing. The former perspective ignores what the latter perspective appreciates; doing requires a "whole person in a whole environment in relation to other whole persons, embedded in time, with all actions viewed as concrete processes, and the entire process thoroughly suffused with turbulence and change" (p. 115). "Management as a performing art" is a metaphor well-suited to this holistic perspective on management and leadership.

This metaphor provides the manager with several unique managerial insights. First, the performing arts do not confuse competency in function with the whole performance. The dancer's technical skills are subsumed within the entire display. Second, performing arts' functions are related to a particular performance and are not generalizable across performances. Third, successful performances result from functions done correctly, with the necessary resources, and sufficient rehearsal until the performance is ready. Fourth, critics to the contrary, the definition of a quality performance is established by the performer. And the process of performance is the major concern, not merely reaching some objective. Fifth, performers take pleasure in performing. Sixth, every performance is unique. Seventh, a performer brings a variety of human skills to a performance, and performers develop "an organic unity of *feeling* . . . (to) bring a coherence and flow to what would otherwise be only a loosely related collection of parts" (p. 121). Finally, success in the performing arts depends on the context of the performance. A strong supporting cast and ample resources can yield heroic performances from otherwise mediocre talent. Successful productions view cast and crew not as interchangeable pieces to be transferred between roles at the whim of a director, but as highly interdependent contributors extremely sensitive to disruptive changes in context.

The performing arts also offer insights into the role of creativity in organized endeavors. Spontaneity is valued, but only within the framework of a script or musical score. Performing artists are able to generate creative efforts within the confines of a highly interdependent system. Similarly, the arts allow and encourage the spontaneous generation of new and innovative ideas. All of this occurs within a culture of quality and creativity. Ideally, managers and corporate cultures would accomplish the same things.

❖ IT'S ALL PEOPLE

Management and leadership revolve around people. Why, then, is our thinking about people in organizations so superficial? The behavioral sciences have been trying to understand the behavior and attitudes of people for years, but the theories that have evolved all seem to be about someone called "Superficial Man (SM)."

Until recently, SM was a white, male, middle-class adult, engaging in observable and classifiable behavior. He was unlikely to undertake any novel actions, so his behavioral tendencies were predictable. Everything about SM could be labeled and explained. This is the image of individuals and individual behavior that is frequently communicated to managers and students of management. And the list-of-functions approach is how we study SM in his managerial role.

Such theories of SM are inadequate, however, because they are evaluated in terms of their utility and parsimony. What would our theories of human behavior look like if they were judged on levels of *stewardship* or ethical foundations? In other words, to what extent does a theory *value* the individual it aspires to explain? Toward a more "robust" stewardship, theories should meet the following criteria:

1. The theory realizes it is a theory (and not untestable dogma).
2. The theory takes a "process" view of human beings and not a static view.
3. The theorist believes the theory applies to him- or herself.
4. The theory will be accepted by those whom it is to explain.
5. The theory avoids "scientism" and a preoccupation with methodology.
6. The theory appreciates the inherent tensions between conformity and freedom.
7. The theory makes it easier to appreciate and love those to whom it applies.

Theories that meet these criteria will exhibit a concern for the inherent value of the individuals who are their focus. We have few of these theories now. We need new ones.

❖ THE END OF CULTURE AND THE DIALEXIC SOCIETY

Culture has been a popular topic recently for a variety of reasons. Discussions of culture are "juicy." We can talk of things we know well and feel strongly about. These discussions are not psychologically threatening. They provide a means to talk about attitudes, values, and actions of those in the culture, allowing managers to move from discussions about culture to discussions about using culture as a management tool.

Culture is oversold and unreliable. By definition,

> Culture is a *system* of attitudes, actions, and artifacts that *endures over time* and that operates to produce among its members a relatively *unique common psychology (UCP)* (p. 147).

To change an organization's culture requires changing the UCP. This requires a much more intense change effort than current culture change programs can provide. But culture is dying. Ours has become a "dialexic" society—one with a compulsion to speak dialectically and to assume that the world is not as it seems. Events, actions, or individuals that might become parts of our culture are undercut by expert analysis, by parody (simplification, standardization, and commercialization), and by ennui (the inability to take events of culture seriously).

Dialexic discussions do not benefit organizations. They merely give reasons for noninvolvement in what is happening in the organization. Unfortunately, technoholism and dialexia have become major elements of the UCP and they are mutually reinforcing. Given this, it becomes easier to understand the difficulty in actually changing an organization's culture.

❖ WHAT SHOULD THE TOP TEAM BE TALKING ABOUT?

Strategic management is *what* the top team should be talking about. However, it is easier to talk about strategic management than to do it. The issue of *how* to implement the results of the strategic management decision is the *most* important topic for top team discussion.

To achieve a position on a top management team, team members develop strong action orientations, are competitive, have an understanding of organizational politics, and have learned to suppress their feelings. This last quality prevents team members from truly understanding what is happening on the top team. An inability to express feelings leads to the almost ritualistic discussions that characterize dialexia. Top management teams need ways to unblock feelings. Options for unblocking include team development offered by a trained OD consultant, immediate intervention, or "going back to school together."

Immediate intervention might take the form of the top team considering the problem of blocked feelings within the larger organization. Consideration of how to unblock the rest of the organization may create a spill-over effect where the same issue is discussed within the context of the team. An alternative is to find or develop an educational program for the entire team designed to consider such issues as strategic leadership, organizations and their environments, anticipating the future, and personal assessment and development.

Successful top teams contain members willing to contribute *time* (long hours), *focus* (a thorough knowledge of relevant activities), and *feeling* (respect for, and devotion to, both the work system and the people in it). Time and focus are in ample supply on top teams. But time and focus without feeling yield competent, yet shallow, teams. Feeling and time without focus yield spirit without content. Feeling and focus without time yield wisdom but lethargy. The top team *should* be talking about ensuring that its members are competent, wise, and spirited.

❖ TAOIST MANAGEMENT

The concept of "wu-wei" or "nonaction" is central to Taoism. *Wu-wei* refers to the idea of not forcing something, or going with the grain. There is much that Western managers, in their desire to take action, can learn from Taoism and nonaction.

In sports, being "in the zone" is frequently cited as key to peak performance. A oneness of mental, physical, and spiritual energies often surfaces in descriptions of peak performance. This may be the closest Western thought comes to the concept of wu-wei. But the Taoist would not use words like "peak" and "performance." Language differences create some of the problems in translating the subtleties of wu-wei for Western managers. Western language and imagery extol victory and triumph. Terms like "cutting our competition off at the knees" reflect this toughness in managerial image and language. Wu-wei views such terminology as "forcing" in nature.

Myth	Wu-Wei Interpretation
1. A single person called the manager	Managing occurs throughout the organization
2. A single free-standing organization	Organization is a temporary abstraction from the totality
3. Control via chain of command	A more democratic leveling of power differences
4. Organization as pure instrument	Organization as a field within which many purposes and processes play out
5. The irrelevance of culture	An understanding of synergies available from many unique common psychologies
6. Primary output is a product	Awareness of all the organization is and does to produce its outputs
7. Rational analysis for understanding	Rational analysis in the service of philosophy of life

Westerners tend to split the present from the future, thought from action, and the manager from the system managed. Wu-wei maintains the unity of time, of thought and action, and of self and environment. A wu-wei interpretation of the seven management myths discussed earlier reflects this desire for reduced fragmentation.

❖ MANAGEMENT AS SNAKE HANDLING

How much of a manager's work is done with as strong a faith as that held by those who handle snakes as part of a religious ritual? The five categories of values discussed earlier contain the bases for determining an organization's definition of effectiveness. Good judgment is needed in that process, but also faith in oneself and one's organization. What is crucial is the basis for one's faith. To this end, the author shares a fanciful conversation between himself and five deceased spokesmen, one for each of the five value categories. Adam Smith speaks for Economic Values, Frederick W. Taylor for Technological Values, Elton Mayo for Communal Values, John L. Lewis for Sociopolitical Values, and Ralph Waldo Emerson for Transcendental Values.

One powerful question is addressed to each participant: "How much faith is involved in the acceptance of the premises and major assertions of your respective fields?" The outcome of each conversation suggests that our modern managers do have faith in theories and ideas, but too many of them have not stopped to think what that really means. *Managers are insensitive to the underlying assumptions of these theories.* It has been faith in the general correctness of what managers are trying to do that protects them when particular snakes bare their fangs.

❖ THE REQUISITES OF VISIONARY LEADERSHIP

Just as a becalmed sailor retains his faith in the wind, a manager needs faith in his/her personal and organizational excellence even if it has yet to appear. To continue one's pursuit of managerial breezes, one must work spiritually smarter. *Spirituality* is seen as the pervasive yet elusive force that energizes individuals. While difficult to define, everyone has experienced the spirit associated with an all-engaging project. But the permanent white water in which managers operate can drain the spirit. As a river floods its banks, so spirit can flow out as quickly as it flows in.

How can managers renew their faith and spirituality in the work place? How can they make work more inspiring? The workaholic, technoholic, or powerholic approaches to working smarter are not the answer. Ignoring Satchmo's Paradox and practicing dialexia are not the answer. Where might the answers reside?

Spiritual leadership can come from any level in the organization. Vision alone is not enough, for it is the spirit within the vision that energizes the visionary. We need new metaphors and symbols to complement the rather sterile psychological terms we use in today's organizations. *Role model, facilitator,* even *CEO* have little in the way of spirit attending them. What about *voyager, knight, quarterback,* or *servant* as alternatives?

True leadership is spiritual leadership in the sense that it brings out the best in others. Accomplishing this becomes a quest; it is seeking a goal without a map, and the spirit can be discovered as the search progresses. Living in this way at home or in the office will force new and different relationships. Old ones may fall by the wayside, but new ones will be stronger. This quest is an intensely personal one. It cannot bring spiritual answers to others. But such a quest will insure that work and relationships will be more spirited in the future.

READING 3

Does New Age Business Have a Message for Managers?

Martha Nichols

In the ideal New Age company, employees are self-directed yet inspired by a visionary leader. The transformed workplace of the 1990s includes a flat organization chart, social responsibility, and good, clean entrepreneurial fun. It feels like a family or a friendly village, where everyone has flexible schedules to accommodate their personal lives. Managers encourage employees to do community work on office time, and everyone creates products that they themselves love.

This appealing picture has been drawn by Tom Chappell, founder and CEO of Tom's of Maine; The Body Shop's Anita Roddick; Esprit's Susie Tompkins; and many other alternative businesspeople. Through rousing tales of personal awakenings that lead to business success, New Age entrepreneurs hope to offer an introspective vision of work that allows for both individual and organizational growth. "The 1980s were all about style and lifestyle," says Susie Tompkins of Esprit. "The 1990s are about soul-searching."

But though these well-intentioned gurus tout a new understanding of work, the current crop of alternative business books is an oddly nostalgic blend of Horatio Alger, Abraham Maslow, Zen Buddhism, and self-help confessional. Largely the autobiographical accounts of successful entrepreneurs, New Age books often take the form of highly structured morality tales. They assure a cynical business world that companies can serve the common good and still make a profit. And they steadfastly assert that you can build an almost utopian community of workers at the same time that each individual employee reaches his or her developmental peak.

It's easy to scoff at such unrealistic visions. Yet mired in paradoxes and contradictions as they are, New Age ideals have become increasingly popular among baby boomers and busters, who find their futures uncertain in the wake of layoffs and restructurings. In the fingernail-biting realm of networked organizations, the continual competitive push for faster production now vies with employees' calls for flexible work schedules and more meaningful lives. How you define yourself—both on and off the job—is up for grabs, as companies become ever more decentralized, diverse, and unstable.

After the organizational fallout of the late 1980s, the plight of individual managers and professionals has yet to be addressed fairly or fully by most corporations. The news may not be good or the future predictable, but companies can't afford to ignore the current epidemic of white-collar job angst. Young professionals feel personal control and security slipping from their grasp every day, and they're naturally drawn to New Age discussions of creative work and supportive communities. Given the popularity of such ideas, senior managers would do well to consider what these alternative writers and maverick entrepreneurs have to say about the emotional tenor of today's workplace.

Indeed, companies must find ways to harness soul-searching on the job, not just gloss over or merely avoid it. As many of the New Age books reviewed here suggest, creating meaning may be the true managerial task of the future. Although their particular message may be flawed by moralistic assumptions or 1960s definitions of human potential, the overall New Age message comes through loud and clear: the old order is crumbling. In this, alternative business books can give executives an energizing nudge—or even a necessary whack on the side of the head.

❖ THE NEW MORALITY TALE

Perhaps the best way to understand what New Age business is about—paradoxes and all—is to follow Tom Chappell's personal odyssey. In *The Soul of a Business,* Chappell, CEO and president of Tom's of Maine, describes how his company grew from a tiny natural soap and toothpaste producer that sold only to health food stores into one fighting for space on supermarket shelves. In the process, Chappell says, his company lost its focus, and work—once the center of his own life—became an "unfulfilling exercise." Surrounded by MBAs and mired in quarterly reports, Chappell was left with a waning sense of company mission and personal purpose.

Chappell saw two options: he could sell the company and pursue other, more meaningful avenues on his own; or he could stay with Tom's and find a way to change both the company and himself. At the beginning of his story, Chappell expresses an uncertainty and desperation that will resonate with many of today's managers and professionals. His odyssey is compelling precisely because he acknowledges his own emotional misgivings, then shows how his strong feelings became a springboard for change.

Looking for both professional and personal renewal, he took the unusual route of attending classes parttime at the Harvard Divinity School. While reading the works of Immanuel Kant, Martin Buber, and Jonathan Edwards,

Chappell came to believe that "common values, a shared sense of purpose, can turn a company into a community where daily work takes on a deeper meaning and satisfaction."

This definition of community is now the bedrock of New Age management, expressed in a variety of ways by people as diverse as Robert Coles, M. Scott Peck, Stephen Covey, and Hillary Clinton. As Tom Chappell says, "We all need to feel part of something, some entity that is, intellectually and emotionally, both manageable and imaginable."

Nice as this sounds, however, it doesn't match contemporary business reality. Even in New Age companies, owners and senior executives benefit disproportionately from the profits. As a result, they share unequally in the power and incentives. At Tom's of Maine, for example, Chappell's first attempt to form a community—or a "clan" or "friendly village"—didn't pass the test with workers.

Fired up by his newfound mentors at the Divinity School, Chappell assumed all his employees would be just as inspired by his ideas. But after creating a new mission statement for the company, with the input of everyone from board members to secretaries, Chappell was shocked to learn that "fear and distrust were rampant throughout company, among management as well as labor. . . . They wanted to do a great job, but didn't have the power, didn't have the respect, weren't getting the direction they needed—except to make the numbers."

Like so many executives who have tried to impose empowerment programs, Chappell found the new mission could work only if employees took on new responsibility. Ironically, he discovered that as he spent time away from the office at the Divinity School, employees began implementing their own suggestions. For example, some manufacturing workers persuaded suppliers to ship items in reusable corrugated boxes. And when the marketing and sales departments recommended recalling a new deodorant that loyal customers didn't like, Chappell authorized the recall at a $400,000 loss. Even with such errors, in 1992 the company's product sales went up 31 percent, and profits increased 40 percent.

So what's wrong with this picture? Obviously, the 85 employees of Tom's of Maine and their search for community bear little relation to a large corporation. And while many managers would benefit from some executive education, most won't spend their time at the Harvard Divinity School. In fact, such moralizing can disguise a paternalistic vision of what a company should be—a place where the good father expects his kids to uphold the "family" work ethic and its "shared" mission.

One of Chappell's many realizations, for instance, was that he had taken his wife, Kate, cofounder of the company and vice president of R&D, for granted for many years. But however laudable this acknowledgment is—and his subsequent efforts to increase the number of female managers at Tom's—Chappell remains CEO, and it's the Tom Chappell image that sells the toothpaste. Although the employees of Tom's of Maine do appear genuinely inspired by their company community, this nostalgic longing for family values,

1950s corporate loyalties, or even a clan of like-minded souls can't keep pace with most current organizations.

In *The New Individualists,* social researchers Paul Leinberger and Bruce Tucker contend that the communities of the future are going to emerge from far-flung networks of professionals battling time-zone differences, not from a yearlong study of Immanuel Kant and Martin Buber. For Leinberger and Tucker, the "shadow networks" that are evolving from the latest information technologies represent a more realistic vision of community: in their words, "The possibility and hope for community lie not in some worked-up commitment or idealist revival of selected traditions but in the everyday working assumption that one is far more profoundly (and mysteriously) connected to other people."

Leinberger and Tucker focus on what they call "The Generation After *The Organization Man.*" Their ambitious study is based on interviews not only with 175 of the original organization men from William Whyte's 1956 classic but also with many of their children. This insightful book, full of anecdotes about what happened to particular "organization offspring" when they entered the workplace as well as intricate discussions of sociological trends, provides a realistic backdrop for the most paradoxical claims of New Age business writers.

As *The New Individualists* emphasizes, the typical baby-boomer quest for a meaningful life is full of psychological holes. For example, corporate cultures in which "sensitive managers stimulate creativity and caring" clearly appeal to the tribal children of the 1960s—not to mention the hippie entrepreneurs who lead those "tribes." But Leinberger and Tucker cleverly call this description a psychological utopia, or *psytopia,* rather than anything modeled on a real human culture.

According to these researchers, the best electronic communities and networks to date haven't been developed for idealistic or utopian reasons; they were "created cooperatively by people who were under pressure to deal with reality as they found it." For Leinberger and Tucker, then, true community doesn't grow out of a shared higher purpose but evolves through the pragmatic need to solve common problems.

❖ THE QUEST FOR HIGHER GROUND—OR NOT?

Yet defining a shared higher purpose continues to fascinate New Age entrepreneurs. Paul Hawken, the founder of Erewhon Trading Company and Smith & Hawken, is the prototypical alternative businessperson. His book *Growing a Business,* first published in 1987 and accompanied by a series of TV programs on PBS, was enormously influential in popularizing many New Age entrepreneurial ideas.

Hawken's latest book, *The Ecology of Commerce,* calls for nothing less than a complete makeover of the economy. Instead of recounting his personal views about starting a small company, this book takes a macroeconomic view of business and the global environment. In Hawken's New Age terms, "The restorative economy comes down to this: We need to imagine a prosperous commercial culture that is so intelligently designed and constructed that it mimics nature's at every step, a symbiosis of company and customer and ecology. This book, then, is ultimately about redesigning our commercial systems so that they work for owners, employees, customers, and life on earth without requiring a complete transformation of humankind."

While Paul Hawken stops short of calling for complete renewal of the human race, Anita Roddick, founder and group managing director of the natural cosmetics company The Body Shop, seems to search for products that would do just that. She asks: "How do you ennoble the spirit when you are selling something as inconsequential as a cosmetic cream? You do it by creating a sense of holism, of spiritual development, of feeling connected to the workplace, the environment and relationships with one another." In *Body and Soul*, which has just been released in paperback, Roddick claims: "We, as a company, have something worthwhile to say about how to run a successful business without losing your soul."

Roddick's use of the word *soul* is not casual, nor is Chappell's use of *community*. These words have become touchstones in the burgeoning ranks of New Age business books. The rhetoric of these entrepreneurial gurus is politically correct to the letter, even if the results would please any well-fed capitalist.

Indeed, by arguing for personal change as a platform for organizational or global transformation, these "enlightened capitalists" are at their most unconvincing. As a model for success, self-actualization—in which joyful, creative people realize their full potential—works best for entrepreneurs who build their own companies. But when these driven entrepreneurs assume that self-actualization will increase every employee's satisfaction, they deny social reality.

Unfortunately, major organizational shifts don't occur through a bunch of individuals transforming themselves. As many people who came of age during the civil rights movement or the women's movement of the 1970s will attest, social changes happen at a gruelingly slow pace and only through concerted group efforts. In companies, individuals with great organizational authority—say, an entrepreneur like Chappell—can certainly create upheaval, but real change can still take decades. And when social friction and organizational instability come into play, the limits of self-actualization, like community building, are all too apparent.

For instance, if everyone follows their own path to bliss, then anything goes—from a hermetic mountaintop existence to Ivan Boesky's "greed is good." Anita Roddick would agree that the 1980s were morally bankrupt; yet she doesn't make the connection between the greedy grab for personal power and the New Age quest for self-fulfillment. Roddick and others express an unshakable faith in personal change because the myth of self-actualization remains seductive. Everyone likes to think they're in control of their own fate and that they can rely on their "gut" to make the right decisions.

But much as New Agers want to believe in the power of personal transformation and creativity, entrepreneurs like Roddick often confuse themselves—their goals, political beliefs, dreams, and considerable talents—with the companies they create and the people who work for them. This confusion leads to both false humility and misleading assumptions about how their work translates to business as a whole.

At their worst, New Age morality tales mix up an individual's drive for power with a higher purpose. In Roddick's case, the story goes like this: Innocent hippie teacher and poet husband, who know nothing of the evil world of business, forge ahead because, she says, "my sole object was simply to survive, to earn enough to feed my kids." She opens her first shop in Brighton, England, in 1976, never loses her vision of selling cosmetics with natural ingredients at reasonable prices, and never loses sight of her customers.

As "Ms. Mega Mouth," Roddick trumpets political change in the media and other public forums, shuns the 1980s den of financial iniquity, and through sheer enthusiasm grabs a market the "immoral" cosmetics industry never thought was there. By 1984, when The Body Shop went public, the company was worth £8 million; there are now more than 600 shops worldwide. And the moral of the story? According to Roddick, "I see business as a Renaissance concept, where the human spirit comes into play. It does not have to be drudgery; it does not have to be the science of making money. It can be something that people genuinely feel good about, but only if it remains a human enterprise."

Roddick's tale, by turns flippantly direct and disingenuous, is representative of the contradictions that suffuse New Age writing. While Roddick says she knew nothing about business when she opened the first Body Shop, she also describes how she and her husband, Gordon, ran a successful restaurant in the early 1970s. And though she prefers to call herself a "tradeswoman," putting as much distance as possible between herself and the traditional business world, Roddick can fling around terms like *corporate identity* with the best of them.

She may be right to excoriate the immorality of big-time cosmetics companies for everything from false advertising to animal testing to high prices; but she is less than honest when she discusses The Body Shop's down-to-earth image. She claims that The Body Shop invests nothing in advertising, but the media attention Roddick thrives on is part of a larger promotional scheme that has helped mold a strong brand image. As with so many personal care products, the image of the entrepreneur founder means everything to the success of the brand. By this reasoning, Roddick's iconoclastic business approach and politically correct image—indeed, *Body and Soul* itself—are savvy sales tools, not just a gauntlet thrown in the face of "boring bankers."

More important, New Age businesses, which often involve personal care products or luxury items, don't map to most industries. In the current economy, the real issue may be not how you "ennoble the spirit" while selling makeup or ice cream but how you do so while selling consequential products like cars, computers, or commodities such as steel.

Paul Hawken is the first to pick up on these inconsistencies. As he notes in *The Ecology of Commerce,* "Although proponents of socially responsible business are making an outstanding effort at reforming the tired old ethics of commerce, they are unintentionally giving companies a new reason to produce, advertise, expand, grow, capitalize and use up resources. The rationale is that they are doing good. But flying across the country, renting a car at an airport, air-conditioning a hotel room, gassing up a truck full of goods, commuting to a job—these acts degrade the environment whether the person doing them works for The Body Shop, the Sierra Club, or Exxon."

❖ ZEN AND THE ART OF YIELDING

Hawken is correct, of course: the basic actions of the business world remain the same whether companies claim the higher moral ground or merely operate in the name of profit. He is also on the mark in describing a world of limited growth and expectations, one that both corporations and individuals will have to grapple with. In this newly delineated world, self-actualization as a road to personal success no longer fits the needs of either contracting or expanding organizations. And it clearly doesn't match the uncertain situation of individual professionals.

It's in laying the outlines for a new conception of self—and a new acceptance of losing personal control—that the best New Age books ring true. Bill Rosenzweig, coauthor of *The Republic of Tea* and cofounder of a Marin County tea company of the same name, exemplifies an entrepreneurial approach that differs markedly from Anita Roddick's brash, look-at-me onslaught. Rosenzweig, in describing how his business developed, writes: "I was constantly reflecting on my own search for the 'right thing.' I badly wanted this to be 'it.' Although I yearned for the tea to be right for me—to be my true calling—I knew this was beyond my control."

Much of *The Republic of Tea*—subtitled *Letters to a Young Zentrepreneur*—is in the form of faxes between Rosenzweig and Mel and Patricia Ziegler. In this charming New Age byplay, Mel Ziegler, founder of the original Banana Republic, is the "Minister of Leaves"—idea person and mentor. His wife, Patricia, fanciful illustrator and tea tester, is the "Minister of Enchantment." Bill Rosenzweig is the young "Minister of Progress," and much of the drama in the story involves whether he should start the business at all.

In typical fashion, Mel Ziegler, who manages to convey both ethereal wisdom and hardheaded financial sense, keeps his impatience to himself: "It took nerve to start a business. Lots of it. I started to wonder: Where was Bill's nerve?"

In creating a company called The Republic of Tea, Rosenzweig and the Zieglers have tapped into the general desire for a more leisurely, meaningful lifestyle—or what they call "Tea Mind." In a world of limited expectations, that is, where entrepreneurs are less sure of themselves and personal drive is less sacrosanct, selling alternative lifestyles may become more important than selling products. While it's easy to dismiss this idealistic reasoning for why products like Metabolic Frolic and Longevity Tea sell, these Zentrepreneurs do express a less self-centered conception of the individual.

In the Minister of Leaves' words, "Life is business, and business is life. In being a businessman, I find no license to do or be things I could not do or be as a man. It's that simple." The pragmatic Ziegler knows social responsibility can't supersede company profits. Yet he is equally certain that "you cannot bully reality. To yield, the businessperson's ego must be set aside."

"Yielding" has uncomfortable connotations for many executives, because it implies lack of control, not to mention the usual stance of women and other powerless players. But as the Minister of Leaves writes, "The existing business models do not constitutionally pay sufficient heed to the one inalienable fact of our existence: Nothing, nobody, exists except in relationship to something, somebody. *We exist only in relationship to one another.*" Ziegler's emphasis on human relationships mirrors Tom Chappell's realization of community—with one important difference. Mel Ziegler talks of an inevitable reality that businesspeople must learn to accept, not a new vision of shared values that an enthusiastic entrepreneur imposes on everyone else and the world at large.

By opposing the usual ego-driven business approach to relationships with others, the Zieglers and Rosenzweig turn the traditional tables. In social science terms, *agency* and *communion* refer to two approaches to the world that are considered opposites. Having agency means you are controlling, decisive, and self-sufficient—traits generally associated with masculinity and, by extension, entrepreneurship. Practicing communion, on the other hand, means you are open, expressive, and long to be connected with others. Not surprisingly, this desire to be one with everything, religious connotations and all, matches the model for traditional femininity.

In the current era of self-help and pop psychological platitudes, of course, women and priests aren't the only ones practicing communion. Yet even if male entrepreneurs like Mel Ziegler and Bill Rosenzweig are trying a new communal approach, most started out as successful businessmen whose agency has never been questioned. Despite the success of Anita Roddick and Susie Tompkins, few female and minority managers have experienced such power on the job. Instead of increased communion, they want new authority. Clearly, such disparities in career opportunities can complicate the picture of which workers are ready to "set aside their egos."

But more than anything, the growing interest in communion and female perspectives suggests a major shift in how people view the job of management. It involves blending traditional masculine and feminine approaches to handle organizational uncertainties. As such, both male and female executives may end up changing how they work.

In *The New Individualists,* Leinberger and Tucker point out that as women continue to enter the workplace in large numbers, they also bring with them a more inclusive and communal sense of self. According to these researchers, such a new conception of self in the working world challenges "almost daily the more traditionally male conception of unfettered self-sufficiency." And it's the realities of networked, decentralized organizations that are driving changes in attitude: "This transition has nothing to do with men 'getting in touch with' some idealized 'feminine' part of the self, but with adopting ways of doing things that will grow increasingly prominent."

Rather than the work ethic or self ethic of decades past, Leinberger and Tucker suggest that today's employees are adopting a new "enterprise ethic": a paradoxical vision of work that includes a belief in one's own abilities, a pessimism about dwindling opportunities, and an acknowledgment of the necessity of connecting with other people. To be sure, the many baby boomers who have young children find it impossible to focus on just their own problems. But more important, the enterprise ethic is based on a sense of loss—loss of the ideal of self-actualization, loss of an unlimited horizon.

In small New Age companies, shared values and a higher sense of purpose may still make a job worthwhile; professionals may even come to accept the trade-off of more meaningful work for less overall financial security. But as Tom Chappell found, defining company values is no easy task. In fact, the need for a more communal sense of self—for acknowledging one's reliance on other people in organizations with fuzzy boundaries—doesn't necessarily lead to the well-defined communities that New Agers dream of.

The toughest dilemma for today's managers and professionals is that even as they acquire more autonomy at work, they'll lose more control over the diffuse organizations they're part of. Though some New Age entrepreneurs may call for creating tribal psytopias of shared values, the multiethnic and multinational reality is far more complex than that. The real contribution of alternative business writers is not their illumination of a kinder, gentler future but their validation of the paradoxical reality.

❖ MANAGING PARADOX IN THE NEW AGE

Even if managers and professionals have become cynical, they are drawn to the optimism and social justice these books, writers, and entrepreneurs promote. Although New Age business books don't present fresh truths or innovative management techniques, executives can learn a great deal from the emotional chords these writers strike.

If nothing else, they indicate what professionals now fear: isolation as well as loss of self, purpose, and stability. Whether or not companies completely do away with organization charts or pursue "profits with principles," managers will have to contend with the new knowledge professional—an individual who constantly questions the value of what he or she is doing, who feels little loyalty to corporate authority yet still longs for connections in a large organization.

And that's just one of the paradoxes managers must learn to cope with. As Charles Handy admits in his latest book, *The Age of Paradox*, "I used to think that paradoxes were the visible signs of an imperfect world. . . . I wrote books that implied that there had to be a right way to run our organizations and our lives." But Handy has come to realize that "so many things, just now, seem to contain their own contradictions, so many good intentions to have unintended consequences, and so many formulas for success to carry a sting in their tail."

In his elegant plea for meaning and morality, Handy expresses many of the frustrations that now beset individual managers and professionals. In his earlier books, he discussed the new knowledge worker as someone who develops a portfolio of skills to negotiate the evolving information economy. But in *The Age of Paradox*, Handy recognizes that such theories don't apply neatly to everyone: "I am more chary, now, of offering general solutions to our individual predicaments. We must each find our own way. The map, however, will be much the same for all of us, even if we choose to follow different paths."

From this standpoint, it makes little sense for executives to impose monolithic management structures on decentralized organizations of diverse individuals. Yet acknowledging the difficulties of negotiating the current "map"— even offering incentives for more communal work relations—may go a long way toward helping employees adjust to the new networked realities.

In the end, Handy calls for finding a personal balance between the many alternatives, in both work and life. He writes, "Paradox does not have to be resolved, only managed." In this, he embraces the Zen perspective of Mel Ziegler and other thoughtful New Age writers. But like a true Western thinker, Handy keeps questioning the cosmos: "There must be more to life than being a cog in someone else's great machine, hurtling God knows where."

Or as Tom Chappell puts it, "One of the most important messages we entrepreneurs can bring to the business world at large is that freedom from all constraint is a temporary joy. . . . No matter how much money you have, or how much free time, the question nags, 'What's next? How do I find meaning in the rest of my life?' "

GLOSSARY OF TERMS

antecedents Things that precede a behavior, which set the stage for (cue) that behavior. (Daniels)

asset rationalization Meeting competitive pressures by equating human and physical assets with current economics. (Beer, et al.)

assumption analysis A process of categorizing the assumptions that underlie conclusions in light of their certainty and importance. (Kilmann)

automatic listening When the listener doesn't actually attempt to hear what the speaker has to say and instead only affirms his or her own unexamined assumptions. (Barrentine)

benchmark A measured, "best-in-class" achievement, a reference or measurement standard for comparison; a performance level recognized as the standard of excellence for a specific business practice. (Watson)

benchmarking code of conduct A behavioral convention that describes the protocol of behaviors to be used in conducting benchmarking studies. (Watson)

benchmarking partner A relationship between two parties who associate in a collegial relationship involving close cooperation to conduct benchmarking studies—the protocol of this relationship is summarized by the Benchmarking Code of Conduct. (Watson)

benchmarking A method by which organizations monitor the performance of the best of their competitors to use as a standard for their own performance. (Band); A systematic and continuous measurement process; a process of continuously comparing and measuring an organization's business process against business leaders anywhere in the world, to gain information that will help the organization take action to improve its performance. (Watson)

best practice Superior performance within an activity, regardless of industry, leadership, management, or operational approaches, or methods that lead to exceptional performance; a relative term that usually indicates innovative or interesting business practices that have been identified during a particular benchmarking study as contributing to improved performance at the leading organizations. (Watson)

blueprinting A method of analysis for managing all elements of the customer satisfaction process that looks at the basic systems and structures of the organization in order to better understand the process of creating satisfied customers. (Band)

boundaryless organization A form of organization that minimizes barriers and emphasizes cooperation and communication between the different parts of an organization. This includes minimizing coordination problems between different functional departments, product divisions, hierarchical levels, and overcoming external barriers to customers and suppliers. (Tichy and Sherman)

bridge team Group developed from the key stakeholders to monitor the status of revitalization and to resolve issues beyond the scope of the team structure. (Beer, et al.)

bureaucratic A form of organization characterized by an emphasis on management through rational, impersonal means through such elements as clearly defined authority, written records, and a separation of management and ownership. (Tichy and Sherman)

business network unit A venture that assigns roles and functions to separate stand-alone specialty businesses to produce or market a product or service. (Galbraith & Lawler)

CEO Chief executive officer; typically the highest-ranking executive in a corporation. (Tichy and Sherman)

change agent The role taken to ensure that the organization's structure and culture are transformed to be congruent with the organization's vision. (Nanus)

chaos A stage of group development where individual differences prevail, and crisis management may be required. This mode follows the disintegration of a pseudo-community. (Barrentine)

charismatic leader One who senses unexploited opportunities, formulates and communicates an idealized vision, builds trust in oneself and support for the vision, and provides the means to achieve the vision. (Conger)

China mentality The conviction that one *can* change the world, motivating one to reject the usual answers and examine old problems in a new light. (Ohmae)

coach The role taken to motivate and direct work units toward activities that will result in the implementation of the vision. (Nanus)

community The final stage of group development, in which people feel comfortable about straightforwardly expressing their ideas on both an interpersonal and group level. (Barrentine)

companyism An excessive concern for, or loyalty to, one's company, which leads to the inability to critically examine company strategy or past ways of doing business. (Ohmae)

competitive benchmarking A measure of organizational performance compared against competing organizations; studies that target specific product designs, process capabilities, or administrative methods used by a company's direct competitors. (Watson)

consequences Things that follow a behavior and change the probability of that behavior recurring. (Daniels)

consolidation The process that results after numerous small competitors in an industry are reduced in number to one or a few large competitors through mergers, acquisitions, or failures. (Tichy and Sherman)

credibility The leader characteristic that combines the qualities of honesty, inspiration, and competence. (Kouzes and Posner)

credibility gap The difference between what leaders say and what they do. (Kouzes and Posner)

critical path The various stages that an organization must follow (allowing overlap across them) to develop an organization that naturally continues to revitalize itself. (Beer, et al)

culture clash Conflict over basic values that occurs among groups of people with different core identities. (Loden and Rosener)

culture track The first step in an organizational improvement program that emphasizes establishing trust, information sharing, and adaptiveness. (Kilmann)

culture A system of attitudes, actions, and artifacts that endures over time and that operates to produce among its members a relatively unique common psychology. (Vaill); The underlying beliefs and values that are taught to new members of the organization that guide activities within the organization. (Nanus)

customer satisfaction The state in which customer needs, wants, and expectations, through the transaction cycle, are met or exceeded, resulting in repurchase and continuing loyalty. (Band)

deadly diseases A set of chronic ailments that can plague any organization and prevent its success. (Deming)

defensive reasoning Reasoning that occurs when individuals: (1) firmly hold premises of questionable validity yet think they are unassailable; (2) make inferences that do not necessarily follow from the premises, yet they think they do; and (3) reach conclusions that they believe they have tested carefully yet they have not because the way the conclusions have been framed make them untestable. (Argyris)

Deming Management Theory A set of fourteen steps that managers are advised to take to transform their organizations into more successful systems. (Deming)

design team Group of steering team members; may also include supervisors, human resource personnel, union officials, team members, and other functional representatives. This team plans the implementation of the team strategy and acts as champion of the team effort. (Wellins, et al.)

dialexia The compulsion to examine all issues dialectically and to assume that in all cases those issues are not as they seem. (Vaill)

differently abled A term used to focus on a person's abilities, while still acknowledging physical and/or developmental differences. (Loden and Rosener)

discontinuities One-time events that occur within the organization. They can be the result of a number of events including technological advances, legal decisions, and economic conditions. (Mintzberg)

discontinuity The break in progress created by moving from the old to the new (restructured) organization. (Kanter)

discretionary effort More behavior than is minimally required. (Daniels)

disorder The confusion created as a restructured organization rebuilds itself. (Kanter)

distraction The shift of focus and energy from an accent on running the business to solving immediate problems. (Kanter)

diversified firm A company that operates businesses in distinctly different industries. (Tichy and Sherman)

diversity Those human qualities that are different from our own and outside the groups to which we belong, yet present in other individuals and groups. (Loden and Rosener)

divisional structure A model that organizes the business around a product or products where each division operates much like a separate business entity. (Galbraith and Lawler)

dominator A model of social organization, like a hierarchy, that has a vertical structure in which power means power over people. (Barrentine)

double-loop learning Learning that focuses on the values governing the actions that produced the errors. (Argyris)

effective managers Managers who manage themselves and others so that both employees and the organization benefit. (Blanchard and Johnson)

empowerment Helping employees take ownership of their jobs so that they take personal interest in improving the performance of the organization. (Kanter)

empowerment Providing employees a say in how the organization is run and some degree of control and responsibility for their work domains. (Covey)

emptying A stage of group development in which individuals develop a critical self-awareness. This differs from the chaos mode in that rather than simply being aware of diversity and differences in others, workers recognize their own weaknesses and strengths. (Barrentine)

enable The process, practices, or methods that facilitate the implementation of a best practice and help to meet a critical-success factor; characteristics that explain the reasons for the achievement of benchmark performance. (Watson)

enterprise web A group of symbolic analysts who combine their skills so that the group's ability to innovate is something more than the simple sum of its parts. (Reich)

espoused theories The beliefs and values people hold about how to manage their lives. (Argyris)

essential business The basic activities by which an organization defines itself. (Nanus)

extinction The absence of reinforcement, with the result that behavior declines and eventually stops. (Daniels)

fancy footwork Actions that permit individuals to be blind to inconsistencies in their actions, to deny that these inconsistencies exist, or to blame other people for their actions. (Argyris)

feedback Information regarding results of one's efforts (how well one is performing). (Blanchard and Johnson)

feminine The characteristics of compassion, loving, and nurturing, which can be found in men as well as women. (Barrentine)

first-order errors Errors that are caused by not knowing. (Argyris)

fixed costs Costs that are based on commitments from previous budgets and cannot be altered quickly. (Ohmae)

frame A schemata, map, image, metaphor, tool, or perspective that presents a unique image of organizations and allows managers to gather information, make judgments, and determine how to take action from its vantage point. Four frames are the structural, human resources, political, and symbolic. (Bolman and Deal)

front-end/back-end model A model that organizes separately around a "front-end" that deals with customers and service, and a "back-end" that is organized around product development and manufacturing. (Galbraith and Lawler)

functional benchmarking An application of process benchmarking that compares a particular business function at two or more organizations. (Watson)

functional model A traditional business structure that is organized around functions such as human resource departments, accounting, and manufacturing. (Galbraith & Lawler)

gainsharing Systems of financial rewards in which employee bonuses are based on organizational performance. (Lawler)

gap analysis The process of setting objectives, analyzing the difference (gap) between the firm's current position and its objectives, and determining courses of action to narrow or eliminate the difference. (Mintzberg)

gap A difference in performance, identified through a comparison between the benchmark for a particular activity and other companies; the measured leadership advantage of the benchmark organization over other organizations. (Watson)

generic benchmarking An application of functional process benchmarking that compares a particular business function at two or more organizations selected without regard to their industry. (Watson)

global benchmarking The extension of strategic benchmarking to include benchmarking partners on a global scale. (Watson)

global localization The capacity to operate on a global scale while retaining the ability to serve local customers and markets. (Ohmae)

global paradox The strange phenomenon in which the larger the world economy becomes, the more powerful its smallest players are. (Naisbitt)

global web An enterprise web of a high-value enterprise that spans across national borders. (Reich)

globalization The process that results in competition among companies across national borders. (Tichy and Sherman)

globalization The standardization of product design and advertising strategy throughout the world. (Ohmae)

goal setting The establishment of targets (goals) for employee performance that facilitate the conscious intentions of employees to perform. (Blanchard and Johnson)

governance strategy Consciously designed movement toward creating a governance system that dramatically rearranges social and power relationships between the organizational leadership and the core employees. (Block)

grounding A process of meditation and relaxation that encourages personal intuition. (Barrentine)

group dynamics Patterns of interaction that occur within groups that help or hinder the accomplishment of tasks. (Loden and Rosener)

high-involvement organization An organization that seeks to give all its members access to information, the opportunity to influence decisions, and a share in the rewards of performance. (Galbraith and Lawler)

high-performance team A group that meets all the conditions of real teams and has members who are deeply committed to one another's personal growth and success. (Katzenbach and Smith)

inductive thinking The ability to first recognize a powerful solution and then seek the problems it might solve. (Hammer and Champy)

integration Creating conditions at work such that individuals can *best* achieve their own goals by directing their efforts toward the success of the enterprise. (McGregor)

interlinked economy The open and deregulated global economy that is currently emerging, encompassing Japan, Europe, the United States, and other aggressive economies. (Ohmae)

internal benchmarking An application of process benchmarking performed within an organization by comparing the performance of similar business units or business processes. (Watson)

job enrichment Creating jobs in which individuals can be responsible for an entire product or service. (Lawler)

just-in-time (JIT) An inventory-control system that schedules materials to arrive as they are needed on the production line, rather than being stored in inventory. (Tichy and Sherman)

kaizen The Japanese term for continuous, incremental improvement. (Hammer and Champy)

lateral unit Organizational unit that brings related tasks or work groups together across divisional and hierarchical lines. (Galbraith & Lawler)

law of maldistribution Eighty percent of the effort expended in a process is caused by only 20 percent of the input, according to Vilfredo Pareto, a twentieth-century economist; also known as the Pareto Principle and the 80–20 rule. (Hammer and Champy)

leadership A process by which an individual or team induces a group to pursue objectives held by the leader or shared by the leader and his or her followers. (Gardner)

learning disability A way of thinking in organizations that keeps managers and others from making necessary changes and adapting to environmental needs. (Senge)

Maastricht treaty The treaty that calls for European communities to become a united economic power. (Naisbitt)

management skills track The second step in an organizational improvement program that emphasizes development of conceptual, analytical, administrative, social, and interpersonal skills. (Kilmann)

managerial competency A definable and trainable skill alleged to have an impact on overall managerial performance. (Vaill)

MBWA (managing by wandering around) The process of having managers spend a substantial portion of their time meeting with customers, vendors, and employees to learn their needs. (Peters and Waterman)

mental models Deeply engrained generalizations, assumptions, or pictures that influence how people see the world. (Senge)

Mercorsor Agreement An agreement linking Argentina, Brazil, Paraguay, and Uruguay in a common market in order to accelerate their individual and collective economic growth. (Naisbitt)

mission The purpose for which the organization exists; the needs or desires that the organization satisfies for customers or clients. (Nanus)

monitoring Gathering information about how well the vision is being implemented in the organization. (Nanus)

multiskilling Team members are required to learn every job on their team and, in some cases, the jobs on other teams as well. (Wellins, et al.)

negative reinforcement Desired behavior is exhibited and strengthened as a means to avoid punishment. (Daniels)

new-design plants Organization-wide approaches to participative management in which group members participate in selection decisions, the layout facilitates work-group tasks, job design revolves around teams, and pay systems are egalitarian. (Lawler)

newstreams Future products and services. (Kanter)

nichemanship An organizational strategy of fulfilling a segment of unmet demand in a larger market. (Belasco)

objectives Milestones that must be attained in order to implement the vision. (Nanus)

organizational defensive routines Actions or policies that protect individuals or segments of the organization from experiencing embarrassment or threat. (Argyris)

organizational gardening An organic metaphor for a business paradigm that emphasizes the ongoing planning, development, and nurturing of a business. (Barrentine)

others People who are different from us along one or several dimensions such as age, ethnicity, gender, race, sexual/affectional orientation, and so on. (Loden and Rosener)

paradigm effect Process by which practitioners of an established paradigm are forced to reassess their own perceptions as a result of the introduction of new paradigms. (Barker)

paradigm paralysis A description of the state of a paradigm whereby participants are tolerant of the established rules, boundaries, and behaviors, and are intolerant of alternative rules, boundaries, and behaviors. This state is marked by very low levels of expressed creativity and very low levels of innovation. (Barker)

paradigm pliancy A description of the state of a paradigm whereby participants are tolerant of established rules, boundaries, and behaviors, and of alternative rules, boundaries, and behaviors. This state is marked by high levels of expressed creativity and high levels of innovation. (Barker)

paradigm shift A change to a new paradigm having new rules, boundaries, and behaviors. (Barker)

paradigm A model or conceptual framework; a mindset for understanding aspects of reality. (Covey); A set of rules and regulations (written or unwritten) that does two things: (1) it establishes or defines boundaries; and (2) it tells how to behave inside the boundaries in order to be successful. (Barker)

paradox A statement that seems absurd, but is actually valid or true. (Naisbitt); A statement whose parts may seem contradictory but may actually be true. (Vaill)

Parkinson's Law Work expands to fill the amount of time available for its completion. The reengineering revision of Parkinson's Law states that "Work expands to fill the amount of equipment available for its completion." (Hammer and Champy)

participative leadership A type of leadership that emphasizes empowerment and increased employee involvement in problem solving. (Loden and Rosener)

partnership A model of social organization that, as its name implies, is nonhierarchical. This model of social organization is more supportive and productive than a dominance model. (Barrentine)

partnership Situation where everyone at every level is responsible for participating in the definition of the vision and values for their unit. (Block)

patriarchal management Leaders act, and are viewed as, parents of the organization, and the rest of the members are the children looking for structure, guidance, direction, praise, and an appropriate reward for performing desired behaviors. (Block)

performance management Creating the right environment and conditions to bring out the best in people. (Daniels)

permanent white water The condition of continuous chaos and complexity characteristic of contemporary business environments. (Vaill)

personal freedom norms Organizational norms that reflect the organization's position on self-expression, the exercise of personal discretion, and self-satisfaction. (Kilmann)

pinpointing Specifying tangible results and related behaviors that are observable, measurable, and reliable. (Daniels)

planning A formalized system of projecting the future and developing ways to meet organizational goals. (Mintzberg)

plans Outlines of activities necessary over a given period of time in order to achieve objectives. (Nanus)

pluralistic leadership A type of leadership that assumes organization culture must change in order to attain diversity, employee empowerment, and involvement. (Loden and Rosener)

portfolio A mix of businesses used by diversified companies that is designed to fit together in such a way as to provide the corporation with synergy and competitive advantage. (Tichy and Sherman)

positive reinforcement A consequence that increases the rate or frequency of a behavior, because the performer values that outcome and views it as contingent on the behavior. (Daniels)

praise Verbal reinforcement (e.g., compliment) for desirable employee behavior and performance. (Blanchard and Johnson)

primary dimensions Immutable human differences that are inborn or that exert an important impact on early socialization or throughout life. Examples of primary dimensions are age, ethnicity, gender, physical abilities, race, and sexual/affectional orientation. (Loden and Rosener)

problem The difference between what is actually happening and what you want to happen. (Blanchard and Johnson)

problem-identifier Person who has the skills required to help customers understand their needs and how those needs can best be met by customized products and to identify new problems and possibilities to which the customized product might'be applicable. (Reich)

problem solver Person who has the skills required to put things together in unique ways and continually searches for new applications, combinations, and refinements capable of solving all sorts of emerging problems. (Reich)

process benchmarking The activity of measuring discrete performance and functionality against organizations whose performance is excellent in analogous business processes. (Watson)

process A set of activities that, taken together, produce a result of value to the customer. (Hammer and Champy)

productivity Employee output in terms of the quantity and quality of work completed. (Blanchard and Johnson)

program management organization (PMO) A diverse collection of organizational members from varying levels and areas in an organization who spend part of their time away from their formal responsibilities addressing complex organizational issues. (Kilmann)

programmatic change Change made in how a corporation functions, based on human resource issues. This directly opposes asset rationalization. (Beer, et al.)

protectionism The attempt to defend domestic companies from trade or competition with foreign industries. (Ohmae)

pseudo-community A group of people who project the surface, yet lack the content, of true communal spirit; noted for superficial kindness and respect. (Barrentine)

pseudo-team A group that has not focused on collective performance and is not really trying to achieve it. (Katzenbach and Smith)

punishment A consequence that causes behavior to diminish in frequency and ultimately stop. (Daniels)

purposing Continuous leadership actions to induce clarity, consensus, and commitment regarding the organization's basic purposes. (Vaill)

real team A small number of people with complementary skills who are committed to a common purpose, performance goals, and working approach for which they hold themselves mutually accountable. (Katzenbach and Smith)

reengineering The fundamental rethinking and radical redesign of business processes to achieve dramatic improvements in critical, contemporary measures of performance, such as cost, quality, service, and speed; starting over. (Hammer and Champy)

reprimand Negative verbal feedback provided when undesirable employee behavior and performance occur. (Blanchard and Johnson)

reverse engineering A comparison of product characteristics, functionality, and performance with those of similar products made by competitors; the tear-down of competitive products to their fundamental subassembly level by engineers, in order to evaluate design characteristics. (Watson)

revitalization Enhancing the abilities of the individuals and the organization to cope with an increasingly competitive environment. (Beer, et al.)

reward system track The fifth step in an organizational improvement program that develops a performance-based reward system. (Kilmann)

sapp A force that drains energy from people. (Byham)

Satchmo's Paradox The inability of experts to explain their areas of expertise to novices (i.e., "man, if you gotta ask [what jazz is] you'll never know." Louis Armstrong) (Vaill)

Say's Law Supply creates its own demand, as formulated by Jean Baptiste Say, a nineteenth-century French economist. (Hammer and Champy)

scenarios Integrated and interrelated sets of possible future events that will have an impact on the organization's success. (Nanus)

scientific management A field of management thought that emphasized systematically-determined management practices and carefully defined employee work behaviors as the paths to improving labor productivity. (Tichy and Sherman)

second-order errors Errors that humans actively design and produce. (Argyris)

secondary dimensions Mutable human differences that are acquired, discarded, or modified throughout life. Examples of secondary dimensions are educational background, income, marital status, military status, religious beliefs, and work experience. (Loden and Rosener)

self-directed work team (SDWT) An intact group of employees, responsible for a whole work process or segment, that develops a product or delivers a service to an internal or external customer. (Wellins, et al.)

selective adaptation Choice of a method or action that accommodates identified conditions rather than ignoring or going against those facts. (McGregor)

semiautonomous teams Small groups of employees who manage many dimensions of their own work affairs. (Byham)

shadow track A steering committee responsible for monitoring and coordinating a comprehensive organizational improvement program that integrates culture, management skills, reward systems, strategy-structure, and team-building. (Kilmann)

shared vision The capacity to hold a shared picture of the future. (Senge)

single-loop learning Learning that focuses on the presenting problem (symptom) and ignores the causes of the problem. (Argyris)

social relationship norms Organizational norms that suggest the degree to which socializing and mixing work with pleasure are condoned or even encouraged. (Kilmann)

spin-in partnership An enterprise web where strategic brokers in headquarters purchase the best of good ideas bubbling up outside the firm from independent groups of problem-identifiers and problem-solvers, and then produce, distribute, and market the ideas under the firm's own well-known trademark. (Reich)

spin-off partnership An enterprise web where strategic brokers in headquarters act as venture capitalists and midwives, nurturing good ideas that bubble up from groups of problem-solvers and problem-identifiers and then spinning the groups off as independent businesses in which the strategic brokers at headquarters retain a partial stake. (Reich)

spiritual havens Programs of support and education for workers and their spiritual development during periods of transition. (Barrentine)

spokesperson The formal role associated with communicating the vision to both internal and external constituents. (Nanus)

steering committee This group is usually composed of upper and middle management, • union representatives, team leaders, and in some cases prospective team members. This group takes the vision and direction provided by senior management and oversees the design effort for self-directed work teams. (Wellins, et al.)

stewardship contract A social agreement that defines and limit what is to be controlled, the boundaries and limitations of a partnership among participants, and the relationship between employees and the organization. (Block)

stewardship contract Definition of the ground rules for employees to participate in the new governance structure, the results that are required, the constraints within which they must live, and the changes that will be made toward greater empowerment, partnership, and service. (Block)

stewardship Empowering people to be accountable for their own actions, predicated on the idea that people in communities and organizations are willing to choose service over self-interest, while not being dependent on managers. (Block)

strategic alliance A mutually beneficial, long-term, cooperative relationship with another firm. (Ohmae)

strategic alliance Corporations that cooperate closely with their competitors in order to take advantage of the competitors' strengths and make themselves stronger. (Naisbitt)

strategic benchmarking The application of process benchmarking to the level of business strategy; a systematic process for evaluating alternatives, implementing strategies, and improving performances by understanding and adapting successful strategies from external partners who participate in an ongoing business alliance. (Watson)

strategic broker Person who has the skills necessary to link problem-solvers and problem-identifiers, and to manage ideas. (Reich)

strategic management The process by which top management teams identify the unit of interest and determine the mission for that unit via thorough analysis of organizational strengths and weaknesses and environmental threats and opportunities. (Vaill)

strategy The process of seeking competitive advantage for the organization. Strategy can be in the form of a plan, pattern, position, perspective, or a combination of the four. (Mintzberg)

strategy-structure track The fourth step in an organizational improvement program that focuses on aligning objectives, tasks, and people. (Kilmann)

subsidiarity Retaining power at the lowest possible level within an organization. (Naisbitt)

superficial man A rather bland, composite, unreal individual that most behavioral science theories attempt to describe and explain. (Vaill)

symbiotic customer relationships The close relationship of suppliers with customers, in which customers may be involved from product conception to delivery. (Peters)

symbolic analyst Person who provides symbolic-analytic services, generally the problem-solver, problem-identifier, and the strategic broker. (Reich)

symbolic analytic services Services typically provided by people who trade worldwide the manipulations of symbols—data, words, and oral and visual representations. (Reich)

synergy Creating a whole that is greater than the sum of its parts. (Kanter); The process of combining all the strengths of the organization so that the sum is greater than the whole. (Mintzberg); Working together, cooperating, combining in a cooperative action to yield an outcome that is greater than the sum of its parts. (Covey)

systems thinking The ability to look at the whole and see how one part affects another. (Senge)

targeted interviewing A technique that focuses on gathering facts about the applicant (instead of theoretical information). This approach looks at past behavior as a predictor of future behavior. (Wellins, et al.)

task alignment Balancing the organization's behavioral and business concerns and focusing on the core tasks rather than on the organizational structure. (Beer, et al.)

task-driven organization An organization in which roles and responsibilities are assigned based on the task, rather than on an established hierarchy. (Beer, et al.)

task-innovation norms Organizational norms that focus on creativity and innovation and reflect the organization's stance on status quo versus change. (Kilmann)

task-support norms Organizational norms that focus on information sharing, helping other work groups, and efficiency concerns. (Kilmann)

teachable moment The period of time when a person is most likely to understand, and accept, the material being taught. (Wellins, et al.)

team gaps The difference between actual and desired dimensions of work-group functioning. (Kilmann)

team-building track The third step in an organizational improvement program that emphasizes managing troublemakers, team building, and inter-team building. (Kilmann)

technoholic One who believes all of the world's problems can be solved by the rational development of a plan and the application of appropriate technologies. (Vaill)

TGR (things gone right) Product improvements and innovations. (Peters)

TGW (things gone wrong) Defects and other quality errors. (Peters)

theories in use The actual rules or master programs that individuals use to achieve control. (Argyris)

Theory X A set of assumptions that explains some human behavior and has influenced conventional principles of management. It assumes that workers want to avoid work and must be controlled and coerced to accept responsibility and exert effort toward organizational objectives. (McGregor)

Theory Y A set of assumptions offered as an alternative to Theory X. Theory Y assumes that work is a natural activity, and given the right conditions, people will seek responsibility and apply their capacities to organizational objectives without coercion. (McGregor)

tracking Gathering information about the effectiveness of the vision in the external environment. (Nanus)

transformational cycle A dynamic sequence of phases through which a master manager journeys toward excellent performance, encompassing initiation, uncertainty, transformation, and routinization. (Quinn)

transitional stages of growth The phases through which organizations move across time as they emphasize different values—entrepreneurial, collectivity, formalization, and elaboration of structure. (Quinn)

triad The combined market of the industrialized world (Japan, Europe, and the United States. (Ohmae)

tribalism The belief in fidelity to one's own kind, defined by ethnicity, language, culture, religion, or profession. (Naisbitt)

"true north" principles Basic truths and natural laws that govern human existence. Like a compass, they always point the way. (Covey)

value creation Combining all the tools and techniques for quality, service, and customer satisfaction into a program that will create and deliver value to customers. (Band)

variable costs Costs that are closely associated with the volume of the business. (Ohmae)

virtual organization A disembodied organization that functions as a series of loosely connected networks of specialists that combine to complete a project and then disband. (Peters)

virtual worksite A workplace that does not exist in a physical location, but instead is created through the use of computer networks and other information technology. (Galbraith and Lawler)

vision A mental image or a dream of a highly desirable future state for the organization. (Conger); An engaging yet realistic image of what the organization could become. (Nanus)

visionary leadership Developing an engaging image of what an organization can become and then creating organizational systems to attain the vision. (Nanus)

work teams Groups of employees who are given considerable responsibility to decide how the group will operate. (Lawler)

world class Leading performance in a process, independent of industry or geographic location, as recognized using process benchmarking for comparison to other worldwide contenders. (Watson)

wu-wei An element of Taoism that suggests that more can be accomplished in the world by nonaction than by forcing action. (Vaill)

zapp A force that energizes people, enabling them to seek and obtain continuous improvement in their jobs. (Byham)

BIBLIOGRAPHY OF INCLUSIONS

Argyris, Chris. (1990). *Overcoming Organizational Defenses*. Needham Heights, MA: Allyn and Bacon

Band, William A. (1991). *Creating Value for Customers: Designing and Implementing a Total Corporate Strategy*. New York: Wiley.

Barker, Joel A. (1992). *Paradigms: The Business of Discovering the Future*. New York: HarperCollins.

Barrentine, Pat. (1993). *When the Canary Stops Singing*. San Francisco: Berrett-Koehler.

Beer, Michael; Eisenstat, Russell A., & Spector, Bert. (1990). *The Critical Path to Corporate Renewal*. Cambridge, MA: Harvard Business School.

Belasco, James A., & Stayer, Ralph C. (1993). *Flight of the Buffalo*. New York: Warner Books.

Belasco, James. (1990). *Teaching the Elephant to Dance: The Manager's Guide to Empowering Change*. New York: Plume.

Blanchard, Kenneth, & Johnson, Spencer. (1981). *The One Minute Manager*. La Jolla, CA: Blanchard-Johnson.

Block, Peter. (1993). *Stewardship*. San Francisco: Berrett-Koehler.

Bolman, Lee G. & Deal, Terrence E. (1991). *Reframing Organizations: Artistry, Choice, and Leadership*. San Francisco: Jossey-Bass.

Byham, William C., & Cox, Jeff. (1988). *Zapp! the Lightning of Empowerment*. New York: Harmony Books.

Collins, James C., & Porras, Terry I. (1994). *Built to Last: Successful Habits of Visionary Companies*. New York: Harper Business.

Conger, Jay A. (1988). *The Charismatic Leader*. New York: Jossey-Bass.

Covey, Stephen R. (1992). *Principle-Centered Leadership: Strategies for Personal & Professional Effectiveness*. Bellevue: S & S Trade.

Daniel, Aubrey C. (1993). *Bringing Out the Best in People*. New York: McGraw-Hill.

Deming, W. Edwards. (1986). Out of the Crisis. Cambridge, MA: MIT Press.

Drucker, Peter F. (1989). *The New Realities*. New York: Harper & Row.

Galbraith, Jay R., & Lawler, Edward E. (1993). *Organizing for the Future*. New York: Jossey-Bass.

Gardner, John W. (1989). *On Leadership*. New York: Free Press.

Hammer, Michael, & Champy, James. (1993). *Reengineering the Corporation*. New York: Harper Business.

Kanter, Rosabeth Moss. (1989). *When Giants Learn to Dance*. New York: Simon & Schuster.

Katzenbach, Jon R., & Smith, Douglas K. (1993). *The Wisdom of Teams*. Cambridge, MA: Harvard Business School.

Kilmann, Ralph H. (1989). *Managing Beyond the Quick Fix*. San Francisco: Jossey-Bass.

Kohn, Alfie. (1993). *Punished by Reward*. Boston: Houghton Mifflin.

Kouzes, James M., & Posner, Barry Z. (1993). *Credibility*. San Francisco: Jossey-Bass.

Loden, Marilyn, & Rosener, Judy B. (1990). *Workforce America! Managing Employees Diversity as a Vital Resource*. Burr Ridge, IL: Irwin Professional Publishing.

Manz, Charles C., & Sims, Henry P. Jr. (1989). S*uperleadership: Leading Others to Lead Themselves*. New York: Prentice-Hall.

McGregor, Douglas. (1985). *The Human Side Of Enterprise*. New York: McGraw-Hill.

Mintzberg, Henry. (1994). *The Rise and Fall of Strategic Planning*. New York: Free Press.

Naisbitt, John. (1994). *Global Paradox: The Bigger the World Economy, the More Powerful Its Smallest Players*. New York: Morrow.

Nanus, Burt. (1992). *Visionary Leadership*. San Francisco: Jossey-Bass.

Ohmae, Kenichi. (1990). *The Borderless World*. New York: Harper Business.

Ouchi, William G. (1981). *Theory Z: How American Business Can Meet the Japanese Challenge*. Reading, MA: Addison-Wesley.

Peters, Thomas J., & Waterman, Robert H. Jr. (1982). *In Search of Excellence*. New York: Harper & Row.

Peters, Tom. (1994). *The Tom Peters Seminar*. New York: Random House.

Quinn, Robert E. (1988). *Beyond Rational Management: Mastering the Paradoxes and Competing Demands of High Performance*. San Francisco: Jossey-Bass.

Reich, Robert B. (1991). *The Work of Nations*. New York: Alfred A. Knopf.

Senge, Peter. (1990). *The Fifth Discipline*. New York: Doubleday.

Tichy, Noel M., & Sherman, Stratford. (1993). *Control Your Destiny or Someone Else Will*. New York: Harper Business.

Vaill, Peter B. (1989). *Managing as a Performing Art*. San Francisco: Jossey-Bass.

Watson, Gregory H. (1993). *Strategic Benchmarking: How to Rate Your Company's Performance Against the World's Best*. New York: Wiley.

Wellins, Richard S., Byham, William C., & Wilson, Jeanne M. (1991). *Empowered Teams*. San Francisco: Jossey-Bass.

INDEX